GRINGO:
THE MAKING OF A REBEL

The author, age 8 years, and his mother at Bryant Avenue.

GRINGO

THE MAKING
OF A REBEL

Emil Willimetz

Peter E. Randall Publisher
Portsmouth, New Hampshire
2003

Design: Peter E. Randall

Peter E. Randall Publisher
Box 4726, Portsmouth, New Hampshire 03802
www.perpublisher.com

Distributed by
    University Press of New England
    Hanover and London

ISBN: 1-931807-16-7

Library of Congress Control Number: 2003109601

To Joie

Acknowledgments

There are many, many people who encouraged Emil during the long years of his writing and researching *Gringo*. I know he especially would have wanted to thank Carol Brightman, his marvelously supportive editor, who cheered the completion of each chapter; his publisher, Peter E. Randall, whom Emil found to be a true kindred spirit; and skilled copyeditor Kathleen Brandes, who also generously assisted me in sorting and selecting photographs after Emil's death in July 2003.

Mary Emma Harris, the stalwart custodian of Black Mountain College history, saw to the early publication of Emil's Black Mountain College material in the *North Carolina Literary Review*. Keats and Evans Smith urged Robert J. Cottom, editor of the *Maryland Historical Society Journal*, to read Emil's war chapter that led to its being published there. Candie and Guy Carawan offered their support and encouragement about notes on Zilphia and Myles Horton and the Highlander Folk School.

During ten years of writing there were countless friends who read and critiqued excerpts and I know Emil would lovingly want to thank them all.

Joanna Willimetz

One of the reasons I'm doing these books is so people can know those of another time. Two key movements in our history were the Depression and World War II. The Depression proved that our society is fallible, that people who run things aren't perfect. The New Deal helped millions of families survive but it did not end the Depression until World War II. The young today don't know about the Depression or the War.

—Studs Terkel, master interviewer of ordinary folk

Author's Note

GRINGO—"Green Grow the Rushes"

In the 1845 war, in which we divested Mexico of half of its territory, U.S. soldiers around campfires at night would sing, "Green Grow the Rushes":

> *I'll sing you one-O*
> *Green grow the rushes-O*
> *What is your one-O?*
> *One is one and all alone*
> *And ever more shall be so.*

The Mexicans shortened this to "green-grow," which in turn became "Gringo," a *Norte Americano*—a foreigner up to no good.

I was born into an immigrant family, with parents speaking broken English—undoubtedly "greenhorn" Gringos.

Uncircumcised in a Jewish neighborhood, I was a "goy" Gringo.

Living in the South, I was a "damnyankee" Gringo.

Today in the North, in Maine, I am an "away person" Gringo.

As an ex-infantry member of the Greatest Generation, I am an "anti-war" Gringo.

Living in Peru, of course, I was the real McCoy—a pure "*Norte Americano* Gringo." So . . . "Green Grow the Rushes."

> *I never travel without my diary. One always should have something sensational to read on the train.*
> —Oscar Wilde

CONTENTS

PREFACE

The past is a foreign country, they do things differently there.
—H. P. Hartley

Dear Jamie and Andy,

You boys have grown to know and love Maine. As do I. You have gotten to know some of your mother's numerous kith and kin—the Creighton/Copeland families who inhabited and made fruitful the mid-coast region of Maine. MADE FRUITFUL? You can't throw a stone around Thomaston and Cushing without hitting a relative! Your families' genealogy goes back to Priscilla Alden, who came over on the *Mayflower*. From them you inherited English, Scottish, and Irish blood—picking up a trace of German along the way.

Through the Creightons you know cultured middle-class folk who speak proper English and live the educated American lifestyle. Your mother's father was an executive of Bethlehem Steel in charge of the open-hearth furnaces in the great Lackawanna plant. In her childhood, she saw labor violence through her father's eyes. An incident on the picket line— where strikers ran a telephone pole through the car of a worker "who was just trying to get to work"— was presented to her as a horror story. For me, it would have been just an awkward solution to "stopping scabs from taking the bread out of an honest worker's mouth."

My parents were immigrant working-class folk from the bottom of the economic ladder. At home, they spoke broken English to their children and preferred speaking German to each other. From them you inherited Austrian blood. I would like you to get to know them.

Being born on the Tennessee Cumberland Plateau, growing up in Peru, and working in Brazil and Korea (not to forget New York and

xi

Maine), has given you both unique life experiences. Wouldn't it be great if you both would write them down—only please don't wait until you're in your eighties!
Happy reading,
Emil

One Last Admonition . . .

A solitary wanderer was lost in the forest. After days and nights of anguished walking, he met an old man. "It is God who sent you," exclaimed the wanderer. "Help me find the way out." And the old man, with a smile, his finger pointing behind him, said: "I myself am lost. All I can tell you is—do not go that way, I just came from there."

—Elie Wiesel

PROLOGUE

MY POP, LEOPOLD WILLIMETZ, grew up in the Austro-Hungarian Empire, a multilingual goulash of ethnic diversity—German, Czech, Slovak, Hungarian, Polish, Gypsy, Slovene, Croatian, Serb, and Bosnian Muslim. Present as well was the residue of occupations by Napoleon's French, Ottoman Turks, and Genghis Khan's Mongols.

Austria had an army in which it was notoriously easy to avoid conscription—until, in 1857, an event occurred that cast a dark shadow over young men's lives. It was the year census-taking was instituted in the Empire—recruitment into the military was no longer an avoidable hazard, but a preordained certainty.

In 1914, the Empire produced Europe's most complex army—Hungarian Hussars, Tyrolean riflemen, Viennese Socialists, and Bosnian infantrymen garbed in the fez and baggy trousers of their former Ottoman overlords. A good percentage of the army was Slavic. As an enemy to their great Slavic brother, Russia, they couldn't be counted on for any degree of Hapsburg patriotism. The army in Austria was not as popular as in Germany, and heavy losses against much larger Russian armies were said to be due to the soldiers' lack of morale. By December 1914, the Austro-Hungarian armies had already lost 1,268,000 men out of 3,350,000.

In my father's family, there were nine brothers and (big joke!) each one had a sister. In the summer of 1945, stationed in the U.S. Army of Occupation in Vienna, I was to meet that sister and learn about the fate of her brothers.

Brother Emil, my namesake, died in Vienna in 1912. I wonder how he would view my stewardship of his name?

Brother Alfons came to New York in 1913 with my grandmother. He

Soldier Karl Willimetz, the author's uncle, who never came back from the war.

must have been in real poor shape for the Austrian draft board to let him go. He died sometime before I was born.

The ruthless draft of the Austrian war machine in 1914 swept up the remaining six of the Willimetz brothers. Of these, Karl, Adolf, Gustav, and Viktor never returned from the war.

Uncle Josef, a jeweler, returned without his right arm and without a trade.

My uncle Franz malingered his way through all four years of World War I and lived to make it to the Bronx in 1922.

Brother Leopold, my Pop, with his young bride, Franziska, my Mom, went into exile in New York City in 1913 to avoid the draft. My Pop was an ardent antiwar Socialist. They were desperate enough to have left their first-born, my sister Marianna, with my grandmother, Hedwig Willimetz, until they were settled in New York.

Pop before the Great Depression.

BOOK I

ELLIS ISLAND AND BEYOND

To get to Ellis Island, you have to duck the outstretched, torch-bearing arm of Ms. Liberty, Mother of Immigrants. "Give us your poor," she says.

Pop in Vienna.

INTRODUCTION

AUS ÖSTERREICH (FROM AUSTRIA) TO ELLIS ISLAND, 1913

WHEN ELLIS ISLAND OPENED IN 1892, an Austrian was the first immigrant in line, but he stepped aside and gallantly allowed a young Irish girl the honor. Courtesy in Austria, it is said, can be in the nature of a malady.

My Mom had the Austrian malady in full measure; she was the quintessence of courtesy and gentility. Every once in a while, I would catch her in a pensive mood, her face relaxed, looking younger, her eyes focused on a far-off place. Vienna? Her home in Strass? It wasn't until I made it to the village of Strass in 1992 that I could build a faint image of her past. Life on her small vineyard, growing up in the Thoma family with three sisters and her brother Josef, must have been hard. The land behind the farmhouse rose steeply in a series of terraces on which they grew grapes.

Vienna, a distant 50 miles over poor roads, must have always been the dream. Her world expanded when, as a raw country girl, she went to work as a domestic for a wealthy *Graf* (Count) in a large manor house outside of Vienna. Later, living with her sister Rosa in Vienna, she worked as an aide in a mental hospital.

I never had a clue as to what made my father tick, but I never would have accused him of carrying the Austrian malady. He had grown up in Ottakring, a working-class district of Vienna. After retirement, when my wife and I led African safari tours, I mentioned Ottakring to an Austrian couple staying at one of our camps. They burst into laughter. Ottakring, it appeared, was the Bronx carried out to the nth degree. Working for a living was strictly *Verboten*—one lived by one's wits.

Mom in her wedding dress.

I visited Vienna in 1992 and toured Ottakring with Irene, my Aunt Anna's niece. Entering a telephone booth, I found that the phone book and the earpiece had been ripped off. Irene smiled ruefully. "Ottakring" was all she said.

Yet from plebeian blue-collar Ottakring, my Pop had found a splendid live-in job in Vienna in a grand Victorian hotel, the Bristol. How he contrived this transition is unknown. My parents never talked about life in Vienna or why and how they left it, but his photo from those days shows him looking distinctly like an elegant hotel manager.

Wine is what lubricates the social life of Vienna for rich and poor alike. One night Mom met the handsome Leopold Willimetz in the *Zehnermarie* (Ten Marias) *Weinstube*. It was to the elegant Hotel Bristol in 1912 that Leopold took his young bride to live. Their first child, Marianna, was born there. Life must have looked good for the newlyweds.

Sudden disaster! Pop, age 31, was about to be drafted into the Austrian army, and it was 1913. With the black clouds of war pending, they decided to leave their beautiful Vienna. Marianna was just a few months old, so she had to be left behind with Pop's mother until they were settled in the New World. They were fleeing to the Mother of Exiles—the Statue of Liberty next to the sunset gates of Ellis Island.

> *Here at our sea-washed, sunset-gates shall stand*
> *A mighty woman with a torch, whose flame*
> *Is the imprisoned lightning, and her name*
> *Mother of Exiles.*
>
> —Emma Lazarus, 1883

I can visualize Mom on a second-class train to Hamburg, sitting in a stiffly upholstered coach seat, stunned by the sudden turn of fortune and filled with sick apprehension. Would she see her baby again? What was in store for them in New York? Was her marriage a mistake?

The lowest-price ticket on the Hamburg-American Line was about $35 (a lot of money in 1913!). The shipping line had an immigrant center in Hamburg, where the dorms were arranged as on a ship. Stays there were short, until the next ship sailed—about four days. Room and board were cheap or included in the price of the ticket. Steerage passengers were given a disinfectant bath and a physical by a doctor, and their baggage was fumigated. The steamship companies had good motivation for all this—those who failed the immigration inspection at Ellis Island had to be returned at the shipping company's expense, plus a $100 fine.

The passage, in steerage, took 8 to 10 days under unbearable conditions. For companies like the Hamburg-American Line, immigrants were a profitable business—self-loading, like cattle. And, like cattle, some 1,000 immigrants were rushed down a long flight of narrow, slippery iron stairs and crammed into a large, open hold.

The dark, dank, nauseous hold was a dormitory divided into two sections—one set of bunks for men and the other for women and children. It must have been terribly frightening for Mom, separated from Pop just when she needed him most! The hold was a continuous babel of languages, and negative rumors were passed around with relish. All day, but especially at night, the hold creaked and moaned from unseen machinery. In stormy weather, it was sheer hell. One person would throw up and start a wave of vomiting through the dormitories. In the dim hold, Mom must have known she would never get out if the ship went down. Most of the time, Mom was so sick she didn't care if it did go down. She must have cried alone in her bunk: "Let's go back home, Leopold!"

It wouldn't take long for the hold to fill up with strange smells; unfamiliar food, smoke, body odors—lots of garlic. The disinfectant must have reminded Mom of the mental institution in which she once worked. Washrooms were small, each with a basin whose faucets ran only cold sea water. They were used for everything: washing greasy dinner pails and soiled underwear, shampooing hair, and for seasickness. Knowing Mom, she would have spent hours cleaning basins so she could use them. The narrow toilet rooms were even worse. No seats, just an open iron trough like those used to feed pigs, with an iron step and a slanted back that made one sit forward. There were six of them in each dormitory, and they were hardly ever cleaned.

You had to stand in line for food, never mind what kind, ladled out from 25-gallon containers. It was hard to be polite with people speaking so many different languages. You had to be pushy to get anything—such as getting up on deck in nice weather. Luckily, peaceable Mom had Pop, who was strong and pugnacious and could hold his own.

Finally they reached a great bay and the Statue of Liberty!

Emma Lazarus, who wrote the famous inscription, "Give me your tired, your poor, your huddled masses yearning to breathe free," was a wealthy Sephardic Jew who had helped many Jewish refugees fleeing Russian pogroms. Her poem has an honored place on the Statue of Liberty. The immigrants who passed it to land on Ellis Island were the poorest of the poor. First- and second-class passengers bypassed the island to be landed directly in Manhattan.

So . . . to get to Ellis Island you practically have to duck the outstretched, torch-bearing arm of Ms. Liberty, Mother of Immigrants. "Send these, the homeless, tempest-tossed to me," she says.

We hear you, Lady, we're on our way from Vienna, Austria, and we qualify. We are a young father fleeing the military, a country girl/wife/mother. Left behind, with agonizing foreboding, is our baby Marianna, most of our possessions, and all our beloved kith and kin. Our son Emil, and two more, are on the waiting list to be born.

Ellis Island was the primary port of entry into America for immigrants. Across the bay was Mecca—New York City. About 5,000 were processed per day—the pressure was enormous. Everyone off the ship. Hurry, hurry, hurry! From the Customs wharf, the apprehensive immigrants were hustled off the dock and herded into the great hall to join the long lines forming there. Inspectors were yelling at them in several languages. The most dreaded moment of all was the physical exam. People suspected of carrying a dangerous disease, or likely to become a public charge, were marked with blue chalk and set aside for closer scrutiny. If you failed a test, you were sent back to your homeland.

If Pop had to go, both would go, but if only Mom had to go back, would Pop, with the Austrian army and the war waiting for him, go too?

No time to think . . . hearts beating fast . . . push . . . a new line . . . a check for TB and . . . push . . . a doctor with a shoe buttonhook grabs Mom's eyelid, turns it over, and stares intently into her eyes. Mom was warned about this, but it happened so quickly she almost fainted. They are looking for trachoma, a European disease that leads to blindness and is unknown in America.

My Pop had an additional test, which was to approach a doctor with his pants open, to be examined for venereal infections. In the U.S. Army, we called it "short-arm" inspection. My "E" Company sergeant would stand us in rows and order us to take out our nongovernmental equipment. As the doctor passed, he would curtly say, "Milk it," by which he meant, like a cow. They were looking for gonorrheal discharge. It was a humiliating and totally ludicrous moment for me, and one my father experienced long before I was born.

Finally, they had to show at least $25, which Pop had carefully kept safe for this purpose. ($25 was a lot of money then—a week's salary for an Ellis Island inspector.)

Mom and Pop passed all the tests but proved poor bets anyway— the family had to go on welfare during the Great Depression when Pop became unemployed and Mom twice came down with TB (a disease of poverty), becoming a ward of the city.

Customs officers had a hard life. For one, they had to deal with the overpowering odor of ripening cheeses, such as limburger and gorgonzola, stashed away in luggage. Was this innocence or a ploy by knowledgeable immigrants so that their luggage would not be handled by the officers and would be stowed until the immigrants were dismissed?

With all tests passed, Mom and Pop were taken by ferry to the Battery Park dock in Manhattan. With the sickening suspense of Ellis Island behind them, they were insecurely ensconced in New York, the future darkly unknown.

I am haunted by the fact that the New World Willimetz home had no generational attic, only what Mom and Pop could carry from the old country. It must have been a heart-wrenching moment of decision for

Mom. Leaving home for good and yet restricted to a small amount of baggage—what would she take?

I can remember only a few personal items from the old country—a small Bible with filigree ivory cover, and a filigree ivory fan. I wish I could report a mother lode of Old World rural Austrian genealogy from the pages of the ivory Bible, but it was virgin, unmarked. What, then, was it doing among the few precious bits of memorabilia so painstakingly carried to the New World? It was certainly not carried by Pop, that fiery Viennese Socialist. Mom, then. But she was indifferent to religion, or so she said.

And the ivory fan? I can see that as a keepsake, carried to the undoubtedly crude society of New York City, to remind them of the cultural elegance of the sophisticated Vienna they had to abandon.

There was a wooden coffee mill and a porcelain drip-o-lator. Coffee is a very Viennese institution and a familiar family ritual. The beans are poured into the metal chamber of the mill and cranked vigorously so the grounds drop into a small drawer. The grounds and a piece of chicory are dumped into the drip-o-lator, and boiling water is poured through it. The hot coffee is poured through a second time, making a full pot of strong coffee meant to last the whole day. Each of us was included in the ritual, the smallest receiving a tablespoon of coffee with a cup of hot milk, the next two spoons of coffee, and the adults half and half. It seemed fair.

A deck of outsized playing cards with strangely shaped hearts and clubs and even stranger Austrian kings, queens, and princes, would appear on rare Sunday afternoons. The card games were played with loud exclamations in racy Viennese German and accompanied by hard thumps of cards slapped onto the table. On these occasions, I was frequently asked to run down to the bar with a gallon canister to be filled with prohibition tap beer. "Rushing the growler," it was quaintly called. But not by us. By us it was, "Emil! *Bier!*"

There was a collection of photos—kinfolk and friends dressed in funny clothes—which brought home to me the loneliness that immigrants face when separated from beloved family and long-term friends, from prized possessions and the sights and sounds of familiar streets.

As children, we knew absolutely nothing of the earliest New York history of the Willimetzes—two out of the million who immigrated into the United States through Ellis Island. Being "Square Heads," my parents' New World was filled with Hunkies, Polacks, Litvaks, Dagos, Wops, and Yids. With these non-WASPs we shared heavily accented English, strange names, and abject poverty. We were spared the humiliation of being foreigners in a pristine WASP neighborhood, for what then was the Bronx but a swamp of immigrants.

Those lines by Emma Lazarus, "The Wretched Refuse of Your Teeming Shore," described the scope of compassion included in America's open-hearted immigration policy. Yet there were those in our democracy who invoked the literal meaning of "wretched refuse" to rally support for halting the flow in the 1920s.

My parents came in early 1913. Marianna, age 12 months, arrived in October of that year with her grandmother, Hedwig, age 50, and her son Alfons, Pop's brother. They arrived from Trieste, a port on the Adriatic, on the ship *Carpathian,* whose claim to fame (other than bringing my relatives) was rescuing 750 survivors of the *Titanic.* My uncle Franz, the only brother to survive World War I intact, arrived at Ellis Island in 1922.

1913 was the last great year of immigration through Ellis Island and the second highest ever—892,653 people. By 1915, the influx of Emma Lazarus's "wretched refuse" had dropped to 178,416. In 1921, Congress imposed the first quota law on immigration. Nothing like slipping in at the last minute, eh Pop?

After 1924, Ellis Island started to reverse its function. Anti-alien hysteria led to immigrant limitations and new deportation laws. Unemployment during the Great Depression accelerated the deportations. Between 1930 and 1936, only 159,000 new immigrants were allowed in, while some 300,000 were booted out. The anarchist writer Emma Goldman was arrested for distributing abortion literature. (Hey, Emma, times haven't changed that much!)

Fortunately, Pop with his Viennese Socialist background escaped the net—he already had his citizenship papers. By 1954, Ellis Island was closed.

1.

GROWING UP
IN THE SOUTH BRONX

*Where you are born is the most important thing determining the
outcome of your life.*
                    —Jared Diamond

*I was born on the corner
of Poverty and Injustice
my parents were Dignity
and Maybe Tomorrow*
                    —Homero Aridjis

*The New York City borough of The Bronx was named after Jonas Bronk, who
settled there in 1639. People would say, "Sunday, let's go out to see the
Bronks." But most folks really didn't know any Bronks, and it became insti-
tutionalized as "The Bronx." A farm region for New York City, it had a population of 88,908 in 1890. In 1904, the IRT subway system was extended into
the Bronx, which then became a haven for upwardly mobile Jewish immigrants seeking a better life beyond the ghettos of Manhattan's Lower East
Side. They were to be my neighbors and fellow citizens in the Bronx.*

An Immigrant Laborer's Lament

I came to America because I heard
The streets were paved with gold.
When I got here, I learned three things:
First, the streets were not paved with gold;
Second, many weren't paved at all;
Third, I was expected to pave them.
                              —Ivan Chermayeff, *Ellis Island*

My father, I'm sure, never expected to see streets paved with gold—his prime motivation was to move beyond the reach of Emperor Franz Josef's army recruiters. Nor did he, I suspect, feel that he was expected to pave them. Not speaking English, my Pop knew he had no chance of duplicating his hotel-management skills in the New World. Instead, he pinned his hopes on the hottest Vienna Woods technology of making birch-bark-and-acorn flower stands. It turned out that this was part of a Victorian lifestyle long outmoded in the United States of America.

Pop tried a number of other unsuccessful ventures about which very little is known in the Willimetz chronology—a candy store (failed before I arrived) and a convoluted shirt scheme in which Mom would sew quality shirts to be shipped to Vienna as a high-class export. Poor Mom. Pop was in no way an entrepreneur, just a deeply disappointed man.

Good jobs for immigrants were hard to come by. Fortunately, during World War I, Pop lucked into a job camouflaging ships in the Brooklyn Navy Yard. After the war, as a member of the AFL Painters' Union, he continued to work with union crews.

I was birthed at home August 2, 1918. My mother was 31 and my father 36. I had an older sister aged six and an older brother aged four:

My mother groan'd, my father wept,
Into the dangerous world I leapt.
                              —William Blake

You don't know someone until you follow them home. Welcome, then, to the South Bronx! We lived in the lower-class section of the South Bronx—north of Tremont Avenue and bounded on the east by the Bronx Zoo—known as "Li'l It'ly." Immigrants tend to flock together in ethnic groups—not my Pop. How and why we ended up in the Italian section of the Bronx may never be known.

In searching for my first true memory, I found not an incident but an emotion:

I am completely engulfed in shock . . . guilt . . . disbelief . . . abandonment . . . emotions that wash over me in continuous waves of paralyzing fear. The strongest of these is abandonment.

Grossmutter Hedwig, Leopold and Fanny with baby Hedy.

The incident that caused the shock, told to me later by my grandmother, was never mentioned in family folklore. Apparently, at the age of four, I was standing on the sidewalk, accused by an angry, hysterical mother of severely hurting her son, hitting him with a stone and causing him to bleed. I stood frozen until the arrival of my own mother. A witness was found and the truth revealed—I had wildly thrown a stone that hit the tire of a passing car and was spun into the face of the wounded boy with ten times the force that I could ever have mustered. I was not then, nor ever have been, the violent type.

I have no memory of these details, but the paralyzing emotion of terror and abandonment is still, today, a component of stressful happenings in my life. It came back in full force when I was in combat in World War II.

My earliest memories are of my grandmother, my father's mother. In late 1913, she arrived in New York with Onkel Alfons, bringing my sister Marianna, who had been left behind in Vienna. Alfons died before he entered my awareness—he must have been in bad shape for the Austrian Army to have let him escape. My Onkel Franz, another of Pop's eight brothers, came after World War I, in 1922. He and my grandmother were the only kinfolk, outside of the immediate family, I knew as a child, and they compose almost all my memories of life in Li'l It'ly.

As the baby of the family, I was indulged by both of them. Sunday mornings, I ran down to the corner store to buy my Onkel an egg and my Grossmutter a tin of Copenhagen Snuff. There were always a few pennies of change, which I got to keep.

I would watch as my Grossmutter opened her tin, placed a dab of snuff in the hollow between thumb and forefinger, inhaled deeply. and exploded a great sneeze into a large, red bandanna. From time to time, she would dig into her apron pocket and hand me a piece of hard candy liberally coated with Copenhagen. You might say I was addicted to tobacco at an extremely tender age.

When Grandma was dying of stomach cancer, she lived almost entirely on calf's-foot jelly and beer soup. The jelly was actually made from calves' feet, with sweet port wine added to it. I got an occasional taste, and it was heavenly. The soup was made by heating beer and whipping it into pure foam. This I could do without, and did.

Onkel Franz, who hoped to stop the decline of his thinning blond hair, would crack his Sunday egg over his head and vigorously rub it into his scalp. He loved magic and bought tricks with which to bamboozle us kids. This wasn't hard to do, and it gave him great satisfaction. The egg rub proved less than magical.

In later years, as a waiter in the famous Hotel New Yorker, he would save the dregs of quality wines and spirits in his locker. With his prestidigitator talents, I suspect he disappeared more than dregs. In my teen years, invited to tea, I would be served half tea and half brandy. I seldom left his house without a buzz.

BRYANT AVENUE, 1923

When I was about five, we moved to Bryant Avenue, on the edge of Li'l Italy. Why the move? More privacy in a single house? More room? Cheaper rent? Probably the latter. It was an old structure with creaking floors, a small coal stove, and ancient pull-chain plumbing. We bathed in a washtub. It was a one-block street with a row of small, wooden houses attached to each other with an umbilical cord of a common porch—like Southern slave quarters. Each house had a small backyard, with a back gate that opened into a common alley. So many years of ashes and clinkers had been dumped in the yard that all attempts at a garden ended in failure—the sole exception being radishes, which will grow anywhere.

The biggest event in the Willimetz family at Bryant Avenue was the birth of my kid sister Hedy, on January 27, 1924. Mom was 37, and this was to be her last child. I was too busy exploring the world around me to pay much attention to the new arrival. (My time with Hedy was to come in about five more years, when she became my sole care in an orphanage.) I have no sense of having any sibling rivalry; my place in the family was always very secure.

Most of my early memories are of life on Bryant Avenue. From our house, the Bronx River was only two long blocks down a steep hill. For a young boy, the river added new dimensions to the South Bronx. One late spring day, I went down there. I had taken an old window screen, doubled it over, and sewed up the sides to make a crude pouch. Loaded with old bread, it soon attracted a load of "killies." I strung them on a necklace of wire and stashed them in the rocks to mellow in the heat. Come Sunday,

Lee, Emil, and Mary.

the family traipsed down to the river— Pop lugging a big pot of good Bronx water and Mom a hamper of picnic supplies. My brother Lee loaded up on firewood as we went along, and I ran ahead to bring out my fragrant killies—they weren't hard to find. Tying one to a weighted line, I dropped it into the river and in a surprisingly short time felt the tug of a crab. The trick was to pull the predator to the surface slowly enough so that it would keep hanging on. Near the surface, I would yell for the net, and Lee would quickly scoop up the prize.

By then, Mom had a pot of water cooking over a small fire, and in would go the crab. I was taught to discard the "dead man's fingers." Who would want to eat those ugly yellow fingers anyway? (The liver, was it?) But the rest of the crabmeat was great, eaten along with thick slabs of dark bread heavily smeared with salted chicken fat. Those were good days for Pop. He was working steadily, and on the edge of a blanket his first-born, Mary, sat with his newly born, Hedwig, rocking her to sleep. Pop had swapped his elegant mustache for a short bristled one, which I still remember for its sting every time he bussed me.

Upstream, the river was blocked by a dam—the water above the dam being fresh and below being the tidal flow that passed our house. In the rocks below the dam, at low tide, we became avid stalkers of crawdads. I can't remember whether or not we treated the crawdads to the same brutal boiling-water exit to life that we did the crabs.

Unbeknownst to the elders, Lee and I went swimming in the Bronx River—usually above the falls, where the water was clean. Once we tried diving for coins under the busy West Farms Road bridge. Lee did the diving and I treaded water, looking up eagerly at the bridge. "See that li'l blond tadpole!" It turns my stomach today to think about our swimming in that ugly, dark tidal sewage. The payoff wasn't that good, either.

In winter, the two steep blocks to the river offered high adventure. Somehow we had acquired a beaten-up sled. It was a high-speed ride, with the moment of truth waiting at the bottom of the hill. It took a great deal of body English and dragging of feet to negotiate a turn and stop at the river's edge. One day, Unk invited his Anna for a spin. (Unk had married an immigrant girl, Anna, from Vienna and no longer lived with us.) I tried to explain to him the mechanics of stopping, but he was impatient.

"Ja, ja, Anna, push off."

When next seen, they were sopping wet, dragging a sled that seemed to be in need of repair.

After World War I, there was a surge of political and religious right-wing repression, and one of its more obnoxious offshoots was Prohibition. The result was a national epidemic of lawbreaking that opened a window of opportunity for the Mafia. For thirsty families, the making of wine was commonplace, the techniques involved simple. You could buy a cask of prefermented grape juice that came with a little label saying something like: "If you put a hose into the cask, pass it through a bottle of water, and let it stand for one month, it will become wine, and that is against the law."

Whenever I went into Onkel Franz's apartment, I was assaulted by the strong, sour fumes of fermenting hops. Aunt Anna would shrug her shoulders and roll her eyes to the heavens, an indication that her Franz was up to some nonsense. It was a gesture she made often.

Unk also made cordials. He bought gallon tins of pure spirits of alcohol and added extracts of pear, banana, licorice, coffee, and chocolate. He was liberal with his cordials around Christmas time, giving away a sample rainbow of flavors. I was told they almost took the enamel off your teeth.

> *Mom's in the kitchen, washing out the jugs,*
> *Lee is in the kitchen, bottling the suds,*
> *Pop's in the cellar, mixing up the hops,*
> *Emil's on the porch, watching for the cops.*

And then there was the wine caper. One night, when bedtime came and I wasn't hustled immediately off to sleep, I became aware of an air of anticipation in the Willimetz household, like waiting for midnight on Christmas Eve. We weren't waiting for Kris Kringle, but rather for our friendly neighborhood Italian fruit vendor. It was all very hush-hush. I was warned not to tell anyone. When I was told this several times over, I knew it was a true family secret.

Almost precisely at midnight, I heard the long-anticipated clip-clop of a horse and creak of a wagon coming up the back alley. We all rushed out to unload a whole wagonload of grapes. The Italian on the wagon handed a flat crate of grapes to Pop, who handed it to Lee, who dashed into the house with it. Vendor to Pop to Mom, then Pop to Mary, and, finally, vendor to Pop. To me? No, to Lee again. My anguished screams of protest shattered the midnight air . . . and brought me my crate.

We stacked the crates in a storeroom we had emptied of trunks, suitcases, and bedding. I never saw so many grapes in my life! Plucking a stem of the sweet grapes, I danced gleefully around the room, but I stopped quickly when I spotted Pop's baleful glare. This was not a matter for joking; this was serious enterprise, involving Pop's capital and Mom's planning.

Pop had bought a wine press and, despite his businesslike manner, couldn't resist an unscheduled start on operations. We quickly filled the press barrel with grapes. Pop clapped on a heavy lid and turned the screw to compress the grapes. To my great delight, the juice ran down gaps in the barrel staves into a bucket. To my great disappointment, I was told, no, it wasn't wine—not yet—and I was trundled off to bed.

Of the actual winemaking, I remember few details, but I can vouch for the recipe—the vat full of fermenting grape juice had a tube running out of it and into a bottle of water. I would watch the trail of bubbles, waiting for something called "wine" to happen. It must have happened when I wasn't looking, for one day Pop started siphoning off the vat into bottles. Holding the corked bottles up to the light, he would say, with considerable satisfaction—"Wine!" He was proud of his product, but we all knew it was Mom who engineered the successful result.

By adding extra sugar to the old grape mash left over after the wine was siphoned off, Pop also made brandy. One day, a broken bottle of brandy sent a tantalizing odor throughout the connected porch system, and soon people were out sniffing. Poor Mom! She, too, had to go out on the porch, sniffing the air from the east and from the west, exchanging puzzled glances with her neighbors. Duplicity, Mom, duplicity! You should have stood proudly by your work: "Smells great, doesn't it!" Pop's boast was that he sold enough brandy to pay for the entire operation. When we had visitors, he would bring out the wine or brandy, but I never saw him drunk.

In the storeroom, where the illicit deed was done, my father kept the remains of a 100-pound bag of brown sugar. I invited a young friend, also about six, to join me in raiding this sweet treasure. We lingered in this dark room also to research our latent sexual drives. Mom surprised us, just smiled, and sent us out into the sunshine.

One time, all of the Willimetzes were invited to an Austrian celebration in a Brooklyn hall. Around three sides of the hall were long trestle tables loaded with dark breads, cheeses (some you wouldn't want to get too intimate with), meats, and *Wurst* of all circumferences and lengths. In each corner sat a barrel of beer. An oompah band pounded out music of sorts. Playing up to the crowd, waltzes predominated. The waltz originated in Vienna, and Johann Strauss composed 400 of them. Don't think of dainty gentlefolk gracefully sweeping around a ballroom. In the middle/late 1800s in Vienna, waltzing was all the rage; it was sometimes wild and infectious (like the Charleston in the 1920s). Lord Byron labeled it "disgusting and disgraceful." This was my Grandma Hedwig's era, so when the waltzing began in that Brooklyn beer hall, she grabbed me and pulled me out on the floor. While everyone else in the room circulated counterclockwise, each couple whirled clockwise. It was an exhilarating moment for a young boy—my head swimming both clockwise and counterclockwise. I've loved dancing ever since. Thank you, Grandma!

CAMP ST. PAUL, 1926/27 ("I'll be back in two weeks, Mother.")
While Mom had few personal friends in our Italian, Jewish, and WASP neighborhoods, she was well respected and frequently received help. Somehow she got Lee and me, when I was eight years old, accepted by the Big Brother Fresh Air Movement. We were sent off for a camp experience in distant New Hampshire—for two weeks, two summers in a row.

What a great hustle and bustle there was at Grand Central Station, kissing Mom and Mary goodbye and loading onto a train. It was like a war movie. Many of the other kids who were going with us from the Bronx were real streetwise smart asses! Being on the timid side, I was glad to have my own big brother on this Big Brother excursion.

After a long train ride, we arrived in

The author, Camp St. Paul bugler.

Boston and had to carry our barrack bags from South Station to North Station. Boston police, at the time, wore brown uniforms and were greeted with catcalls: "Hey, Western Union, if ya see an officer, have 'em call a policeman, tell 'em we need a cop." (The things that stay in memory!) You may not have the imaginative ability to believe it, but 70 years after that camp journey, Boston's South and North Stations are still not connected!

The train ride to Danbury, New Hampshire, was even longer than the New York-to-Boston leg. It was an older train that poured out thick yellow smoke, and the stiff green nap covering the seats was coated with scratchy cinders. It became a tiresome ride, but I remember being fascinated by the station names, particularly the one at the end of the line, White River Junction, a place I never did get to see. I couldn't imagine what the camp would be like. The farthest I'd gone before then was on a boat ride up the Hudson River to Bear Mountain Park, 50 miles away.

We were met at the station by a bevy of camp counselors—college students, we were told—and were duly awed. The glory of the camp was a small lake with rowboats and canoes. Rowboats we rented in Crotona Park and Pelham Bay, but canoes! That was Indian stuff!

In a shoebox of letters my kid sister Hedy saved, I found a postcard I sent home from New Hampshire:

> Dear Fambly . . .
> I am having a great time in camp and the counslars like me.
> I passed the canoe test and go canoeing a lot. This is a picture
> of the camp.
> Emil

The lake at camp contained all sorts of exotica: beautiful, fragrant water lilies; long-nosed pickerel, and ugly black leeches you learned to body-search for and destroy. Directly across the lake was a girls' camp, a further bit of exotica more interesting to Lee than to me. The girls' camp proved a magnet for rowers, paddlers, and swimmers. I had learned to swim in the Bronx, and Lee put me up to a marathon swim across the lake to the girls' camp—a good half mile. Under his urging, I breaststroked, side-

I conquer Mt. Kearsarge.

stroked, and backstroked, and we made it! The girl campers, who had been watching this epoch swim, cheered us as I flopped, exhausted, on their dock. Drawing this small audience for my brother Lee earned me double points.

Another sunny day: "Well, guys, today we have a paper chase."

"A wot?"

"Clues will be left in various places and they will lead you to the prize. Okay?"

Off in a meadow by myself, I found a most cunning clue, missed by everyone—a trail of small dabs of shaving-cream suds that led across the grass. But it was messy and fluky, with the trail wandering off in every direction.

I was saved by the hullabaloo of the treasure found. (Years later, I found that the suds had been made by perfidious insects! You can't always rely on nature to be honest!)

You can't even expect grown-ups to be honest. One day, they stood me up on the camp office steps, put a bugle in my hand, and told me to blow. The start of a musical career? Don't you believe it—just be glad you weren't anywhere close by. I ended up on the cover of a fund-raising pamphlet. And did it work? Well, they evidently made enough from my bugle call to send Lee and me back the following summer.

One night, we sat around a campfire till long after midnight, and the counselors scared the pants off us by telling ghost stories. In the wee hours, they fed us toast and cocoa, and we started off on a hike down the road to Mount Kearsarge, singing lustily to stay awake. By dawn we were on the mountain and then on the summit. Wow! Above the timberline! It made me feel like a real explorer!

At the foot of the mountain, the camp trucks met us, and we wolfed down breakfast sandwiches. It sure beat the Bronx! Camp was an experience that opened another part of the world for me—was there more?

For Mom and Pop, the Bryant Avenue days (as far as my awareness goes) were the best years of their adventure in the New World. Pop had some entrepreneurial success in his wine venture. Mom, too, must have felt extra fulfillment with her new baby and her role as a wine expert. Things seemed to be going smoothly for the Willimetz family.

But were there shadows on the horizon? Yes, there were!

2.

THE GREAT DEPRESSION

The worst peacetime crisis to afflict humanity since the Black Death.
—Piers Brendon

IN THE UNITED STATES, the 1920s were the years of so-called Prosperity. It was a frenetic time—the heyday of the flapper, whose entire weight of garments, it was said, totaled about 32 ounces. A world of bootlegging and high crime, of selling securities and making big money on the stock market. The Willimetz family had little participation in the above activities— the weight of our garments was well above the flapper minimum.

The year 1929 stands out as the start of the Great Depression. The 1920s had many alarming weak spots—in agriculture, in coal mining, railroads, and textiles. There was an average of 600 bank failures per year. Large numbers of textile and shoe workers in New England had no jobs. The Willimetz Depression started in 1927, when my Pop, who was working as a painter, became unemployed. He was 45 years old. We moved some ten blocks to a hilly, predominantly Jewish neighborhood. Here we lived as janitors in the basement of a five-story apartment house. In the lobby, we were not listed along with the tenants; we had a separate mailbox labeled, "Willi Metz: Ring Bell For Superintendent."

To sidestep the blacklist, the name on our mailbox was Willi Metz, the name under which Pop hoped to paint as a freelancer (about which more in a moment). Our living space was below-ground and dingy, but with Pop out of work, it was a bargain—free rent and a $20 monthly stipend. After 1929, we would have had a lot of competition to get that place. With no Social Security or "safety net" in those days, it gave us time to breathe.

Using the hysteria left over from World War I, industry had mounted a battle strategy to destroy unions. This opened the way for industrial racketeering, which became so lucrative as to attract such leaders of "enterprise" as Arnold Rothstein and Al Capone.

According to Louis Adamic, in *My America*, "Building-trades union officials were silent partners in paint, lumber, hardware, and general building-supply concerns, and the union members who got the best jobs were those who induced their employers to buy the largest quantities of material from these concerns."

When my father's painters' union split, I figured that my Pop, a stout Viennese Socialist, had backed the wrong half, the anti-racketeering part. Anyway, he was blacklisted.

Our family had many of what my sister Hedy called "long noodle spells." We ate "poor" but never really went hungry. Finally, in 1929, we were forced to join the biggest industry in the country—Home Relief. Mom and I went weekly to pick up a bag of depression food: pasta, rice, beans, flour, lard, sugar, salt, and other basics. Unpacking these bags at home was—at least for me—a bit like Christmas, for there might be such special treats as dried fruits and packaged pudding, possibly a jar of apple butter or prune whip. The Bronx had a large bakery with a side door where you could buy cheap bread and cake that had been returned from grocery stores. The stuff didn't have a long shelf life, but who needed that?

We lived and worked in a five-story apartment house. Of the janitorial tasks during our first years of underground residency, the heaviest chores were done by Pop and Lee—with me included only as needed. The house had a dumbwaiter garbage system, two shafts that ran from the top floor to the basement. Lee serviced the right side and I serviced the left. Each kitchen had a hatch that opened onto the shaft. Rough hemp ropes, about an inch thick and hard on one's hands, pulled the dumbwaiter. The ropes were heavy enough to lift tons—talk about your margin of safety! The dumbwaiter was invented by Thomas Jefferson for use in the home he built at Monticello. Although I discovered this many years later, it does add a degree of prestige to our labors.

We'd peer up through the gloom of the five-story building, to approximate the small hatch at each apartment, and ring that bell. Then we'd hear: "A LITTLE LOWER, PLEASE," or just "UP." The dumbwaiter had a limited capacity, and the third floor usually had to ask for a return trip: "IT'S FULL!" or "WE GOT MORE!" Bags and cans were emptied into receptacles and up we'd go. Occasionally a tenant would put a note on an item or just yell down the shaft: "THE SWEATER'S FOR YOU," or "THE CAKE IS STILL FRESH," or "IF YOU CAN FIX IT, IT'S YOURS."

We were early recyclers; trash was worth a small amount of money. Four-foot stacks of newspapers, bundled and tied, and huge burlap bags of rags and bottles, went to the man who patrolled the street with a donkey cart, mournfully intoning, "Bottles and rags!" His high, shrill cry penetrated even the thickest basement walls. Soda bottles were three-cent and five-cent returnables. Interesting that after many long years, we are now back to bottle deposits—five cents was worth a great deal more then, however, than today. Five cents bought an ice-cream cone. Garbage and ashes were put out in large galvanized cans fitted with tight lids. The garbage collector's struggles with these cans were guaranteed to roust you long before wake-up time. In those days, there was a multitude of newspapers—the *Daily News,* the *Mirror,* the Hearst *Journal-American,* the *Telegram.* Forget the *New York Times* and the *Herald Tribune*—they had no comics. I got to read the funnies from every paper in town. Come Monday, I was the best-read boy in the neighborhood, and the envy of all.

During this period, the fantastic mayor of New York, Fiorello LaGuardia, personally helped the young Willimetz sprouts endure the ordeal of a newspaper strike by reading the comics over the radio every Sunday morning.

LaGuardia went to law school at night, and during the day he worked at Ellis Island. He was working there when my Mom and Pop arrived in 1913, and I fondly imagined he helped them through. As a practicing politician, LaGuardia was the best—one of the few public figures who knew to what extent the "prosperity" of the twenties was a bitter joke. A congressman from a district of poor Jewish immigrants in East Harlem, he ran on both the Socialist and the Republican tickets. His Jewish opponent in the 1922 race accused him of being Italian and an anti-Semite, so LaGuardia challenged him to a debate in Yiddish. He had an agnostic Italian father and a Jewish Austrian mother.

Sweeping the sidewalk and the backyard was also one of my regular chores. If I didn't have something better to do, I found a certain satisfaction in sweeping dirt into neat piles with a wide push broom. Sidewalk dirt went into the gutter; it shouldn't have, but it did. Professional street cleaners—each with a trash can on wheels and a broom with stiff, Hitler mustache-like bristles—pushed up the street with authority, melding trash with donations from the vegetable vendor's and the milkman's horses. I used to watch my competition with interest—it hadn't occurred to me that sweeping could be a career. An epic scene in a Charlie Chaplin movie: Charlie, as a street cleaner waddling up a street, sees a circus parade coming down it with elephants and wheels abruptly off into a side street. I knew the feeling!

Next door to our building was a duplicate five-story apartment house. The neighboring janitors were a Polish family with a son slightly older than me. The only area we had in common was a small section of backyard with no dividing line. The Polish boy and I scrupulously kept this square clean. When we met during this task, we acknowledged each other warily. We were willing to be friendly but didn't know how. One windy day, wielding my push broom, I realized that the Polish trash would quickly be blown into Austrian territory, so I cleaned both sides. When next we met, the Polish boy questioned me. "How come ya did my side?" When I explained, he grunted, "Thanks." I never had to do my patch again. He became less stiff, even friendly, and occasionally began to appear socially with me and my Jewish friends. I sensed he was uncomfortable with the neighborhood gang, that he could have been a bit of an anti-Semite (or his family could have), but my being in the group made it possible for him to join us.

Steaming piles of horse buns were a fact of life in those Bronx days: something to avoid when playing street games, something to scoop up if you had a garden, and something to inspire little ditties:

> *Purty little horse manure,*
> *99 percent is pure.*
> *See the little boidy*
> *Peckin' on the turdy,*
> *Purty little horse manure!*

Accompanying the manure were great mobs of tough little streetwise sparrows. Hated by many, they were called "hoodlums," "dirty tramps." But they were my gringos, fellow immigrants—eight pairs of English sparrows introduced into Brooklyn from Britain in 1850 to take care of a caterpillar problem. You had to admire the bold dexterity with which they dodged traffic to feed on undigested oats. Totally aggressive and intelligent, they would snatch the food from a starling's mouth. In the spring, the mate-seeking males would spread their wings in the street dust, bowing and shaking for female attention. Circling the females, the males viciously fought each other for recognition. Successful couples adopted streetlights, telephone poles, and traffic lights for nesting sites. In the evening, their shrill bedtime exchanges made an unholy din.

In captivity, they say, sparrows learn to imitate canaries. They are classified as songbirds (perhaps in an English garden), but all I ever heard was cheep-cheep-cheep. When horses no longer trod the city streets, the great numbers of sparrows declined. They were my kind of bird: "Hey, look at da boid!" "That's a sparrow!" "Chirps like a boid!"

The heart of our basement was a great furnace. One day, a huge truck arrived at our house full to the brim with hard, glistening, black anthracite coal. From the sidewalk, a flight of iron stairs led to a downhill alleyway. About halfway down the alley, a window opened to the coal bin. Unloading was an operation that required gravity and all the truck crew's skill. It took about 50 feet of chute, hooked together, to run the coal to the bin window. One man operated the hydraulics that tilted the truck bed, a second kept the coal moving down the chute with his shovel, and a third was stationed at the critical juncture where the coal needed to be persuaded to turn right—through the window and into the bin.

I used to stand entranced, watching the coal rattling noisily down the chute. Every once in a while, one of the men (in black face) would catch my eye and flash me a grin. It was doubly fascinating that these men, I was told, were bootleggers.

The coal industry, pushed to overproduction during the war years, saw the workforce decline between 1920 and 1927. By 1927, many mining towns in Appalachia had almost total unemployment. For many of those still working, take-home pay amounted to less than $2 per day. Thus, many miners turned to bootlegging coal. They dug the coal illegally in the anthracite fields—an act of desperation to keep their families alive—and trucked it to the cities.

The door to our apartment, at the foot of the iron steps, also turned right off the alley. To enter our flat, we had to cross the dark and grimy room containing the enormous, asbestos-covered furnace. On the face of the great furnace was a series of pipes, valves, thermostats, and gauges. When I scrutinized all the gadgets, it was as an engineer. But only one of these gadgets had any real significance—a glass tube of water showing a red level that said DANGER. I was told to inform either Lee or Pop if the water reached the red zone. I wasn't told what specifically would happen, but I envisioned an explosion that would send the top five stories of our apartment house into nearby Crotona Park.

I was sometimes called on to stoke the great furnace—when my father and brother were otherwise occupied. I would open the furnace doors wide, pick up a long iron hoe, and rake the red-hot coals until the clinkers were loose enough to shake through the grate or be raked out into a pail. The coal bin was uphill from the furnace and friend gravity and I would drag the loaded scoop down to the open doors. I would lift and swing the load with all my might into the fiery red gap. There was a certain satisfaction in bracing myself, swinging the shovel, and hearing the coal slither smoothly off into the furnace. It took numerous swings to cover the big glowing bed, and as I got tired, I would occasionally hit the door edge and coal would fly everywhere. How I hated that! I was nine or ten, and it revealed the child in me when I was trying so hard to be a man.

But the worst was not the spills. The cellar was lit only by a dim, 60-watt bulb hanging at the end of its own electric wire. The bulb made absolutely no impression inside the black coal bin. I would grab the large coal scoop, lay it flat on the floor, and run it up into the dark until it hit the coal pile. Coal would slide down and fill the shovel. This brief journey took all my resolve, because on top of the pile lurked unseen monsters noting my every move and waiting for some unknowable moment to swoop down and envelop me in their dark evil. It was the stuff most of my nightmares were made of. I would have to force myself awake before the climax could destroy me. It must have been powerful stuff, for these dark evils surfaced at rare times in my adult dream life as well. Was this "dark evil" a follow-through of the "paralyzing fear . . . guilt . . . and abandonment" of my earliest childhood? It joined me again later, in the foxholes of World War II.

MY SOCIAL SECURITY CARD

My father is a butcher,
My mother cuts the meat,
And I'm a little hot-dog
That runs around the street.

Not exactly! My father wasn't a butcher, he was an unemployed house painter. My mother had very little meat to cut, and running around the streets, for me, was secondary to working. In the Depression, for us and millions of other families, work was the ultimate goal. So when my chance came to work as a delivery boy for the *Bronx Home News,* I did it with a pride way out of proportion to the smallness of my contribution. Saturday was payday, and I would solemnly turn over my money envelope to Mom. Whenever she bought me some clothing, she let me know that it came out of my earnings.

My $10 monthly contribution, at a time when our family income was at its lowest ebb, certainly helped—at least I thought so. At one time, I was the only one in the family with steady employment—until Lee dropped out of high school later that year and could pick up odd jobs. Average per capita income in 1929 was $14.18 per week. By 1933, it dropped to $10.50, and at one point, 34 million people had no income at all!

I was an uneasy nine-year-old when I showed up for my job as a delivery boy for the *Bronx Home News*. At the neighborhood station, I was given a route outlined in red crayon on a cellophane-covered map of the Bronx and a small notebook containing a list of customer names, addresses, and door numbers. Also, free of charge, I received a light canvas *Bronx Home News* bag in which to carry my 80 or 90 papers, plus free samples for potential customers. I was to roll up each paper and wedge it between the customer's doorknob and doorjamb. I was told to leave the thick Sunday paper flat before the door. That first day, I was so immersed in learning the directives governing my new job that I was totally unaware of my fellow workers. The second day, the other boys circled me like members of a wolf pack.

"What did ya do wid the samples?" challenged one.

"I just put them on door knobs, like they told me."

"Do you always do wot ya told?" sneered one of the old hands.

"You cover just the first two or three stories of the building," explained a more compassionate voice. A possible friend, I thought. "Why work? Do you think the inspectors ever check above the first two floors?"

"But what do you do with the leftovers?" I asked.

"We throws 'em down the sewers," laughed another.

I gradually found my own means of profitable sample disposal. I gave several copies to local candy stores to sell along with the big city papers. For this, I would get a glass of chocolate egg-cream (chocolate syrup, a dash of milk and seltzer—no egg in sight) or a paper cup of flavored ices or even a small candy bar. (My favorite was a Maryjane—molasses taffy filled with peanut butter. Maryjane came to designate marijuana, but not in my day.)

A free newspaper was cheaper for wrapping than brown bags. The Italian fruit and vegetable vendor gladly accepted my papers in exchange for a banana or an apple. He cruised our home neighborhood daily with his horse and wagon, and I was never sure if he thought the papers were a fair exchange for the fruit or, knowing I was a janitor's kid, he figured I needed the nourishment. The local fish market made a donation of a small fish every Friday. When I was in London, fish 'n' chips was delivered in a twist of newsprint—I wondered which kid was working the scam.

As I broadened my horizons, I added a saloon. Prohibition was still in effect, and they served only near-beer, 1.2 alcoholic content . . . wink . . . but not with Dutch Schultz working the Bronx. It was a classic saloon—dim, cool, and beery, with sawdust on the floor, a brass rail, and a dark mahogany bar. The bar was loaded with heaps of crackers, squares of pumpernickel and rye bread, and small slices of cheeses, liverwurst, head-cheese, and chunks of fragrant salami. Also frequently found were gallon jugs of pickled eggs or pigs' knuckles. For a couple of papers, I would earn a piece of bread and a choice of tidbit. Once, when the bartender was in a good mood, I was allowed to spear a toothpick into the gallon jar and make off with a whole dripping pickled egg.

I would take home any leftover papers to add to the stacks from our garbage collection. Bundled and tied, these papers were sold to the rag man for pennies a pound.

My first Sunday of work, I showed up at 5 a.m. to assemble sections of the Sunday edition. Not exactly the size of a *New York Times,* it was still a substantial Sunday paper. When I had the stack piled in front of me, I found I had assembled a problem—I couldn't possibly carry the huge pile. The others had all brought wagons and recycled baby carriages. As they left, I got alternate looks of derision and concern. I had to return to head-quarters three times.

The following day, my sympathetic new friend offered to help: "You have to have a cart for the Sunday delivery."

"I guess so," I agreed.

"Know where we get 'em? Out from under the ground-floor stairwell of apartment houses. Some people, too lazy to carry baby carriages upstairs, just leave 'em there."

"You mean steal them?"

"Yup, but you gotta go pretty far from your own route. All you need are the springs and wheels—even then, disguise it by building a box on it.

Look, I've spotted one on my route that's just the ticket; let's get it."

It was a light, folding carriage that should have been easy to carry upstairs.

"See," the boy said, "they're just lazy."

So I learned to be "street smart" and was led into sin. Mom had set a moral code for us, but life didn't always seem to allow it. I had constant guilt feelings (and still do), because I felt that the cheapest carriage might very well belong to the poorest family, lazy or not!

With a Jewish friend, Shlomo, I had a Saturday enterprise—window cleaning. We kept a short list of repeat customers in the back of my *Bronx Home News* notebook roster. Our capital investment was minimal—a bucket, a cake of Bon Ami soap, and a roll of newspaper. Wet newsprint rubbed with the Bon Ami made a splendid (and cheap) glass cleaner. Dry newspaper finished the job without smears. We took turns doing the outside. You trusted your partner to hang onto your legs as you sat out and pulled the window down on your lap. It was 10 cents a window—whether first floor or fifth. But hey—remember that 10 cents would get you into a movie house!

THE BRONX ZOO: A FAMILY FRANCHISE, 1929+
The great Bronx Zoo was only a short walk from our house, and at one time the Willimetz family had taken it over, Sundays and holidays. My sister Marianna (now Mary), age 18, was a cashier at a refreshment stand; Lee, 16, was a soda jerk; Emil, age 11, a busboy; and Mom, 42, was cleaner of the zoo's public toilets. Hedy's turn came several years later, with a full-time job in the New York Zoological Society office. Pop, of course, was a freeloader customer.

Lee and Mary always were able to work, even on rainy days, but a busboy wasn't needed when things were slow—nor was a barker. The barker was the one who moved through the crowds with a megaphone: "GET YOUR ICE CREAM, SODAS, SANDWICHES, HOT DOGS . . . . THE STAND IS OPEN JUST DOWN THE STREET . . . . NO WAITING FOR SERVICE." (Oh, yeah?)

On cloudy days, the barker and I would wait on a park bench to see if the weather would clear. The barker was my first truly dirty old man. He would avidly tell me sex stories that made him gleeful and me sick. He also worked down by the Bronx River, where there were rental rowboats and a refreshment stand. One day when he noticed some activity under the wooden boardwalk, he crawled under to discover a pair of young teenagers making out.

"Well," he said, "did I have a time with them. I made them do things with me they never heard of." And he proceeded to tell me in loving detail.

But the tale that made me leave the bench was about a friend's seven-year-old girl for whom he was baby sitting—and making her have oral sex with him.

To get away from the bench, I took to hanging around the neighboring Reptile House, making friends with the attendants and helping them clean the glass cages—me on the outside, naturally. One day a gang of keepers carried a huge sleeping python out on the lawn. As they stretched it out full length, one keeper rammed a pole lined with skinned rabbits down the snake's throat to its stomach. Then back it went into its cage to coil up and slumber away for another few months. Watching all this beat working.

On overcast days, with threats of rain and no work, I would wander desolately around the zoo. It was on one of these gloomy walks that I discovered that camels spit. (Later in life, I found out that their cousins, llamas, do too.) The animals had cropped the grass close to the chain-link fence, and they stared at the lush bounty just outside, trying to tongue some in. Helpfully, I pulled up grass and fed it to them through the fence. At one point, some dried leaves got included, and the camel made a disdainful face and gathered his mouth to spit. I spun away and remained unblessed. My feeding efforts attracted a number of passersby who seemed to want to be entertained, so I slipped in some dried leaves and stepped back. I would like to point out that unemployment is detrimental to one's character.

As a busboy in the stand that employed my brother as a soda jerk, I had my pick of any of the delicious productions offered for sale—and some that were not offered for sale but were the invention of my fevered sweet tooth. In a very short time, believe it or not, I lost interest in most of the baroque concoctions—I was happy to settle for hot cocoa and grilled cheese sandwiches.

Occasionally there would be a small disaster. Items like Eskimo Pies would melt down enough to become deformed. Instead of throwing them away, we would take them with us on the way home and throw them, unwrapped, at parrots in an outdoor stand. Lee's baseball training stood him in good stead—a target properly hit would reward us with a bedlam of satisfying squawks. It would also net the parrot an Eskimo Pie.

One September, when it was starting to get dark early, we were almost all the way home when I discovered I had left my pay and tips in the pocket of my apron, which I had thrown into the laundry bag. Too embarrassed to tell Lee, I told him I was off to see friends. Then I returned to the gates alone. It wasn't easy, but I managed to find a dark corner where I could scale the fence. As I stumbled down the path to the pavilion, I kept brushing up against fences bordering cages and was greeted by sudden hisses, snarls, and growls. The camels uttered no sound as I passed their enclosure, but the squawking parrots increased my heartbeat. At least they let me know I was still on the right track. The thought of meeting a night patrol kept my nerves fine-tuned to hysteria. Finally I made it. Fortunately, the dirty laundry bin was outside the locked stand, and I rapidly fingered my way through the sticky, smelly stuff until I gratefully felt an apron with a pocket of nickel and dime tips and an envelope with a few dollar bills. Of course, I had to rerun the same gauntlet, but with a somewhat lighter heart, for I had my money and an envelope with the zoo imprint on it to prove I did indeed work there.

The year I was baptized, at age 11, I started to go to the 4 a.m. Catholic mass on Sunday—4 a.m. because I had to be at the *Bronx Home News* at 5 and the zoo at 10. It was known as the "working man's Mass," which added to my pride as a member of the proletariat. At the service, I noticed a scarcity of workmen. Most of the congregation seemed to be drunks parking their bottles outside in the bushes and going through the routine so they could get home and sleep it off. I felt very virtuous going to church (hoping to confess my sins?—such as stealing baby carriages?). I felt even more virtuous abandoning the church because of the hypocrisy of the drunks. I guess my heart was never in it at 4 a.m.!

John Galbraith says that the number of stockbrokers and wealthy entrepreneurs jumping out of Wall Street windows in 1929 was exaggerated. The suicide count, however, was minor compared to the great number of men whose will to live was destroyed by the Depression. Deprived of their traditional role as family breadwinners, seeing the havoc starvation created among their loved ones, they lost their reason for living. Immigrants, like Pop, speaking poor English, were hit extra hard. Many, like Pop, turned to gambling.

> *There was, interestingly enough, an upswing in playing the horses: half dollar bets, six bits: a desperate examination of THE RACING FORM. While lost blacks played the numbers, lost whites played the nags.*
> —Studs Terkel, *Hard Times*

Unemployed, Pop had time to play the horses—only not like anyone else! He was obsessed with the notion that all horse racing was fixed. Not just fixed, but fixed so that any gangster worth his place in gangsterdom would have the secret formula that gave him instant access to any day's daily double. Pop felt he could redeem his inability to support the family by decoding this lucrative Golden Horseshoe secret code. He bought the *Racing Form* every day, working out all the possible next-day results, placing $2 bets. He bought his spectacles across the Hudson in a Hoboken 5 & 10 store, using the *Racing Form* as the ultimate eye test. As the Depression deepened, he spent more and more time with his *Racing Forms*. When he could no longer make money bets, he kept track on the edges of the newspapers. I can still see him sitting at the dining-room table, in a marked state of despondency, obsessively tabulating race results. Year after year, the newspapers piled up in a corner of the living room. The Golden Horseshoe dream died only with Pop's death in 1967. I grew to hate gambling—even Bingo.

At least we avoided the double poverty of those who had seen "better days," Our "better days," in the rickety Bryant Avenue house, were not that much better, so the family settled in the basement without great trauma. Although many of my friends came from more financially secure families, I never felt inferior as a "janitor," but my sister Mary did. In her vulnerable teens, Mary was ashamed of living in the basement, descending the flight of iron stairs, and going through the furnace room. A dismal entrance, yes, but the apartment was clean and decent. One day she had a tea party, and Mom fixed all kinds of special things. The girls left early and Mary cried. Her unhappiness made me aware of the devastating effects of the Depression on our family. Mom kept it to herself, but she suffered on Mary's behalf.

Mary was born in October 1912, and Mom and Pop fled Vienna in 1913. Mom's mother-in-law had raised 10 children and was clearly competent to care for Mary. I can envision that the baby was still getting mother's milk when the decision was made to leave—or, at the very least, Mom would still have been strongly emotionally tied to her daughter.

It took several long years to get out of the cellar apartment, and it was Mary herself who made the move possible. Mary never finished high school; she dropped out to go to a secretarial school. The huge amount of paperwork generated by corporations opened doors for women workers. As a teenager in the Great Depression, Mary became a steady breadwinner, getting $12 to $15 a week. She worked for a time at a large insurance agency and later at a truck delivery company.

Dinner was a major source of family bonding. Everyone had equal rights at the dinner table, but Mary usually dominated—who could compete with her breathless tales of office intrigue? "I was standing by the water cooler . . . ." I preferred her truck company job, since, along with the intrigue, she also brought home ice cream and cookie samples from the salesmen.

My brother Lee was also a high school dropout—in his freshman year. Growing up, Lee had multiple jobs. The one as a Western Union messenger required a bike. Bikes being expensive, we bought up wrecks and rebuilt them. It wasn't necessarily the best of ideas. On one bike, Lee attached the front wheel to the main frame with a broomstick. Always pushing his limits, he was speeding downhill one day on a cobblestone street, and when he applied the brakes, the broomstick broke. Lee finished the hill on his backside. The experience made him painfully unemployable for a time.

His next big job upgrade was as a taxi driver. I don't know how the dates coincide, but when I saw Clifford Odets's epic taxi-strike play, *Waiting for Lefty,* I thought of my brother Lee's terse comments about his long hours and small paycheck. Some of the play's action even took place in our South Bronx neighborhood.

With anything requiring coordination, Lee was always superbly confident. One winter day, the long, steep hill on Bryant Avenue leading down to the Bronx River was a sheet of ice. Inviting me out in his cab, he careened down the hill. Suddenly braking, we spun around in several complete circles. Once was enough for me, but he had to do it a few more times before he would take me home.

In 1932, Lee and his friend Jack pooled their resources and bought an old car for $70. The Hutchinson River Parkway had just been completed, the very model of a modern superhighway. Lee proudly took the family for a Sunday drive on the new road. We rode the Hutch in that old car like royalty, but we never made it all the way home. About ten blocks from Crotona Park North, the gears quit. I spent the afternoon watching Lee and Jack strip the transmission system—fascinating! I can still see the bucket of kerosene filled with shining gears. They learned enough about keeping that old car running to take it out to the West Coast. The journey west ended (or the car did) over the mountains in a Washington State apple orchard, where they picked fruit for a living. This was a time when Burma-Shave signs edged the highways. (More of this later, when I take to the road.)

RIP A FENDER
OFF YOUR CAR
SEND IT IN
FOR A FIVE-POUND JAR
BURMA-SHAVE

One day, we received a crate of Washington Delicious apples, each piece of beautiful red fruit separately wrapped in tissue paper. The wonderful apple smell permeated our basement flat for about a month, as we slowly depleted the crate Lee had sent us.

Those great-looking Washington apples were sold by desperate jobless men on street corners. The Western Apple Growers Association, finding itself with a surplus of apples, decided to sell them on credit to the unemployed.

5¢—BUY AN APPLE A DAY AND EAT THE DEPRESSION AWAY!

Each man had to pay $1.75 for a crate and would make a profit of $1.85—assuming, of course, that he sold all his apples and found no rotten ones in the crate. Skilled, educated men selling apples became a symbol of the Great Depression. But not to everyone. President Herbert Hoover made probably one of the most astonishing remarks of his life when he wrote: "Many persons left their jobs for the more profitable one of selling apples."

In those days, without today's mechanical labor-savers, daily household chores were backbreaking for Mom. Monday was wash day, with corrugated scrubbing boards and washtubs. Water was boiled and clothes were presoaked, scrubbed, rinsed, and hand-wrung. Wet overalls became unbearably heavy to handle. In the backyard was a pole onto which clotheslines were hooked—one for each floor of the apartment house. I remember hearing about a four-year-old kid flying a kite on the roof being pulled over the edge, falling through consecutive levels of clotheslines, and living to tell the tale. In the winter, the clothes were brought inside so frozen that Mom could have walked them into the house.

Ironing was a difficult chore, and almost everything—from clothes to linens—was ironed. Mom had two detachable irons, one always heating on the stove. I remember the hiss of the iron going over damp clothes. Mom was never one to skimp or cut corners on any task, no matter how odious, and our shirts were always picture-perfect—mine for a short time, anyway.

Mom did all the house cleaning, made the beds, and, of course, did all the cooking. We had no frozen or convenience foods in those days, and precious few canned goods that Mom deigned to use or could afford. She never stopped. After a full and exhausting day, she would sit down and mend socks with a wooden egg. Often she layered thread over previous worn-out mends. Or she turned a collar, patched a ripped shirt or pants. The American concept of planned obsolescence had not been included in her Austrian peasant upbringing.

But in addition to her household chores, Mom also had numerous janitorial duties, like washing down the stairway of our apartment house. Unfortunately, my mother was a perfectionist—instead of cleaning five stories of marble steps with a mop, she went down on her knees and scrubbed it all with a brush. She also worked at times as a hotel chambermaid (as well as cleaning toilets in the zoo). It was a hard life, with few social or recreational compensations. As I grew older and more aware of life around me, my mother's increasing age lines tore at me.

When one of us was sick, Mom treated us at home, or we took our chances in the charity wards of city hospitals. Twice we called for a personal doctor to come to our house—once when Hedy had scarlet fever and then again when I had rheumatic fever.

My tonsils were taken out in the old Lincoln Hospital—where I, of course, was totally apprehensive and mistrusting. Between Mom and the doctor, I was calmed down and Mom left the operating room. The doctor had a cone into which he said I must blow hard to test my wind. I blew, my head spun, and I was out. I had been deceived—the cone contained ether! When I came to, my throat was painfully sore. Mom and the doctor were looking down at me, smiling. I had no time for the Doc—he was a deceiver! I wasn't even sure that Mom hadn't been in on the plot. Mom left the room and returned with a large dish of cool, soothing ice cream. It was easy to forgive a Mom like that!

At the NYU Dental College, I remember long rows of dental chairs with equipment trays, "rinse please" bowls, and drills. The master dentist professor would march down the rows, peering into mouths, criticizing the work. Just get it over with, please! I went several times to have my teeth repaired (and all four wisdom teeth were yanked out).

Mom came down with tuberculosis twice.

Mom had several operations that I was not privy to, but I do remember her telling us how angry she became when, after an operation to cut out a diseased kidney, the doctor asked her who had removed her appendix. She had no idea that it had ever been removed! Charity wards kept us alive, but they were never very obliging.

At the age of 11, I had become very aware of her failing health, her thinning face, and her wasting body. Although I never articulated my fears, even to myself, they had been building up in me. One day, coming home from PS 44, I saw Mom unconscious on the front stoop. She was surrounded by several of our tenants, all with that grave and studied look that people wear when facing someone else's disaster. She was dead, I knew she was, and I pushed past the group and knelt beside her. Her hand was icy cold.

"Your mother just fainted." "She'll be fine in a moment." "We'll take her into the house."

As I held her head in my lap, her eyelids began to flutter, and she gave me a wan smile and weakly squeezed my hand. With the help of our tenants, we helped her down the iron steps and through the furnace room to our apartment. As we tucked her in on the couch, she said, *"Mein* pail *ist* on the stoop."* As I started off to get it, she added, *"Kannst du* the floor dry *machen?"* She looked anxiously at me, insisting her job needed to be finished. I nodded and left.

I visited Mom in the old Lincoln Hospital. She was in a huge Victorian-era ward with dark wood-paneled walls and long rows of iron bedsteads. Curtains surrounded beds of patients being worked on or at death's door. Mom looked pale and lost, her dark hair spread out over her pillow. Pop and Mary looked solemn. I was engulfed by apprehension.

Mom, they said, had tuberculosis and would have to be away at a sanatorium for two years. With Grossmutter needing help in her old age, Mary and Lee working, Pop painting for the bank, no one could be at home to look after Hedy. She and I were to go to St. Agatha's Orphanage. Since Hedy was only five years old, I, at 11, was to go with her and take care of her.

I broke suddenly under the tension and, bursting into tears, fled the ward. Mary came after me. "It's not that bad, Emil. It's only for a short time, until Mom can come home. You won't be in the actual orphanage, but in a separate place with other children your age."

When Mary and I returned to the ward, Mom reached out to pat my hand, which started a laughing jag and another dash out of the room. I guess I finally calmed down, ashamed that with my hysterics I was causing my mother further stress when she clearly had more than she needed.

I'll never know the quality of the health care my mother received, but I do know that she was a strong woman from sturdy peasant stock. Her major source of illness, TB, was from the ceaseless toil and the constant tensions of poverty. TB was a killer during the Great Depression, and it almost took my Mom.

For me, the image of my mother lying "dead" on the front steps of our apartment stoop was the defining moment of my total awareness of the Depression, and my growing hatred for the system that treated poor people this way.

The main building and playground at Nanuet.

THE ORPHANAGE AT NANUET

Nanuet was across the Hudson River, near the village of Nyack, New York—not more than 30 miles from the Bronx. St. Agatha's Orphanage was a large outfit draped on the top and sides of a hill. Our unit was separate from the main complex but connected with it—we were fed from the same kitchen. The "temporary" orphanage (I believe it might have been called the Preventorium) consisted of a dorm, a dining room, a one-room school, and a large play yard.

Hedy, her first night in strange surroundings, afraid to leave her bed, wet it. The Matron rubbed the wet sheet under her nose. It was not a good beginning. Along the bathroom wall was a row of sinks, where the Matron would station herself with a giant bottle of cod-liver oil and an outsize (seemed like) tablespoon with the plating worn off. She would fill the spoon and you would step up and have it jammed into your mouth. The spoon would be perfunctorily rinsed under the hot-water faucet and the next protesting kid would be hauled up under the baleful eye of the Prefect, our male guardian. Some kids would hold the oil in their mouths, slip into a toilet stall, and spit it into the bowl. What's the sense of that? I guess I was old enough to know that this indignity was in the name of our good health.

The Matron had large, square black buttons on a white uniform that stared at some kids at eye level. Hedy says she still feels nauseous whenever she sees large, square buttons on a white dress. The large bathroom was split by a makeshift plywood partition that separated the sexes. As we prepared for bed, I strained to hear sounds of Hedy but never did. One night, the bathroom was rent by terrible piercing screams and much frantic activity coming from the girls' side. Terrified, I rushed to the partition door, but the Prefect had gotten there first.

"Stay here and keep the other boys out!" he ordered, as he slid past me into the other room. His appearance gradually calmed the troubled waters and after a time he returned to us.

"Nothing to worry about, fellows," he said with a sheepish grin. "It was all my fault. I reached through the partition to open the window, and some girl saw my hairy hand and screamed. I guess you know how girls are." I longed to comfort my sister, but on the other side of the partition, she was hopelessly out of my jurisdiction.

At 3 p.m., after school, we lined up again for another health break. This time, it was a battered metal cup dipped directly into a large milk can. The milk had eggs, sugar, and vanilla beaten into it, and I liked it. Hedy hated it—it did have its occasional glop of raw egg white.

Our hot meals came to us from the main orphanage in large, round, insulated containers. Our daily breakfast was oatmeal, with milk, butter, and sugar to liven it up—plus toast and cocoa. On Sunday, it was cornflakes and milk. For lunch we had peanut butter and other types of sandwiches, and for dinner we had boiled potatoes, turnips, and cabbage— with butter, salt, and pepper, the cabbage and potatoes were acceptable, but turnips left the dining room in kids' shirt pockets. There must have been other things, but that's all I can remember. At the foot of our hill were great manure piles—insulation cover for cabbages. Every day, we could see them digging for dinner in the huge piles.

In Nelson Mandela's *Long Road to Freedom*, he describes how, whenever journalists visited the prison on Robben Island, the prisoners were given a pile of worn shirts to repair instead of the daily rock pile. Most Sundays at the orphanage, we had a weak beef or lamb stew with potatoes and carrots, but when we had official visitors (and for Thanksgiving and Christmas), we had chicken or turkey with sweet potatoes.

We spent our evenings in a huge, fenced-in playground with swings, teeter-totters, and slides. These were the most difficult hours for Hedy and me. Hedy's severe depression expressed itself in frequent tears, which of course depressed me, and I spent most of this time trying to keep her amused. Since being pushed on the swings seemed to give her pleasure, she was swung incessantly. As we reached the apogee of the push, Hedy would shout in exultation. The higher the arc, the more full-throated the glee. It was one of the few moments of solace I was able to give my young sister, and I flew her in sync with her upbeat mood.

This, at times, involved the playground Prefect, who was intent on flagging down the high flyers. The Prefect was a hard-nosed character, and it took a certain amount of finesse to avoid his wrath. Asking to go to the bathroom earned a whack, just to make sure you were committed.

The main buildings were surrounded by high walls, and because we could never see the orthodox orphans, the happenings behind the wall took on a sinister aspect. A major infraction of the rules brought threats of being shipped to the main orphanage next door, with Dickensian details of the harsh life to be found there.

Fear was a constant companion, fear for my mother's life—a heavy weight of lead that settled on my chest. During the day, when I was busy with tasks and school, it lay hardly noticed. In the evening play yard with Hedy, when the bells tolled for the Angelus, I would stop to look at the main orphanage, where the sound came from. Then recurring thoughts would engulf me. What if our mother never came back? What would life be without her? Would we be sent to the neighboring orphanage? I didn't really think so, but then . . . ?

There were only three boys in the oldest age group—an Irish kid named Bill Gannon, me, and a guy whose name I can't remember but will call Bully, since I felt he was a born one. Fighting with fists was one of the major infractions. One evening, I had my little sister in a happy mood, romping around the yard, when along came Bully and knocked her down.

Hedy, left, about the age when we went to Nanuet.

I will never be sure that this was a purposeful act, but it infuriated me, and I grabbed his coat and flung him to the pavement. Bill quickly got between us and led us to the back of the school building, out of sight of authority. I had my first fistfight, which ended in Bully's nosebleed. A bloody shirt would be hard to explain, so the fight was prudently called off. It was no great victory for me, but it did keep Bully off my back for the rest of our Nanuet stay. Bill and I became good friends. He came from a much poorer, depressed area of the Bronx than we did. His tales of life made me feel very fortunate.

We had visits from Mary and Pop, which upset Hedy more than ever but netted us gifts from home—mostly clothes, cake, and books. Money sent by the families was placed on account in the commissary, which was open each evening. We could buy candy, cookies, toothpaste, and so forth. I also bought more than my share of batteries, since I did most of my reading by flashlight in bed under the blanket. Bill never went to the commissary, since he knew the cupboard, for him, was bare. By getting him to help me entertain Hedy, I convinced him that he was part of the Willimetz family, and he reluctantly agreed to share our loot with us.

In the winter, we had three old Flexible Flyer sleds, one without a steering device. On the broken sled, it took heroic measures and a lot of body English to avoid the dung piles at the foot of the hill. How I longed to have Anna and Unk share the sport with us!

The schoolhouse was a single, square building—a one-roomer for all grades. A nun who had been put out to retirement pasture was our all-grades teacher. It would be hard to remember what I learned in my two-year stay. There are missing elements in my primary schooling—like grammar and spelling. Hey! What's a past participle?

Some unthinking architect designed the school building with a circling belt of windows—each window divided into countless square panes. I know they were countless, because my only firm memory of school was washing those tiny panes.

We were at Nanuet for about two years. When Mom came home from the sanatorium, we came home from the orphanage. Mary arrived at St. Agatha's to get us, and as happy as I was, leaving Bill was a downer. We both knew that the chance of his moving permanently to the orphanage next door was very real.

3.

Growing Up in the Bronx

OUR LIVING SPACE MAY HAVE BEEN BELOW-GROUND and dingy, but instead of being hemmed into a slum area with poor schools and high crime, it was in a respectable Jewish neighborhood. Many of our neighbors were active union members employed in the garment trades. The apartment house was adjacent to Crotona Park—the setting of many Indian rituals, Zionist dances, adventures, and misadventures. It was a large green space, with hills and dales, woods, mammoth rocks, playing fields—even a small lake complete with rental rowboats. Indian Lake, being a dump for unwanted goldfish, was a sportsman's haven for underage Izaak Waltons. In winter, the lake froze over for ice-skating, and the hills were great for sledding and skiing on barrel staves.

The average American boy is good at catching balls. With me, it was not always a foregone conclusion. I don't want to give the impression that I had a deprived childhood, with all work and no play, but the truth is that I wasn't always available to be part of organized games like baseball and street stickball, so I failed to develop the needed skills. Stickball was a Great Depression game, since all that was needed was a Spalding ball, a broomstick, and bare hands in lieu of baseball gloves. The game started with choosing sides. With my reputation, I was always taken last and positioned out in left field.

However, without boasting, I can say I played schoolyard baseball with the best of them. In those days, we wore knickers that fastened just below the knee and had buttons instead of zippers for the fly. The game required a bit of stealth and firm, quick fingers. Sneak up behind your opponent, reach around his legs, grip the edge of his fly with hooked fingers, and rip. Popping one button was a first base, two a second, and four a home run. Home runs were rare, and were accorded much acclaim. I remember asking Mom, after an active day in the schoolyard, if she could use a double thread to sew on some new buttons. She never questioned me, but with a slight smile, she made them invincible.

Paramount Pictures had a movie lot in our neighborhood, a square city block surrounded by a high wall. Occasionally, objects would be visible above the wall. One time, we watched a World War I dogfight, with small toy planes battling on thin, invisible wires, smoke pouring out of their tails.

We had another use for old tennis balls and Spaldings, a game called stoop-ball. A short flight of some six marble steps led up to the front door of our apartment house. The game consisted of standing in the gutter and hurling the ball at the steps. If you hit the side of a step, it would return bouncing on the sidewalk. If you hit an edge, it would arc back without a bounce. The point was to accumulate the highest percentage of arcs before you missed a toss. It was the sort of mindless game to pass the time waiting for something else to happen. Sidewalk solitaire.

One day, I was listlessly throwing the ball against the stoop when a movie crew truck pulled up. I was persuaded (with the offer of a $20 bill) to continue playing while they filmed the arrival of a large luxury car. I recognized the actor immediately—it was Lewis Stone. My role was to stop playing to watch this elegant man enter our humble apartment house. The film was to be released as *Too Much Money,* and it had to do with Stone's problem of having—you guessed it—too much money (a problem unbelievably improbable to us). I never did see the movie, so I can't comment on my appearance as an actor. I might even have been the face on the cutting-room floor.

As a youngster, I was painfully shy, but don't think being in the movies made me any less so. It took a long time of growing up to come to grips with it. When I was about 10, someone gave Mom a complete white sailor suit, which she laboriously cut down to my size. The shirt had a large, square collar with a rim of blue piping. The pants had a full U-shaped panel, like winter underwear but with the flap in front. It was closed by a rim of 13 buttons, one for each of the 13 colonies. Hey, sailor, want to play schoolyard baseball? The white Dixie Cup hat was a lifesaving device—it would float to mark a man overboard. The only thing missing were the gold earrings that Old Tars wore to pay for their funerals.

I really felt like somebody, as I paraded around the house in full uniform. One of my secret delights, when I went to bed, was to invent stories wherein I played heroic roles—a Walter Mitty thing. For the next many nights, I sailed the seven seas and had many great adventures, all in my white sailor suit.

One summer day, I decided to wear it outdoors. In the bright sun, it was dazzling, a suit of light. Too much. A great torment. I couldn't be seen in it, but could I hurt my mother's feelings by not wearing it? Before my friends could see me, I raced back down into our basement apartment and tore it off—never to wear it again. So much for Walter Mitty! Poor Mom, she had to put up with a lot with her son Emil.

The Austrian Christmas differs in that it is celebrated not the morning of the 25th, when folks get out of bed, but one minute after midnight of the 24th, before folks go to bed. At our supper table on the 24th, there was not a sign of Christmas. Out of sight, but thickly present, was anticipation.

After supper, Mary, as the oldest, would take us to the movies—two feature films, a Looney Tunes cartoon, a newsreel, several previews of coming attractions, and a serial. The serial, such as *The Perils of Pauline,* would end abruptly just as Pauline was tied to the tracks, her eyes bugging out in terror, with the whistle shrieking loudly as the train was about to cut her in two . . . . "TO BE CONTINUED NEXT WEEK." It would be close to midnight before we returned home.

The kids gone, Mom and Pop would spin off in high gear. Pop would rush down to pick up a tree at next-to-nothing last-minute prices. After setting it up in the apartment, he would do a whirlwind tour of predetermined stores to buy presents (also at last-minute prices). Mom would decorate the tree. She'd hang a few Christmas bulbs, Santa Clauses, and angels; drape strings of food-colored popcorn; and attach walnuts, Hershey kisses, and oranges to the branches. (Oranges in those days were a treat.) She would then clip about a dozen small candles to the outer tips of the boughs. It was a virtuoso performance, and we would return home to be dazzled.

At one second after midnight, presents would be distributed. Lee once received a Flexible Flyer sled, and I a Tinkertoy kit. We managed simple presents for Mom and Pop. When all of us were working, we would get together and buy Mom some labor-saving kitchen gadget, like a motor-driven clothes wringer, an electric beater, or a pressure cooker. But she used only some of them, whipping eggs with a fork and cream with a hand beater. When Joie and I returned from Peru in 1970, we lived in Hedy's house in Queens. Hedy took many of these 25-year-old appliances out of storage and we added another 15 years to their service.

But the major emphasis at Christmas was mostly on haberdashery. Were clothes really gifts? Or just necessities? For us, new clothes were not an everyday happening, so they were very much appreciated.

As part of his last-minute shopping, our "half-price" Pop bought a five-pound box of assorted chocolates. A ritual before going to bed was the selection of two agonized-over pieces—and no spit-backs! The big advantage of the Austrian Christmas over the American tradition was being able to sleep late on the 25th!

BRONX INDIANS, 1926-1930

There were no books in our house, but there was a public library on the far side of Crotona Park, and I was able, at a tender age, to get a library card. The books I liked the most were stories about fictional Indians—the adventures of Running Fox and Spotted Deer stay in my mind. (Later it was James Fenimore Cooper.) My animated reading of exciting Indian adventures to my older brother Lee turned him on, and at the age of eight, I was the resource person for the authentication of an Indian tribe.

It hasn't made the anthropology books, but during the Great Depression, an Indian tribe of some 10 to 15 members existed in the Bronx. I was the youngest member of the tribe, and my brother Lee was the undisputed Chief. To advance up the tribal ladder—Papoose, Squaw, Brave, Warrior, Chief—one went through a series of qualifying tests. Sure, this was an urban Indian Society, but our initiations were tied in with whatever nature was available to us—Crotona Park and the Bronx River, which ran through a part of the Bronx Zoo and the Botanical Gardens. Crotona Park had a huge rock the size of a house, brought down from Canada by glaciers for our tribal use. The rock had a slope that gradually increased in steepness, ideal for an initiation—namely, to see how far you could run up before having to use your hands for support and balance. It was a matter of speed and stamina. At this, I made "Brave."

To spy out the land, tall trees had to be climbed. Lee selected a straight, smooth-bark hickory that went up about 75 feet before the first branches. You were graded on the distance you could shinny up this tree—no small task, and it had an element of danger. Under Lee's urgings, I got about halfway up the tree when my strength gave out. I had pushed myself beyond my limits and clung to the tree exhausted and in panic. "That's far enough, Emil," yelled Lee. "Hold on and rest. You've got more than enough to make Brave." (Brave being my tribal status thus far.) As I regained confidence, Lee talked me down a few feet at a time, but on the last yards I couldn't hold and slid down so fast I burned my legs and tore my pants. This wasn't too popular with Mom, but it didn't detract from my making Brave.

According to tribal rank, we followed our chief, whooping and growling menacingly, through crowded Bronx streets, in and out of traffic and into the woods of Bronx Park—about a three-mile expedition. The Bronx River had a 15-foot waterfall, below which the water was tidal. The jumble of rocks at the foot of the falls afforded us good hunting for crawdads and crabs. When the tide was low, it was a slippery and wet ford to the other, less inhabited, side of the river.

One day, arriving at the falls, we found the tide high, which meant a walk downriver to cross a bridge. Lee held us at the falls, took off his sneakers and socks, and walked out to where the river poured over the edge. As he gingerly worked his way out for about 10 feet, his confidence increased. Turning, he danced back to us.

Lee: stalwart leader of our Indian tribe.

"It's duck soup," he boasted. "The top of the falls is lined with slate slabs, and the rush of water keeps the last foot or so clean. Farther in, the water seems deeper and green with slime or somethin', so keep to the edge. Indians have courage, so let's go."

Jack, Lee's immediate rival for Chief, stripped off his shoes and socks and started off. Others followed. Seeing my hesitation, Lee slapped me on the shoulder.

"Come on, Emil. It's safe and easy, I'll help you."

I tied my sneakers together, stuffed my socks inside them, and hung them around my neck. I didn't have to roll up my pants, since I was wearing knickers, which buckled just below my knees. Lee held my hand and we started across. It was as he said—duck soup. My bare feet seemed to stick to the slate, the rushing water whipping past my ankles but without menace. I shook loose from Lee's helping hand. It felt exhilarating to be making it on my own and gaining me points toward Warrior status. I even stopped looking down at the rock below. The few no-goes shamefully hiked down to cross the bridge, dropping their Warrior status to Brave—at least for a time. The falls became part of the tribal initiation.

One day, initiating two new tribal members on the dam crossing, Lee invented a new task for us. Upstream, out of sight of the boat rental docks, the river was lined with dense bushes, a site Lee chose for our new challenge.

"True Indians," he announced, "running along their trails, were never stopped by rivers or streams. They stripped off their clothes and swam across bare-assed."

"But what do we do with our clothes?" we asked.

Never daunted, our Chief invented rules as needed. "We tie our clothes on top of our heads. Poor swimmers can hang onto logs, but this earns a downgrade in status."

Sunday rowers were a major obstacle, so timing and speed were of the essence. We stripped, tied our bundled clothes to our heads with shirtsleeves, and huddled in the deep bushes for the last rowboat to round the bend. My swimming experiences at St. Paul's Camp stood me in good stead. Trying to keep my head high above the water, I kept up a strained breaststroke that left me last in the race. "Rowboats coming around the bend. Hurry, Emil, hurry." With the great extra effort, my clothes got soaking wet! Nothing new. They would dry in the sun while strewn all over one of the great boulders gifted us by Canada.

Two (more urban) tasks were included in the initiations. A good Indian was stealthy enough to steal horses from under the noses of the Palefaces. This task came in two parts: One was to swipe a potato off the vegetable stand and the other was to sneak into the movie house (stockade) on a Saturday matinee. The vegetable stand was easy—all it required was good timing. The movie was not so easy, because ushers (Blue Coats) were employed as sentries to prevent illegal entry. Loitering near the theater exit when the show let out, I snagged a discarded ticket-half. In those days, the entire theater didn't empty out after a show; many were waiting to see the second feature. In the melee, I managed to find myself inside. Unchallenged but with an un-Indian beating heart, I wandered back to sit next to tribal members who awaited me there.

The stolen potatoes were cooked in the hot coals of an evening campfire in Crotona Park. The potatoes, with a quarter-inch charred crust, were super-delicious; we called them mickies. Mickie was an Irish term—didn't everybody know potatoes came from Ireland? We would have been prouder had we known that potatoes were basic to New World Indians.

Being an Indian had its downside. When I was nine, I had been winter trapping with the tribe in the wild swamps of Van Cortlandt Park, breaking through the thin ice and stalking wild game all day with cold, wet feet. After that, I had to stay home from school for several months with rheumatic fever. Fortunately, the disease didn't affect my heart, as it frequently can. I mistakenly mentioned it to an army doctor one time, and he had me doing gymnastics trying to detect a damaged heart. I guess he thought I was trying to get away with something.

As Urban Indians, we lived in an urban village—namely, in the 2-by-4 scaffolding that held up a large billboard. Here we had built cardboard wigwam houses and held our powwows. Standing high on the billboard scaffolding, with elbows on the billboard's 6-inch-wide cap, we could peer into the windows of passing elevated trains (wagon trains to Oregon). Two stories below us ran a hard river of concrete—the sidewalk.

Lee's principal rival for Chief was his good friend Jack, who mirrored him in physical dexterity—almost. One day, viewing the wagon trains from the top of the two-story billboard, Lee invented a new initiation rite. You were to be graded on your Indian bravery by perching on the 6-inch cap—sitting, kneeling, or standing. I warily maintained my position as Brave by cautiously straddling the cap. Several of the Warriors managed to get up on their knees, but only Lee and Jack had the true Warrior bravado to stand erect. Seeing Jack standing up, Lee dropped to his knees, grasping the 6-inch board, and guaranteed his position of Chief by doing a handstand. It all happened so quickly that it was only afterward that I became weak with fear. If anything had been wrong with my rheumatic heart, I'd have dropped dead there and then. I guess I loved my brother, but how much of my deep sense of responsibility for him came from my dread of having to report to Mom some disaster that I didn't prevent?

Lee and I had gone to the Big Brother Camps, which had this objective: "By removing the boys from the distraction of crowded city living, it is possible to change the course of their poor habits and tendencies and redirect them into natural and constructive channels." Despite their pretensions of remaking my poor character, I was molded by only one Big Brother—my sibling Lee. He was truly a great Indian chieftain and a first-class brother. I never fully realized how noble he was to include me, even though I was four years younger, in so many of his activities. I was proud of him and proud to have maintained my position of Brave in his tribe. He pushed me to dare more than was my norm, building up the drive that later took me wandering throughout the United States and beyond.

The tribe broke up when Lee began to date. As much as he hated to see the tribe disband, you can't take a tribe on a date—there was no Brave category for his kid brother in this activity! I reluctantly blew taps for the tribe on my mute Big Brother Camps bugle.

4.

How Odd of God to Choose the Jews

Roses are reddish,
Violets are bluish,
If it weren't for Christmas,
We'd all be Jewish.

In my early years in the Li'l It'ly section of the Bronx, when I was about five, our gang accosted a Jewish kid who was naive enough to wander into our territory. He was immediately surrounded, rough hands gripping his shirt.

"Hey, Yid, you believe in Christ?"

The boy, eyes wide with fright: "Huh?"

Whop! "Stay outta Li'l It'ly, ya fuckin' Christ killer!" Whop!

I guess I was almost as shocked as the little boy. I can still see his frightened face. I kept my mouth shut, relieved that they had never asked *me* if *I* believed in Christ. Who? HE was a stranger to the Willimetz family, my father being a Viennese Socialist and my mother anti-Catholic. I was willing to acknowledge HIM if it meant so much to my friends, but the violence made me uncomfortable. Was HE somebody you needed to beat up on a fellow for?

One time we tied a small Jewish boy to a billboard, knowing that his big brother passed that way going home from the elevated station. We watched with glee as the boy was released and led home in tears. But then we scattered. We knew vengeance would soon be coming back down the street in the shape of the older brother and his friends.

A few years later, our family moved across the line to the predominantly Jewish neighborhood adjacent to Crotona Park. I made my mark (and a few dimes) in the Bronx as the neighborhood *Shabbat* (Sabbath) *goy* (non-Jew). I was called in to light fires in cookstoves and to do other small jobs for pious Jews who couldn't "work" after sundown on Fridays. As a *goy*, I was an intimate witness to the culture of my Jewish friends. I'd be sitting in a living room with a friend when an ancient rabbi would come shuffling in, long white beard and all, nod to my friend, and disappear with him into another room—for Bar Mitzvah lessons, I was told. Letters of the Hebrew alphabet flowed through the door . . . *alpha, beta, gimme dollar* . . . well, something like that. (Actually, it was *aleph, beth, gimel, daleth,* and so on.) Hebrew was the language of the ancient Jews and of the Torah (book of Jewish laws), and now it is the official language of Israel. It is said that one prayed to God in Hebrew but pleaded with Him in Yiddish! Even though I grew accustomed to talk of Passover and Hanukkah, I was always the stranger at the table.

The 174th Street elevated ("el") train station and almost all the stores in our neighborhood were on Southern Boulevard, at the foot of a steep, three-block-long hill. This hill was quite a chore for many of the older folk, so I had a thriving Sunday morning business of bringing up Sunday papers, cigarettes, and fresh bakery goods. With the tips, I would buy slices of pineapple cheesecake for the family—super delicious, and a stroke of pride for me to be a provider of such luxury. The Depression wasn't all Hell.

The only store at the top of the hill was Schechter's Grocery. On the window was a sign in large, gilt Hebrew letters. It gave Mr. Schechter's store a mystical aura. I never grew comfortable seeing Hebrew lettering on shop windows—the signs always seemed strange and cabalistic to me.

"Mr. Schechter, what does that say?"

"Kosher."

"Oh."

"Kosher means," he said, "that a licensed Jewish *schochet* (butcher) killed and blessed the meat and that the meat is clean." This put a new light on the contents of the store for me. The chickens Mom bought were always kosher. She said she trusted them to be fresh.

Mr. Schechter himself was anything but a mystic, just a prosaic purveyor of groceries. We had a white-enamel two-quart milk bucket, which I would take to the store to be filled at 5 cents a quart. Mr. Schechter had a multigallon milk can straight from the dairy. Prying off the heavy lid, he would thrust in a long-handled, one-quart dipper and carefully decant it into my bucket.

One spring day, he said, *"Kindila* (little boy), would you be too busy the next days?"

"Well, Mr. Schechter, I have school and the *Bronx Home News,* but I could work after and practically all day Saturday."

"OK by me, it all helps. Come in tomorrow when you can. I have many deliveries. You know Passover?"

"Yeah." A big Jewish holiday for eating.

The deliveries, stacked up for me, were in large bags, and I was glad I brought my illicit cart. Actually, weight had no relation to size—large boxes of matzos seemed to make up the bulk. One of my stops was at my friend Shlomo's apartment, and his family invited me to join them in a *seder.*

"What's a *seder?*"

Shlomo's father, who usually mostly ignored me, was today in a teaching mood.

"It's a feast at Passover celebrating the Jewish Exodus from Egypt," he intoned. "Matzo was the unleavened bread eaten by the Jews on their flight."

Because, I gathered, they didn't have time for the bread to rise before they fled. He would have gone on in this vein, but Shlomo broke in with a piece of matzo and a small glass of thick, sweet Manischewitz wine. Surrounded by the jovial family, amid jokes about the *Shabbat goy* who delivers unleavened bread to the fleeing Jews, I learned also: "Passover lasts eight days and only Passover foods are eaten."

"That's why, you *schlemiel*," butts in Shlomo, "your grocery bags are so big—we eat lots of matzos!"

"Hey!" I jumped up. "I left my wagon downstairs full of Passover groceries. I gotta go." Amid a chorus of farewell *shaloms*, I fled. The groceries were untouched. Could you do that today?

Many of my Jewish friends in the Bronx had split personalities, divided between religious Jewish home life and Christian America's secular rituals. The great hoopla of Christmas was particularly upsetting, and many admitted shamefacedly to participating in gift exchanges or feeling envious of their non-Jewish friends.

Like me, many had immigrant parents, and I constantly heard:

"On the subway, I would pretend that the couple reading a Yiddish newspaper wasn't with me."

"My parents were helpless when it came to helping me with homework."

"I hated it when my parents had to come to school, with their heavy Yiddish accents."

One of my wife Joie's fellow schoolteachers had a Jewish immigrant mother who was valiantly struggling with English. On the subject of racial tolerance, she stated: "Some of my best friends are 'Genitals'!"

Children were pushed by their parents to become doctors and lawyers, professions not available to Jews in their original homelands.

A grandma out with her two grandchildren stopped to talk to the *rebbetzn* (rabbi's wife). "Aye, such lovely boys," the *rebbetzn* crooned. "Tell me, how old are they?"

"The doctor is four," explained grandma, "and the lawyer is six."

Jewish culture infiltrated almost every facet of life in the Bronx. Yiddish words were sprinkled into joshing conversations, and ribald jokes had enough German for me to get the gist of them. Jewish vaudeville and plays were common in the city, and stars such as Molly Pickens, Sophie Tucker, and Fanny Brice had their faces plastered large on the walls and billboards of our neighborhood. Al Jolson, Eddie Cantor, George Burns, Groucho Marx, Irving Berlin, and George Gershwin—all Jews—were stars in the entertainment world.

An immigrant Romanian Jew waiting tables in my favorite Bronx restaurant would profess utter boredom: "Menus we don't have. You wanna read, go to the liberry!"

But if you picked something from his recited menu that he didn't recommend, he'd say, "Personally, I wouldn't eat that, but you can have it—you want?"

His Jewish brashness added flavor and character to the restaurant—fortunately, the food was good.

Here's a story collected by Jonathan Williams, a poet I knew at Highlands, North Carolina, and met again at a Black Mountain College reunion in 1995:

A man on a streetcar in Kansas City sat behind a distinguished-looking black man wearing a little yarmulke and reading a Hebrew newspaper, right to left, right to left.

He couldn't resist, so he tapped his companion on the shoulder: *"Du bist a Yid?"* (You are a Jew?)

The black man turned around and shrugged heavily, *"Oy vey, duss iss alles vuss fehlt mir!"* (Oh, man, that's all I need!)

There are, of course, black Jews, like Sammy Davis, Jr., in the United States. Black Ethiopian Jews have settled in Israel. And there are tribes in Africa that claim to be descendants of a lost tribe of Israel.

Crotona Park dominated nine years of my life; it's where I learned to grow and to play, how to approach girls and how not to approach girls. The park was also a focus for the restless young folk who lived around its perimeter, an Africa to be carved up and exploited by imperial forces. I learned about tolerance and intolerance. It wasn't all that easy.

One day, our gang (veterans representing Crotona Park North) was wandering around the park's eastern flank. We came across a square hole in the ground about the size of a boxing ring, neatly excavated, and about four feet deep. We puzzled over its function. For some inexplicable purpose, I had jumped down into the pit just as a Freeman Street posse (Crotona Park East) arrived.

I was paying no attention to the upper rim when suddenly a heavy object landed on my back. I guess the temptation was just too much for the Freeman Streeter, who wrapped his feet tightly around my waist and clamped an arm in a chokehold around my neck. It was The Old Man of the Sea and Sinbad, and great fun—for him! Whenever I tried to slam him against the wall or pinch his arm, he would tighten his chokehold. Then, as suddenly as he had appeared on my back, he was gone. It was the Polish boy, my fellow backyard sweeper, who happened to be roving around with us. He had jumped into the pit and yanked the boy off my back by his hair. Standing close to him, I was shocked and frightened by the savage look on his face. Pale and taut with anger, he lashed out at the boy with his fist. It was a deadly blow, with the full force of his body behind it, and the boy fell to the ground, unconscious.

The Pole helped me out of the pit and scrambled up after me. Then we sauntered off northward, leaving stunned Freemanites administering to their fallen champion. It was getting dark when, passing the flank of a small hill, we were met by a hail of rocks—a Freeman Street ambush. I was struck full in the eye, and blood poured down my face. I howled in anguish—convinced I had lost my eye! Taking me with them, our gang retreated out of the park. The Pole took me into his basement, where we washed out the wound. Fortunately, the stone had been flat where it struck. It cut me on the eyebrow and nose but missed the eyeball. From the pain, I was also convinced that my nose had been broken. (It wasn't.)

With a bloody handkerchief held to my eye, I had little hope of getting past the family to the bathroom for further tidying up. My main concern was Mom, wanting somehow to ease her pain at my pain. But, as always, Mom was made of sterner stuff, and she was very matter-of-fact yet soothing in her ministrations.

The Pole never tried to collect on the debt I owed him—the violent action seemed to be its own reward. Instead, he drifted away from our ken completely. Years later, I heard that he had been drafted or had volunteered in the early days of World War II. He was killed in the invasion of Sicily, one of the first in our neighborhood to die in that war.

A tiny scar in my left eyebrow is not the only memento of those early experiences. I have similar scars in my scalp. When I lived in Little Italy, I had learned about religious intolerance, but the Crotona Park inhabitants were largely of the same faith. The motivation for our gangs was xenophobic nationalism—a disease that infects most nations in the world, not excluding Israel.

Under the influence of my friends, I become an ardent Zionist in the 1930s. We sang in Hebrew (sort of) and circle-danced the *hora* in Crotona Park—evoking a new state for Jews into being! Israel became a state in 1948, and now, when I read about its many trials, I still feel involved. They have always seemed to be infected with the same diseases from which Americans suffer: right-wing, narrow-visioned politicians; orthodox religious fanatics; and lack of compassion for poverty-stricken Third World neighbors. I bear no ill will against Israel today, although the joy has gone out of the dancing.

5.

LIFESTYLES OF THE POOR AND UNKNOWN—THE FAMILY WILLIMETZ

MY SISTER MARY

Born October 7, 1912, in Vienna, Austria
Died June 6, 1987, in Bethpage, Long Island, New York, age 75

ALTHOUGH BORN IN AUSTRIA, Mary was, of course, automatically a U.S. citizen, since her parents were. Always independent she went to get her own citizenship papers. A high school dropout, after World War II she studied to pass her high school equivalency test and became the Bethpage, Long Island, town librarian.

When Mary retired, overweight and wearing a pacemaker, she went on a travel binge that took her around the world—several times. Her doctor advised her to slow down. He admonished her, "Stay home or else!" Mary replied, "Doc, if I stop, I'll die." At the age of 75, she was forced to stop, and her prediction came true.

MARIANNA LEOPOLDINA WILHELMINA FREDERIKA

My sister's name? Oh, yes—my sister's names! My older sister is not really Mary—not by a long shot. She was born in Vienna and was only a few months old when Mom and Pop had to leave her to come to New York. She was baptized as Marianna Leopoldina Wilhelmina Frederika Willimetz, a heavy burden laid on her by male relatives wanting their

Mary

names to make the momentous journey to America. She called herself Mary in pure self-defense.

With all her grandiose names, Mary was brought to the New World some time after her first birthday by Pop's mother. I don't think Mom ever got over her guilt of having to leave her behind when they first came to the States. Hedy says Mary had a heart murmur as a child. Growing up, as I knew her, she was a lithe, attractive girl. I know so little about my sister Mary. Being six years older, she was usually way beyond my ken, but I got along pretty well with her—apart from the time, as her best man, that I arrived late to her wedding. (You'll hear from her about that!)

For years, a beautiful zither hung around the Willimetz apartments—a strange, foreign musical instrument I would listlessly strum on rainy days. The zither, for me, stands for the many details about our family history we never thought to ask about. Was it a treasure brought from

Vienna? We'll never know. The zither, evidently, spoke to our Pop. Chock full of Viennese genes, we all must have fine musical talents, right? Wrong!

Mary was tethered early to a piano, but by the time I was becoming aware of things, she had already admitted defeat.

MARY'S WEDDING, MAY 1, 1937

Mary no doubt had experiences that weren't aired at the dinner table. Of her serious boyfriends I only knew Victor, who was studying to be a naval architect. When I worked the summer of 1937 at the hotel on top of Mount Washington, he came to visit me. We had a great race down the mountain together. He was my kind of guy, but I think he had too many years of schooling ahead of him for Mary. I voted for him but lost the election to Charles Buxton. Victor played the piano at Mary and Charlie's wedding, which proves my point—a great guy.

I happened to be the best man at all Willimetz family weddings. I could have done better! But it wasn't all my fault. Mary chose to get married on MAY DAY, the day of the Great Workers' Parade! And in the ROCKEFELLER CATHEDRAL!

In any case, I was the hit of the parade, the only one in a blue serge suit, white shirt, and tie in a sea of blue jeans and work shirts. Wouldn't you know, it turned out to be a bright, sunny day—and hot. I opened my tie and shirt and carried my coat over my arm, but I still sweltered.

I figured that by dropping out of the march at 12:30, I could catch the 7th Avenue West Side line, exit at 110th Street, and get me to the church on time (1 p.m.). It didn't work out that way.

But the 110th Street exit on the 7th Avenue line is a long way from 110th Street and Riverside Drive. More than that, the long way is totally uphill, steeply uphill. Luckily I was in good hill-climbing shape and arrived only a little late, hot and dripping in my blue serge suit. But I was nowhere near as hot as my sister Mary!

The Buxtons lived for a time in Denver. Sometime during the World War II, they moved back to New York, and Charlie joined the U.S. Navy. After the war, they moved to Bethpage, Long Island, where Charlie worked at Grumman Aircraft as a controller and Mary worked as the town librarian. With two good jobs, the Buxtons saved their money. When Grumman, having sold a goodly number of planes to the Shah of Iran, needed a controller out there, they offered Charlie the job. Mary was enthralled with the two years they spent in Iran, and it started her off spinning around the world.

In 1986, I managed to stop Mary long enough for her to come with us on a Willimetz Travel tour of Peru, Ecuador, and the Galapagos Islands. It was a Willimetz sibling reunion: Mary, Lee, Hedy, and Emil—the first since Pop's death 19 years earlier.

Charlie, at times, had a tendency to be voluble in his opinions. In Lima, the fine Larco Herrera pre-Columbian museum had an imposing collection of erotica in a separate building. Seated outside, taking admissions, was a delicate, elderly, white-haired British lady. Incongruous? Just wait and see.

The ancients had a pottery figure for every sexual event known to man (more than was known to this man, in any case). Upon exiting the museum, Charles pontificated: "I didn't see anything new!"

"Oh! You didn't?" The elderly British lady remarked archly. "Please, let me take you back inside." Intrigued, we all trooped after her. She led us to a case with a piece of pottery labeled, "Hermafrodita." The image was that of a man, face twisted in agony, in the process of cutting off his penis. Under the penis was an obvious vagina.

The old lady turned to Charlie: "It's a hermaphrodite changing his sexual orientation. Have you ever seen anything like this before?"

A much subdued Charles admitted he hadn't, and we all silently departed. A great educational museum.

(On another visit, my mother-in-law, on exiting the museum, whispered to her daughter: "If that guide hadn't followed us so closely, there were a lot of questions I would have liked to ask you.")

I learned a lot about my grown-up siblings, too, on this tour. On the plane trip down, Mary came sidling up the aisle to ask us the Spanish word for "love." Glancing back, we saw her in deep conversation with a Spanish-speaking nun who lacked English. In what language did they communicate? I have a photo of Mary, deep in conversation with an

Indian woman, in an Otavalo Indian market in Ecuador. Her interest in and ease with people enlivened her world travels. I certainly gained more respect for my older sister.

On Mary's third world cruise, during a transfer from the ship to a dinghy, she slipped and broke her knee. It was mended in Singapore, but when she returned to Bethpage, it was found to be infected. She had to have bone surgery, which left one leg shorter. Mary would have had to wear a prosthesis, and with her considerable weight, that would have largely immobilized her. On June 12, 1987, at the age of 75, the morning she was to leave the hospital, they found that she had died peacefully—as she had predicted to her doctor. Was it the power of suggestion or suicide? Her children think it was suicide, figuring that she probably saved up her pain medication until that last night. A few years later, a despondent Charles hooked up a hose to his car's exhaust and committed suicide.

MY BROTHER LEE
Born February 11, 1914, in the Bronx
Died April 16, 1999, in Kansas City, of a stroke at age 85

Even though Lee dropped out of school in his freshman year to help out the family during the Great Depression, I suspect he was more than happy to do so. Lee was no scholar. Like Horatio Alger, he rose from rags to riches and became financially more prosperous than all of the Willimetzes combined. He was also clever enough to choose a splendid wife and have two fine children. He was, as you already know, a great brother!

My brother was named Leopold Albin, a regal Austrian name that really didn't suit him. Leopold in Austria is a princely name—literally. There is a beautiful alpine lake, Leopoldsteiner See, and just above Vienna is the small town of Leopold Dorf. Leopold is my father's name, even one of my older sister's names (Leopoldina!), but not my brother's name. His own children knew nothing of Leopold—he called himself Lee.

Growing up, Leopold Albin was handed a violin. Lee was a natural-born athlete who excelled at all sports—just not fiddling. He advanced far enough to do a barely recognizable, *O Tannenbaum, O Tannenbaum, wie*

Lee and Gertie.

grün sind deine Blätter. ("Oh Christmas tree, Oh Christmas tree, how green are your leaves/branches"—better known in these foreign climes as "O Maryland, My Maryland.") By this time, I was old enough to hear and wince at his many ill-conceived notes, but Lee was called upon to render it with some frequency.

Above all artistic endeavors, Austria excels in music. The Hapsburgs were patrons of music, and many members of the royal family were gifted musicians. Leopold I was a composer. That we were *aus Wien* ("from Vienna") was never spoken, but it was implicit in Pop's, "This is my son Leopold, he plays the violin!"

Lee's meager repertoire and lack of progress never seemed to bother Pop, and he gave Lee $2 every Saturday morning for lessons. But instead of playing the fiddle, Lee played baseball, betting the $2 on the game. His musical career ended abruptly when his team got into a free-for-all over a point of procedure and he got whacked across the nose with a bat. The damage couldn't be passed off as the result of violin lessons, and the violin was sold.

> *Lee, Lee, the painter's son,*
> *He learned to play when he was young,*
> *But all the tune that he could play*
> *Was in the ballpark far away.*

LEE'S WEDDING, MARCH 30, 1940

I arrived in Kansas City on a freight train. After several hot showers in Lee's flat, I became wedding-acceptable. At the age of 26, Lee was to marry Gertrude Miller. This was three years after my fiasco with Mary's wedding, so I stuck close to Lee all the way to the church in Parnell, Missouri. (Missoura is it, Gertie?) I count this "best man" gig as my most tranquil.

Lee was a sound sleeper, and it took a large-size Big Ben alarm clock, set across the cold floor and placed in a tin washbasin—to wake him and keep him awake. I sensed that this might prove to be a conflict of interest with his bride, a farm girl used to waking with the roosters. Roosters were not part of Lee's Bronx upbringing. Doctor? Lawyer? Indian Chief? INDIAN CHIEF, you betcha!

After 10 long, dreary years the Great Depression had ended with the advent of war-production jobs. Lee and Gertie moved out to Long Beach, California, where Lee found work in shipbuilding. (It would have made a better story if, instead of welding, he had gone to work camouflaging battleships, like his father had done during World War I.)

At war's end, he moved to Kansas City, welding air-conditioning ducts and ending up as a shop foreman. Moving into a dilapidated old house, he completely renovated it with new plumbing, wiring, painting—even digging out and putting in a complete basement.

"Then," says Gertie in despair, "he rented out the house and we moved out into another old one."

At his peak, Lee was renting and maintaining 20 units. He also proved adept at working the stock market to his financial advantage. No other

Willimetz could equal Lee's income, but then no others worked as hard.

In 1996 or so, Lee took his entire family on an Alaska cruise. On his way home, he suffered a stroke. Although he lost his ability to speak, with Gertie's help he was able to maintain himself for a few more years. But Gertie's health also deteriorated, and Lee had to go into a nursing facility, which completely bewildered him.

On March 10, 1999, Gertie died. At her bedside in his wheelchair, Lee wept disconsolately. A few weeks later, he too died.

MY SISTER HEDY
Born January 27, 1924, on Bryant Avenue in the Bronx (I know, I was there, around somewhere.)

Hedy is six years younger than I, and I wasn't as good a brother to her as Lee was to me. As children, six years puts you on different planets. The closest we ever came was our two-year stay in the Nanuet orphanage, when she was 5 and I was 11. Later in life, she became our landlady, and much more.

My younger sister was named Hedwig Amelia. Hedwig was our grandmother's name, our father's sister's name, and our cousin's name. Just not my kid sister's name. Her name is Hedy! (For her fresh and upbeat personality, she was Hedy Lamarr to our fellow travelers on an epic Galapagos trip.)

HEDY'S WEDDING, JUNE 12, 1948
Against her better judgment, Hedy also asked me to be her best man. She blames me for bringing her groom to the wedding late and dressed in a motley manner. If she keeps this up, I'll tell everyone that her real name is Hedwig Amelia.

"I shouldn't have trusted Emil," says Hedy, "to see that Tony dressed properly and got to the church on time—not after what happened to Mary."

Anyway, that's what Hedy says. I was at Tony's apartment in plenty of time. How was I to know he had bought a shirt (since his jacket was a 37) with a 37 sleeve—long enough for an orangutan? A 37 sleeve was so unusual that the clerk in Bond's had to go to the basement to find one. When he put it on, fresh out of the box at the last moment, the sleeves hung inches beneath his fingertips. It took precious time to find rubber bands to bind them up enough to reveal his fingers.

It was dark in the bedroom when he put on his suit, and I never noticed that his jacket was purple and his pants blue, each with a different pinstripe. I pushed him to leave, but when we hit the street, he announced that he needed a new pair of shoes. That started us on a real downward slide, and I began to sweat again in my one and only refitted blue serge wedding suit.

Finally we were in a taxi: "Where to, Buddy?"

"It's on 5th Avenue," says Tony. "Go uptown to about 96th Street and come back down 5th Avenue. I'll recognize the church when I see it."

Norman Vincent Peale's Marble Collegiate Church is actually at 29th Street and 5th Avenue. Needless to say, we ran up a good taxi bill and arrived a little tardy.

Tony's parents were as immigrant as ours. Their Italian/English was understandable, but just barely—we were the Willa Nutses. To Mom and Pop, the Paternos were the Pa Tonys. A typical dinner conversation, with the two immigrant families present, frequently lapsed into a mix of Italian, German, and English—much to my wife Joanna's total confusion.

Hedy, like Mary, had a checkered work career, although not until the Depression had slipped into the war-production years. Starting out at Metropolitan Life, she also worked in the New York Zoological Society office. Her house in Queens overlooks the Flushing Cemetery, where she also once worked. Mom, Pop, Mary, and Charlie are buried there.

Hedy and Tony's love of animals was well known in their Queens neighborhood, and strays were constantly left on their doorstep. At one time, she had three neurotic dogs, two cats (aren't all cats neurotic?), and a few fugitive parakeets. Kids returning from vacations brought them little half-dollar-size turtles with "Souvenir of Florida" painted on their shells.

The turtles Hedy raised in a tank. In the back of her cellar was an

Hedy and friend.

earthen bank, and in the winter she would hibernate the turtles there. In the spring, she would put a heat lamp over the bank and watch their expectant little noses poking through the dirt. She kept them until they were the size of dinner plates, then packed them in damp moss and shipped them back to a ranger in Florida. Her favorites she gave to the Queens Zoo, where she could visit with them.

Tony and Hedy were constantly engrossed in campaigns. Dressed in black, these two dangerous radicals would go downtown to the 7th Avenue fur district, set a stencil on the sidewalk, and quickly spray-paint: DON'T BUY FURS!

Shortly after their marriage, Tony came down with lupus and developed several deadly associated illnesses. He died in 1974 of heart failure. Hedy's tender care and steadfast attention to the details of his illnesses gave Tony many extra years of life. He was a sweet person. Together they managed to buy a two-family duplex in Queens and a cottage in the Catskills. When we returned from Peru, we rented an apartment in Hedy's house, and later she was landlady to a second-generation Willimetz—our son Andrew!

After 10 years of widowhood, she met and married Frank LeVoci, another Italian who looked like and was the same age as Tony, but born in Italy. Frank, a polite and gracious man, was one strange character. Inviting her out to tea, he would buy and share a single muffin. He gave her money for groceries, but none for clothes or vacations. When she came with us to the Galapagos, she paid her own way. After 10 years, she finally divorced him, not asking for a financial settlement. Tony, who had been a sign painter, did considerably better by Hedy than Frank, who made good money as an aviation design engineer.

EMIL JOSEPH WILLIMETZ
Born August 2, 1918—and getting older, but not wiser, by the minute

I had no middle name until I was 11, when I was baptized. Religion was never a big family thing. My father, the old Socialist, dismissed religion as the opiate of the people. One of our devout Catholic neighbors, finding out that I had not been sanctified, persuaded Mom to have it done.

So one day, looking like an Irish wolfhound in a line with newborn puppies, I stood waiting my turn at the baptismal font. Each time a baby was hit by the cold holy water and cried, I giggled—to the great discomfort of my gentle mother, who nervously yanked on my arm. When I stepped up, the priest, who seemed happy to have a subject he could communicate with and who maybe wouldn't cry, paternally asked, "Well, my son, and what good name can we give you today?"

Caught by surprise, I blurted out the first thing that came into my head—"Ernie," the name of a cop on our block who allowed me to help fly his pigeons. The priest frowned and my mother rolled her eyes.

"There is no such saint as Ernie, young man, I baptize thee Emil Joseph Willimetz." I could have cried.

Flying pigeons from flat Bronx rooftops was more than a sport, it was war. You flew your pigeons off the roof with a long bamboo pole, hoping to shanghai a few strays from a neighboring flock or to pick up a solitary bird flying by. Then you called your birds home. When a new bird is captured, it can be kept, returned, or eaten, depending on your relationship with your neighbor. So you see that my request to be named Ernie, Mr. Priest, was not frivolous—it stood for a friend who trusted me to fly his cherished birds.

Winnie the Pooh had two names—"in case one gets lost!" How lost can I get now with three? And so ever after. But, when I studied writing in college, I thought how nice it would have been to publish as . . . e e **willimetz.**

Emil was derived from one of Pop's brothers who died the year before they came to the States. There is not much you can do with Emil but grin and bear it. Or, like in the army, be called Willi, short for Willimetz. On the Tennessee Cumberland Plateau, I was introduced to a local mountain man. "Emil?" he asked. "There's no such name, must be Amos!" And he called me Amos for seven years. Emil is subject to great variation: Emile, Emiel, Amal, Amial, Aimial, Aim, Amo, and, not to be ignored, Emilio. The "E" in Emil is, of course, pronounced as a Germanic "A." Unsophisticates say it as an "E." Our postmaster topped all by calling me E-mail.

Emil was bad enough, but all through school I had to teach most of my teachers how to spell and pronounce both names. However, better Willimetz than my great-grandmother's Kosibradka.

Brother Leopold's children were rewarded with Emmitt and Ann. Sister Marianna's children received Edmund, Charles, and Carol. My boys were given good stout Scottish names, James and Andrew. Willimetz, however, stays the course.

On the other hand, had my children's mother stayed in the strict Puritan line of descent for names, you boys might have not have fared so well. David Fischer, in *Albion's Seed,* lists some of the names the early

When I graduated from P. S. 44, I was thirteen, tall for my age, and ready to go.

Puritans gave their children: Kill-sin Pemble; Small-hope Biggs; Be-courteous Cole; Humiliation Scratcher; Mortifie Hicks.

Paul Revere, our great New England hero, might not have made it into the history books if his father hadn't changed his name from Apollos Rivoire. Who knew that Rockefeller came from Roggenfelder?! Franklin Delano Roosevelt's middle name came from De la Noye. Try that out on some of our redneck voters: Franklin De la Noye Roosevelt!

My wife, Joanna Jordan Creighton ("Joie"), comes from a prominent Maine family that traces its ancestors back to the 1600s. It's a good thing Maine has a small population (only a little more than a million), or Joie's genealogy would get out of hand. If you're from Maine, she's probably related. Just don't look us up, though. Enough's enough!

Our son James, having married a lovely Peruvian, Silvia, gave our bloodlines some new gene tracks—Spanish, French, and, possibly, Inca.

Their first child, Andrea, has a name that sort of works in both countries, although I don't suppose Ellis Island would have allowed it to get by unscathed.

Son Andrew, having married an attractive Chinese woman, Wenjuan Fan, adds yet another cultural dimension to the global Willimetz family experience. Wenjuan being more of a name than boorish Americans can cope with, is known to all as Fan. Her child is called, affectionately, Nonito. Nonito was eight months in Wenjuan's womb when her husband died in an auto crash. Urged to name her child upon leaving the hospital, she picked Andrew from a proffered list. Married to our son, she gets the attention of two by calling just one.

Whenever I saw Pop eye me speculatively, with music on his mind, I quickly reminded him that I had been classified in school as a "listener." In the second grade, we studied "music," which meant going to the head of the class where the teacher sat at a piano. I was to sing a few bars of "Jingle Bells." Red-faced, I stood mute before the piano, was graded a "listener," and have spent the balance of my life as a non-singer. However, life is indeed strange—I am the only Willimetz to have sat in an orchestra and performed before an audience.

My school, Black Mountain College, was small—75 students. In order to put on a play or an orchestra recital, it was necessary to impress numbers of students. Needing an oboist in a work by Hindemith (or was it Stravinsky?), Leslie, the student flutist, came back from Christmas vacation with an old oboe. I was forthwith given the instrument, an instruction book, and a kerosene stove and taken to the most remote empty cottage on the campus and told to master the art. I tried, seriously and professionally keeping a spare oboe reed soaking in a glass of water at my feet.

As the day of the concert drew near, the orchestra began to panic at my lack of progress. The conductor hired a teacher of wind instruments from Asheville to evaluate me. He took one look at the old oboe, lit a cigarette, placed his hand over the bell, and blew smoke out of several hairline cracks.

Was it the oboe, then, or the oboist?

It was decided that if I could muster a passable A-flat, the score could be rearranged so that I could still contribute. I was given some sheets of music so I could follow the score. My A-flat was connected in a series of long, graceful swoops across the page. By dint of constant practice, I passed the A-flat test. But since the score was in a language I only faintly understood, in concert I sat next to the flutist. At his nod, I placed the reed in my mouth and my fingers on the assigned stops. When he poked me with his elbow, I hit a loud and full-throated A-flat . . . until he poked me to stop. We toured at least one college in the nearby North Carolina area—the only New World Willimetz to perform in concert. Pop vindicated! BLOOD WILL OUT!

> *Whene'er the oboe sounds its "A,"*
> *All the others start their tuning*
> *And there is fiddling and bassooning.*
> *Its plaintive note presaging gloom*
> *Brings anguish to the concert room.*
> *Even the player holds his breath*
> *And scares the audience to death*
> *For fear he may get off the key,*
> *Which happens not infrequently.*
> *This makes the saying understood*
> *"It's an ill wood wind no one blows good."*
> *—Lawrence McKinney, People of Note*

My Grandmother never learned English, so German was a mother tongue for me. It was also the only subject I ever flunked in school. It was to be a snap course, but my teacher, Ms. Goertz, spoke *Hochdeutsch* (high German). I spoke *Plattdeutsch* (low German). Worse, I spoke Viennese *Plattdeutsch*. Worse yet, I spoke Ottakring (Pop's working-class neighborhood) Viennese *Plattdeutsch*. It was like a Bronx boy taking his accent and street vocabulary to Oxford. My personable, nonguttural Viennese language didn't make the grade—Ms. Goertz had apoplexy every time I recited.

Prejudice aside, I must confess I failed also because of the grammar. Forgive me, Ms. Goertz, what was it you said a "dative" was?

I also must confess that I lied when I said I never sang. Ms. Goertz took her class down to Bryant Park, behind the New York Public Library, where we stood before a statue of Goethe and sang German *Lieder*. Come to think of it, my singing that day might also have contributed to my flunking German!

I was more successful in college. In my German class, I had the honor (no doubt to the horror of A.A. Milne) of translating *Vinne der Pooh* into German.

Finally, by chance, I ended up in Vienna, surrounded by kinfolk all refreshingly speaking proper Viennese—my kind of German. Replete with jazzy Viennese/Ottakring slang, it was music to my ears! Potatoes were no longer the harsh German *Kartoffel* but the melodious *Erdäpfel* (apple of the earth); tomatoes were no longer *Tomaten* but *Paradiesen* (fruit of paradise). All were translations from the French, Napoleon having once occupied Vienna.

As a boy I spoke German at home, studied it in school, and used it frequently in the army and with my kinfolk in Vienna. But after a 50-year hiatus, I returned to Vienna and was completely unable to converse with my beloved remaining cousin, Minni. Joie says that whenever I started speaking German, it came out Spanish. (We had lived in Peru and I had struggled with Spanish there.) She claims I spoke better Spanish when under the illusion I was speaking German.

MY POP, LEOPOLD LUDWIG WILLIMETZ
Born August 31, 1882, in Vienna, Austria
Died September 17, 1967, in Queens, New York, at age 85

Pop was raised in a family of 10 children in a working-class, blue-collar neighborhood—he must have seen his share of poverty. Seeing his New World family sliding into destitution could not have helped but to destroy his self-esteem. The best he could do (and it saved us) was to get a janitor post in the Bronx. In Vienna, he worked in an elegant hotel. Should he have stayed in Vienna and risked the war that killed four of his brothers? Did he ponder on that? Did Mom?

The smartest thing my father ever did, I figure, was to come to the New World. I often wonder if he felt that way. I don't think so—but was the Bronx then that different from Vienna? Life in postwar Austria after World War I was probably as hard or harder than in Depression America. Look at it this way, Pop, it's hard to avoid fate—we did get involved with the Austrian Army after all, just not as anticipated.

My father was an angry man with a short fuse, frustrated by the many slings and arrows of the Depression. He was short and stocky, with thinning dark hair. Despite Pop's short temper and daily jobless frustrations, he rarely took it out on his kids. Pop was a chain smoker. I remember one day he sent me out for cigarettes and I got involved in some tomfoolery with the gang and was an hour or so late in returning. He was shaking with anger and took a wild swing at me, which I easily ducked and fled. I never imagined he meant to connect and didn't hold it against him.

Pop was a great one for a bargain. He bought Mom a coat with a fur collar. It looked good but smelled like goat in the rain. He bought a watch in a busy subway station. The man had his watches in a fancy leather jewelry case that looked like it contained expensive stolen goods. Hidden on his wrist was a loudly ticking watch. Looking furtively around, he held a "stolen" watch to Pop's ear. "Hear that watch? Seven jewels! Only one dollar. Got to get rid of them in a hurry—quick, hide it." The watch Pop hid in his pocket never did a tick of work in its life—it was a toy.

My lifetime covers the advent of radio as well as TV. One day Pop brought us a homemade radio in a cigar box. I remember little about the mechanics, only that it worked. It had a stiff wire on a spool you turned to pull in a station—very tricky. Some of my friends had Philcos, but they weren't any prouder of their sets than I with ours. We spent evenings with Amos 'n' Andy, learning that Negroes speak funny and are dumb. From FDR's Fireside Chats we learned that we had nothing to fear but fear itself. While his talks helped the morale of some people, he never reached Pop.

In 1931, there were 200,000 home evictions in New York City, and in the first three weeks of 1932, there were 60,000 more. Pop finally got work, of sorts, renovating houses for the local bank—in brutal competition with other freelance painters. They desperately bid against each other, lucky to break even. Occasionally, when Pop was in a bind for time, Lee and I would have to pitch in to help. I hated scraping off ancient layers of wallpaper or washing ceilings. It made me realize what a hard worker Pop was, painting all day with a heavy 6-inch brush. It was backbreaking, unprofitable work, but it did bring in a certain amount of cash flow that kept us going.

House paint, before 1950, contained as much as 50 percent lead by weight. Studies reveal how lead poison-

Pop.

ing affects behavior, increasing irritability. Not only was Pop involved with paint day in and day out, but he also inhaled the dust from sanding and scraping old lead-painted walls. What with the Depression, in contrast with the prestigious job he had had in Vienna, how could he not have been irritable—even without the lead in his system!

Pop was at the apex of his career as a house painter when we learned that he was a victim of achromatosia, or congenital color blindness. He couldn't tell enough red from green to get a driver's license! When he had worked in painting crews, a master painter mixed the colors and Pop got by. But now he had to discuss color with the bank agent. A true son of Ottakring, he worked out a chancy system that got him by. He bought a fat, accordion-type wallet with more than a dozen partitions. On each he put a label: PARLOR, PARLOR TRIM, KITCHEN, KITCHEN TRIM, etc. After dinner, he would solemnly take out, one by one, paint chips surreptitiously removed from an empty house, for us to identify. As he passed them around the table, he heard: "It's tan." . . . "It's more like dark cream." . . . "It's buff." . . . "Beige." . . . until he would explode. "*Verdammdt!!!!* Make up your mind!"

When we concurred, he would write it in chalk on the proper partition and memorize it for the morrow's discussion with the bank agent. Finally, someone had the sense to bring home a set of Glidden Paint color charts against which we could match his chips. That made Life with Father much easier.

If he couldn't get the keys to a house in advance, either my brother or I would have to help him break in, usually through an unlatched cellar window. One of my less-than-happy childhood memories: going from room to room with a small flashlight, an ear cocked for police sirens, muttering, "Walls: light green." . . . "Molding: forest green." . . . "Cabinets: cream."

Pop was a whiz at matching shades. He used several small cans of strong pigments: raw sienna/burnt sienna, raw umber/burnt umber, etc. He knew pragmatically what color would result when mixed with white.

During the war years, with 16 million folks in uniform, Pop managed to get a job working in a change booth of the New York subway system. The Great Depression was past history, and working made a great improvement in Pop's morale.

Just after Joanna and I were married in 1949, we took Mom and Pop to visit her family in Hamburg, in western New York near Niagara Falls. I had my reservations about taking Pop—a foreign accent, not noticeable in the Bronx, was outstanding in Hamburg. On political themes, he could be more dogmatic even than I, and much louder. I hoped I could dampen him down if need be. It never happened. He wore hearing aids attached to a large battery, which hung around his neck on a piece of dirty string and had loud/soft, on/off switches. When he found the conversation of little interest, a loud click cut him out of the conversation circuit. He would sit with a bemused look until he sensed people getting more animated and . . . click . . . he was with us again. Was he trying to avoid conflict? I think so.

The Creightons acquitted themselves with honor, won over I suspect more by Mom than by Pop. Mom was duly impressed by the Creighton family *joie de vivre*. Coming home in the car from dinner at the Supervisors' Club at the Bethlehem Steel plant, the Creightons all harmonized on "Good Night, Irene." For Mom, this was a family in perfect harmony, a harmony she and Pop hadn't had for many years. Mom confessed a year later that she still cried every time she heard someone singing good night to Irene. Crying for the loss of harmony in the Willimetz family? Or because Joie's father died in 1950 at the youthful age of 59—shortly after our visit?

Despite his deafness, Pop wasn't the least beaten down. At Niagara Falls, he turned to Joie:

Pop: "You know that river's salt, don't you?"

Joie, who had spent most of her life on the Niagara frontier (but very little time with Pop): "I don't think so."

Pop, firmly: "It's salt!"

We crossed back over the river from Canada, and as we came up to U.S. Customs, I suggested, "Let me do the talking."

A head appeared at my window: "All of you U.S. citizens?"

"Yes, sir!" I earnestly replied.

"*Jawohl,*" added my father.

"Pull over," suggested the agent. To Pop: "Do you have your passport?"

"*Nein,* but I have my subway pass."

"You need a passport to prove citizenship.

"With the war I traveled all over Canada with just my subway pass!"

By this time, Pop was out of the car, standing toe to toe, his chin about 6 inches from the agent's chest and getting more and more agitated. Mom, of course, was sinking deeper into a dark corner of the car.

The give-and-take went on for a while, but the content didn't vary much. His match met, the weary agent surrendered:

"You may continue. Next time bring your passport," and, plaintively, "please?"

They stayed that night in a local Niagara Falls tourist court. Joie and I had to return to Tennessee. We received a card from Mom—I could just see her weary look: "To see the Falls from Canada at night, we again crossed the bridge!"

Pop, however, had truth on his side. He did indeed go to Canada on the subway pass he had from when he worked during the war as a change-booth operator on the IRT subway line. His travel tactics were commensurate with his travel budgets. He boned up on a target city and went there by bus or train. On one occasion, in a Canadian city, he started his explorations by riding a streetcar to the city line. On the return trip, with passengers gone, he stood up front to tell the driver about his city.

Pop: "You know this city has 712,000 people?"

Driver: "I hardly think so."

"With the whole metropolitan area, it has over 2 million."

"Nothing like that."

"It's the biggest city in Ontario."

"Actually, Toronto is the biggest."

"Isn't this Toronto?"

As he told the story on himself, he had gotten off the train in Hamilton! He must have had his hearing aid turned off. Easy to tell funny stories about Pop, but he could be dauntless. How else could a color-blind house painter face up to that reality and get by with it?

Come to think of it, Pop's odysseys to strange cities vibrate to something deep inside me. Pop had the adventure gene that underwrote my travels—it was Mom's genes that brought me home again.

In 1967, I flew back to New York from Peru—Pop was dying and the family was gathering around him. He had been diagnosed with stomach cancer; they had opened him up and closed him again—it was too late.

For our inheritance, Pop had amassed $200 for each of his sons and was fully prepared to transfer the results of his 50 years of research on the gangster code. We thanked him but said we didn't have his patience. The money went into Mom's small account.

When we had a moment together, Mom reached down to hold my hand. In her quiet voice, she told me that she had become incontinent, which upset Pop, and he poured some urine on her head. Pop had gone completely sour. Poor Mom. Poor Pop. I could only hug her to me tightly.

After Pop died, Hedy tried to care for Mom at home. But Mom, being incontinent, needed frequent attention. Hedy and Tony both worked, so they put Mom into the Neponsit Nursing Home, a city care facility. Tony's father and our Mom were in the Neponsit Nursing Home together, but unfortunately they had very little in common. But it meant that Joie and I, when we returned to live in New York, could alternate every other week with Hedy and Tony to visit them.

For a birthday surprise, we had taken the aging Leopold to the track at Roosevelt Park. He was furious because we hadn't given him time to research his bets! Adding insult to injury, Mom bet on a horse that carried her birthday date—and won!

As a young boy, I took for granted—almost didn't notice—the figure of Pop hunched over his *Racing Forms*. In high school, when I was more perceptive about the reality of his life, the sight sickened and angered me. Pop had entered the unknown New World with a jaunty, twirly mustache and the hope of making a successful new life. At the age of 84, he was still living in poverty. Clubbed down by an economic disaster, he ended his life hopelessly mesmerized in a search for a mythical Mafia Code. A tragic waste of a good man.

The poverty the family suffered never bothered me personally—it's what it did to my parents that hurt. And what it did to my sister Mary and people in the world around me. People object to the violence of protest, but I hate more the violence of poverty. My father, Leopold, lived a hard life and died a hard, painful death.

But all is not lost, Pop. You gave the world Mary, Lee, Hedy, and Emil, and all their progeny. You left the New World richer than you found it.

MY MOM, FRANZISKA THOMA WILLIMETZ
Born January 26, 1887, in Strass, Austria
Died October 15, 1971, in Queens, New York, at 84 years

Typical family scene: Mom, sitting in a straight chair and threading a needle, a basket of clothes and socks in her lap. When Studs Terkel taped interviews with people all over America, he would get them to tell about their fantasies. I often wondered what he would have gotten Mom to fantasize about as she sewed. Would she dream about the captivating Leopold as he was in Vienna, or about the small vineyard in Strass, with her parents, her sisters, and their children and grandchildren? Did she feel her marriage to Leopold a mistake? And, Mom, what about us?

When my wife, Joanna, was introduced into the Willimetz household, she learned that my mother had been voyaging through the New World under a pseudonym. We had called her Fanny, but her real name was Franziska. It became Fanny under the provincial hand of an Ellis Island immigration clerk. Language communication on Ellis Island was strictly Tower of Babel, and strange indeed were the results. But Franziska? What a great name!

Mom was a gentle and accepting woman who added dignity to scrubbing stairs and cleaning toilets in the Bronx Zoo. She was of average height and weight; her hair, brown with streaks of gray, was pulled back in a bun. Her sensitive radar to our needs, emotionally and physically, was uncanny. Extremely patient and loving, Mom was the one who held the Willimetz family together—until, grown-up, we drifted to separate parts of the country. She must have lost her Leopold somewhere back in the early Depression; they lived together but had become totally estranged. Jobless in the Great Depression, Pop had become hard to live with.

Mom had to contend with a family of seven—including Grossmutter. You have to remember that Mom had her mother-in-law living with her for 22 years! As much as I loved my grandmother, I don't remember her taking on much, if any, of the household work. Of course, Grandma had given birth to and raised 10 children and deserved some rest—but 22 years?

When Mary and Lee started to work, our culinary repertoire became more advanced. I would guess that the biggest part of the family income, 70 to 80 percent, went into food. Almost every night we sat down to a full dinner. Didn't everyone eat like this? No, they didn't! (Today, in the

Mom.

United States, about 10 percent of the average family's budget goes into food.) Mom was a *Mehlspeisköchin* (a born Viennese cook)! She was a no-recipe cook—it was a handful of this, a pinch of that, stir until it felt right, and flavor to taste. Her art appeared to be instinctive, as she deftly assembled ingredients into a finished dish. She found it difficult to write down a recipe for me—her dishes just flowed from her hands.

Fruits and vegetables came around by horse and wagon. In the cold weather, the horses breathed out smoke, stomped their feet on the cold paving, and left calling cards in the street for the sparrows. But in the market, where Mom did most of her shopping, we had a much greater variety. Believe it or not, fruit in those days was sold dead ripe, although only in season. What a joy it was to bite into a ripe Georgia peach! Or to have them sliced into a bowl of sour cream!

Occasionally I would get to go with Mom to the Bathgate market. It was about three miles from our house, but it was kosher, and that was where the best food was to be had. Kosher chickens cost more but were freshly killed. By buying them unplucked, we saved 25 cents. We returned home schlepping heavy shopping bags—walking to save 10 cents on the trolley car, 20 cents if I went along.

Up Bathgate Avenue, just a few blocks from the market, was a large brick factory building with massive iron-rimmed doors. They looked to me like great castle gates, large enough for giant wagons pulled by teams of horses to enter and leave at a full gallop. It loomed magical yet sinister—it was the brewery of Dutch Schultz.

Bread came in large round loaves and was sold by the pound. We would buy a quarter or a half at a time. It was very tasty bread, and I especially loved the crust. The bakers' union glued a large union label to the loaf, which Mom carefully cut off. I discovered that the label didn't diminish the taste of the crust underneath, and I devoured both with equal gusto.

I loved the kitchen. When I discovered how the outside "greasy spoon" world ate, I was horrified and spent as much time as possible learning from Mom. While I sat in the kitchen defrocking a chicken, Mom would give me a running commentary on what she was cooking—plus a wee dollop of behavioral advice. (She would also let me lick the spoons and beaters coated with chocolate or icing.) Unfortunately, I learned but a fraction of her art.

Mom really awed me in a butcher shop. Buying a piece of meat was a conference of equals. In two minutes, she had the busiest butcher deep into the virtues of his meat, often causing him to run to the locker to cut a choice selection from a hanging carcass and exhibit it with pride before her. The Viennese are said to use 40 different cuts of meat for boiled beef!

Mom would ask for a special cut and describe where it came from on the carcass. "Coarse grained," Mom would say, "but *saftig* (juicy)."

The butcher would suggest a fillet of veal for *Wiener* (Vienna) *schnitzel*, but Mom would say, "No, too expensive," or "Too soft, please cut from the inner part of the leg." *Schnitzel* cooks agree that the cooked color should be a light golden brown, like a Stradivarius violin. Not that Mom knew of this criterion, but I'll bet her schnitzels were not far off the mark!

My major grievance against Pop was his treatment of Mom. The economic pressures of the Depression destroyed any chance they had of continuing a successful marriage. Mom and Pop finally split. I was away at college and never really got the straight story, but apparently Pop lost a $100 bill. Somehow blaming Mom, he ended up hitting her.

My sister Mary moved out to Denver, where her husband Charles had a job with the *Rocky Mountain News*. Brother Lee followed on their heels and worked for the same paper as a lead puddler in the linotype room. When I bummed out to Denver and visited him at the plant, he showed me how well he calculated the quickness of the hardening factor in his molten lead.

"Watch this!" he said, dropping molten lead, which hardened before it hit his shoe. Typical Lee!

In 1938, Mom cashed in a couple of insurance policies and flew with Hedy to Denver, where she found a live-in job as a housekeeper. Hedy, who was about 13, not only was accepted for room and board, but the woman of the house, Lois LaVoe, practically adopted her.

Pop was left behind to live a bachelor existence in the Bronx. He rented a small, cheap flat on a level with the elevated subway tracks. Coming back to New York that first Christmas vacation, I stayed with him. When trains went by the window, we would automatically raise our voices, then drop them when they passed. I wasn't sure, and neither was Pop, how we would relate to each other on the Mom question. It was just never mentioned, but I'm sure he knew, in a toss-up, which side I would choose. I spent my time cavorting with friends but usually made it back home for supper. Pop was no chef, but I learned bachelor cooking from him. On Sunday, he would make a big meat stew. On Monday, he would add small new potatoes . . . Tuesday, peas . . . then mushrooms . . . carrots. The stew kept getting richer by the day. We ate quickly, without unnecessary conversation. We never did have much to say to each other.

The time sequence is confusing, but after three years, the LaVoe family had to sell their rather large house and move downtown to an apartment. Soon thereafter, Mom and Hedy left Denver, ending up back in the Bronx with Pop—but it was never good. Charles went into the U.S. Navy and Mary also returned to the Bronx. Lee stayed on to marry Gertie and spent the war years working in Long Beach, California, building ships.

Mom did a spell as a chambermaid at the elegant Hotel Tuscany under the tutelage of Onkel Franz's Anna, who had worked there for years. Just how it came about, I'll never know, but somehow the famous violinist and fellow Austrian, Fritz Kreisler, learned about Mom's talents. Kreisler (1875-1962) was an Austrian-born American whose musical wit, elegance, and richness of tone were the envy of his peers. Kreisler remains—like Caruso—the most frequently lauded "historic" exponent of his art.

Mom did extra duty cooking for parties in Kreisler's upscale apartment on Sutton Place. Frequently she was given the keys to the apartment to clean up when the Kreislers went out of town.

Occasionally teenage Hedy went along with Mom and was pressed into service at large affairs as majordoma of the cloakroom. As Hatcheck Hedy, she was both a success and a failure—coats were no problem to keep apart, but hats often got married to the wrong customer. One kindly lady suggested that she pin the check numbers on the inside instead of the outside of the mink.

At one point, Kreisler had a taxi accident that kept him away from the concert hall for a spell. He thought so highly of Mom that he honored her with one of the best boxes at Carnegie Hall for his first return concert. It must have made her proud to be able to invite Hedy, Anna, Onkel Franz, and others to her box. It was an overflow crowd, and Pop, being deaf, was invited to sit on the stage along with Kreisler's closest friends. If someone like Fritz Kreisler would honor Mom for the comparatively few meals she gave him, what must we owe her for the lifetime of excellent cooking she gave us?

Kreisler donated his Guarnerius violin to the Library of Congress, where it is used by guest violinists in the library's recital programs. It is considered to be the very finest violin ever made . . . but did it have the right schnitzel color?

One evening we received a call from Neponsit that Mom had come to the clinic complaining of a headache, sat down in a chair, and died. Her arteries had calcified and burst. She had a hard life but a quick and painless death.

6.

THUMB TRAVEL, 1932

Riddle: Name the longest snake in the world!
Answer: The road.
—Laurens van der Post, *A Story Like the Wind*

I DISCOVER WHY GOD MADE THE THUMB

I DIDN'T GRADUATE FROM PS 44 MAGNA CUM LAUDE, but I did pass everything—despite missing two years of instruction when I was in the Nanuet orphanage. I was 13, tall for my age, and ready to go. My first thumb-travel adventure was that summer, with my good friend Stanley (Shlomo) Cohen. By the time we returned home, after my August birthday, I was a much more mature 14.

Shlomo was a calm, even-tempered boy, not exactly type-cast for adventures. (I think he became an accountant.) On the other hand, I was about the same—a quiet type, and shy to boot. But as I ventured forth to explore the world, things just seemed to crop up, despite my introverted ways. But not through boldness. I just seemed to find myself in places and positions where things happened, frequently much to my surprise and sometimes to my dismay. I wanted to see, I wanted to know. My brother aided and abetted this search by including me in his Indian tribe, but I guess the thirst must have been there from the start.

Gone are the days when the road was lined with Burma-Shave advertising signs, placed a block or so apart. A bit of roadside Americana of my youth. We were glad to get rid of large billboards, but we loved the Burma-Shave signs.

Every shaver
Now can snore
Six more minutes
Than before
By using
Burma-Shave

My favorite road northward was 9W (now I-87, the New York State Thruway). We were picked up by a man in a derby who had a bulldog face like J. Edgar Hoover. I sat in front, Shlomo in the back. We hadn't gone far when I found a hand in my lap. I moved over tight against the door and admonished him to stop. But he tried again, and this time Shlomo tapped him on the shoulder and told him to pull over. It was an unexpected beginning to our summer adventure that deterred us not a bit.

Our journey took us through the Catskills to Albany. Turning west, we crossed New York State on Route 5, through the roller-coaster hills of Cherry Valley, just in time to sample the lush purple bing cherries. Our goal was Niagara Falls. That first rainy night, our ride left us at the junction of Route 20 where it splits off to Buffalo. At this juncture was the tiny office of a real estate firm. Finding shelter on the porch, we wrapped ourselves in a pup-tent shelter-half and cowered behind the balustrade. I felt heartsick and afraid. I was happy to have Shlomo for company. Cars swished by in the rain, headlights sweeping the porch. Anxious not to be caught by the real estate agents coming to work, we stayed awake most of the night.

College boy
Your courage muster
Shave off that fuzzy
Cookie duster
Burma-Shave

The next day, at Niagara Falls, lured by the promise of free samples, we toured the Nabisco Shredded Wheat factory. After the tour, our young girl guide seated us at a table and set out small bowls of shredded wheat topped with slices of banana, and a milk pitcher. By the time we finished our cereal and the contents of the pitcher, a line was forming for another tour.

"Let's take it again," suggested Shlomo, grabbing my arm. With great interest, we watched once more all that can be done to shape wheat into edible Brillo pads. Back down at the table after the tour, we now had the full attention of the young female guides, who gave us double measure. Under a barrage of teasing, we emptied the milk and sugar containers. With our limited funds, a meal was worth any price. We even went through the tour a third time, red faces and all!

> *He had the ring*
> *He had the flat*
> *She felt his chin*
> *And that*
> *Was that!*
> *Burma-Shave*

Our tummies taut with Nabisco biscuits, we hiked into the land of honeymoon dreams—Niagara Falls. It was tremendous, thunderous, and extremely violent. I was glad that my brother, aka Chief Lee, wasn't there to invent some outrageously brave tribal initiation. The falls of the Bronx River had been enough for me. On the Canadian side, we stood in awe, watching pigeons swooping through the heavy mist in an ecstasy of daring flight, barely missing the full weight of the falls. (Were they picking up insects swept over the brink?)

We camped for weeks in several Adirondack Park camps. At Tupper Lake, several young ladies from close-by Gloversville, on vacation from a local factory, were neighbors to our pup tent. One was a tiny, very delicate, appealing girl. It seemed improbable to me that she could really work in a factory, but she said she did! I had just finished reading W. H. Hudson's *Green Mansions* and had fallen in love with Rima, his elfin bird-girl rainforest creation. I became enamored of this ethereal factory girl, but all she wanted to do was go to the camp dances, and Shlomo and I didn't have the money to join them. The romance went nowhere, but was I in love with the factory girl or with Rima?

All too soon, they left for the factory and we moved on to another campsite. The mighty Adirondacks, with 6 million acres and 2,800 lakes, held attractions besides Rima.

> *If Crusoe'd*
> *Kept his chin*
> *More tidy*
> *He might have found*
> *A lady Friday*
> *Burma-Shave*

At Saranac Lake, we fell in with George and Martha, a middle-aged couple from Florida. Martha was a genuine southern belle, already faded at age 40 but still well endowed, as soft to the touch and as white as Wonder Bread. Living in a trailer, she was good with the skillet, and, in exchange for small tasks, was liberal with her victuals. She was no Rima, but we were well pleased with her orange marmalade and grapefruit wine. George was a dapper taciturn sort, always inappropriately dressed for the wilderness.

They wintered in Florida in their trailer and made jewelry—mainly butterflies, created from bits of colored paper and silver wire. They arranged a dozen of the butterflies attractively on a card that said, "Souvenir of the Adirondacks." Each day, George would take off in his car to canvass trading posts, grocery stores, and gas stations—any place that sold souvenirs, which was every place in the park (which is bigger than Yellowstone, the Grand Canyon, or the Olympic National Park). We frequently kept him company, while Martha stayed at base to make dinner. It was a great way to see the Adirondacks, and, of course, any car heavy enough to pull a trailer was super comfortable. We were summer hedonists.

So one morning I was surprised when, at the last moment (I was already in the car), Shlomo said he had decided not to go with us. Later, he told me why. The night before, he had gone with Martha to the camp grocery wagon to pick up some supplies. The post wagon was a short walk through the woods, and on the way back, they sat down together on a log and Martha masturbated him. When George and I took off that morning, she invited him into the trailer and they had intercourse, Shlomo seated in a chair. Both of us being virgin, this of course was a momentous event, but he seemed reluctant to go into details. I had the impression that losing his virginity with Martha wasn't the great thrill he had anticipated. Shortly thereafter, George and Martha departed for greener pastures.

> *The answer to*
> *A maiden's*
> *Prayer*
> *Is not a chin*
> *Of stubby hair.*
> *Burma-Shave*

With the last of our money, we bought a peck of potatoes. Fishermen would give us surplus catches and occasionally we would be invited to a family barbecue. Getting desperate, we decided to move on to Lake George, which, with a campsite close to town, offered the best possibility for work.

In Lake George village, I got a job washing dishes at the Blue Mill Diner. It wasn't the best of jobs, but it paid in food and a modicum of cash. I had my three meals and could take a doggy bag back to Shlomo, who was hustling odd jobs around the campground. The most difficult part of the job was putting up with the cheeky waitresses, who too quickly learned my penchant for blushing. The dishwasher station, in the back of the kitchen, became a great place for waitress leisure-time sport. "What! You sleep in a tent? Poor boy, come home with me tonight, I'll keep you warm."

"Emil, are you a virgin?"

"No."

"I'll bet you are. Hey, girls, look at him blush!"

"I wonder how far down he blushes."

With wild shrieks of laughter, they grabbed to open my shirt buttons. I didn't dare wear shorts to work, for fear of the consequences. I liked some of the girls well enough, but they all had full-time boyfriends in town and a shy, barely 14-year-old dishwasher certainly was no great catch.

From Lake George, we took the road north to the head of Lake Champlain, the gateway to Montreal. With less than $5 each in our pockets, we knew we would be turned back, so we hiked around the Canadian border post on a secondary road. Six miles into Canada, we were caught and taken to headquarters by the border patrol.

"Where you boys going?"

Me: "Going home. We couldn't get into the States and we're going back home."

"Your address?"

Shlomo: "Montreal."

Taking up a pad and pen: "Address!"

Shlomo: "St. Lawrence Avenue, 1422." Had to be a St. Lawrence Avenue, right? Wrong!

The patrolman picked up the telephone, obviously calling Montreal. It was all in French but we could cull out a St. Lawrence Avenue here and there. A series of *oui . . . oui . . . ouis,* and then *non. . . non. . . nons.* He hung up. The patrol-station atmosphere, never friendly, turned hostile.

"Identification!"

Unceremoniously searched, uncovered as agents from the Bronx , we were locked up for the night. The jail bunks consisted of wide steel bands covered by a thin leather pad. Not upscale quarters. Not the only inhabitants in the cell. The next morning, after being dumped at the U.S. border, we swam in Lake Champlain in the buff, drowning Canadian fleas. I proudly carried my deportation papers in my wallet until they wore out and became illegible.

> *Within this vale*
> *Of toil*
> *And sin*
> *Your head grows bald*

But not your chin—use
Burma-Shave

Near the end of summer, Shlomo and I parted company—I had become
emboldened enough to take off on my own. After all, on August 2, I had
turned 14! What lured me next was a handout offering jobs in Aroostook
County, Maine, picking potatoes at 7 cents per barrel. A potato is a big
item—how many could it take to fill a barrel? So Shlomo returned to the
Bronx and I went to Maine.

I knew less of Maine than I did of picking potatoes, least of all its size.
I remember an endless crossing of the state on narrow, winding roads.
Reaching Sebago Lake in late afternoon, I stopped to talk with a family
packing a large touring car, ready to start home. Full of family, the car had
no room inside for me, but they offered me the running board for the 30-
or 40-mile trip to Portland. As I hung onto the roof rack in the gathering
dusk, every insect in Maine wanted to greet me . . . splat . . . and I was glad,
for once, to be wearing glasses. It was a fine family—they fed me supper
and put me up for the night. Great state, Maine! Although who would
want to live so far from New York?

Early the next morning, I thumbed along Route 1 out of Portland and
by that evening found myself in Aroostook County. A farm truck stopped,
and I was told to hop in the back. As I struggled to climb the tailgate, a
hand reached out and pulled me on board. I still find it difficult to believe,
but . . . IT WAS MY BROTHER LEE!!!

Just as astonished as I was, he grabbed me in a tight bear hug, but as
the truck accelerated, we were thrown back onto a pile of empty potato
sacks. It seems he had also seen a notice about jobs in Maine; in the middle of the Depression, it was hard to pass up a chance to earn money and
to see more of the country. Neither of us had a clue that the other was in
Maine. What are the odds for such a chance encounter?

But Lee wouldn't let me pick potatoes, although he admitted he was
lonely for company. "In my bunkhouse, they're all Canadian, everybody
speaks French. Who understands it? I just sit there and eat."

It was stoop labor, backbreaking, he said, and it took a good many

Emil, right, and Shlomo, on a winter trip to New Hampshire, 1934.

more potatoes to fill a barrel than I had imagined.

"It's the end of August, Emil, school time. Get on home. You know how Mom worries and Pop's pissed off about your bumming around all summer."

We left the truck just outside the farm and Lee camped out with me by a river. Swimming in our undershorts, Lee displayed his usual Indian Chief bravado by diving head-first off a railroad bridge. I, as a Brave, jumped feet first. We spent much of the night talking—he really was starved for communicative company. In the morning, a farmer backed a cow up against a nearby fence and started milking. Lee picked up my empty army canteen, sauntered up to the fence, and engaged the farmer in conversation, all of it from Lee to the farmer. Finally he got to the point:

"You're pretty good at that milkin'; bet you couldn't get that stream to go through this little canteen hole."

The man said nothing, reached for the canteen, and filled it without difficulty. Returning the canteen, he turned away from my brother and continued milking into his bucket—not acknowledging Lee's thank-you. A Maine character, I thought. Is this what is meant by taciturn?

Reluctantly, I hugged Lee goodbye and we parted. Maine had to wait 17 more years for me to return!

7.

PUBERTY: IT'S NOT EASY

HIGH SCHOOL YEARS, 1932-1936

IN HIGH SCHOOL, sometime when I wasn't paying attention, I grew tall and my hair turned thick, bushy, and brown instead of thin and blond. (Joanna, my barber-wife, cuts my hair on the porch in the spring. She says I am growing nesting material for all the birds in Cushing!) Back in the Bronx, in my teenage years, I bothered the local barbers as little as possible. I had other things bothering my head—puberty, for one!

James Monroe High School had an enrollment of some 6,000 students. I don't remember learning much about Mr. Monroe—evidently he was one of the stalwarts who backed the revolt against Great Britain. He was also a slaveowner. Our coach/physical ed teacher, who was a pleasant neuter in the gym and probably OK as a coach, was definitely not adept at public speaking. I guess no one in the administration had a clue that his brusque, masculine exterior hid a painfully shy public figure. Standing before more than 1,000 nasty male teenagers, in a talk billed as "Sex Education," he turned beet-red and stammered out a number of inanities, such as:

"Stay away from girls until you're older [and presumably wiser] . . . . Uh, ya know, fellers. . . about girls . . . ya gotta be careful . . . you can get sick . . . they can get knocked up . . . get you in trouble . . . ."

"And ya know [appropriate gesture of masturbation], don't do it so much . . . especially before big games."

To give the coach some credence, masturbation was still a dubious act in those days—the *Official Boy Scout Manual* (1910-45) said so in no uncertain terms. But then I never did become a Boy Scout.

But with 45 painful minutes to perform, he soon was at a loss and fell back on a "spare that towel" routine worthy of a top-flight stand-up comedian. First he told us to take frequent showers.

"Keep clean," he admonished us. "Ya know, clean is good." He urged us not to let the poor towel do all the heavy-duty drying. "Your hands can do a lot of the work, too!"

In a forlorn race against unfulfilled time, he went through his entire "hand-as-squeegee" routine, ardently pressing the mythical water off his chest, each leg, reaching around to his back, forcing the water from his hair. I could see the water spurting as he ran his agile and talented hands over his body—several times. It certainly was convincing. Being shy myself, I vibrated with him in his agony. But the other members of the keyed-up audience, emboldened by the absence of girls and irritated by the lack of sex information, hooted, whistled, and threw pennies on the stage. Throwing pennies on the stage was an accolade we had reserved for our much-despised, authoritarian principal, Dr. Hein, and I resented down-grading the gesture for such a trivial cause. We were dismissed with time to spare.

To tell the truth, while I learned absolutely nothing about sex from the coach, I have conscientiously spared my towel every time I've taken a shower for the past 70 or so years—and think of him as I do it. By that standard, it must rank as the most memorable lecture of my career.

The only other fixation that has lasted throughout my life has to do with pants. My mother caught me (age seven or eight) painfully forcing my shirttails into my trousers without opening my belt. All she said was, "Acht, liebe, macht your belt open!" Not only have I done it faithfully over the years, but I think of Mom every time I do it. In the contest for memorable items, Mom wins hands down—I tuck in my pants more than I shower! Mom was gentle and patient with us, but her quiet word had more authority than any amount of bluster from Pop or Dr. Hein.

In the Massachusetts Colony of the Puritans, masturbation was a capital crime. They found a direct order in the Bible against it: Genesis 38, where Onan "spilled his seed upon the ground" in an effort to prevent conception, and the Lord slew him.

Had the Lord been keeping his eye on the Bronx, we wouldn't have lasted a day!

With my peers, I used to gather in the remote regions of a lumberyard to masturbate. But alas, I had the will but not the way. The only one of the gang who hadn't reached puberty, I tried valiantly to climax but to no avail, though the smell of fresh sawdust still arouses me. I was also unique in another way—the only one with foreskin. Besides the Jews, at that time, only the Xhosa of Africa and a few other groups practiced male circumcision as a cultural ritual. My family didn't.

My brother Lee was my bedmate for all the years we lived in the basement apartment in the Bronx. I had established a nightly ritual: whenever I was sure Lee wouldn't show up early, I would scoot down to the foot of the bed, where I could see the window across the alley. About 10 p.m., a young lady would appear in that window to get ready for bed. From my vantage point, I could see only part of her bedroom, the side with her night table and mirror. She would take off her dress and slip and, uncharitably, pass out of sight, only to reappear in her pajamas to sit at the mirror and apply cold cream to her face. One eventful night, she stripped completely to stand before her mirror and examine her body. Carefully lifting her breasts, while standing sideways to her image, she was evidently making an assessment of her charms. I have no idea what her assessment was, but mine was A-OK, since she was the only completely naked lady I'd ever seen. Of course I was, as usual, exuberantly trying to masturbate, but this time a startling and exciting reaction occurred—a sharp tingling went through my body. At last! I was one of the boys.

The girls of my teen years were children of first- and second-generation immigrants. Most were smart, sharp, and liberated—some aggressive with boys. Being a *goy* didn't seem to matter or was a subject for good-natured joking. With some, however, I could sense, even though we kissed and petted, that there was no serious future—they were expected to marry fellow Jews.

There was also a leavening of delicately shy girls like Henrietta. Shy? No, just extremely sensitive and lacking in social skills. She was studying the violin and was said to be a child prodigy. I would walk her home from school but never entered her house or engaged her in any after-school activity, for all of her free time was set aside for practice. Standing at her apartment-house door, holding hands and exchanging earnest talk, was as far as our "affair" went.

One day, she seemed very upset and withdrawn. Finally, as we were parting, she spoke in a rush:

"We can't go together any more."

"But why, Henny?"

"That's what my father says."

"But why?"

"He says I can't go out with a *goy!*" She ran into the house.

And that was the end. She was adamant—no walks home from school, no more holding hands. I never even heard her play the violin!

James Monroe High School, with a population of some 6,000, overflowed the main building, so I spent my first year in an annex. This part of the South Bronx was on a steep slope—a couple of miles or so down to the Bronx River and the same or so up the opposite slope to the school. The Tremont Avenue trolley made the journey, five cents each way, but even 10 cents was money. So I clamped my roller skates to my shoes and went to school on wheels. Actually, I went half the distance (the downhill grades) via my wheels. For the upgrades I used trolley wheels—me clinging to the rear cowcatcher. I make saving the fare money sound virtuous, but in truth I split the trolley fare with a little bakery near the annex. My favorite was a five-cent custard-filled flaky pastry that I remember as a "napoleon." I would eat it as I zoomed down the hill on my skates. The sidewalks in those days were mostly rough slate slabs, and by the time I got down to the river, I was covered with pastry flakes and powdered sugar— a snowy Napoleon on the way back from Moscow.

The Monroe annex was dullsville, with the exception of my excitable science teacher. I discovered her true character one day when I brought to school a round oatmeal box containing a handsome ribbon snake—to swap for a pair of white mice. The boy in the seat behind me became interested in my box when he saw it move. Putting his foolish hand into the box, he let out a yelp of astonishment and pulled out his hand with my otherwise-friendly pet attached to his thumb. He flung his hand wildly to one side, sending the snake flying off to land on top of an equipment closet loaded with retorts and other science stuff. Pandemonium in the classroom—with the teacher leading the chorus. She dashed out of the room, firmly slamming the door behind her. I recovered the snake much sooner than we recovered our teacher. I can still see her pale face peering through the glass panel in the door. At the end of that term, I didn't do so well on my report card in science—or in conduct.

During the 1970s, Joanna and I lived again in New York, this time in Queens. We had been members of the Queens County Bird Club for five years when one of the members suddenly turned to me out of the blue:

"Emil, weren't you in my freshman science class at Monroe?"

By dint of hard thinking, I furrowed up a shy, young girl in our science class. She probably would have recognized the snake immediately but had to look at me for five years before she could properly place me.

THE GREAT CHICAGO WORLD'S FAIR

In August 1933, the end of my first uneventful year in high school, I decided I needed the excitement and educational benefits of the Great Century of Progress Chicago World's Fair. The slogan of the fair was "Science Finds . . . Industry Applies . . . Man Conforms . . . the transformation of life through science." If science equals progress, the German Tiger Tank and the atomic bomb changed all that for me.

The fair boasted many fascinating science exhibits and modern labor-saving machines. But many millions of the workers who built these marvels were out of work in 1933 and without the means to buy them.

Traveling alone that summer, I crossed the Hudson River on a ferry and planted myself on Route 9W.

Stopping a car, I settled in and looked at the driver, instantly realizing he was my good friend, the J. Edgar Hoover look-alike of the previous year. He glanced over and caught my eye.

"I know you," I said.

"I don't think so."

"Last year on this same road. I think you'd better pull over."

"Oh, come on. I'm not going to hurt you. We'll just have a little fun." He reached over to grab me between my legs: "I'll give you $5."

I pulled the keys out of the ignition and held them out the window. He pulled over. I retrieved my pack from the back seat and tossed the keys into the car. He left. Hoover types, apparently, appeared to be one of the hazards of the open road—although such encounters were rare, and I never had a dangerous one.

Drunks were a more serious menace to my hitchhiking career. I never gave it much thought until I saw the smashed wreck of a coupe. Drunken teenagers, they told me—the two in the rumble seat were decapitated. When confronted with a drunken driver, I would wait only as long as the next town or likely hitchhiking spot and then ask to be let out on the grounds that I felt sick and could vomit at any minute.

> *Here lie the bones of Marvin Gray*
> *Who died maintaining his right of way*
> *He was right, dead right, as he sped along*
> *But he's just as dead as if he was wrong*
> *Burma-Shave*

Most of the people I met on the road were OK folks, obliging types. On Friday afternoons, I would get rides from salesmen in need of company to keep awake as they drove three or four hundred miles to make it home for the weekend. I met a few really exceptional people. After bailing out of "J. Edgar's" car, my very next ride on this same 9W was a touring car with New Hampshire plates driven by a retired science teacher-turned-farmer, with his wife and children. I squeezed into the back seat, putting one of the boys on my lap. When I told them I was going to the Chicago World's Fair, they all became excited about it—the kids were full of questions.

At Bear Mountain, we pulled over by the bridge and got out to peer down the gorge. We dropped stones, leaves, sticks, and feathers from the bridge while the former teacher lectured us on the velocity of falling objects. Who knows what else we chattered about, but the upshot was that when we came to where he had to turn east to New England, he gave me his address.

"Around Easter vacation we'll be maple sugaring. Why not come up and help? Be an interesting experience for a New Yorker." Under the excited chorus of the kids and the welcoming smile of his wife, I told them I'd really like that, and they pulled off.

That winter, I wrote them to see if I could come visit with my friend Shlomo. The answer was yes, bring your friend. It was spring in the Bronx when we left, but still winter in New Hampshire. The first night of the trip, we slept on a sawmill platform surrounded by snow and sawdust.

Maple sugaring was a unique experience for two Bronx boys. The farmer had already tapped the trees and was hauling buckets of sap to the sugar house. We dumped the fresh sap into the first of a descending series of large, shallow pans. One of our duties was to keep a fire going under the pans. The syrup would be ready when the sap hit the final pan and had been reduced in volume about thirty times.

But I am keeping us away from the World's Fair, the main point of this chapter of my life. A travel veteran, I had little trouble hitchhiking out to Chicago and was duly impressed with the fair and its Science of the Future. I had intended to sleep in the lakeside park, but even at midnight, it was still buzzing with energies generated by the fair. I discovered that the most tranquil and secluded spot was just over the seawall edging the lake. Huge rectangular slabs of granite, used to hold back the water, had been just tossed over the wall in seemingly haphazard fashion. I finally found one that was relatively horizontal and not too craggy. Fortunately, it was a quiet night on the lake, and in contrast to the hubbub on the other side of the wall, the gentle lapping of the waves was soothing. Exhausted, I slept the night away.

The next day, having spent most of my money at the World's Fair, I headed home. I rode out of Chicago with a salesman who took me to the Lincoln Highway. There he thought to leave me, since he was headed west to Dubuque, Iowa. Well, Lee had been west of the Mississippi, and here was an easy chance to duplicate his feat, so I stayed put. The Illinois roadsides were dry, and huge cornfields were turning brown. The great drought of 1930 had returned with a vengeance in 1933.

Fortunately, the salesman bought me some lunch. On the lunchroom counter was a container with watermelon slices so cold they were white with frost. In contrast to the hot, dry air outside, they seemed a miracle of happiness. Seeing the subject of my intense inspection, the salesman treated me to a slice. This was one of the last sparks of happiness for the summer. From Dubuque, I started the endless trek home, turning back eastward with just enough money to buy a loaf of bread and some cheese. It was to be one of the harshest experiences of my hitchhiking career.

The great cornfields of Iowa, Illinois, and Indiana were fast withering away, and there was little joy in the cars that picked me up. One night I slept on the edge of a dusty cornfield, and I found some good-size ears of corn that had survived the drought. They were not fully ripe, but in my hunger I ate a couple of them anyway—raw. That same day, I ate an unripe melon, creating a nightmare that followed me on the entire trip home. My stomach protested in an uproar—I had the runs complete with cramps. Riding with a farmer, I had to ask him to let me out. I spent long stretches of time behind bushes, afraid to hitch rides.

By the time I got to Pennsylvania, my stomach seemed to be getting under control. I had been riding through the Alleghenies with a genial salesman when he said:

"Do you like to eat, son?"

"OH, YES!"

"Well, I'm on my way to a family reunion, western Pennsylvania style. It's a very fertile group, and there'll be a great many folk. Wanna come?"

"But they'll know I'm not family."

"It doesn't matter. Being Quakers, they'll feed you anyway. Are you game?"

"OH, YES!"

It was a huge, wealthy-looking farm, and the great dining room, crammed with cloth-decked sawhorse tables, overflowed into the kitchen and through open doors to a veranda. There seemed to be a hundred kinfolk—most had eaten, so there was immediate seating. My salesman benefactor didn't even have to lie—I was accepted at face value, no questions asked.

They were the sweetest people I've ever seen—at least the best cooks. It was my first experience with the meaning of *the groaning board.* It seemed to me that every meat known to man (China and Africa excluded) was lined up in front of us: fried chicken (or was it guinea hen?) roast turkey/beef/lamb/sliced ham/sausages galore; mashed/roasted sweet potatoes; cole slaw/lettuce/potato salads; and many vegetables—some, such as rutabagas, were unfamiliar to me. There were biscuits/dark breads/corn bread; pitchers of cider/raspberry juice/iced tea/coffee, and more. And, wow, desserts were planted thick around the rim of the dining area, and I knew I should leave room, but I was like a deprived cocaine addict and sucked it all in.

When we left the dining area, my friend the salesman steered me away from the gregarious multitude to an apple orchard,where he filled a bag with huge, warty, yellow-green apples saying, "They may look ugly, but they're best you'll ever taste. When you can walk, just high-tail it down the farm road; it's two miles to the turnpike."

I groaned my thanks, put my hat over my face, and tried to sleep. The transition between the high point of my life to the low point was rapid. My friend had hardly disappeared when I twisted to my knees and all that gourmet repast went out the same way it went in, past my nose.

The waste, the waste! The food was wasted—or was it? I still remember the good Samaritan and his Quaker kith and kin. Did they think I really was kinfolk? I doubt it. Did it make any difference to them? Not a bit.

When I could, I staggered down the road, like Odysseus, on my endless journey home. I never did get as far as the highway that afternoon—I spent the rest of the day behind an old barn, moaning with sickness. Foolishly, I had had an apple for breakfast; it was everything he said it would be, but it didn't help my diarrhea.

For the last days of my trip, going through Pennsylvania and New Jersey, I practiced, for the first time, cadging food hobo-style.

"Lady, do you have work I can do for something to eat? I lost all my money and need to get back home in time for school."

Only a few times did I have to stack wood or do some simple manual task. Mostly I was given sandwiches. Once I was given thick slabs of bread loaded with raw onion slices. I appreciated the bread, but, with my stomach still in an uproar, I didn't dare eat the raw onions.

When I arrived home, there was a wreath on the front door—Granny had died. Mom was gone again, with a second bout of TB. There were other times I wished I hadn't left home, but nothing ever came close to the experience of this trip.

Back in school, in my sophomore year, I was moved to the main building. The move hardly changed my attitude toward education. It wasn't until my senior year that I had a teacher to whom I could really relate—the only one who ever moved me in any significant way. Anne Rizack was a tiny, plain, Jewish lady in her late twenties who became more beautiful every day I knew her. As our senior-year English teacher, she had, in short order, even the most brutish of my fellow classmates avidly memorizing Shakespearean sonnets. She was the first to awaken in me the value of creativity. It was as if a partition had been lifted, allowing new light to pour in. It was love at first sight—for me and for most of my fellow students. We deemed her actually not much older than we were, for in spirit she elevated us to her level.

John Rice, my writing professor in college, wrote about his favorite teacher: "A boy who has such a teacher will fumble for a word; *love* is too narrow, *worship* too wide."

When Anne Rizack asked us to write something for our English class, I wrote about the trip I had taken to the Chicago World's Fair. I really put my heart into it, and I was very proud of the A+ she awarded the paper. It was published in *The Monroe Doctrine,* our school magazine . Toward the end of the semester, Ms. Rizack called me up to the front of the class to present me with a medal. My story had won first prize in a nationwide high school writers' contest. The story appeared in the *School Press Review,* published by the Columbia (University) Scholastic Press Association. It was another thrill for me that Eleanor Roosevelt officiated at their convention.

Normally, I would have received the medal in an auditorium ceremony, but a student about to graduate with a 35 in citizenship was not about to be so recognized. On the other hand, I couldn't have been more proud for having it presented by Anne Rizack in front of my friends in our classroom.

When I asked Ms. Rizack for a letter of recommendation for Black Mountain College, I was embarrassed by her overgenerous praise—and still am. After much inner debate, I decided to include it in this book. It was part and parcel of my sudden discovery of an unknown creative ability that was appreciated by journalistic scholars, by my closest friends, and by my highly valued teacher. It was overwhelming, and it changed my life in many ways yet to come.

320 East 176th Street
New York, New York
July 3, 1936

To Whom It May Concern:
I have known Emil Willimetz for the past year. He was a contributor to the literary magazine of the James Monroe High School, *The Monroe Doctrine,* of which I am Faculty advisor, and he was a student of my senior English classes last term. I have, therefore, had double opportunity to observe Willimetz in the performance of creative as well as of regular work. He deserves the highest praise for both.

Emil Willimetz can be recommended only in superior terms. As a student and writer for the school's magazine, he revealed the possession of a sensitive, delicately attuned mind, of a real literary talent, of brilliant sympathies in various fields of the world's thinking, of a highly eager and curious and loving spirit. I have seen him demonstrate these qualities outside of the classroom, too. His living is original, adventurous, responsive to beauty. His contacts with people, singly and in mass, reveal a deep-rooted social responsibility.

I feel that I have been most fortunate in knowing Emil Willimetz. I feel a deep personal regret that he has left New York, for I know how he makes richer the place in which he is. For further information I can be reached at the address above, and, after September 11, at the James Monroe High School, Boynton Avenue at 172nd Street, the Bronx, New York.

Yours truly,
Anne G. Rizack

The Monroe Doctrine, our school magazine, had been largely beyond my ken. With the publication of my story, its staff and authors had become my focus. Intellectual egghead endeavors were new to me, and I entered into them with considerable excitement. As a group we read books, including some that would daunt me today: Proust, *Remembrance of Things Past;* James Joyce, *Portrait of an Artist as a Young Man* and *Ulysses;* Dostoyevsky, *The Brothers Karamazov.* None of this reading and discussion was for school credit, although some of it was inspired by our friend and teacher, Anne Rizack.

Thomas Mann's *The Magic Mountain* was a book that moved me strongly. In the book, tuberculosis was depicted as a disease of wealthy people, who were battling it out in a super-luxurious sanatorium high in the Swiss Alps. My heroine was a lovely young woman whose being radiated a spiritual and erotic power. A beautiful way to die. It took some time for me to remember that my mother fought through two bouts of consumption, and that TB was primarily a grim disease of poverty. Not that I loved the young heroine less—it's just that she had nothing to do with the Great Depression.

One of our favorite authors was a contemporary British writer, Storm Jameson, whose sensitive writing predated today's feminists. One of my schoolmates, Jeanette Gootzeit, was a dark-haired, aggressive girl with a reputation for being a bit on the hyper side. Here's an excerpt from a story she wrote about herself for *The Monroe Doctrine:*

> Her friends were discussing Storm Jameson. One of them said, "Oh, gee, isn't Storm a beautiful name?" "If she's Storm then I am Fury," said another. Suddenly something burst in her heart and she said, "Well, I'm Drizzle." They all laughed and laughed and said it was classical. Then one repeated it with a Jewish accent, saying Drizzele." And then like harpies they took up the chant calling her "Drizzle, Drizzle." And she wondered why her heart was crying.

Hildreth Freiberg was my girl through my senior year in high school. She wasn't my first girl but at least the first most serious one. We never went on dates, at least not in the formal sense of "dating." Money was a sometime thing, not always available. When we went out to movies, shows, meals, or campouts, whoever had money paid or shared the cost. She introduced me to cultural aspects new to me, and we went together to see Picasso and Van Gogh exhibits.

Hildreth had a petite figure with barely perceptible breasts and a pretty, round face with the high cheekbones of the Russian steppes. We were both active on the school magazine, both adored Anne Rizack, and were mutually attracted to leftist ideas. Music played an important role in our young relationship. We would gather at a friend's house, put a stack of classics on the turntable, and then huddle on the carpet in pairs. In those days, it was called petting, and it was always laden with the fear of a key turning in the front door—clothes had to be manipulated so as to be rearrangeable in an instant.

In those days, adolescent boys and girls sometimes met as if each were from another planet. Sexual prohibitions in society created feelings of shame and anxiety. Not with Hildreth, of course—we were very advanced in sex, for we had studied Havelock Ellis's *Studies in the Psychology of Sex* (an abridged manual, of course).

The big problem we always faced was, "where." One night, we were doing "homework" together at her house and were getting pretty close to

Hildreth and Emil.

one of the advanced chapters in the Ellis manual, when we heard her older brother at the door. We had hardly had time to get to our books when he marched sternly past us. Had he noticed how flushed we were, he would have known we were into pretty exciting homework.

One June day, toward the end of my junior school year, we were desperate enough to go to my apartment. My family, by this time, was out of the basement and into a larger, five-story walk-up apartment. At two in the afternoon, everyone was out working or at school; my brother Lee was driving a taxi. I had, of course, gone through the prescribed embarrassment of buying condoms—they were not openly available, so one had to ask for them, holding back until nobody else was at the counter.

It was a total fiasco. Not only did I fail to penetrate but also ended up with what our manual called "premature ejaculation." Suddenly, we were horrified to hear the outside apartment door open and my brother Lee walk in. We quickly disappeared under the sheet and held each other in total shock. Fortunately, by this time I had my own bedroom, and in a short time we could hear Lee under the shower. Quickly and silently, we dressed and left the apartment. I walked Hildreth down the long hill to the elevated station. We never said a word, hardly looking at each other's drawn faces. She said a weak goodbye and rushed up the station steps.

About 11 that night, after the night shift at the New York Public Library, where I was then working, I decided to walk off my frustrations and feelings of impotence before going to bed. From 42nd Street, I hiked up Fifth Avenue, through Harlem and the Mott Haven freight yards, past Hildreth's house at 148th Street, to 176th Street, arriving home long after midnight. As I walked, I thought—should we have waited? But waiting really wasn't an option—at 18, we were at the peak of excitement and a deeply felt need to complete our explorations of each other. We were in love, and in the proper setting, I was convinced we could have had the good experience it should have been. Under the pressure, it was as opposite to making love as it was possible to get. So much for Havelock Ellis.

In my last two years at Monroe, I worked as a night page at the New York Public Library, Music Division. It was not too complex a job—fetching books for patrons. I was also, of course, responsible for returning books to their homes on the shelves. During slack periods, I was obligated to stay busy in the back rooms shelf-reading, checking to see that the books were all in proper Dewey Decimal order. Our rarest books were stashed away in deep underground stacks. Lit by small bulbs and rarely inhabited by other humans, these stacks were strangely haunted—not quite like our coal cellar, but close. I was always glad to find the book I needed and run!

I almost missed one Sunday night shift because of being apprehended by the police. In good weather, our *Monroe Doctrine* gang went as a group on picnics—and once or twice on overnight campouts. Our favorite picnic site was Palisades Park. Hiking up the Jersey shore, we settled down one day on the end of a dock for our picnic. Another boy and I climbed the Palisades. Returning all grimy, we stripped to our shorts for a swim. Apprehended by the Park police, we were taken to Park headquarters. I was due to work by 6 p.m. at the library, so I was frantic with anxiety. We were freed in the nick of time, but not until memorizing the

20 park rules—among them, no climbing the dangerously crumbly palisades and no swimming off the piers.

During my senior year in high school, I was engrossed in American Student Union activities, so I had to do my homework either on the subway or at the library. At first I was apprehensive about being caught doing homework, so I positioned myself on top of the ladder platform, where supposedly I was shelf-reading. When my ruse was discovered, I was subject to a good deal of kidding and occasionally even received some help with my homework.

The librarians, who made out the slips for books I was sent to hunt up, were always deep in concentration at the front desk working on 3x5 index cards. I thought them a stodgy lot until I found out that they were writing epitaphs on those cards—of all our customers and each other. The only one I can remember:

> *Here lies the Greasy Scholar,*
> *Whose neck was dirtier than his collar,*
> *His collar was dirtier than his shirt,*
> *Ashes to ashes and dirt to dirt.*

One of our steady readers was a woman who always wore a red beret; she was "The Red Frying Pan," but I don't remember the epitaph. Willimetz had them stumped for a while, until someone worked it out with "bets" and "Willi nilly nets."

I had been hired for this job, after a brief interview, by the Music Division boss, Charlton Sprague Smith. One night, he invited me to a special in-house performance of ancient music played on ancient musical instruments, one of the many cultural WPA programs for unemployed musicians. The group was also transcribing ancient music for modern instruments. It was a fascinating experience, and it gave me a good deal more respect for music and musicians. It is one thing to sit at a formal concert and watch the orchestra plowing through a symphony, but it's much more exciting to sit informally in a room of shirtsleeved professionals who are making and enjoying the awakening of long-dormant music.

I'm sure my musical ignorance was clear to my boss, but he kept up a running commentary on the ancient music and instruments as though I were a fellow musicologist. He impressed me with the importance of this WPA project. I didn't realize the status Charlton Sprague Smith had in the music world until after I left the job. His recommendation of me to Black Mountain College was certainly above and beyond the call of duty.

8.

SENIOR YEAR, 1936: THE AMERICAN STUDENT UNION

The lessons of youth can be so powerful that they tend to override all subsequent experiences to the contrary.
        —Jared Diamond

SATURDAY AFTERNOONS, IN WARM WEATHER, I had a seed business—bags of sunflower seeds, pine nuts, and pumpkin seeds, which I doled out in three- and five-cent wooden measuring cups. My best customers were a circle of old Jewish immigrants in Crotona Park, passionately debating 1905 Russian revolutionary politics in a mixture of Yiddish, English, and Russian. When they left the park, through a deep ring of shells, you couldn't tell Bolsheviks from Mensheviks, but the passions engendered in these debaters stayed etched in my mind.

The immigration of European Jews to the United States was the result of persecutions that occurred long before Hitler. Czar Alexander II was assassinated in 1881, and Russian Jews bore the brunt of the backlash. Most were forced to move to an area bordering Germany, Austria, and Romania, called the Pale of Settlement. Large numbers were killed in the pogroms of 1881-82, 1891, and 1905-6. This savage treatment started shock waves of immigration to the New World. They settled on Manhattan's Lower East Side, one of the world's most crowded districts. Many worked in the garment trades—in sweatshops or alone at home.

The 1911 fire in the Triangle Shirtwaist Factory affected me profoundly even in the 1930s. The fire killed 145 workers—mostly immigrant women, many Jewish. Despite the fact that the factory doors were locked and escape was cut off, the sweatshop's owners were acquitted of negligence. Some 300,000 people marched in the funeral parade. It was the start of militant unionization and the radicalization of the garment trades in New York City.

When an extension of the subway system opened up Harlem, many of these unionized Jews moved uptown. And when an elevated extension opened the Bronx, they established themselves there. This move, in turn, opened Harlem to the flood of blacks migrating from the deep South. During the Great Depression, the trickle-down allocated to the sparrows completely dried up. New Deal patches on the economy brought a modicum of relief to many people, but the yearly per capita income kept falling—in 1933, it was $495.

Our basement flat in the Bronx was surrounded by large apartment houses, the habitat of members of the International Ladies' Garment Workers, the Amalgamated Clothing Workers, and the Furriers Unions. Every Sunday morning, our courtyard would reverberate with the incendiary strains of the "Internationale," rendered in brass. Not the Communist "Internationale" but the Socialist version—a minor difference in wording but a major difference in political thought and action. It was the theme song of the popular socialist Jewish newspaper, the *Forverts (Daily Forward)*. Many of my high school friends were the sons and daughters of these unionists.

When I arrived at James Monroe High School on my first May Day in the main building, there were so few students in attendance that the teachers invented non-curriculum subjects just to pass the day. The following May Day, I persuaded my good friend Shlomo to take me with him to 14th Street and Union Square to see the big parade. May Day emptied the Bronx—it was a sacrosanct workers' holiday, and subways were only a nickel! When we got to Union Square, it was awash with humanity, and workers carrying all manner of signs and banners were still marching down Fifth Avenue into the square.

I had expected to be marching with Shlomo's father's contingent of the

Furriers Union, but instead I found myself in a group of students carrying antiwar signs. Suddenly we were charged by a squadron of mounted police, the horses trained to turn sideways, tumbling us backward. Very intimidating, until we learned to plaster antiwar stickers on the horses' rumps and the riders' boots. Turnabout, we figured, was fair play. It was an exhilarating experience that seemed to express my growing negative feelings about war. On the return trip, the subways belonged to the riders, who were carrying signs and singing songs in seemingly every language in the world.

Instead of going home, the students took me to their headquarters. They were not all strangers—I knew many of them from my English class and the school magazine. The name of the organization was the American Student Union (ASU)—an organization I knew existed but never connected with. The Furriers Union had a hall on Westchester Avenue, just a few blocks from the school, and the father of one of the ASU gang was an officer in the local, so the students obtained a key to the hall. Forthwith, they had a rent-free headquarters complete with typewriter and mimeograph machine. From a literature rack I was able to get some background about the ASU and about some of the history of May Day. A few years earlier, a group of protesters in Union Square had demanded Depression relief. The *New York World* wrote: "Women were struck in the face with blackjacks; boys beaten by gangs of police, and an old man was backed into a doorway and knocked down time after time." It was the part about "boys beaten by gangs of police" that impressed me. I took home a few pamphlets and magazines to read.

But statistics alone don't tell the story of the Depression. During my high school days, newspapers and magazines were filled with the human side. Women were terrified of becoming pregnant. Many men, bearing the shame of not being able to provide for their families, became impotent.

In 1933, one out of every five children in the nation was not getting enough of the right things to eat. You can starve for a long time without dying.

Edward Robb Ellis, in *A Nation in Torment: The Great American Depression, 1929-1939,* related a string of sorry tales:

A teacher in a coal-mining town asked a little girl in her class-room whether she was ill. The child said, "No. I'm all right. I'm just hungry." The teacher urged her to go home and eat some-thing. The girl said, "I can't. This is my sister's day to eat."

In an interview with Studs Terkel for *Hard Times,* Virginia Durr said of the Depression:

> It was a time of terrible suffering. Have you ever seen a child with rickets? No proteins, no milk. And the companies [to raise the price] pouring milk into the gutters. People with nothing to eat and they killed the pigs. [In 1936, six million piglets were slaugh-tered.] If that wasn't the craziest system in the world, can you imagine anything more idiotic?

When the steel companies closed down in Birmingham, Alabama, thousands were thrown out of work. Virginia Durr was acquainted with some execu-tives, and she argued with them: "You feed the mules which work in your company. Why don't you feed the people? You're responsible." She continued:

> There was a small number of people who felt the whole system was lousy. The kids came along and they want to change it, but they don't seem to know what to put in its place. I think it has to be responsive to people's needs. And it has to be done by demo-cratic means, if possible.

According to Piers Brendon in *The Dark Valley:*

> The Depression had cast a pall over the world. During the 1930s the globe was enveloped by something like the fog of war. The Depression wrecked the Weimar Republic and brought Hitler to power in Germany. It smashed the fragile internationalist, parlia-mentary consensus in Japan, opening the door to the militarists. The Spanish Civil War became a national struggle that seemed to

be a prelude to a world war. [It was.] The World Depression ended only with the World War II blood bath. It was the worst peacetime crisis to afflict humanity since the Black Death.

I had been sickened by the Great Depression and the state of the world into which I was born, and I desperately needed to do something about the tensions building up in me. Surrounded by a sea of misery, I, too, wanted to change things. Contrary to John Kenneth Galbraith's notion, I felt that if you made the sparrows prosperous, their prosperity would find its way up through every class resting upon them. This was the democratic ideal and radical notion that motivated me in high school. How to get it done was the problem.

Our *Monroe Doctrine* student magazine group had grown more radical as time went on, and when the great movement against War and Fascism swept through the colleges in my senior year, we were swept into the eddy. While I had not been a joiner, never having had the after-school time (and probably not much inclination), I did become active in the American Student Union, organized against war, fascism, and racial bigotry.

Our literary selections changed from the classics to antiwar novels. We read John Dos Passos's *Three Soldiers;* Hemingway's *A Farewell to Arms;* Erich Maria Remarque's *All Quiet on the Western Front;* and Dalton Trumbo's *Johnny Got His Gun,* the powerful and shocking story of a legless, armless paraplegic soldier and his thoughts on war.

It was about this time (1933) that "The Scottsboro Boys" became a celebrated cause and turned our heads to the South. Here we found a depth of causes to protest—the Ku Klux Klan, lynchings, and other actions of brutal violence. We were shaken by the dreadful conditions of the Harlan coal miners in Kentucky. We tried various ways to raise money for these causes. (I even spent some hours riding the subways, shaking a can labeled, HELP THE SCOTTSBORO BOYS.)

The horror of World War I seemed not to have satisfied those who like to settle things in that way, and a second chapter was a-building, only 20 years after that first bloody and senseless debacle. Roosevelt's New Deal was trying to patch up the old economic balloon, but the Depression per-

sisted until Hitler solved the problem with World War II. To a young boy
growing through his teens to maturity, it was fertile ground for protest.

The American Student Union was against war as well as strongly
against the rising tide of fascism. We were not pacifists. By 1936, in addition to dancing the hora for a new homeland for the Jews, I was singing
Spanish Loyalist songs in Crotona Park. People I knew suddenly disappeared, breaking the boycott to go illegally to Spain. Swept up in the fever
to join them, I fortunately was deemed too young. Actually, the events in
Spain caught up with me between 1943 and 1945, when I was drafted to
fight the same Germans who learned their trade so well there. In 1944, I
was to hear Loyalist songs in a coal mine on the border between Holland
and Germany.

In 1896, Italy had been defeated by Ethiopians with primitive
weapons. On October 3, 1935, Mussolini avenged that defeat by sending
mechanized troops against the untrained and poorly armed Ethiopians.
Bombs erupting in the African villages were described by Count Ciano as
the opening of beautiful flowers. Clearly, what the Italian Fascists were
doing in Ethiopia was terribly wrong—even to a 17-year-old high school
boy. And although there was a boycott, U.S. petroleum companies sold oil
to Italy and FDR did little to discourage Mussolini.

According to Sean Cashman, in *America in the Twenties and Thirties:*

> Allied terms at Versailles were harsh. Germany would be dis-
> armed, forbidden to maintain more than 100,000 troops or have
> any major warships, submarines, warplanes or tanks. Germany
> would have to pay all war damages, a sum estimated at more than
> $600 billion in today's dollars. Until the Germans accepted these
> terms, the Allies would continue the strangling naval blockade
> they had imposed in 1915.

The Allies continued the blockade a full year after the war's end. Many
thousands more died of hunger or illnesses due to malnutrition. The
Germans signed! In 1923, inflation swept the country and the German

mark began plunging: in January, it was 7,000 to the dollar, and by August it was one million to the dollar. It was not worth the cost of the paper to print a stamp, so postage was free. The mark finally fell to an all-time low of 4.2 trillion to the dollar, and all savings were destroyed. (As children in the Bronx, we played with million-mark notes, brought over by my uncle as souvenirs.)

Germany had lost nearly two million men in World War I and, with the inflation, was in a state of despair. It was fertile ground for Corporal Adolf Hitler, a dedicated soldier who had found himself in a hospital at the end of World War I. In *Mein Kampf [My Battle]*, he wrote: "In vain the death of 2 million . . . . Hatred grew in me, hatred for those responsible for this deed . . . . I decided to go into politics."

Adolf Hitler took power in 1933 and thumbed his nose at the Allies by building up the German army, navy, and air force. The democracies did not react, except for Great Britain, which concluded a 1935 agreement that permitted greater German naval strength and unlimited submarines. In 1936, Hitler violated the Treaty of Versailles by marching into the Rhineland. The Germans had only three battalions, and the army had orders to retreat if opposed. They were not opposed.

> *The forty-eight hours after the march into the Rhineland were the most nerve racking in my life."* Hitler later admitted. *"If the French had then marched into the Rhineland, we would have had to withdraw with our tails between our legs.*
> —Blanche Cook, *Eleanor Roosevelt*

Sensing the approval of the Allies, Hitler then took over Austria and Czechoslovakia and sent arms and men to Franco's Spain. There was little feeling that the world valued democracy. But it was all grist for our active ASU anti-Fascist campaigns.

The James Monroe main building was east of the Bronx River, with few crosstown transit possibilities for students in my neighborhood. One could go downtown to Manhattan via the Lexington Line and then return uptown on the Westchester Line, but it took longer than walking the three or so crosstown miles. In the rain or snow, the exposed bridge crossing of the Bronx River was murder. I still have scabs on my ears from frostbite. When a family effort was made to upgrade my winter wear, I received a lined, horsehide leather coat. Not only was it warm, but it was handsome and I loved it.

But it wasn't just the walk that caused my frostbite. The American Student Union had started an antiwar campaign in the winter of 1936, leading up to a school walkout and demonstration on April 22. Since a large percentage of our student body had to cross the bridge, we distributed most of our leaflets there. Was Valley Forge as miserably cold as our bridge?

In my final year at Monroe, my spare cash went into paper, mimeograph ink, and stencils. Leaflets to cover 6,000 students didn't come cheap, so lunch was as frugal as I could make it. Across the street from the school was a convenient deli, and I could run over during lunch hour. On the window, in large gold Hebrew letters, was the usual sign that said, "Kosher." On the counter was a dish containing bits and end pieces of fragrant salami, with a sign, "A nickel a stickel." My favorite, also a nickel, was a spiced, mashed potato knish, painted with egg yolk. Kept on the hot grill for many hours, the bottom of the concoction would build up to a tough, thick crust that was a treat to nibble on in the more boring classrooms. (I did, at times, love the Bronx!)

Our large school lunchroom also had food bargains, the cheapest being three slices of rye bread for a penny—meant, of course, as an adjunct to a purchased meal. Frequently, my lunch consisted of three pieces of rye liberally coated with free butter, mustard, pickle slices, and other condiments.

One day when I went up to buy bread, my leather coat was lifted from the back of my lunchroom chair. I was devastated. It was not just a coat, it was months of careful planning by my parents, setting aside money from other needs, and it represented a real financial disaster to the family resources. I hated the person who stole it; even more, I hated to break the news to my mother; and most, I hated the lifestyle that made a leather coat such a big item in our lives.

As a son of Austrian parents, I have always identified with that small country. "It was sweet to live here," wrote the author Stefan Zweig of his youth. In the coffeehouses of Vienna, he found a basis for outbursts of creativity. For the price of a cup of coffee, one could sit all day with friends and enter into passionate discussions on a variety of subjects.

My library closed at 10 p.m., and by the time I cleaned the reading-room tables and rode the subway to the 174th Street station, it was almost midnight. Near the station exit was a Bickford's cafeteria, where my left-wing friends would be gathered in a far corner. But while Bickford's didn't have the *Gemütlichkeit* (coziness) of a Viennese coffeehouse, coffee was only five cents. Engrossed in bitter arguments over "party-line" changes, my friends would hardly notice me when I sat down at the table.

I guess I was the idealist type who wanted my coffeehouse warm and friendly and my revolution dramatic but pure. It was during this time that Stalin was purging his old Bolshevik comrades. This, of course, aggravated the anti-Communist factions. I looked over at Saul. He just shrugged his shoulders:

"You can't make an omelet without breaking the eggs."

"Just breaking eggs doesn't make an omelet!" someone else jeered.

Saul laughed: "Comes the revolution it will rain borscht—but only communists will have spoons! Gotta spoon?"

Big joke—assuming, of course, that everyone loves borscht. Original ideas—which might have led to a better understanding of our political world—were obliterated by one faction tying to score points against another, earnest Liberals vs. Socialists vs. Communists vs. Trotskyites. We even had a Lovestoneite, whatever that was. But I had little time, and even less inclination, to read the many pamphlets that were being circulated, and I felt "out-pointed" in these cafeteria debates. Hey, teach, wot's a polemic? I turned away from the doctrinaire political factions.

The nationwide student strike took place April 22 of my senior year. More than a million students responded, mostly in the universities. The classroom walkout was called for 11:30 a.m., and I must confess that I remember little about those morning classes. I knew that at least five students in my late-morning classroom pledged to walk out with me. By 11, I was feeling a little sick to my stomach.

I kept shooting furtive glances at the others. When the classroom clock reached 11:30, I made a great show of gathering my papers, standing up, and marching stone-faced past the frowning teacher and out the door. With relief, I sensed others stirring behind me. Actually, we had at least nine or ten from the class, and the corridors seemed to be filled with students. Of the few high schools that participated, ours had the largest response—some 350 students put down their books and left their classrooms to hold a rally in the street outside.

Soapbox oration has gone out of style, but in my youth it was the essence of the First Amendment. Large organizations had portable platforms and loudspeaker systems. The ASU had a box, and the portable loudspeaker was a student with a stout voice. That I never took a turn on the soapbox had to do with having a soft voice—and painful shyness.

Our antiwar rally outside the school consisted simply of several student speakers. We were excited and elated by the number of students who had elected to defy the authorities. I went around shaking hands and distributing leaflets. In about 30 minutes, back into school we went.

In the colleges, the strike was accepted by the authorities—at least no harsh treatment was meted out. But in our high school, the reaction to the strike was traumatic. The next day, we were all ordered to report to the principal's office. To the mob that crowded the hallways outside his office, the principal, Dr. Hein, made an ominous announcement: Because of our terrible breach of conduct, none of us would receive diplomas.

But as a result of all the publicity and the multitude of petitions we engendered, the New York City Board of Education agreed that if we had passed all the educational requirements, Dr. Hein couldn't refuse to sign our diplomas. But you can't keep a good disciplinarian down completely—Hein limited his decree to just two honor students. Jeanette (Drizzle) Gootzeit and Isidore Auerbach were not to graduate. Jeanette was superbright and did her senior year New York State English Regents exam in blank verse. She was the only one in the state that year to receive 100 percent in the English Regents.

Being an officer of my local ASU chapter, I was told in no uncertain terms by the principal that, although he had to sign my diploma, he would give me a 30 in citizenship. (Something must have weakened his resolve—I ended up with a 35.) He added that he would see that there would be no college for the likes of me. Mean-spirited man! I had the feeling that he doubly resented the fact that I was in bed with a largely Jewish crowd. He only served to reinforce my belief that in 1936, Fascists were everywhere!

Dr. Hein called me irresponsible, but I resonated more to John A. Rice, my future guru at Black Mountain College, whose definition of responsibility was: "By responsibility I do not mean pliability, an over-nice attention to the wishes of others. Heretics are often the most responsible of men."

The graduation ceremonies were less than tranquil. With 1,100 graduates that year, there would be no proud students marching up the aisle to receive their sheepskins. There would, of course, be speeches of congratulations and optimism about the future (1936—the heart of the Depression!).

The main speaker, Dr. Alberto Bonaschi, a member of the Board of Education, refused to give our graduation address. He cited the two honor students who were banned from receiving their diplomas because they participated in a "peace strike" at the school on April 22: "I do not desire that my presence in any manner be regarded as approval of an action of yours [Dr. Hein], with which I heartily disagree."

I was scheduled to intervene during the ceremonies and lead a denunciation against the principal. But that was also not to be. A *New York Post* reporter described the scene:

> Because of my strong faith in the police, and because I don't care to make enemies among them, and because "police brutality" is such a dreadful thing in a time of Fascist tendencies, I am heartsick over what I saw in James Monroe High School, 172nd Street and Boynton Avenue, The Bronx.
>
> Right after Dr. Hein announced the bestowal of diplomas a

man rose from the audience and began to speak. Several men in plain clothes ran to him, seized him and dragged him out. They had to do that. They took him into an elevator and I entered too. The elevator descended slowly, two floors to the cellar.

All the way down at least three men punched and kicked the disturber. He made no resistance. The elevator stopped, the door opened and he was pushed out. Again he was punched and kicked many times.

"That's enough fellows," I finally shouted. "Don't kick him any more."

—Henry Becker, reporter

The *New York Post* also ran an editorial:

LESSON OF THE MONROE HIGH SCHOOL OUTRAGE

For an object lesson as to what happens when Fascist repressive measures and gag law take the place of orderly process and civil liberties, we call the attention of our readers to the situation at James Monroe High School, The Bronx.

There, as in a microcosm, we can see clearly what has happened in the same way, if on a larger scale, in the goose-stepping countries of Europe.

The police were in Dr. Hein's school, aware of Dr. Hein's attitude, conscious of his determination to suppress all opinion in opposition to his own. They acted accordingly.

All this week, in schools where principals met peace-demonstrating students halfway, there have been happy and peaceful commencements, without picket lines, without recriminations, without cellar beatings. And Dr. Hein's excuse for what he has done is that he wants to preserve law and order!

After I left New York for my trip to the South, the ASU held a *Trial of Dr. Hein.* The WPA had a Theater of Action, a truck that could drop its sides and rear end and convert into street theater. Through Heywood Broun, a syndicated Scripps-Howard columnist and head of the Newspaper Guild, we were able to get the truck, and Broun came to take part. The trial took place in front of James Monroe, and, although the school was out, it gathered a crowd and was first-class publicity. As a result of this action, the newspaper protests, and pressure on the Board of Education, Jeanette Gootzeit and Isidore Auerbach received their diplomas.

That I was deeply emotionally involved in the antiwar strike is not reflected in the above barebones outline of events. I had planned on spending the summer exploring the South, but before I left New York, I felt compelled to take the time to write about my more personal involvement in the events. When I returned from the South in September, I took a free WPA course in writing and polished the account that follows.

*****

A PERSONAL REPORT: GRADUATION COMES IN JUNE

We start off, excited and enthusiastic; the leaflet distributors drop out, one for each street centering at the school. We arrive at the main entrance holding signs high and the long, narrow chain of pickets begins its first circle. I feel strange in my new graduation clothes, boys in blue jackets, white pants; girls all in white with a red ribbon.

Over the facade of the building is an engraved quotation: "WHERE LAW ENDS, TYRANNY BEGINS." We use it in our picket line:

> *Here law ends, tyranny begins*
> *Here law ends, tyranny begins*

Many police are around. They ride up and down on horses, are lined up around the entrance and in the school. We change our chant:

> *Keep the cops out of Monroe, since when do cops go to school?*
> *Keep the cops out of Monroe, since when do cops go to school?*

Some of the cops near us look sheepish, others belligerent.

"What they need is a good spanking," one of them says loudly to his neighbor. Some people near him laugh and nod their heads in agreement.

The cop looks pleased, he walks away with a smile on his face.

I suddenly leave the group, my mother and kid sister are coming down the street, they are looking for me. I run to meet them. It is June and my mother looks young and pretty in her light spring coat and straw hat. She looks happily at me, at my new clothes. I am going to graduate, the first in the family, there is a great career ahead of me; she sees it in the clear, warm sky, in the smart blue-white of the other students.

Then she sees the picket line, she knows how much I am a part of it. My sister has a leaflet in her hand, but neither of them has connected this handbill with trouble in the school, neither of them has read it. My mother reaches for my hand but says nothing. Together we watch the line go round and round, together we listen to them chant:

> *We want a principal with democratic principles*
> *We want a principal with democratic principles*

People are beginning to file into the building, and with them my mother and sister. They go into the assembly hall to a prearranged program—a program in which I have sworn to play a part. I have helped arrange this program really well, so well that despite me it will go on, yet so well that my failure in it would break me in the eyes of my friends and take down the structure of my beliefs.

Suddenly the chant stops. I look up quickly—we have to line up for the march into the assembly. A fellow student grabs my arm. She is very excited and waves a newspaper clipping: "Bonaschi has written an open letter to the principal, he refuses to address the graduation. He calls the principal unfair and against academic freedom. Bonaschi's name is on the program and he won't be here. Isn't that great?" she cries. "Isn't that great?"

We march into the assembly. Row after row of the seats are filled—the overflow goes on to the stage. I am a "W" which puts me directly behind the speaker's dais. This is part of our plan, my being seated there. In my seat I close my eyes. Somewhere out in front is a light spring coat and a straw hat, happy with the graduation. Around me are hundreds of expectant students.

I glance at the program. Next is Bonaschi, a distinguished member of the Board of Education. He is obviously not present. There is a stir in the audience, a wave of whispers. A faculty member fills in for him. Next is Dr. Hein, next I am to act, to stand up and protest—to be joined by other students in the assembly. From all around comes the rapid clap-clap of applause. The principal raises his hand for silence. The assembly becomes quiet. I feel my hands are cold. He begins his address, his first words are muffled by the throbbing of my temples. I cannot move. Suddenly in the balcony a man stands up. His voice is loud, it breaks clear in the silence. People are startled. "Friends, this is not a fair graduation," he shouts. "Two students are not graduating today who in all fairness and justice . . . ."

His words are cut off by the rising rumble of sounds from the audience. Several cops and detectives rush to his seat and knock him down. A woman begins to hit one of them and is pushed away. They put handcuffs on the man and half push, half drag him out of the balcony.

Everyone is talking, some start to applaud the man, some to hiss him. Deep in the graduate ranks a voice yells out: "Where is Bonaschi?"

I recognize the voice but I can't move. In front of me the principal is holding onto the speaker's stand, his face is red, he is trying to be calm: "Parents, do not let this outrageous performance upset the graduation."

I feel a great impulse to push him off the platform. He talks for some time, I am not conscious of what he is saying. After a time the students rise, they are about to be graduated in bulk. I remain seated. A teacher hurries up to me, we are conspicuous on the platform. I tell her softly to go away. She tells me to stand up. I say sharply, "Go away!" She leaves me. Dr. Hein continues:

> . . . and because you have successfully completed four years of scholastic achievements, it is my privilege [great relief?] to graduate you, class of 1936, from James Monroe High School.

Applause . . . and the orchestra strikes up a few notes of "America the Beautiful." I go over to where my mother is sitting, her eyes are red with fear and excitement. I stay and reassure them that all is well. They start to go when I suddenly remember my diploma and tell them to wait a minute. I run upstairs to my homeroom. Since I am a "W," I have to wait in line for my diploma. I run quickly back to give it to my mother. She looks up at me, I keep my eyes down but squeeze her hand. They leave.

I sit for a moment in my mother's seat—tired. The auditorium is almost empty. Members of the band are putting instruments away, a few of the faculty are talking in small groups. Outside I hear faintly the chanting of a reinforced picket line. I hear, too, the approaching wail of a siren. The siren dies in a whine outside the entrance, the even chanting breaks down into angry confusion.

I go outside. Students are grouped around a police wagon. The police had given a man a bad beating. There is a cut on his face, his lip is almost torn off, and blood is coming out of the corner of his mouth. With his handcuffed hands he wipes it away, his hands are shaking. The picket line breaks out in loud angry voices:

> *This is New York, not Berlin*
> *This is New York, not Berlin*

They push the man inside the wagon and bang the door shut. A student next to me is crying with anger and pity. She says to me that he needs a doctor, he is bleeding at his mouth and may be hemorrhaging. Our strike committee goes off to call the IWO (International Workers' Organization) for a doctor and the Civil Liberties Union for a lawyer.

We have a contact with Heywood Broun in the Newspaper Guild, and we make plans with him for further help with publicity. The afternoon passes quickly. I forget my fatigue, my sense of failure—there is so much to do.

It is dark when the last of the work is done. We go to Bickford's cafeteria to eat. Because of the excitement we are not hungry. They tell me they are glad I didn't stand up to protest, that it was much more effective the way it played out. But I knew better. I'll never be sure whether or not I would have stood up to protest.

I break away from my friends and take the subway to the Battery and then to the Staten Island ferry. It is a ride we have often taken to cool off on hot summer nights. The ferry vents a long, loud blast as it moves away from the slip—a lonesome sound. It is June but the wind still blows cold in the dark, almost everyone goes inside. I am alone by the time we pass the Statue of Liberty. Across the bay is Staten Island, off to the left is the channel out to the ocean, a dark bare slit in the horizon. I feel strongly my loneliness. I feel, too, my loneliness in the family. I feel a great need to get away, to leave the city, to leave the family for a time.

BOOK II

LIVING THROUGH THE TEENS

As a kid hatched in the Depression, I came out of high school in 1936 with few expectations—no thought of college or a career. I fully believed that war loomed in my not-too-distant future, to engulf me in a fearsome blackness—like the black hole of my childhood coal cellar. I drifted, never dreaming my wanderings would offer me choices.

Emil at 18.

9.

ADRIFT IN THE SOUTH

IN JULY 1936, AFTER GRADUATION, I decided to spend the summer wandering around the South—a shadowed land where whites treated Negroes with indifference, scorn, and, too often, brutality. I had read books and pamphlets on the subject and raised money to free the Scottsboro Boys. Josh White had an album of chain-gang songs that I played with some frequency. And there was Bloody Harlan, stories of the epic struggle of Kentucky coal miners. I had to see it for myself!

I left early in July in my usual expeditionary outfit: tan pants and shirt (faintly reminiscent of a Boy Scout uniform), army knapsack, pup-tent half, $10 in cash in my pocket, and a like amount secreted in my clothes. Late in starting, I made poor time getting out of New York. Stationing myself at the Holland Tunnel, I finally got a ride on an empty produce truck, across the dreary Jersey flats via the Pulaski Skyway. In the days before cars, carriage roads went the shortest distance from town center to town center. Auto roads built on the coach roads meant there were few bypasses, and cities such as Philadelphia were a time-consuming drag— heavy traffic, stoplights, and endless streets. Baltimore, with its long rows of cloned houses, astonished me.

I denned for the night behind a billboard on the far side of Baltimore. Rolled up in my half-shelter in the dense weeds and surrounded by tin cans, old newspapers, and outhouse smells, I wept softly into my sweater pillow. I was consoled by my knowledge that this wave of fear and homesickness would pass—it was a common denominator of almost every trip I took. I had a sack of a dozen prune-filled Viennese yeast buns called

Buchteln, my mother's contribution for the first week of my journey. (Were they Mom's none-too-subtle reminder of the good things awaiting me near the home hearth?) All night long, I dipped into the sack for the comfort it gave me. I ate the last one for breakfast.

Soggy with *Buchteln,* it took me all morning to get to and through Washington. I took in the Capitol and the Washington Monument but didn't linger over them. I would rather have paid homage to the Bonus Army Veterans, who had had the bloody hell and self-esteem kicked out of them by General MacArthur at Anacostia Flats. The Great Depression was my era, and I nursed its historic monuments in my bosom.

Finally, southward over the Potomac, across the Mason-Dixon Line. There were no magnolia trees (or poplar trees) that I could recognize— only mile after mile of scrub pine. The drivers were very much like those on the northern side of the line. Southerners talked funny but had pretty much the same concerns as Northerners. Farmers would worry about crops, parents about children. I was a quiet listener, someone they would never see again, and they frequently vented their preoccupations. Salesmen, away from home for a week at a time, would bitch about their wives, worried about their virtue. Others, with a wink, would tell me, sometimes in great detail, about their conquests away from home.

When I tried to get them to talk about the blacks we drove past, working on farms or standing about in small, dusty towns, I sensed nothing but indifference or the good-natured tolerance awarded children. I knew that there were deeper feelings, but I lacked the courage to challenge. In those days, few blacks had cars, and my chance of being picked up by a black driver was almost nonexistent. Going through Richmond and Petersburg, Virginia, to Raleigh, North Carolina, I turned west on Route 64, the rolling Piedmont of cotton farms and tobacco patches.

It started to grow dark and threatened rain. I asked a farmer to let me out at a railroad crossing. Hunkering behind some bushes, I settled down to wait. A light drizzle began to fall, and the night became black. Cars and trucks swished by the STOP/LOOK/ LISTEN sign, going bump, bump over the tracks and receding into the distance. I was becoming mesmerized and about to fall asleep when I finally heard the sound I was waiting for—the smooth, heavy whine of an approaching Greyhound bus.

I hitched my pack over my back and peered out through the brush. The bus's illuminated forehead announced its destination as STATESVILLE. This suited me fine, as Statesville, North Carolina, was the first large city on Route 64 and a good distance down the pike. I hoped the bus would have few customers along the route. As the bus slowed to a stop before the tracks, I dashed out to stand behind the rear luggage ladder. I heard the whisper of the pneumatic door opening. Good man! He was looking and listening. The door hissed closed, the bus started moving, and I attached myself to the ladder. As it went bump, bump over the tracks, I scampered up the ladder and sat on the edge of the luggage rack. Apparently the driver's mind had been on trains and not on illicit passengers, since he kept on accelerating into the night.

I pulled the rope loose (it was kept as usual in a handy slipknot) and ducked under the canvas with the luggage. For a while, I remained tense, my hand clutching the rope, ready to abandon ship every time the bus slowed. Finally, the warm, dry nest and the gentle patter of rain lulled me to sleep. Twice the bus came to a full stop—I was awake and halfway out from under the canvas in seconds. But both times, it was a passenger departing the bus without needing luggage from the rooftop. In Statesville, I eased down the ladder and held on there until the center of town, departing the bus as the driver slowed for the turn into the terminal.

Hoping to spend this wet night in the terminal, I mingled with the disembarking passengers. My luck was bad. No bus until the next morning, and since this was the last arrival, the station would soon be closed. I used the restroom and went out into the night.

Down the street was a Greek diner, and I headed for it. It was "greasy spoons" like this that horrified me my first year on the road. Do people really eat like this? Yes, indeed! Seated at the counter, I ordered one of the cheapest things on the menu, a hamburger and coffee. Salt, pepper, and a thick layer of catsup went on the burger, and all the sugar and cream I could get into the coffee cup. When the Greek wasn't looking, I added more cream.

Over in a booth, a man was watching my culinary skill with amusement. He motioned me to join him. He had been drinking beer, but it was hard to tell how long he had been at it.

"A Yankee," he grinned as he caught my accent, "and what part of the great North are you from?" I admitted I was from the Bronx—a fact I had been super-cautious about revealing ever since I crossed the Potomac. Yankees, especially from New York, were purportedly not popular in the South.

While he wore the coveralls of a dirt farmer, he turned out to be a very literate man. Although the beer had loosened his tongue, he remained very cogent. We spent about an hour on Faulkner, Tom Wolfe, and the Southern literary movement—heady stuff for a young Bronx boy! I admitted I wanted to be a writer but said that I had many doubts. My literate farmer had spent a few years at the University of North Carolina, as had Thomas Wolfe before him. "Wolfe was the Deity of our lit and writing classes. He was a big man, with a tremendous appetite for food and everything else. Hey, I've got a college magazine with one of his short stories. It's really jackleg, full of Southern pride and phony heroics. You should read it—it'll give you all kinds of hope as a writer. Look," he said, "if you don't have a place to stay, why don't you come home with me. You can read the Wolfe story."

He must have caught some shift in my composure and smiled. "I live on a farm not too far from here and we have a wide veranda that goes clear around the house. It has a glider you can sleep on."

When we got into his old pickup, I was relieved that his driving was meticulously careful. He lived on what appeared to be a dairy farm, with milking sheds, silos, and fenced corrals. On a slope near the house was a large tobacco patch.

The kitchen needed a female touch—dishes, although unwashed, were stacked neatly by the sink; a basket of eggs sat out on a counter garnished with magazines and newspapers; clothes were draped over most of the chairs. It was a kitchen that definitely lacked attention to detail. He swept aside a set of overalls and made room for me at the table. Then he proudly set before me the magazine with Wolfe's story. "Well," he smiled, "from the way you ate that sandwich, I suspect you could eat some chili. Made it myself."

As I read, he deftly and ceremoniously extracted a bowl of chili, bread, butter, and a jar of honey from the ice chest. Back he went for a mason jar of milk, but the glass, beaded with moisture, slipped from his fingers and crashed to the floor. He put a finger to his lips, smiling sheepishly, and we both bent to pick up the pieces. The kitchen door swung open and an elderly man stood there, a Southern John Brown. He looked at me with some surprise and then at the person I took to be his son, his face tightening with disgust. After he closed the door without comment, I heard his slippers going shush-shush into a back room.

For a moment, my new friend looked completely dejected, then he winked at me. "My old man doesn't approve of me; he's not a devotee of Thomas Wolfe. As a farmer, he thinks the only book he needs is the *Farmer's Almanac* . . . . Oh, mustn't forget the bible." The chili was excellent. While the bread was a store-bought white, it made a good medium to hold the butter and honey. I finished the story and agreed it was stiff and filled with Southern clichés. (A few years later, Robert Wunsch, a teacher at Black Mountain College, was to show me another copy of the same magazine.)

The porch glider was all he said it would be, with a thin mattress, a pillow, and a blanket. I slept soundly until I was awakened at first light by a hand shaking my shoulder. It was John Brown, the father, and I jumped up, prepared to gather my effects and run.

"Hate to rouse you out so early, son, but a farmer has early chores and I thought you might like to share breakfast."

In the morning light, close-up, he no longer was John Brown, just a kindly old farmer.

"Sorry we made such a loud mess last night," I ventured, "but that milk jug was slippery."

"Don't give it a thought. My boy is not a happy farmer; he'd rather be a bookworm. Had a couple years of university at Chapel Hill and can't forget it. Goes out Saturday nights and drinks beer."

We went into the kitchen, where he quickly fried eggs and thick bacon. He brought out a pan of corn bread, and the coffee was already hot.

He continued: "The Depression hit us, but hard. Everything seemed to go wrong; his mother died, and the sheriff was about to auction off the

farm." His mouth tightened. "What saved us were two Nigra families."
("Nigra?" First I'd heard that—was he being careful not to upset my
Yankee sensibilities by not using "nigger"?)

"Ya know, lots of Nigras got money. Real money. Rich! One of the
buyers has a brother in the Nigra insurance business and the other is related to a funeral parlor family. Between them, they got enough cash to buy
a section of my land. I had to sell them part of my tobacco allotment, too,
and it was the allotment that paid for my son's college. To make do on the
piece I had left, I needed to pull my son out of school. This Depression is
a killer!"

He put a small slab of ham and some corn bread in a bag (he called it
a "poke"), for me to take on the road. We got into the old farm pickup and
he ran me out to the main highway.

"Don't mistake me, my son's a good boy, just educated beyond a farm
that ain't got the money for school. Maybe someday he'll get what he
needs so bad."

"I hope so," I replied, as we said goodbye. "Tell him I said so." I liked
the old man, and his son, whose names I can't remember. The son stays
firmly in my mind. I thought of him and Thomas Wolfe—especially his
immature short story—every time I became discouraged as a writer.
Which was often!

It was a beautiful morning, and I was in an upbeat mood as I set my
pack down on the edge of the road and waited for my first ride. I was not
disappointed, for almost immediately I was picked up by a government
car, a Water Conservation man. We had a lovely trip through the foothills,
and he spent the time convincing me that no one, but no one, least of all
me, should let life go by without spending time hiking in the Smokies. He
gave me a trail map and full instructions on how to get to the trailhead via
the Newfound Gap road, then under construction. He let me out in the
town of Morganton, North Carolina, within sight of the Blue Ridge
Mountains.

In my senior year at James Monroe, I had an extroverted school friend
who got us thrown out of the library by arguing too loudly about Black

Mountain College. Thus, I was on alert when I espied the village of Black Mountain, just east of Asheville, on my road map. Buoyed by my evening with the literary farmer and my breakfast with his father, I looked forward to the Blue Ridge Mountains and a visit to Black Mountain College.

One of the amusements among the staff at our high school magazine was collecting absurd statements by politicians. A eulogy of Southern women by the late Representative Rankin of Mississippi stayed with me on this trip to the South: "Fashioned in paradise, wreathed in graces and virtues that blossomed like flowers plucked from the green fields of Eden, led down to earth by angels along a pathway of stars, to be the joy, the blessing, the inspiration of noble men."

On my second ride of the day, it happened that Southern womanhood was revealed to me. I was standing just outside a gas station when in pulled a small Ford roadster tightly packed with six young female camp counselors in dazzling white summer uniforms (trim cotton T-shirts and shorts). With three in the front and three in the rumble seat, I knew my cause was hopeless, but I took up the challenge—which went something like this, I'm ashamed to say:

"How about a ride?"

"But where would we put you?"

"It isn't every day you can meet a genuine Yankee from New York City."

"We really would love to, but . . . ."

"So this is what Southern hospitality amounts to . . . " etcetera, with more sparkling repartee.

Much to my great surprise, when they packed back into the car, they offered me the middle of the rumble seat; the smallest settled down on my lap. Double names flew around the car like butterflies: I'm Mary Lou; my name is Virginia Ann; mine is Johnny Mae; etc. etc. Emil, of course, slowed them down for a moment. Would it have helped if I'd offered Emil Joseph?

A recent discovery of David Fischer's great book on the British settlement of the United States, *Albion's Seed,* has been a major factor in a belated understanding of my Southern experience. The preponderance of double first names goes back to the way those who peopled Appalachia lived in Merrie Old England:

> For seven centuries, the kings of Scotland and England could not agree who owned the border lands between them. From the year 1040 to 1745 every English monarch but three suffered a Scottish invasion, or became an invader in his turn . . . . Both sides of the border were brutally sacked and burned.

As a result of hundreds of years of brutality and treachery, these border people withdrew into tightly knit kinship groups—opposed to government and pledging loyalty only to family. It was these border people—Scottish, English, Irish—who settled Appalachia. Due to the great number of children needing given names, the double first name came into practice:

> In North Carolina's Catawba County, the first U.S. Census of 1790 listed 300 nuclear families named Alexander. These concentrations of kinsmen, all bearing the same surname, created endless onomastic confusion . . . . Our roll-call includes Sally's Mary and Cripple John's Mary and Tan's Mary, all bearing the same surname; and there is, besides, Aunt Rose's Mary and Mary-Jo, living yon side of the creek.

In my mind's eye, I can still see those six Southern girls in their clean white camp uniforms. The only name I clearly remembered was the one on my lap, Mary Lou. So I think of them as the six Mary Lous.

They were on their way to someplace west of Chattanooga—so much for Black Mountain College! As Mary Lou squirmed to settle on my lap, I was suddenly embarrassed that she might be conscious of the excitement she was causing there. With faces all aglow, hair blowing in the wind, and smelling faintly of fragrant soap, I could give Representative Rankin his Southern women who "blossomed like flowers plucked from the green fields of Eden."

They were eager to learn all about me—New York . . . my mission in the Southland. I'm afraid that my description of life in New York would go better in a work of fiction rather than autobiography. But it was all in high spirits, and I calmed down enough to give a full recital of "The Ancient Mariner" and "The Cremation of Sam McGee." I had an oilcloth-covered *Golden Treasury of English Verse* and had memorized these and others during my long waits between rides. I dug the book out of my pack (which hung on the attached spare wheel), and we took turns reading Shakespearean sonnets—"Shall I compare thee to a Summer's day?" How else can a Bronx boy entertain six young Southern belles?

At Old Fort (which, a year or so later, turned out to hide a treasure trove of moonshine at $5 per gallon) the road started up the mountain in an interminably winding lane studded with redundant SHARP CURVES AHEAD signs. Get behind a grinding, wheezing coal truck and you could fall asleep on the job. (These were the days before Interstates, when a driver really had to stay alert and drive!)

Mary Lou was tiny, but on this laboring, swinging ascent, she turned into the dead weight of a 100-pound sack of cement. My legs and feet tingled with pins and needles. I couldn't jiggle my legs to relieve the pain—it might have caused a panic. It was very unromantic of me, but as much as I loved Mary Lou (and I did), the long haul ahead to Chattanooga appalled me. So I reinstated my original decision to visit the college. At the village of Black Mountain, I voiced my deep regrets and bid the young ladies a fond adieu. No matter how active my imagination, six-to-one was daunting!

VISITING BLACK MOUNTAIN COLLEGE

In the tiny village, I asked about the college. Rising abruptly out of the town was a dramatic sweep of a ridge, and halfway up this ridge, a great white building was pointed out to me: "That's Blue Ridge and that's the college." Crossing the railroad tracks, I was picked up by a bread van. So it was as one with Wonder Bread that I made my first ride up the long hill and was delivered to Lee Hall and Black Mountain College. The great porch, with its huge white pillars, was filled with elderly folk comfortably ensconced in rocking chairs.

"Black Mountain College?" I asked tentatively, and was told, "Inside, through that door, you'll find their office." In the college office, several people were busily working. I wondered if I could get information about the school. A professor, Ted Dreier, sat me down at his desk, where I expressed some bewilderment about the people on the porch. It turned out that in the summer, the complex was a YMCA Conference Center, and for nine months it was leased by the college. Either the college group wasn't totally immersed in what they were doing or they were interested in what I had to say about my travels and checkered high school experiences—at any rate, we talked for at least an hour before even getting to discuss the fascinations of young Black Mountain College. The upshot was an invitation to stay and have dinner with Ted, his friendly wife Bobbie, and their two children. Being faculty, Ted had a small house away from the main building. I rated them solid New England ethical puritan types—without the stiffness.

One of the many enthusiasms of Ted Dreier was the prospect of the school's becoming self-sufficient by growing its own food. To this end, the college had leased an adjacent 25 acres of apple orchard and farmland. As a result of my interview, Ted hired me to work on the farm's pasture fence. He took me down to the farm to meet a black teenager named Charlie. The postholes had been dug, and it was a question of setting the posts, dragging 12-foot split rails to the site, and nailing them up—three to a section. Charlie had been struggling valiantly to put up the fence by himself, but it really needed two.

I bunked down in the corner of an old barn. The only part of the structure not about to collapse contained a horse stall—complete with horse. In Western literature, a man always loved his horse and call it "Old Hoss." "Old Hosses," at least not the Western saddle type, are not often bred in the South Bronx, and even though the creature shared my bedroom and my working day, I had no special reason to love it—I just addressed it matter-of-factly as "Horse."

It was an uphill battle, though, with Horse. I quickly discovered, that first night in the ammonia-drenched old barn, that horses belch, fart, and void in heavy streams all through the night—not to mention stamp their feet and shake vigorously. It has been revealed to me that horses need only five hours of sleep—which was OK for Horse, but after 10 hours working on the fence, I needed more.

Here's a haiku written by an ancient Japanese poet, about staying in a low-class inn. So is life here that much different than in old-time Japan?

Fleas and lice did bite
And I'd hear the horse piss water
Near my bed at night.

The pay was 20 cents an hour, and I was glad to get it. Charlie got the same, but it was a form of discrimination—he had the skills and I just provided muscle under his supervision. That first night, after he had put Horse into his stall, Charlie sug-

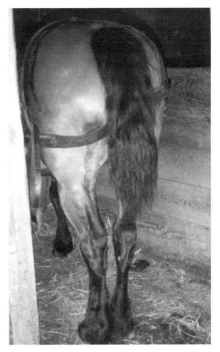

The only part of the barn not about to collapse was the horse stall, complete with Horse.

gested, "Bring the horse with you in the morning." Yeah, Charlie . . . and you take the B train to Times Square and shuttle over to Grand Central. After several unsuccessful attempts at feeding the bit into Horse's mouth, I just led the critter up the road by threatening him with the harness every time he stopped. Charlie was scornful of my inability to relate to Horse, and he turned up each morning, making a noisy show of the simple workaday routine of harnessing.

One of my job requirements was to take Horse to the stack of split rails, gather up a bunch, encircle them with a chain, and attach the chain to Horse. One time, I decided to ride back to the site. I backed the animal against a fence, scrambled on board, and said "Giddyap." Apparently this was not the Southern way of starting a horse, and nothing moved. Increasingly strong kicks in the ribs started motion—until we had to cross a small stream. Horse stopped, pulled over, and abruptly lowered his head to drink, almost sliding me off over his neck. It was a hot day, and I tolerated his thirst—until I became alarmed at the great quantity of water going into his barrel. Trying to lift a reluctant horse's head proved beyond me, but in time we moved ahead. I was sure Charlie would notice the extended belly and announce that so much water on a hot day would probably kill him. But he didn't, and the horse survived nicely.

I had hoped to learn more about the plight of the Negroes in the South, but Charlie was reluctant to enter into a discussion about Jim Crow.

At the foot of the slope on which we worked was a small lake, and at the end of a hot, muggy day, I suggested that we go for a swim. Charlie seemed reluctant, and I assumed it had to do with skinny dipping, so I suggested going in our underwear. We had a great swim and were relaxing on a raft when he suddenly looked alarmed and quickly rolled off the raft. He disappeared underwater and came up under the bushes at the lake's edge. It was then that I noticed a dusty pickup coming down the road. When it passed, I swam to join Charlie. He looked at me wide-eyed.

"That was a local redneck. I'm not supposed to swim in this lake."

That was all he would say about the incident. We dressed silently and he took off. We never again went to the lake. I really liked Charlie, but he was reluctant to make a personal connection.

I had dinner with the Dreiers one more time and was questioned in detail about my bona fides. The college was keen about getting a cross-section of American youth, and I seemed to fill in several blanks—Depression poor . . . immigrant family . . . wanderer . . . radical. My winning the 1936 *School Press Review* award also held their attention. Ted asked if I would like to apply for a scholarship.

But what did I know about Black Mountain College? I had read Louis Adamic's *Harper's* magazine article (*Education on a Mountain*, April 1936). It was his great enthusiasm about this small, educationally radical school that had caught my attention.

So it was that on my last night I stayed up with Horse, debating the pros and cons of the big decision. I needed someone with whom to share my debate. Turning and tossing, I ignored the acrid, pungent smells that went with our deliberations.

"Well, Horse, to apply for a scholarship I have to pay $10 as a registration fee! And as you surely know, $10 was five hard days on the fence; $10 would cover my travel expenses for two weeks or more in a pinch. And, of course, the scholarship is a very iffy thing. On the other hand, Horse, anyone with my kind of luck to get a ride with six Southern belles might just be lucky enough to win out on a scholarship. It wasn't exactly 'easy come, easy go,' but it was unexpected money and probably worth the gamble—and I still would have about $10 or so of fence money left."

Horse shook his head up and down, stomped his feet in approval, and the "pros" won! What other college would offer a $1,200 scholarship to a poor wandering boy? The registration was writ' out, paid for, and I was on my way—eager to further investigate the Southland. It had been more than interesting thus far!

At the Indian village of Cherokee, I stocked up on a few cans of food, a loaf of bread, and some George Washington packets, the first of the instant coffees. Standing in front of the store was a Cherokee Indian in full Sioux regalia, with whom I was invited, for a small fee, to have my picture taken. I knew he needed the money, but then so did I, and I resisted. Souvenir shops lined the street and Western-style tepees were scattered around. Most of the highly talented Cherokees had long since been chivied out of the verdant Smokies and transplanted to the barrens of Oklahoma in the Trail of Tears, when thousands died walking the long way West.

A new road was being cut over the Smokies from Cherokee through Newfound Gap to Gatlinburg, Tennessee, so I had no trouble getting a ride up on a construction truck. The map given me by the Water Conservation man indicated a foot trail heading south to Georgia—the first 35 miles of the famous Appalachian Trail, which now covers 2,000 miles between Georgia and Maine's Mount Katahdin.

My hike along the trail turned out to be a three-day jaunt, and I met only a few other trekkers—all going north. The first day, coming around the side of a mountain, I met a black bear picking berries. He took one look at me and barreled off down the hillside, tearing up the scenery as he went. This gave me the confidence that night to keep all my food in my pack and use it for a pillow. I could hear a bear working over my empty cans by the cold fire, but fortunately for me, I have since been told, he didn't contest me for my pillow. I ended my idyllic hike at the start of the AMC trail on Mount Oglethorpe, Georgia. Thank you, Mr. Water Conservation man—for your map and your enthusiasm. I went back to harnessing the power of the thumb.

In the next few weeks of travel, I crisscrossed with my future—although I didn't realize it at the time. As I went from the rain-forest foliage of the Smokies through Ducktown, Tennessee, the vegetation along the road went from heavy green to stunted trees and bushes . . . to weed and grass patches . . . to deeply eroded washes of cinders and clay. Pathetic little patches of kudzu vine had been planted to cover the scars, but these only served to emphasize the devastation—the result of sulfuric acid fumes spread far and wide by the tall Tennessee Copper Company chimney. As I passed the complex, I hadn't the faintest inkling that one day I would sit astride that chimney photographing the plant and its grim surroundings.

> The postcards of Ducktown, Tennessee, give only a faint idea of the devastation which goes on. Imagine an area of 50 square miles so poisoned by the fumes of the Copper Plant that everything is killed off and the earth itself made to look like a convulsive red scar! Like a Dante illustration of the Inferno.
> —*The Diary of Anaïs Nin*
> (she had visited Black Mountain College)

In 1936, in the Tennessee/North Carolina highlands, a painted house was rare indeed. The region was peppered with poor houses, unpainted clapboards, or decaying log cabins, surrounded by eroded cotton fields. As late as 1939, there were still 270,000 occupied log cabins in the United States, mostly in Appalachia.

The Tennessee River ran brown with silt from eroded farms, and frequent floods damaged the towns and cities on its shores. Downriver, at Muscle Shoals, Alabama, the Tennessee Valley Authority (TVA) had opened the 37 miles of rapids that had cut off navigation to large cities such as Chattanooga and Knoxville.

Within a few decades, this large area, the size of England and Scotland, had gone from a farming basket case, draining the nation of tax money, to a green, prosperous region that poured money into the U.S. Treasury—thanks to this regional program. Roosevelt tried to develop several more regional programs but was stymied by Congress.

Knoxville was settled in 1786 and named after Major General Henry Knox, who commanded the artillery during the Revolutionary War. I had absolutely no premonition of the prominent place Henry Knox would play in my life—that in this small, red-brick city of Knoxville, I was to work for CIO unions . . . kiss my future wife on the bridge over the Tennessee River . . . live there with my wife and two small children for two years . . . and live in Knox County, Maine, in my retirement.

Just north of Knoxville, I witnessed the final construction stages of the Norris Dam and the model town of Norris—the country's first all-electric town. The glare of floodlights on the huge dam face, and the strings of naked lights along the streets and roads, made for an awesome scene. But despite all the liberal views of J.P. Morgan and others involved with the TVA, no blacks were allowed to live in the new town of Norris. In back of the dam, a large lake was forming. The TVA was transforming a 40,000-square-mile basin into "the Great Lakes of the South"—a wonderful recreational area. I was to swim and fish in Norris Lake not too long in the future.

Leaving Norris, I picked up a short ride to Jellico, on the Kentucky border. It was a late Saturday afternoon, the sky was dark and threatening rain, and I knew I had to quickly find shelter for the night. But I was riveted to the road by a tragicomic show. A white line had been painted across the highway with a Tennessee road marker on the south side and a Kentucky marker on the north. Tennessee was dry; in Kentucky, the first buildings were drinking establishments.

Gathered on the "wet" side was a knot of boisterous coal miners engaged in a tug-of-war with blue-uniformed Tennessee police. The dare was to step south across the line while waving a whiskey bottle. The challenge was met by sudden dashes of the police to capture the miner and drag him into Tennessee, where a paddy wagon awaited. A captured man was aided by his buddies, who joyfully tried to drag him back to safety. Watching it all with a grin was the Kentucky sheriff, complete with plaid shirt, black hat, and black pants tucked into boots, plus a star on his galluses and a heavy revolver strapped to his leg.

Needless to say, I was completely fascinated and quick to take sides with the miners—until the game was called off by rain. As I looked around wildly for shelter from the deluge, I spotted an old man in a rocker on the porch of an old house behind me. He beckoned to me, and I dashed up to join him.

"It'll be an all-night pisser," he said.

"Sure looks like it," I agreed.

"Set a piece 'n stay dry."

I put my pack down against the wall, pulled over a chair, and sat next to him. He rocked quietly for a few minutes, slid his chew to the other cheek, and nodded in the direction of the white line and the receding paddy wagon.

"Ever see anythin' so darn stupid?" he asked.

I nodded sympathetically, agreeing to myself that the performance didn't tally with my image of embattled Harlan County miners.

"Break their backs all week, get Saturday afternoon off jest to spend their pay on licker and that foolishness. The caught ones get fined $10—their kids'll do with less to eat."

He went on to allow that he, too, had been a miner until he got leg pains and black lung disease and couldn't work. Sensing my intense interest, he told me some about being a miner.

"The coal bosses," he said, "fought us [the United Mine Workers union] with every dirty trick, even hired killers. The miner that could stand on a stump and preach union, while scabs with rifles took potshots at him from the surrounding hills, was a man we trusted to follow when the call came to strike. Such a man," he said, "was William Turnblazer."

"Turnblazer don't talk so good these days," he added. "At a meetin' in the Cumberland Gap Hotel, scabs set the hotel afire and tossed tear gas through the windows. It kinda ruined his voice." Years later, I worked with Turnblazer and can confirm the sorry state of his vocal cords.

In the last hundred years that records of mine accidents have been kept, more than 120,000 miners have been killed mining coal. (These are only partial records.) Much later, I learned of the additional great waste of life in mines from so-called natural causes. Among men 60 to 64, the "natural" death rate of miners is eight times that of any other industry.

> If we must grind up human flesh and bones in an industrial machine—in the industrial machine we call modern America— then, before God, I assert that those who consume coal, and you and I who benefit from that service—owe protection for those men first, and we owe security to their families after, if they die. I say it! I voice it! I proclaim it! And I care not who in heaven or hell opposes it!
>
> —John L. Lewis

Darkness was coming on, and the rain showed no sign of letting up. The miner sheepishly allowed that he'd put me up for the night, but since he had been laid off, his wife had a notion or running a boardinghouse, so if I had a dollar, they could put me up and feed me supper and breakfast. On a rainy night, this seemed a great bargain. I agreed but asked if I could sleep on the veranda. "I'm used to sleeping outdoors," I told him. I didn't tell him I disliked getting used to sleeping with bedbugs.

His wife was, as they say, a dour lady. I sat at the table with my talkative friend and a couple of nontalkative miners and ate my share of corn bread, string beans cooked to death with fatback, and boiled potatoes. Breakfast was biscuits and grits. The coffee was coffee only because she said it was.

I left early the next morning, passing through Harlan County and its bleak mine camps without further incident. It occurred to me that I had learned more about the miners' poverty level from eating that dismal dinner than from anything else I did in Harlan County. It's difficult for me to dissociate what I learned that night from the crippled miner and what I learned years later working in Tennessee. After Joanna and I were married and lived in Knoxville, she worked for the United Mine Workers Welfare and Retirement Fund. Then I was to learn a great deal more about accidents, black lung disease, and other mine workers' problems.

Because I was out of touch with home and getting antsy about missing out on my improbable scholarship, I cut short my Southern junket and hurried back to the Bronx. But I was to return to the South and live there on and off for some 12 years. Looking back, I realize it was something of a progression from boyhood to manhood. I discovered I could survive the unknown, satisfy my innate curiosity about things of the world, and open up opportunity through travel. It endeared me to the South: led me to Black Mountain College, Highlander Folk School, the CIO, marriage, children; honed my skills as a photographer. It was a jumping-off place for Peru and the wide world of foreign travel. (It also dragged me to the infantry in Mississippi, like the Cherokees to Oklahoma—my own Trail of Tears.)

When I returned to the Bronx, there was no news from Black Mountain College waiting for me, and as the months went by, my hopes faded. I had now turned 19—manhood approached, yet the future was a void. My conviction that another world conflict was fast approaching—that the United States would be in it, that I would be in it—clouded my need for career decisions. What career was out there anyway? This was still year 1936-37, deep in the Great Depression.

I took the first job I could get, wrapping musical instruments at the Progressive Musical Instrument Company. I handled tiny fifes, bulky drums, saxophones, and fiddles. There seemed to be a run in New York for conductor's batons. The job also entailed deliveries around the city, bulk shipments at the post office, running errands, and cleaning up at night—

all my great skills. It paid $12 per week and was boring. I couldn't seem to make any kind of contact with my boss or fellow workers.

I quit and went to work at a picture-framing shop, upgrading my weekly salary to $15. While the work was no more demanding—wrapping and delivering framed pictures—I found the environment more congenial. The actual work was done by two small, middle-aged, lively, Russian immigrant Jews. They were very quick at what they did and kept up a lively repartee as they did it. When I laughed at one of their first Yiddish jokes, I was accepted into the family. One of them ran to the back and returned, wiping dry a mug that she handed to me in a ceremonial gesture. She told me it was mine to keep. Every afternoon we took a break, sipping hot tea through a lump of sugar and munching crackers. They soon realized the meagerness of my Yiddish and spoke immigrant English whenever I was nearby.

Mr. Goldberg, the owner, did the accounting and paperwork. He had a bad case of diabetes, which affected his circulation, so he had to walk with crutches. He lived in a hotel close by, and my first duty of the day was to pick him up and help him to the shop. Because of his considerable weight, the crutches cut off his circulation, making his hand movements slow and awkward. Frequently I needed to help button his shirt or knot his tie. His room always smelled of spicy after-shave lotion, something unknown to the male Willimetz establishment. It reminded me of an item I'd found used as a placeholder in an old library book:

> *When I was a boy*
> *I often watched*
> *as my father shaved,*
> *which he did daily*
> *in the bathroom*
> *on the second floor.*
> *One nite as he finished*
> *he poured a liquid*
> *into his hands*
> *and splashed it*

onto his face.
I asked my father
what it was
and he said, "Cologne,
to make me smell nice."
Then I asked,
"What is cologne?"
and he, my own father,
said "Toilet water."
I never ever used the
Second-floor toilet again.
                                    —Author unknown

Mr. Goldberg and I would stop downstairs in his hotel at a small cafe, where he would always order the same breakfast—coffee, toast, and two soft-boiled eggs stirred in a cup. The counter man would butter the toast and cut it up into strips. Mr. Goldberg would butter, salt, and pepper his eggs and use strips of the toast as a spoon. It looked and smelled delicious. He was a quiet, introspective man, and while we spoke some during our morning ritual, I never felt I reached him.

During this period, I took free WPA evening classes in writing and speech. The speech teacher was a mystic who had us all sit on the floor in a yoga position with closed eyes and hum . . . mmm . . . mmm . . . mmm . . . mmming while he intoned:

"Let your toes relax and now your arches." Slowly he worked his way up our torsos. "Now," persuasively, "relax your larynx . . . . You are totally relaxed and eager to talk without tension or embarrassment." We took turns standing before the class and making short speeches. I wasn't totally relaxed and eager to talk—I still turned beet-red and um/uh-ed tensely through my recital. I managed to overcome the blush and hesitations when I worked for the CIO, but I never quite made it as an orator of any note. Today I do better narrating slide shows in public places, knowing I can depend on the slides to keep me on track.

I made better progress in my WPA writing class, but I have no remnants of anything I ever wrote there. The teacher, as I vaguely remember her, tried but lacked the spark and personal interest of Anne Rizack at James Monroe. I would sometimes hang around after class and exchange ideas with fellow students, but we all worked full days, and any creative energy generated during class was quick to sputter out.

SPRING 1937

My high school friends and neighborhood buddies mostly had gone their own ways—some to colleges, others holding down jobs that fully occupied them or took them out of the city. It was a year of loose ends and frustrated hopes. So, in the spring of 1937, when my wanderlust sap was beginning to rise, Uncle Franz (now called Frank) offered to take me with him to Europe. I was elated. Every summer, my Uncle Frank would take leave from his job of the moment—paperhanging, waitering—and take off for Europe. He would get hired as a waiter or steward on the Holland-American Line, leave the ship at Rotterdam or Le Havre, and work his way around European resorts waiting on tables. He claimed to menu-speak in six languages, and I believed him. As an alternative to wrapping drums or framed pictures, I was to go along as a busboy—mute in six languages. (Actually not—I did speak some German.) It was a golden opportunity to make the traditional Grand Tour of Europe that only wealthy youngsters made in the early days of the 20th century. In the 1940s, millions of our youth made the Grand Tour during World War II. Today there is greater sophistication and much more freedom for young people to travel the world on shoestring (or even champagne) budgets.

I justified going to Europe as I did to go South—to see the problems for myself. We were to go to more than one fascist country: Nazi Germany for sure (my Uncle Josef was in Berlin); Austria, our family homeland, of course; probably Italy, Hungary, and Czechoslovakia. Austria had been a Socialist country, but a right-wing dictator had taken over and the Socialists had been driven underground. I looked forward to seeing how these things really worked. Weren't my uncles Frank and Josef, and my very own Pop, old Viennese Socialists?

It was the middle of May. I had ordered my passport and Unk was negotiating my berth on the SS *Statendam* when a letter arrived from Black Mountain College:

> May 11, 1937
> Dear Mr. Willimetz,
> As you may already know, applications are first passed upon by the Admissions Committee, without reference to the financial status of the applicant. If their decision is favorable, the application then goes to the Treasurer.
> Since the amount of student aid that we can grant depends upon variable factors, it is difficult to say at this moment how things would turn out. You can be sure, however, that we shall give your application our most serious consideration. Mr. Dreier is also writing you.
> Frederick R. Mangold
> Registrar

Ted Dreier's letter said, in effect:

> Dear Mr. Willimetz,
> The Scholarship Committee has approved a full scholarship to begin the Fall of 1937, but it still has to be approved by the Financial Committee. If you haven't made any commitments to another school please consider this possibility.
> Ted Dreier

It was another BIG DECISION time—go on to Europe, as I so fervently desired, or give up my Grand Tour and stay to earn pocket money should the still-uncertain scholarship materialize. When the entire family opted to forgo Europe, I didn't even have "Horse" to commiserate with. Through my good farmer friend in New Hampshire, I got a job that summer of 1937 working as a waiter in the hotel atop Mount Washington.

Arriving at the hotel a week early, I was put to work carrying blankets, kerosene, and food from the hotel down to the Lake of the Clouds

Appalachian Mountain Club hut. That entailed several trips a day over a distance (as I remember it) of about a mile or so, carrying 100 to 120 pounds (at 1 cent per pound). I found going downhill with a load much more difficult than going uphill—hard on the knees. But it was good money for those days, plus I had the opportunity to hike the beautiful and dramatic peaks of the Presidential Range—Madison, Adams, Jefferson, and Washington.

Mount Washington, the highest peak in the northeastern United States, rises to 6,288 feet. It had numerous hiking trails, a dirt road to the top, and the world's first cog railway, built in 1869. Known for its severe climate, it has been described as having the worst weather in the world. The mountain is the site of a weather station that has recorded many of the strongest winds in the United States. In 1934, the wind was clocked at 231 mph, a world record. The observatory buildings were held down by heavy chains.

Even in the 10 summer weeks that I worked on the mountain, the weather was wild and dangerous. In gale winds, we would go out on the bare summit, open our jackets, and lean into the force. Turning in the other direction, we would open coats and leap Olympic distances. Wild!!!

Sheets of heat lightning would illuminate the long valleys below, and one night the air was so electric that light bulbs exploded, fireballs dashed to the ground in bursts of sparks, St. Elmo's Fire raced along the power lines. Exhilaration!!!

White Mountain summits are above timberline, and there are intimidating signs where the trees disappear:

> STOP
> Weather Conditions Above Timberline
> Are Sudden and Severe.
> Turn Back at the
> First Sign of Bad Weather.

Being above the timberline in fog is like being inside a bottle of milk—total whiteness, without points of reference. At best, you feel hopelessly lost; at worst, you stagger with nausea and vertigo. In cold weather, this fog can exist in a condition called "rime," where moisture freezes on warm surfaces. Your eyes freeze shut, you stumble around in a blind panic, and you can easily fall off cliffs or into crevices. Mount Washington is known—with good reason—as the "killer mountain."

McKinley: 20,320 feet; death toll: 8
Rainier: 14,410 feet; death toll: 67
Washington: 6,288 feet; death toll: 116

Many are killed in winter climbs on the mountain, and skiing down Tuckerman Ravine. Others die even in the summer months from exhaustion, or from hypothermia due to sudden storms. On July Fourth, I helped litter-carry Harry Wheeler, age 55, dead of a heart attack on the Cap Ridge Trail, to the cog railway tracks for transportation off the range. On August 3, we had a severe hailstorm.

The cog railway's steam engine, built to be more or less level on the slope, looks mighty peculiar on the flats. The engine drives a large cog wheel, or gear, which fits into a series of linked sockets. Running up the center of the track, these sockets have flanges under which a braking device is fixed. I was told that the tracks were laid mostly by French Canadians. Tough, reckless men, they built wooden sleds with wood friction brakes that fitted under the flanges, then they held races to see who could whiz down the mountain the fastest. Being clocked at more than 70 mph, it was no wonder that many of them lost their lives. These are not tallied in the 116 official deaths, but in 1873, 1900, and 1919, men were recorded as being killed trying the same hair-raising stunt on boards.

During the summer of 1963, on a visit from Peru, my family had ridden to the top of Mount Washington on the cog railway. I suggested to my wife that she return to the base station and bring the car to where a road crosses the Mount Jefferson Trail. We would take the Cap Ridge Trail to Mount Jefferson and drop down to meet her. Not to worry, didn't I know these trails like the back of my hand?

Cap Ridge takes its name from a series of rock ledges above timberline that look like the spiny backs of stegosauruses. It was hard going, but in the woods we went through a majestic fairyland of moss-covered fallen trees. The ground underfoot was smooth and soft, like a moist velvet carpet. It was a great trail, but my kids' strides were a lot shorter than mine (and my 40-year-old feet less resilient than my 19-year-old ones), so we were a couple of hours later on arrival than I had predicted. Joanna had gone through her fingernails, was working on her toenails, and was contemplating calling out the National Guard. I reckon I had filled her with too many stories about the "killer mountain." But it was the two half-dollar-size turtles, souvenirs from Florida, sitting in a cottage-cheese carton in the back window of the car, that paid the ultimate price. The wax had melted from the carton, completely encasing the poor critters and suffocating them.

Of the ten waiters on Mount Washington, eight served the restaurant and two worked the counter where the hikers ate. Numbered 1 through 10, we moved the numerical order up one digit each day to give everyone a chance to serve the low-tip counter. Most of the restaurant clientele came up via the afternoon cog and stayed overnight. We would take the same customers for both dinner and breakfast, so there was a hustle to get good ones. We each had spies on the cog, sizing up the approaching customers, and they would give us ratings. Then we would use this info in bidding with each other for customers. "I'll give you 50 cents to take my turn." "You can have this great family for a dollar." A group of four or five was better than a single or double. I found out that poor folk can be the best tippers.

Hikers would come in, cold and wet: "What! You don't serve drinks? I'm going to complain to the Humane Society. I'd give a fortune right now for a drink!"

So on my day off, I set out to rectify this inhumane situation. I took the morning cog train down and hitched to Littleton, where, with my sophisticated farmer friend fronting for me, I bought several bottles of applejack. Not knowing much about liquor, I thought applejack sounded great. It was dark when I got back to base camp, too late to attempt the trail, so I started up the tracks. In January 1992, Louis Nichols died climbing up the cog-railway trestle. Even though I did it in July, the trestles can get very windy, cold, and scary—especially at midnight on Jacob's Ladder, which has almost a 45-degree slope. As it was, I had to climb it like a ladder, bent double with my fingertips just brushing the ties, the bottles clinking in my pack. What I hated most were the sudden gusts that tested my balance. I would, of course, be cleansed by alcohol if smashed on the rocks below.

Now when cold, wet hikers asked about a drink, I would serve them, without comment, about a fourth of a coffee cup of applejack. This philanthropy, somehow, boosted my take from the low-tip counter service. We were all college students (or wannabes), about the same age and intellectual attainment. We played poker every night, and, by the end of the summer, ended up just about even, as though we had never gambled at all. I know, because I kept a record of my tips on my locker door—a heady $300+.

Finally, in a photo finish:

August 3, 1937
Dear Mr. Willimetz,
I am very glad to inform you that the College will grant you student aid to enable you to attend during the academic year 1937-8.
    As you know, College begins on September 9. We are looking forward with pleasure to having you here.
Frederick R. Mangold
Registrar

I had to work on the mountain until Labor Day, barely enough time to hurry home, pack a few things and Greyhound down to North Carolina.

10.

BLACK MOUNTAIN COLLEGE

To me Black Mountain is one of the most fascinating places in America.

—Louis Adamic, *My America*

THE BLACK MOUNTAIN RANGE, a spur of the Blue Ridge, runs north-and-south for 20 miles. Across the valley from the college, we could see the Craggies, in all their glory. These unglaciated mountains of western North Carolina are the highest of the Appalachian system. Mount Mitchell, at 6,684 feet, is higher than Mount Washington but with a kinder climate. This majestic scene was our daily view and was in itself part of our curriculum.

THE FIRST TWO YEARS, 1937-39

On September 10, 1937, I arrived at Black Mountain on a Greyhound bus—fare paid, as befitting my new lifestyle. I was met at the village bus stop by a tall, soft-spoken student, Bill Reed. I had, of course, seen Lee Hall before, but as I drove up to it now as a student, the white-columned building loomed above me, hugely overwhelming and intimidating—a far cry from my dilapidated bed-and-breakfast barn! The building was truly outsize: Each student had his own study and shared a bedroom, and there was still plenty of room to spare for classrooms, offices, and guests.

My empty study room had to be furnished—cots and bedding were available in the attic. I even scrounged a floor lamp. Bill took me to Asheville, where I bought, among other things, yards of red burlap for the

The campus of Black Mountain College.

cot, pillows, and drapes. The result was pleasing aesthetically (sort of) but terribly unpleasing, I was to realize, to the epidermis. Two orange crates and a hollow door made me a desk. At James Monroe High School, I had found that my handwriting wouldn't do, so I had invested in an old Standard Royal typewriter. This machine I centered on my new desk.

I took classes in Plato, Literature, German, World Affairs, and, one night a week, Writing. Each afternoon, we went out on a work program. (I picked apples across from my 20-cents-an-hour fence.) When the Lake Eden summer-camp property was purchased, we trucked across the valley to prepare the site for eventual college occupation.

Coming back from work, we found tea and cookies laid out in the lobby. A congenial practice—a time to pick up mail (seldom), swap news with friends, and relax before dinner. Each floor had a large lavatory with multiple showers, sinks, and toilets. After an afternoon of work, a stinging hot shower and a change of clothes set the mood for dinner and whatever evening programs were ahead.

Bill Reed became my mentor, introducing me to students and faculty and acquainting me with the routines. After dinner, students disappeared behind study doors (presumably to work). I had no idea which door belonged to which student—and if I did, would they resent a visit? I had been told we were expected to honor DO NOT DISTURB signs, but I saw none as I walked down the long hallway one lonely evening. As a new student, I found the long, empty corridor forbidding and hostile. Bill had told me that if I had any questions please to drop in on him at any time, so I carefully lined up a few questions and knocked on his door.

He was working on a painting, and I apologized for disturbing him, but he seemed pleased by my visit and by my interest in his work. He was completely dominated by art and tried to educate me in his style of painting. I watched intently as he carefully laid out color shapes on a canvas with egg-tempera paint.

"When this is dry," he said, "I overlay the shapes with a second coat of another color. I get a rich, velvet tone, an interaction of soft color and soft shapes." I completely forgot to ask him my list of questions.

In the Bronx, writing and politics had dominated my high school years, although I did see a Picasso retrospective at the Museum of Modern Art. Seeing Picasso's art style change as we walked up the ramps from the Blue Period to the Woman in the Mirror enabled me, if not to understand, at least to accept the legitimacy of modern art. But until I went to Black Mountain, I had never known a working artist in the process of creation, and it intrigued me.

Bill was unlike anyone I'd ever known, and we became close friends. I knew, almost from the start, that he was homosexual, but he never imposed his feelings on our relationship once it was clear that I couldn't reciprocate. All this evolved through mutual understanding, since we never spoke about it. I sensed that many eyebrows were raised about my own sexual status, although nothing was ever said—nor did I care.

Bill came from a wealthy family, allowing me a glimpse of a lifestyle I never knew and had always resented. He once took me to visit his aunt at her apartment on Park Avenue (maybe it was Fifth Avenue) for tea. Later in life, on a visit to Japan, I witnessed a Japanese tea ceremony. Auntie's tea was just as much of a ritual and just as fascinating. A beautiful sterling silver tea set was arranged on a small, round table circled by fragile cups and saucers. A delicate china teapot was covered with a quilted tea cozy; a silver kettle with hot water sat on a spirit lamp, ready for action. Filling the table space were a saucer of sliced lemons, a silver creamer, a tiny bowl of lump sugar, and a cut-glass brandy flask. In addition to a platter of bite-size cucumber sandwiches made with white bread with the crusts carefully cut off, there was a colorful platter of tiny pink and blue cakes which I thought might be bonbons but turned out to be *petits fours.*

As always with strangers, I was at a loss for small talk. Should I describe my Onkel Franz's tea ceremony—tea laced with a third of a cup of brandy, thick slices of black bread, and slabs of bologna, salami, or limburger cheese? Or chatter: "My father paints under a pseudonym; my mother is in the Tuscany Hotel, an expert on beds."

Well, I wasn't *that* bad. I might even have talked about teatime at the college—how welcome tea and cookies were after the work program. In truth, I even managed finally to feel comfortable, balancing my delicate teacup and eating the tiny cucumber sandwiches—although I knew the cucumbers would upset my digestion. Evidently she was Bill's favorite aunt, and I liked her. Probably one of the few of his kin who accepted his homosexuality. And she accepted me, even if under false pretenses, thinking no doubt that I was Bill's lover.

In time, I began to feel that I shouldn't continue with a relationship that would never culminate in any happiness for Bill, so in our second and third years we drifted apart. This *précis* of our three-year friendship falls far short of the reality, but it's the best I can do in this context.

On his first sight of John Webb, John Rice's favorite teacher at the high school level, he wrote in his autobiography, *I Came Out of the Eighteenth Century,* "I knew that here was something special, here was a man and a man to know."

Seeing Rice for the first time, I had no such epiphany. I only saw a somewhat pudgy man wearing glasses on a round face. It took time to see past this exterior, to see the twinkle in his eyes—at times with humor, occasionally with malice. But when he spoke in class, the full force of his personality became evident, and I knew it would pay me to listen.

John Rice, a native South Carolinian born in 1888, was the heart and soul of the original Black Mountain College—the founding thinker behind the BMC educational philosophy. In high school, I read Louis Adamic's article on Black Mountain's philosophy of education—now I was busy living it at the college, although still not completely rationalizing it.

During my first year, some St. John's College students and faculty came to visit. I remember a session in the large lobby, debating the "100 Great Books" theory of education versus the Black Mountain way of education. I have only a vague remembrance of the terms of the debate. It had to do with the concept that the great books are a common depository of the world's knowledge, and by an in-depth study of these books one gets "educated."

In his autobiography, John Rice wrote:

> The common expression to "get" an education is significant. It lights up the entire fallacy of the prevailing system, for education can only be experienced; one "gets" only information or "facts"— and the "facts" acquired in the average college have to do with the past and are mainly worthless to one destined to live in the future.

Myles Horton (my friend and mentor at Highlander Folk School) debated and collaborated with Paulo Freire of Brazil on education methods. Freire's viewpoint paralleled Rice's: "The teachers pour out information and students are expected to 'bank it.'"

One of Rice's basic educational concepts was that of ". . . Mark Hopkins at one end of the log and the student at the other." Colleges should be small, with as close a relationship as possible between teacher and student. As literal as I was, and as greedy as I am, I held out for two Hopkinses at the other end of my log. It was a course on Form in Literature, and it was given to me by two of the school's top professors, Fred Mangold and John Rice. During the year, I studied the literary forms of 10 writers: Thomas Browne, Dickens, Hardy, Hemingway, Proust, Gertrude Stein, and others. I studied how words were put together for effect—vocabulary, sentence structure, and book format. I then wrote a short story, which I rewrote in the style of each of the 10 authors. It was, without doubt, the most exciting and fulfilling course I've ever taken. In fact, I didn't think of it as a course, but as a life experience.

Still glowing from my Columbia Scholastic Press Association award, I had come to study writing. (I certainly got my money's worth out of that prizewinning English-class paper.) The writing class met once a week on a Wednesday evening; to stay in the class, one had to submit a piece of work. At first this didn't seem too tough an assignment. But it was! Many an hour I sat staring at a blank white sheet, carefully adjusting it and read-justing it in my Royal Standard—in contrast today with my computer, where work flows like water with the greatest of ease. But it was not just the contest between the two machines, it was chronic "writer's block." Rice could be murderously sarcastic, but not often in class with students. He would read our stories and poems aloud and turn us loose to criticize each other, occasionally offering his own evaluations.

I remember one assignment—to write a piece in the pure narrative form. I took this literally and wrote a simple narrative of going out on Mount Washington to bring in the body of a man who had died of a heart attack. In a sea of more elaborate stories, it stood out as being without message or emotion—and was criticized as such. Rice reread a page, emphasizing the rhythm and flow of the narration, making it sound much better than it really was. "It is good narration," he remarked, "and it ful-filled the assignment."

In our writing class, Rice couldn't afford to be too hard on us, since, from time to time, he would read a chapter from his own "work in progress," *I Came Out of the Eighteenth Century.* We had the same carte blanche to tear into his work as he with ours. Well . . . sort of. (It took me 50 years to track down a copy of his book, which certainly gave me a new and deeper perspective on Rice.)

The writing class started at 8 p.m. and was supposed to end at 10, but frequently it didn't. Occasionally the discussions were so animated and creative (or so we thought) that we kept on until midnight. One evening, we were so turned on that Rice was moved to pull a case of beer from under his couch to further lubricate the talk past midnight. That writing class was the core of my Black Mountain experience.

Toward the end of my second year at BMC, trouble arrived at the school. A fellow student, Marian Nacke, wrote about the situation in Mervin Lane's book, *Black Mountain College: Sprouted Seeds, An Anthology of Personal Accounts*:

> There are a lot of machinations going on here, too complicated to explain, but the point is some of the faculty are trying to get rid of Rice and threaten to break up the College if he doesn't leave. Ostensibly their reason is that they can't get money and students as long as he continues to insult people away from here, as he has done all his life.

Rice had been accused of having carnal relations with one of the students. A lot has been made of this episode, especially by Martin Duberman in his *Black Mountain: An Exploration in Community.* But I think that, more to the point, Rice had a caustic, biting wit and couldn't resist using it against less witty faculty members. Sarcasm was Rice's Achilles heel. A number of faculty members delighted in the opportunity to pay him back. On March 7, 1938, Rice was asked to take a "leave of absence" until May 1. Several of us drove down one weekend to visit him in his exile at Folly Beach, South Carolina. It was not a happy journey. The leave was then extended.

It was Rice's expulsion from Rollins University in 1933 that had led to the breakaway and started a new educational institution. It was his expulsion from BMC, and the move from Lee Hall to Lake Eden in 1940, that ended the Rice saga and changed the direction of the college. It was an uncertain, restless time for many of us who admired Rice. Writing was my rationale for studying at BMC, and Rice was the focus of the course—no one else could take his place. The spirit gone, it was the beginning of the end of my own involvement, although other factors in my third year at BMC, such as the war in Europe, became more important.

In his autobiography, Rice wrote: "The sun set on our empire, and we were content to have it so; and school spirit, about which one reads much in sentimental records, was unknown to us by name."

When he left Black Mountain College, Rice left education and started a career as a writer. *I Came Out of the Eighteenth Century* won the Harpers Publisher's 125th Anniversary Award in 1942. It was about his boyhood in the South, bringing to life his uncle, Cotton Ed Smith, one of the prolific breed of bigoted, diehard Southern politicians.

Rice also wrote a number of well -received short stories about blacks. Mary Fiore, a BMC student in the final days of the college, lent me a copy of Rice's *Local Color*—stories that would have received superior grades in our writing class.

In his foreword to *Local Color,* Erskine Caldwell wrote:

> This is the South I know—stripped bare of its magnolias and manners. It has been a long time in American fiction since a storyteller has been able to achieve anything like the fusion of two races of people as John Andrew Rice has done in this volume.

Unfortunately, Rice must have had the same kind of writer's block that kept me staring at blank sheets of paper by the hour. It's too bad that he didn't have more of what he once challenged me about: "The artist is not the man who *can* but the man who *must.*" He never really did justice to his writer's talent—his output was extremely small.

During my Lee Hall years, Josef Albers had shared his influence with John Rice. From 1940 to 1949, with Rice gone, Albers was the school's dominant force.

Albers had arrived at Black Mountain directly from the Bauhaus in Germany. He came highly recommended by Philip C. Johnson, curator of Architecture and Industrial Design at New York's Museum of Modern Art. But Johnson warned of one hitch—Albers didn't speak English. Rice decided that it made no difference. When he saw photographs of work done by Albers and his students, Rice told Theodore Dreier, "This is just the kind of thing we want." Asked upon arrival what he hoped to accomplish in this new country, Albers replied, "To open eyes."

According to Albers, "To distribute material possessions is to divide them, to distribute spiritual possessions is to multiply them."

Here's Martin Duberman's assessment:

> That Rice could appreciate Albers as a teacher was a compliment to both men since, volatility aside, they were very different: Albers, suspicious of words and of psychological probing, intuitive, confident of the reality in any given situation and of his ability to perceive it: Rice, verbal, consciously paradoxical, sardonic and relativistic.

While I had much less to do with Albers than with Rice, I grew to admire his teaching abilities. Just as Rice's writing class required a submission of work in order to attend, Albers's classes met for three hours, twice a week, and everyone had to bring completed work. The work was spread around the room, and each student had to explain his solution to the class assignment.

In the drawing class, a student huddled under a Mexican poncho as the model. Albers admonished one of his students:

"No, no, see! She's a potato!" With appropriate circular gestures, "See, a potato!"

Another, a chunky male student: "See, no neck, a head but no neck." One had to be made of stern stuff to pose for Albers's drawing class!

He was a most serious man, and his sense of humor remained mostly hidden. One day, I was seated next to him at dinner. We were eating oyster stew and Albers began scraping the bottom of the bowl with his spoon. It had a gritty sound, and Albers turned to me, his mouth slightly turned up in a small smile, and said, "Ah, zee beach!"

The humor was latent—one had to be there at the opportune moment.

The culmination of Albers's artistic development was his famous "Homage to the Square" series, on which he worked from 1949 until his death on March 19, 1976.

It is difficult for me to understand Albers's total involvement with his "Homage to the Square" series. When I was with him at the college, he was deeply involved with studying color.

Don Page, who was one of Anni Albers's favorite weaving students, accompanied her to her husband's memorial service. As they waited for the hall to empty, Anni sat in deep thought.

"Who would have believed," she finally exclaimed to Don, "that of all his life he would end up just painting squares?"

There were no "sports" programs at BMC—hiking took their place. Across the valley, the Craggy Range was the goal of an occasional overnight hike. The school itself was halfway up a ridge (part of the Blue Ridge Mountains), and was a frequent Sunday climb.

Bill Reed and I were walking the ridge circuit one Sunday afternoon when suddenly he pounced on an old shoe and exuberantly held it aloft. I thought he'd found a golden treasure. He had! Happily, he pointed out the shoe's great virtues—a patina of mold and two rows of rust-red eyelets on the flanks.

"It's for my class in *Werklehre*—what a find!"

"*Bon appetit,*" I replied, "but don't you need the other shoe?"

"Wait and see what happens to this shoe under *Werklehre!*"

Bill worked hard to explain *Werklehre* to me. "The goal," he said, "is to gain an understanding of the nature of materials by making radical changes in their appearance." He mounted the shoe on a large fragment of bark padded with moss and draped with twigs and acorns. He filled the shoe with thick compost, planted in it tiny, colored toadstools, and sprinkled the whole with various shaped, colored leaves until the shoe lost its utilitarian, manufactured aspect and became something made by mother nature herself. He also showed me another project—small clear-glass marbles mounted on a piece of old mossy wood and made to look like dew.

At one end of Lee Hall, we had a freight elevator that went from the basement to the attic. It was an eight-foot-square open platform operated by a series of heavy ropes. It was used extensively at the beginning and end of the school year to carry student furniture to and from the attic, but it was seldom used during sessions. Since it made a good deal of noise, one had a tendency to pay attention when it was operating.

I have this memory of peering down the hallway to see a regal head slowly appear-

On the porch at BMC.

ing at floor level, neatly coiffured gray hair studded with tortoise-shell combs, rimless glasses pinched on the nose, neck covered by a high lace choker rimmed with gemstones. A floor-length, silken, dark amber-colored gown was gradually revealed. The person, leaning on a cane with an elaborately carved ivory handle, was standing serenely erect. It was a grandma slowly coming into view on the third-floor level, her chauffeur operating the ropes. She was on her way to visit her grandson, Everit, an art student, in his study. If I could only turn vivid mental images like that into photographs!

Everit's grandma seemed a cliché of the Wealthy Grandmother, with a cool way of examining the "others" in her world that belied her keen interest in everything. She refused to fly and traveled the country with her maid in a chauffeur-driven limousine. "Never drive across Texas," she admonished Don Page. "It's too big!"

Everit's grandmother took the art class in her limo to an Asheville auto junkyard. The students, with gleeful shouts, fanned out to pick up old car parts. The grandmother was avidly trying to explain the merits of *Werklehre* to the bewildered dump owner, who was attempting to keep a tally of the items the chauffeur was packing into the limo's trunk.

She endeared herself to the entire assembled college by holding a celebration in our lobby, with the chauffeur mixing a case of bourbon with ginger ale in a huge washbasin. The world could use more grandmothers like that!

According to Anni Albers, "Being creative is not so much the desire to do something but the listening to that which wants to be done: the dictation of the materials." (Mary Emma Harris, *The Arts at Black Mountain College*)

Being Jewish, Anni probably survived by coming to Black Mountain. She had studied textiles at the Bauhaus and taught weaving and textile design at BMC. She was a fine teacher, not at all in the shadow of her more famous husband. I went down to the weaving studio one afternoon, sat at a loom for several hours, and decided it was not for me. It is amazing to me how many of my good friends did study under her—Bill Reed, Don Page, Eva Zhitlowsky, Harriett Engelhardt.

In the 1960s, living in Peru as a filmmaker, I was working on a one-hour TV special on native arts and crafts. The Huancayo region, high in the Andes, had a famous weekly Indian Market that was fertile ground for my film. After about a week of filming silversmiths, gourd carvers, potters, rugmakers, and weavers, I was ready to leave when one of my contacts asked, "Have you filmed the little German lady who is teaching Indians how to weave?"

Well, I hadn't. Teaching Indians how to weave? These gifted descendants of the Incas who knew about every textile technique known to man and could weave hand-spun threads at 400 per inch, the finest cloth in the world? This I had to see!

I drove into a little Andean village and was surprised to find a modern-looking textile studio. The owner was indeed a small German lady, Franziska Mayer, who spoke very good English and showed me her bank of excellent looms, each with a young Quechua girl industriously weaving.

On seeing a display of her personal work, I exclaimed, "The only textiles I've ever seen like these were done at my college by Anni Albers."

She grabbed my arm in great excitement. "Do you know her, did you really know Anni at Black Mountain College?"

"I was at Black Mountain before the war, from 1937 to 1940. How do you know about the college?"

Well, there was nothing to do but go up to her house for coffee and cake and *klatsch* about BMC. I finally got around to filming her studio and its finished products. When I packed up to leave, she gave me a big hug, a kiss on the cheek, and a sample of one of her ties.

I never did get around to talking about native Indian textiles or whether her Indian weavers were into Black Mountain innovations. (Actually, most of them were weaving traditional, classic-quality cloth, using natural alpaca yarns.) What had attracted my attention were some of Franziska Mayer's personal pieces.

She had studied weaving in Europe, she told me, with Anni Albers. Anni had taught her to design directly on the loom instead of working out designs on paper. In the fall of 1946, Josef and Anni went on a sabbatical and Franziska took Anni's place as weaving instructor at Black Mountain.

How and why she elected to retire to this remote Indian village, and why her brother set up a hardware store there, I never knew for sure. Presumably they were Jewish refugees from Germany.

In February 1997, I came across an article on Peruvian Andean weaving villages by Carol Noble. In it, she states: "These villages supply goods to the *Kamaq-Maki,* a center for local artisans . . . . Run by native women, it is renowned for its fine-quality weaving, knitting, braiding and spinning. It grew out of the ashes of the famous [studio] of Franziska Mayer."

I wrote Carol Noble inquiring about Franziska Mayer's studio but never received a reply. I have this sinking feeling that her studio was burned by the infamous Shining Path terrorists who dominated the Huancayo region. Did she herself survive?

The Alberses left Black Mountain in 1949. In 1950, Josef headed the Yale Department of Design. In 1953, he was honored by Germany when they opened the Albers Museum in his birthplace, Bottrop, near Essen. The Vice President of the United States attended the ceremonies.

In Mervin Lane's *Black Mountain College: Sprouted Seeds,* Sue Spayth wrote: "The music, ah the music (in the days before tapes and just a few record players) live music was a dazzling highlight for me: singing in a Bach cantata with Jalowetz, listening to Betty and Allen Sly playing Brahms."

Heinrich Jalowetz (affectionately known as "Jalo") taught music and was greatly respected not only as a musician but also as a person. Martin Duberman quoted a writer as saying, "I would not have appreciated the visual world as much without Albers, and man's love for man without Jalowetz."

The history of the Jalowetzes in Europe is a Nazi classic. Hounded out of Germany in 1933 by brutal Nazi hoodlums, he fled to Vienna, where he had once studied. In 1935, the Nazis murdered the Austrian dictator, Dollfuss, and intensified their drive to take over Austria. By 1936, the Jalowetzes fled again, this time to the Sudetenland of Czechoslovakia. When the Sudetenland was taken over by Germany in 1939, Jalowetz and his wife, Johanna, finally made it to the United States, and he was almost immediately taken on by Black Mountain College.

Their daughter Lisa left Europe with a scholarship to BMC. Lisa later married Boris Aronson, a well-known stage designer in New York. Having been told by my Pop (shamefacedly) on his deathbed that we had Slavic blood, Lisa and I, at the 1995 BMC reunion, traded our Slavic *metzes* and *wetzes*. Their son, Mark, visited us when we lived in Peru.

At Black Mountain, the exposure to great music and a great musician, Jalowetz, was constant. Sitting up close during one of Jalo's piano concerts, I could hear him mouth the music under his breath—almost as if he were conducting an opera. Of course, he had conducted operas all over Europe for more than 30 years.

According to the famous harpsichordist, Yella Pessl, who had performed at Black Mountain, "Dr. Jalowetz had an authority of con-

ducting which could live up to the one of Arturo Toscanini, under whose leadership I had performed numerous times."
—Mervin Lane, *Black Mountain College: Sprouted Seeds*

Jalo's death was very much in keeping with his life. He performed an evening of Beethoven sonatas, walked out on the porch, sat down, and died. There is no doubt that he was the most beloved person at the college.

For music, Jalowetz, yes, but also John Evarts. John had been the music critic for New York's *Brooklyn Eagle.* Being younger than the other members of the faculty, with less actual teaching experience, he always struck me as nursing an inferiority complex. He needn't have, as he was one of the bright notes in the community, the life of the Saturday-night dancing, and very much appreciated by all. John also wrote original music scores for several BMC stage performances.

I had taken one semester of Evarts's music class. We studied Bach, but I dropped out after the first semester to concentrate more on my writing class, something I've regretted ever since. I find that, today, I have a deeper feeling for the music of Bach than any other composer.

> The trouble with a women's college is that there are too many men there, in the thick imagination, so it becomes necessary to vacate on weekends. Nobody left BMC on weekends. On Saturday night there was dancing, pounded out by John Evarts on the piano.
> —John Rice

At BMC, males and females knew each other on the work program in sweaty blue jeans, with careful makeup and hairdos wiped out—possibly a whiff or so of body odor. It is interesting that in my high school, the girls considered blue jeans workingman garments (which, of course, they were) and mostly wore dresses and slacks. I saw my high school friends a few hours a day after school; dates were hard to arrange with so few having telephones. I must have been close to 20 before I even used a telephone.

At BMC, we took more notice of each other on Saturday nights. We combed our hair and changed to suits and dresses and danced in light-footed espadrilles to John Evarts's piano. We took no pity on John, dancing sometimes until midnight. But first John would play "musical portraits," with an uncanny knack for snaring someone's personality with musical passages—it wouldn't take us long to uncover the identities. He also was great at musical farce. One night I remember he did an opera, *Der Alte Schwartzer (Old Black Joe),* in complete Wagnerian mood and then continued in the style of Bach and other composers.

Allen Sly—composer of orchestral, choral, and chamber music; soloist, recitalist, and conductor—was from England. He also taught contradancing, which took place in the gym. The fragrant aroma of fall apples piled in the corner on a bed of straw was the very scent of English country dancing. Light-footed in our canvas espadrilles, we leaped and glided to "Greensleeves," "Christ Church Bells," and "The Black Nag," every step to the precise beat of the music. I thoroughly enjoyed the discipline. (Some 50 years later, a group of English country dancers showed up at my niece's wedding in Cushing, Maine—they had been trained by Allen Sly.)

Bob Wunsch was a Southerner, from Monroe, Louisiana, and also a Rollins College breakaway. Wunsch was one of the lesser intellectual luminaries at BMC, but he filled a very busy, comfortable niche. His main claim to fame, for me, was that he went to the University of North Carolina at Chapel Hill. Not only had he had, briefly, Thomas Wolfe as a roommate, he also had a copy of the same magazine edition my literate farmer had shown me. Bob directed and supervised numbers of plays. In order to put on a play at BMC, almost every available body needed to be impressed. As shy as I was in public performances, Wunsch managed to get me into *three plays*.

I took part in Clifford Odets's *Waiting for Lefty,* about a New York taxi strike—at a time when my brother Lee was driving a taxi in the city. Some scenes, like the 174th Street "el" station, were set in my old Bronx neighborhood, where Odets himself grew up.

I also had a speaking part in Irwin Shaw's bitter antiwar play, *Bury the Dead*. In my third year at BMC, I was severely criticized by Bob Wunsch in a faculty meeting for my militant antiwar stand in 1939, the first year of World War II.

I had speaking parts in the first two plays and can't say I added much to the drama. But I did add an element of suspense to my third play, Shakespeare's *Macbeth*, in which I had no speaking part. Being a May Day production, when the print shop (where I worked) was deluged with printing programs, I had little time for rehearsals. When "Birnam wood" came to "Dunsinane," I was one of the anonymous soldiers that came.

Macbeth took place in the gym without benefit of a stage. All the dining room tables were hauled down, arranged on several levels, and covered by the great lobby carpets. Action, then, could take place on three different levels. The few spotlights we possessed were rigged up in the rafters, along with students to motivate them. Scene changes went on in total darkness.

We had simple costumes made to fit with a few stitches of thread. Auto hubcaps on chains were draped on our chests for breastplates. Long wooden spears completed the illusion of "soldier."

On the big night, I was stitched into my uniform, breastplated, handed a spear, and led off into the wings. Not having time for rehearsals, I depended on following the soldier in front of me. In total darkness, I groped my way up the first level of tables. "Move over," my soldier/guide hissed. Move over I did, kaplonk off the table. My breastplate and spear rang out in the hushed gym like the true start of war. Scrambling back up on the table, I discovered my spear had broken—so I held it as best I could by the break.

When the lights came on, the audience craned to see which of the spotlight manipulators had fallen off his ceiling perch. It didn't take long to notice the soldier with the dazed look, the broken spear, and the disheveled uniform with stressed stitching. Well . . . even Clausewitz had to agree that battles seldom go according to plan.

Thornton Wilder and Clifford Odets came to visit the school, giving readings and taking part in lively discussions. Since Clifford Odets lived in my Bronx neighborhood, I cornered him in the BMC lobby and told him that, having seen the play in New York and having been in it myself here at college, I valued it highly. Particularly I mentioned how moved I'd been with the very effective strike scene, where someone planted in the audience yelled, "STRIKE!" and then another, until everyone in the theater was standing and screaming, "STRIKE!" He was very pleased that I knew his play until we twitted him about selling out and going to Hollywood with his film script, *Golden Boy*. It started out being flippant and quickly engulfed a good part of the lobby around us. I don't think it made Clifford very happy. He allowed that he was writing his first play while living on 10 cents a day. If living on 10 cents a day had any literary virtue, the Great Depression must have spawned a multitude of great writing!

Our faculty was a mixed bag of rebel professors, some from Rollins College, and top-echelon Europeans—gifts of the Nazi regime. The refugees were several cuts above what we could have normally afforded, and they added immeasurably to the quality of the teaching.

Anna Moellenhoff was a refugee who taught biology and German. I took a German course under her. At the beginning of the class, she admonished me: "I will not rate you at the end of the year on your knowledge of German. I will judge you only on how much your German improved."

I was not the only student in her class, but I pursued my own course of study. That she gave me an assignment to translate *Vinnie der Pooh* into German says what needs to be said about Anna Moellenhoff. How about that, Mrs. Goertz? (For those with weak memories, Mrs. Goertz was my high school German teacher who flunked me!)

I had little contact with Fritz Moellenhoff, who taught psychology. (Fritz Moellenhoff left BMC to work at the Menninger Clinic and later joined the staff of the Institute for Psychoanalysis in Chicago.)

In a community replete with artists, writers, and music lovers, Morton Steinau and Bob Sunley stood out as top-notch intellectuals. I served with

Sunley on the student council, and he was my first-year bedroom partner. Some 35 years later, at a lecture in Long Island, New York, by former BMC faculty member Buckminster Fuller, someone tapped me on the shoulder. It was Bob Sunley—he had recognized me by the back of my head!

Irene Schwinsky was a fitting mate to photographer Xanti Schwinsky. In the huge old wooden building, Irene caused a sensation. We had a small room set aside for ironing clothes—the iron and the board were always up and ready to go. One time, Irene left a hot iron sitting flat on the board. It burned its way through, leaving a perfect iron-shaped hole, and dangled at the end of its cord inches from the carpet.

The Moellenhoffs had left Germany, miracle of miracles, with all their huge, overstuffed furniture. It had come from the port in a great van that didn't quite fit under the arch at the foot of the road. After much deliberation, air was let out of the truck's many tires; it oozed through the arch and had to be reinflated by hand pump. The load was temporarily stored in the basement, unfortunately directly under Irene's bathtub. One day, the water was left running and the tub overflowed onto the furniture. That there was no blood was due only to the genial nature of Anna Moellenhoff. All this, of course, was simply the nitty-gritty of community life. Xanti and Irene were only at the college a short time, but they left an indelible impression.

In Martin Duberman's book on Black Mountain, he slides over the advent of Gutenberg at BMC in a less-than-casual fashion, describing it as a money-saver perhaps in line with, say, conserving toilet paper:

> A few students, in the second year, set up a cooperative store open each day to sell cigarettes, paper, candy bars, instant cocoa, and other assorted foods. In additional efforts to save money, the college set up its own print shop.

It was not that way at all, Martin!

David Way, a tall, redheaded student in my writing class, from

We bring Gutenberg to BMC.

Billings, Montana, approached me one day: "My father," he said, "is willing to give us a small press."

"Good, but my father's a house painter—how would those skills go in a print shop? Could I help paint it?"

"Look at it this way," he reasoned, "you help me set up and run the print shop, and I'll help you put out a Black Mountain magazine."

Putting out a BMC magazine to showcase our sterling writing was a dream frequently discussed by members of the writing class, and he had me hooked. But he forgot to mention that we would have to pay the shipping cost. A notice arrived stating that a freight car was sitting on the village siding with a crated press and a due bill of some $150. One of the customers we had lined up to help us out was Steve Forbes. He was interested in having us print a booklet on his "Theory of Musical Scales," so we had him put up the $150 as a job advance.

The machine turned out to be a Chandler & Price Challenge Gordon, a cast-iron foot-powered press with a huge flywheel. I don't remember the net weight of the shipment, but it took a gang of us to load it onto the school truck and haul it up to the basement of Lee Hall. It wasn't exactly a Sears, Roebuck delivery with detailed assembly instructions, but we managed to put it together. That is, Dave did, and I provided grunt power when called for. It looked great, but it didn't work.

"Don't worry," said Dave, "the printer down in the village has the same press."

The night we arranged to inspect his press was the night of a storm that had knocked out the town's electricity. It was a weird scene, examining Frankenstein's monster by candlelight. The printer was an older man with an attitude—"What could these snot-nosed college kids know about printing?" But Dave did know, and he expressed satisfaction with the examination.

Well, it worked, and we mounted it on 2x4 skids. Although it was made for foot power, Dave rigged up a 1/4 hp motor on a block of wood. We greased the block and attached a spring to it. By starting the great flywheel with the foot treadle and nudging the motor to make contact with the wheel, we were motorized. Of course, since it was a hand-fed press, a misfeed would entail stopping the press, cleaning the tympan, and restarting the flywheel and motor. The press seemed like a solid chunk of iron, but it had a temperament, demanding total attention every minute. I don't know what it had against Dave, but it once tore out a snatch of his red hair as he leaned over it. It took some time and some doing on Dave's part, but I became a printer—and grew to love it.

We had a rack of large type trays but not much in the way of type. Albers came to our rescue with several fonts of elegant Bodoni type that he had brought all the way from the Bauhaus in Germany. Like the Willimetz family, he and Anni, I'm sure, were limited in what they could take out with them, and he must have really treasured his Bodoni. Again, I thank him. We printed Steve's *Musical Scales,* but it took some doing, since we had only enough type to print half a page at a time. It was a long, tedious job but I learned typesetting in the process.

We accumulated more Bodoni, and I, too, grew to treasure it—especially the ultra bold, with its fat, round bosoms and bottoms. We did the college printing, playbills, and concert programs, plus we printed private letterheads and Christmas cards for profit.

Albers was our faculty adviser for all school printing. I would take him a proof of a playbill and he would examine it carefully.

"Now, I ask me," he would muse, "is this for me the best? You know, Emil, I believe in the *'tausend* technique.' You do a *tausend* and pick best."

"Mr. Albers," I would say, "that's great for sketches, but I'm not an artist and I do my layouts directly in the chase and run a proof. A thousand proofs?"

"Well," he would say, "better you should learn to make sketches, ja?"

I was never too good at sketches, but I did learn a bit about composition when I took a course in typography from Albers.

We did very well in the print shop but never managed to put out a BMC magazine. After David Way left (he went on to found two book-printing companies), the shop in the basement became for me a haven. I would save up work, especially longer print runs, for the times when I was restless or depressed.

The only problem was that it became known that I worked late, and all kinds of lonely, unhappy, or sleepless friends would come to join me. Frequently, on Saturday nights after dancing, there would be personal little parties in the studies, so anyone feeling left out might end up with me in the basement.

In a small college of only 75 students, it was difficult to be clandestine. At one time, moonshine found its way onto the campus. It was cheap and replete with mysterious, adventurous overtones, which did little to hide the awful taste. Doctoring it with pineapple juice or other strong flavors only made it worse. Having had moonshine experience on the Cumberland Plateau, I finagled some charcoal from an art student and placed it into a jar of moonshine. Overnight, the moonshine fusil oils were seen to gather around the charcoal. Decanting the shine made a less-lethal-hangover drink but not necessarily a better-tasting one. So it, too, was brought down to the midnight print shop—the haven for college derelicts.

May was an exciting time at BMC, when the redbuds, dogwoods, and azaleas were out. The feel of spring on the Blue Ridge was powerful and erotic—and not only for the birds. I found it difficult to concentrate on my studies.

My good friend Sue Spayth, in Mervin Lane's *Black Mountain College: Sprouted Seeds,* summed it up:

> The location of the college was in itself a kind of utopia: these glorious mountains; the gently gurgling, constant bubbling, sometimes crashing waters of the stream below our bedroom windows; the sunsets behind the blue wave of mountain peaks; walking to breakfast in the chill morning air. But it was the insistent calling of the whip-poor-will on a soft moonlit night that really did me in. Someone in worse shape than me must have kept tag of these breathless calls, for he enumerated some 16,000 calls in one night. Of course, poor-will . . . no one ever answers him.

Fortunately, the Dogwood Days were a busy time for the print shop—in the college basement, the cry of the whip-poor-will was not to be heard.

Parents of the students and friends of the college were invited to visit, and months of preparation went into preparing plays, art exhibits, and music recitals. We printed numerous invitations, mailing pieces, playbills, and programs. David and I decided that pink would be a great theme color for Dogwood Days, and we mixed a big batch. The color never seemed quite right, so we kept experimenting. The pot of pink grew big enough to paint Lee Hall. I was still using it for many things a year later. It strained the imagination to invent so many uses.

Robert Haas, a fellow Viennese and well-known calligrapher, printer, and photographer, was at the school and did a hand-lettered program for *Macbeth,* which we printed on heavy, firecracker-red stock. It was stunning. I often wish I had saved some of our work. Haas also instructed several students in photography, but I had no interest—little did I know! I had fastened onto a writing career, and it was hard for me to let go.

At a 1995 BMC reunion, I was accosted by a young lad who noticed my name tag:

"Willimetz? Hey, I read one of your stories in the North Carolina State Archives."

"That's fantastic!"

"Yeah, I liked your story, it was super."

"I had no idea that anything like that was in the files. What was it about?"

"About two brothers on a freight train."

"Icarus the Punk!" I remembered. "The older brother abandons the younger?"

"That's the one!"

I was so flattered by his interest that I forgot to ask him if there were other stories in the archives.

In the Raleigh archives I did find a brief dialogue in faculty minutes between Bill Reed and John Rice—apropos of my final months in Rice's class.

John Rice [about my drive as a writer]: "The artist is not the man who can but the man who must. All his stories are in essence hobo stories. Has almost written himself out."

Bill Reed: "Wasn't Willimetz good at first in your class?"

Rice: "Yes, but started to repeat; no progress."

Bill Reed: "Trying new things which aren't in his own experience?"

Rice: "Yes, but new themes are still decadent."

Reed [good friend and gentle soul]: "A bad start to have at first great enthusiasm and right afterwards suddenly to have equally strong criticism."

I think Rice meant that I branched out with concepts outside my knowledge but encased them in my decadent hobo experiences. I knew he was disturbed by my attempts at free style. *The Dying Outlaw* was for me an unsuccessful experiment in a literary form between narration and poetry. Again I was dealing with feelings I had not been able to resolve and found difficult to write about.

Charles Olson, the last rector of BMC, told one of his writing students, "Concentrate on what you know about. Write from the center." Olson was probably the better guide for my abilities—at that time.

It was, of course, a real question whether or not I had "the right stuff" to become a writer. I was turned in this direction by the completely unexpected success of my high school story (which was a pure hobo tale, a literal happening) and by the encouragement of my English teacher and friends. Apparently I didn't have the "must" stamina to overcome, in my third year, the engulfing threat of war. After the war, by pure chance, I became involved in photography, and that became my career. The training I received at Black Mountain stood me in good stead in writing scenarios for films and filmstrips—and, I hope, in writing this epic.

Part of Black Mountain's uniqueness was the composition of its student body. At BMC, students came from all levels of society, but that was played down. A number of students had transferred from other colleges to take advantage of certain assets of the BMC educational system. There were, of course, Jews, but I would be hard put to remember them as such. I was aware of only a couple of students who might have been on full scholarship and a few that were really wealthy (ownership of a small car was one of the few clues). Isolated as we were, the need for cash was not a real factor.

James Monroe High School was predominantly a Bronx culture. I was unaware that any of my Black Mountain fellow students came from families who spoke immigrant English, but it was common in my high school. I would say that perhaps 90 percent of my Bronx friends were Jewish, and their language was laced with Yiddish expressions. Having money was never a real factor. When it was decided to have a party or go on a picnic, whoever had money contributed.

> BMC was a unique place, but probably very few of its alumni could agree on the actual essence of that uniqueness.
> —Phyllis Josephs, in Mervin Lane, *Black Mountain College: Sprouted Seeds*

11.

MY THIRD
BLACK MOUNTAIN YEAR

BLACK CLOUDS: Excerpts from school year 1939-40

As PART OF MY RESTLESSNESS, brought on by my dread of the impending world disaster, I decided to exhaust my energies by returning to school from New York via bicycle. In our Bronx basement, we had one of the bikes my brother and I had rebuilt from wrecks. It was lightweight, with narrow racing tires, but it had only a single gear. I must confess, though, that I cheated on both ends of the trip. Bill Reed took us—the bike and me—in his small Ford to his mother's house in Rumson, New Jersey, and agreed to drive my suitcase to school. This gave me a start on the 10-day, 700-mile journey. At the other end of the trip, I hitched a ride in the back of a pickup for the long ride up the mountain at Old Fort.

I made good time down coastal Route 1 but lost the daily average going west across North Carolina. Pumping across the rolling hills of the Piedmont, I learned to regret my perpetual urge to travel by novel means. My face became deeply red, and the skin on my nose peeled off. I bought a wide-brimmed straw hat and pinned it with a shoestring to my shirt collar. It sailed behind me, flapping madly in wild downhill rides. Sleeping in fields each night didn't give me the rest I needed for the long days on the bike, and by the time I reached Lee Hall, I was a sun-blistered wreck. Why do I do these things? As Josef Albers would say, "Now, I ask me?"

While I was out of touch with the world, riding my bike from New York, Europe again became enmeshed in bloody war! Almost unnoticed by me, during my first two years at Black Mountain College, life outside had gone on like a steamroller, relentlessly obliterating nations and incinerating people. Although my third (and final) year at Black Mountain was a bad one for me, it was a year of total disaster for the rest of the world—the loss of Spain to the Fascists and the start of a second world war.

The war in Spain came to Black Mountain with the arrival of two Spanish refugees, Fernando and Paco Leon. At the age of 17, Fernando was a sergeant in the Loyalist Air Force. When the war was lost, he escaped to France. He says, proudly, that when Leclerc led his Free French Forces in the liberation of Paris, Spaniards were the largest part of the force. In June 1939, he won a scholarship to Black Mountain. He writes:

> I studied, my first year, only science with Charles Lindsley. My second and third years at BMC were more fun, for I took music with Evarts and Jalowetz, writing with Wunsch, history and Plato with Straus, Cervantes with Mangold, etc. In the Spring of 1942 I applied to the School of Engineering of Columbia University, presenting my three years at BMC as pre-engineering, and Columbia accepted all my credits including the surveying I did for the work program.

He studied continuously at Columbia for 15 months and graduated third in a class of 100 students. "I'm telling you all this," he wrote me, "because I am proud of the quality of teaching at BMC." Fernando subsequently worked for General Electric on the development of airplane engines.

I linked Fernando to the sudden craze at BMC for Spanish rope-soled canvas espadrilles. Not so, says Fernando—they came from Mexico (as Mary Emma Harris speculates, probably from a visit there by the Alberses and Dreiers) and were not nearly as good as true Spanish models. Nevertheless, his wearing espadrilles started the fashion. They were great for dancing.

Although I had expected it, the advent of the war still threw me completely off balance.

BMC was a diverse cultural entity where politics were seldom mentioned. In my third year, the European war became a hot campus topic, but it still didn't involve more than a part of the student body. Ted Dreier was the only faculty member to voice an antiwar opinion, but in a very quiet voice. Mostly I debated individuals on my objections to the war and did a lot of extracurricular reading. In my high school, the issues of war and Fascism had been a dominant feature, and being an activist on current problems was almost a given. I missed this support and felt isolated in my strong antiwar sentiments.

Hearing about an antiwar rally at the University of North Carolina at Chapel Hill, we organized a car pool to attend—an epic journey of better than 400 miles round trip in the days of narrow, ungraded highways. It was a good rally, and we were late leaving Chapel Hill for the trip back to BMC.

I rode with Ted Dreier and Mitzi, a young first-year student. Ted's car was a canvas-topped touring Ford, made extra long with the addition of a large wooden box for camping supplies. About 2 a.m., having been slowed by heavy rain and patchy fog, Ted was exhausted and asked me to take over the driving. He promptly fell asleep in the back seat and Mitzi likewise in the front seat.

At about 4 a.m., we were in the home stretch, the hilly section just before the steep climb at Old Fort. As we came around a curve, a huge magnet gripped the car, slowly pulling us toward the edge of the road. We had hit a wash of greasy red Carolina clay. There was nothing I could do to stop the slide. I was afraid to brake and afraid to turn the wheel any more sharply. The left wheels dropped off the pavement, and I desperately tried to feed more gas. It was the most inevitable event I've ever been in. I knew the consequences and knew there was nothing in the world I could do—and all as slow as a dream. With all four wheels now off the road, I could feel us tilt, turn over, and start to tumble down the hillside. We rolled over and over, crashing through small trees and bushes. I clutched the wheel with all my strength and counted three complete rolls before an abrupt lurch pulled me loose and I went through the canvas roof into a stream bed. The car came to a stop just over me. Desperately I strained my arms against the car frame to keep it from rolling farther and screamed for the others to get out.

Ted was able to get out and help Mitzi. When they were both away from the wreck, I dropped my arms and rolled away, expecting the car to fall on me. It didn't move an inch; it was firmly wedged against the bank. The only injuries I received were strained arm muscles. I reached into the car, turned out the lights, turned off the motor, and we scrambled up the steep hillside. Together we stood on the road's shoulder, trembling, with Ted hugging us in his relief that we hadn't been hurt. We stopped a car, but it was crowded and could only take Ted, holding Mitzi on his lap.

I watched the car's lights winding down the mountainside and then, suddenly, they were gone. I was alone in the cold, rainy night, dazed and wracked with guilt—miserable on the road I had once so joyously traveled in a rumble seat. It was one of my life's low points.

Without Mitzi as a lure, none of the few cars coming by would stop, so I drearily hiked down the road. In the gloomy wet dawn, I arrived at Old Fort and, in time, was able to get a bus to Black Mountain. It was not a happy young man who knocked on the door of the Dreier cottage. Bobbie Dreier helped ease my terrible guilt when she exclaimed to Ted:

"This is the third time we've had skidding trouble. We have to get rid of that big box on the back of the car. We're so lucky that you're all alive!"

Bless you, Bobbie Dreier! Nothing was ever again said to me about the accident. It took two wreckers to pull the car up the slope, and I guess the insurance covered most of the damage. So much for my antiwar activism! Obviously I was warned—drag my feet, protest all I want, roll down hillsides in cars, I had no way of escaping war!

For the first two years, Black Mountain College answered a deep need in me to learn—literature, art, music, writing, and printing. I had quickly, easily, and eagerly adapted to the BMC lifestyle—slipping smoothly from my intensely political Bronx world into one that was intensely personal. Walls between disciplines didn't exist at Black Mountain. The art teacher sat next to you at the dining room table, the music teacher gave concerts in the lobby and talked with you at the afternoon tea table. Like a thirsty blotter, I absorbed it all—art, acting, music, contradancing, literature, printing, and, my dream, writing. Educational and community pursuits occupied me full time—more than full time—or so it seemed.

In my third year, I had my greatest need to know—to find answers to questions about which the school had nothing to teach me. I was left floundering, sometimes in real pain.

For me, at the time, the antiwar side of the coin took precedence, although that decision was tearing me apart. I was a political person, I knew the stupidity and futility of war, but I also knew the evils of Fascism. I took long walks. (Walking seemed to be my way of working through problems.) One time, after midnight, restless, I left the print shop to walk. At the bottom of the hill, I kept going until I reached the old empty road that paralleled Route 70 and walked down it to Asheville—17 miles. I sat in the bus station until morning and took the first local bus back to Black Mountain.

Adding to this hour of my discontent was the absence of John Rice, who had been such a large part of my first two years. I halfheartedly took writing under Bob Wunsch, a second-rate writing teacher at best. I was well aware of negative feelings among the faculty concerning my concentration on the war and the neglect of my studies during this third and last year at college. Years later, going through the BMC material in the North Carolina State Archives, I was to find out the full extent of these feelings.

There was, however, a bright spot in my last semester at BMC. Across the valley from the college verandah were the Craggies, topped by Mount Mitchell, a cosmic view that had for us a multiplier effect. Under its spell, good moods became transcendental and bad moods became suicidal. A late February snow blanketed the ground—a soft, lead-colored sponge teetering on the final edge of becoming water. (This part of North Carolina never heard of real snow, as in Maine!) A thin, cool mist saturated the air around me on the verandah of Lee Hall as I sat in a rocking chair thinking about my constant state of indecision about the draft. Listlessly rocking, I heard the door behind me open, and Harriett Engelhardt stopped by my chair.

"Good morning."

"Define 'good'!"

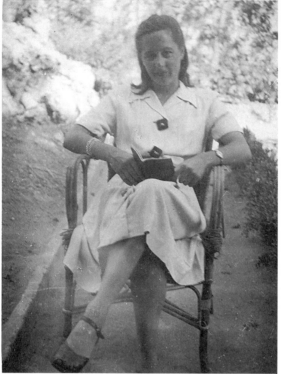

Harriett was destined to re-enter my life at moments and places so bizarre as to be fictional.

"This is what happens when your Yankee climate invades the South!"

"A lost cause. It looks like our Yankee climate is about to go down the drain. Where are you going in all this wet?"

"I'm on my way to church."

"Wow! Well, pray for the world, it's awash with blood." (I didn't write all those antiwar leaflets in high school for nothing.)

"Is that what you've been brooding about in that rocking chair? See you."

"Could be my blood," I muttered, but she didn't hear as she glided down the wide steps and was off on the long walk to town. How was I to know that Harriett would die in the war zone and not me?

I had been aware of Harriett—she was one of the college's "great" dancers, light on her feet and up to all of my dancing maneuvers. But she really impressed me when she walked down the road by herself in the slush, three miles or so to the village church. Faithful Christian in a pagan world! Engulfed in my own wave of depression, a sense of loneliness in her drew me.

Harriett was an art student, a weaver, with a slight, boyish build, short brown hair, a pleasant face, and a quiet manner. From Montgomery, Alabama, she had a light Southern accent but, apparently, no need for her second first name, Pinkston.

With Harriett, "no" was instantaneous, definite, and unyielding. We would lie on her study cot, hold each other tightly, and kiss passionately—everything else was a no-no. She did say once that she had promised her father that no boy would touch her body until she got out of school. Well, this boy never disappointed her father. We were not ones to really talk about our feelings. Two introverts! I never felt that I really "knew" her. Even so, she was one of the few bright spots in my dismal third year.

That damp February day started a chain of events that ended only with her death. Harriett was destined to re-enter my life at moments and places so bizarre as to be fictional.

12.

POST–BLACK MOUNTAIN COLLEGE, 1995

FAST FORWARD: HOW TIMES CHANGE!
Highway sign just outside of town in 1995:

> BLACK MOUNTAIN COLLEGE
> EST. IN 1933; CLOSED 1956
> Experimental School With Emphasis on
> Fine Arts & Progressive Education
> Campus was 3 mi. NW

IN MY TIME, OF COURSE, THERE WAS NO SIGN. Had there been one, it might have read: "BMC Students Go Home."

Actually, although there were some suspicions and antagonisms, the college sat high above the town in splendid isolation and was mostly tolerated or ignored. Today the Black Mountain College Museum and Arts Center, 13 miles away in Asheville, is promoted by enthusiastic young people (most not even born at the time of the school's death). It is amazing to me how the preeminence of BMC's reputation has lingered over the many years since its demise. Probably the most extraordinary thing about BMC is the proliferation of books written about it, and, as I understood from people at the 1995 BMC reunion, more were being incubated.

Headed by Mary Holden, this group of young people sponsored the reunion October 27-29, 1995. It was enormously successful, with some 160 attendees—from a 1933 Rollins College defector (Norman Weston) to last-ditch Olson followers. I went and knew only 12 students, remnants of the Lee Hall old-timers.

At the reunion, they lined us up to take the usual group picture, and I found myself standing next to a guy in a black sweatshirt with BLACK MOUNTAIN COLLEGE printed in bright red. I asked him where it came from, since I had the same sweatshirt sleeping in a bureau drawer in Maine. Apparently his story duplicated my own. In 1994, I noticed an ad in *The Nation* offering the above T-shirts for sale. I sent in my money and asked about the entrepreneurs. This letter came back from Oregon:

> 14 January 1994
> Dear Mr. Willimetz:
> Alas, we are not Black Mountain alumni; we are wannabes. BMC was our dream school. One of us could not go because her parents feared Free Love and Free Thinking, and the other because he learned of it the year it closed. Sigh. We were forced to settle on Hunter and Ann Arbor.
> Sincerely & Enviously,
> VM & MD

In October 1996, 56 years after leaving BMC, I spent some time in the BMC Archives in Raleigh, North Carolina. I had already written my chapters on Black Mountain for this book and was looking to see if I could pick up some additional material. I could indeed! Faculty meeting notes on "Willimetz" were frequent and less than flattering—I took quite a hammering. It was amazing how many of the incidents mentioned in those archival notes I had blocked out of my memory.

FACULTY MEETING NOTES
These quotes came on pages of little snippets, leaving out all the connecting material. It has been suggested that I may have edited these faculty evaluation notes. Absolutely not! I believe I used almost every quote—any editing was done in Raleigh.

Faculty discussion on whether I should return after my third year:

[Clip unidentified]: ". . . good stuff but very difficult" . . . "becoming a problem" . . . "putting College in second place to printery" . . . "unhomogeneous group of Way, Hendrickson, Hill and Willimetz." [I would like to read the notes on these other malcontents.]

Kenneth Kurtz: "The students overrate Willimetz's ability . . . . With Willimetz in a class it really disintegrates . . . ." Doesn't want Emil in his classes.

Charles Lindsley: "He is a source of discontent, yet so many speak highly of his talents."

Bob Wunsch: "Wolpert [Jerry Wolpert, a fellow student, probably in the Student Government at this time] is distressed about his being kicked out and about the high-handed methods of the Faculty. He says Willimetz is one of the most intelligent people here."

Fred Mangold: " . . . his full scholarship be continued only if he should deserve it. This is his third year. He is not going to try to graduate. He is in some ways a parasite."

[The overwhelming majority of BMC students did not elect to graduate. It was one of the benefits of its educational innovations.]

John Evarts: "He isn't as far as the printing is concerned."

BT: "The students say that if he is kicked out it is because he has no money—that he would not be kicked out if he would be full paying."

[Money, of course, was a major factor at BMC. The faculty received very little in pay over room and board. I do remember feeling guilty in not living up to the faculty expectations.]

Lindsley: "Then if we should decide to tell him to leave we should expose him to the students."

Misc.: Mr Albers reports that he has been very hard working in typography [my class with Albers] and takes criticism well, good to work with." "Hasn't done much writing lately, but did before April."

Evarts: "Doesn't he do quite a lot of reading?"

Mangold: "We have no real evidence of it."

Evarts: "He has done some reading for history."

Walter Barnes: "He does a fair amount and in a way that is rather satisfactory— sometimes good." [I was taking his class in history.]

Evarts: "We made arrangements for him to take an examination. Walter will make questions from the bibliography he is handing in."

Barnes: "He took a 2 1/2 hour exam on about 3,000 pages. One question was answered well; the others fair. I should think it would be a passing paper."

[Is this a throwback to the pedantic pass/fail system against which the Rollins radicals rebelled?]

Mangold: "Too mixed up . . . deserves credit for work in printing."

Anni Albers: "General attitudes much better than previously. Much gentler."

Josef Albers: " . . . because he has some practical work."

Anni Albers: "Should say that we see some improvement . . . has something . . . encouraging but not best for him to come back."

Kurtz: " . . . gets students unduly upset."

Wunsch: "Willimetz is somewhat crafty and gives out wrong impressions without actually lying. Wouldn't be best for him to come back."

[And a new can of worms not followed up on: " . . . glad Reed isn't so connected with him anymore!"]

Misc.: "This place [BMC] has taken the desire for hoboing away from him, he says; but he goes off still for hikes during class hours . . . ."

[I hadn't known before how the faculty viewed my travels.]

Wunsch: "He doesn't face things, he is really scared . . . too cowardly to face the world."

Mangold: "He is mixed up about the whole war business. He writes nothing else but about the war, all of which comes down to 'Will I have to go into it?' He is terrified. Emil lives in a world of illusion which he then has to persuade people is true."

In my high school antiwar days, I had memorized and frequently quoted the ghastly casualty reports of World War I and the horrendous disregard for human life with which generals commanded troops to "go over the top" into murderous machine-gun fire. My favorite example was the battle for the Fortress of Verdun:

. . . as the sun began to fall, the first wave of German infantry advanced, debuting their newest piece of equipment: the flame thrower. The Frenchmen who could still move crawled to the tops of their trenches . . . . They soon learned that if they shot the fuel tank, the tanks would explode. Hundreds of Germans were immolated; the others kept coming. In another hour, the Germans were at the trenches. Skulls were pulped by rifle butts. Men were pinned to the cold mud with bayonets. Soldiers from both sides were shot at close range. Others were blown apart by grenades.

Before the siege was over, more than a million soldiers had been devoured by the fighting. And what may be the most grisly statistic ever, only 290,000 bodies were ever recovered— with fewer than 160,000 of them identifiable.

—Donovan Webster, *Aftermath*

The name of the game had become attrition—the side that survived with the most men would win. The Battle of Verdun in France yielded a million deaths so evenly divided between the combatants that there was no declared "winner"—just one million fewer players on the board.

The British suffered a more inconceivable sacrifice of another million at the Somme, and at Passchendaele, a graveyard of liquefied mud, another half million. *Was this the game they wanted me to play?*

In World War I, a young French lieutenant wrote in his diary just before his death in battle: "They could never make us do it again."

You wanna bet, lieutenant?

I had used the horrifics of the Verdun battle to persuade my fellow high school students to protest against the stupidity of war. In the process, of course, I thoroughly psyched myself! So I truly was . . . "really scared" . . . "totally terrified." The coming war was like Ted Dreier's car—a huge magnet slowly pulling me off into my blackest nightmare.

As to being "mixed up about the whole war business," I was that, too. I had protested the black cloud of Fascism as it covered the globe and was dismayed at the lack of interest, even complicity, of the democracies. Now, when it was too late, the European democracies were at total war with the Fascists. With more modern weapons than in World War I, there was more killing, more destruction. Was I to believe that the Allies were truly fighting Fascism? France, with its bloody domination of Algeria and Vietnam? England, with its vast colonies and its abominable treatment of Ireland?

I was also well aware of the Nazi treatment of the Jews, although we were not cognizant of the extermination camps until toward the end of the war. I honored little BMC for sponsoring Josef and Anni Albers, the Strauses, the Schwinskys, Fritz and Anna Moellenhoff, Fernando and Paco Leon, and, above all, the Jalowetzes—Jalo, Johanna, and my fellow student Lisa. But our country was doing less than nothing to help Jews and other refugees trying to flee Germany. How many refugees of the caliber of our faculty or greater could have been saved by a country truly dedicated to democracy?

" . . . [Willimetz] hasn't found the way. . . restless . . . ." Neurotic? Certainly deeply upset!

I couldn't completely throw off my hatred of Nazi Germany for the evil it was doing. Was joining a war fought by historically questionable allies going to solve the world's problems? Or was war itself the greater evil? Although some 80 percent of the American people were against our entering the war, I absolutely knew we would join the Allies. I was indeed completely "bewildered."

That I was militantly antiwar was no secret to the BMC faculty. The summer I worked on the school farm, 1936, was the year I graduated from James Monroe, and I remember talking about my antiwar activities with Bobbie and Ted Dreier. Certainly, I believed, my old high school nemesis, Dr. Hein, wouldn't have failed to blacken my reputation when the college checked my high school records. Being a radical, I gathered, had been no detriment to admission.

Of all the negative criticism by the faculty, I was most offended by that of Bob Wunsch. I thought of him as a small, weak character.

Louis Adamic, in *My America*, quotes Wunsch about his plays: "Dramatics is the nearest thing to experience, and as such a good medium to knowledge, especially self-knowledge." Say! Wasn't it Bob Wunsch who

from "Bury the Dead"

and stagecraft

bury them   they stink!
for christ's sake bury um
bury the dead!
o the lovely army o the
eet army o the god damn a
my what are we going to c
o? where is christ? a gree
and please...   e extra
they're st...   ll
em all tell...it my bar m
husba...   ever for y
rd o bl
mom le
lay down the sword

put on the bitter antiwar play *Bury the Dead* and pressured Willimetz to take part in it? I wonder if any of BMC's World War II dead also participated in the play?

Yet, in reading Katherine Reynolds's *Visions and Vanities*, I got a better slant on Bob Wunsch. In 1932, just before the grand split at Rollins College, Rice and Wunsch, both Southerners, were instrumental in getting a play written by black anthropologist Zora Neale Hurston performed at Rollins. From Winter Park, Florida, President Hamilton Holt gave permission for the play, but without blacks in the audience. Disappointed, Hurston had it performed again at a local Negro school. She still felt it was a breakthrough for the South and for her career to see a sympathetic version of Negro life. Wunsch also helped her get her first short story published.

She dedicated her first novel to: "Bob Wunsch who is one of the long-winged angels right around the throne. Go gator and muddy the water."

I wish I had known this aspect of Bob Wunsch while I was at Black Mountain.

At the 1995 reunion, and from other sources, I learned about what happened to some of my fellow BMC students.

I knew Ike Nakata, an American Nisei born in Hawaii, in my last year at BMC, but not very well. I was too preoccupied with myself that year, and Ike had a retiring personality.

In "Getting By and Through the 1940s," written for the University of North Carolina *Literary Review* (vol. 1, no. 2, 1995), Ike filled in some of the blanks:

> When I was drafted in midsummer (1941), I was to spend eight months in the Army air corps, through the bombing of Pearl Harbor and our entry into the World War, December 7, 1941. In the early spring of '42 I was honorably discharged ("character excellent," it said on my discharge paper) due to "questionable citizenship." Yet I had been born a citizen—the discharge was officialese for "undesirable ancestry." It was shattering to my ego, to

my beliefs. I felt bitter and brittle.

In the early spring of '43, the secretary of war announced the formation of the 442nd Regimental Combat Team expressly for Japanese born in America (and Hawaii) whose patriotism had to be proved. I volunteered. After service in Italy and France, I did not get out of the army until the end.

I know from other vets that the 442nd in Italy, with the onerous task of having to prove themselves, took exceptionally high casualties. It became known as the "Christmas tree" unit, because it had become the most decorated unit in the entire army.

Harriett Engelhardt died in a Jeep accident in France. I learned that a check for $2,011.31 was donated to Black Mountain College for a Harriett Engelhardt Memorial Collection of Textiles. According to Ted Dreier, "This was Harriett's entire estate and included $271.40 contributed by the Japanese 522nd Field Artillery Battalion (442nd Combat Team). We understand that she worked with this unit for several months."

Tommy Wentworth was killed in action in Normandy. Tommy and I trained with Ike and the 442nd Combat team at Camp Shelby the summer of 1943. We both were assigned to the 29th Division, but in different regiments.

In *The Arts at Black Mountain College,* Mary Emma Harris wrote: "After Pearl Harbor Lucian Marquis, a German refugee student, tried to enlist in Buncombe County . . . . he was told that he should obtain letters from 'solid citizens' testifying as to his character. Dreier, Wunsch, and Kocher, all American born, wrote the required letters. To Marquis's astonishment, he was turned down because the names of all three of his sponsors were *Germanic in origin.* His distress turned to amusement when he noted that the letter of rejection was signed by a man named Jaeger."

Derek Bovingdon and Roman Maciejczk were, as far I know, the first BMC students to die in the war. Never leaving the States, they died in air force training flights.

True to his nature, Bill Reed had become a Quaker and registered as a conscientious objector. He changed his name from William F. Reed to

Alexander S. because of a hassle with his father over his CO status. His father, Colonel Latham Reed, was a World War I veteran.

Both Mary Emma Harris and Martin Duberman made the point in their books that Bill was a surrogate son for the Alberses, and I agree. He not only did intensive work with Josef Albers but also took weaving classes under Anni. Bill graduated in art and subsequently returned to teach art at BMC during Albers's 1940-41 sabbatical.

Bill got into his kayak and paddled straight out to sea.

During his time at Lake Eden, Bill had designed and built a small stone building as a memorial to the Dreiers' nine-year-old son, Mark, who had died in a car accident. The stone came from the surrounding area, and he wove the curtains himself. As befitted its character, it was called the Quiet House, a Quaker-type space for reflection and a place for weddings and funerals.

(In 1963, Joie and I and our two young boys came back from Peru to visit the USA. I stopped to see Bill in Cambridge and regretted the visit almost immediately. There was so much to say, and I had time only for a superficial hello and good-bye—strained and awkward at that.)

Bill and several other BMC students—Claude Stoller, Don Page, Bob Bliss, Charles Forberg—went to Harvard and MIT for graduate work in architecture. For a time, Bill taught design at MIT with Gyorgy Kepes. He designed and built, with his own labor, a house on Martha's Vineyard.

Apparently building was *his* release from problems—as walking was mine.

One of my college friends, Don Page, flew with me to the 1995 BMC reunion. He was a neighbor of Bill's on Martha's Vineyard, and from him I learned about my friend's final days.

One day in 1965, Bill got into his kayak and paddled straight out to sea. Several days later, his body and the kayak washed up on the shore—a terrible waste of a wonderful person who couldn't cope with problems imposed on him by the society in which we have to live.

I often feel guilty about my inability to relate more closely to Bill's needs. Was it my male genes that stopped me or cowardice in the face of conventional attitudes on homosexuality? My episodes of male bonding—mass masturbation with my friends in the lumberyard—were not so far in my past. I still suffered from my episode with Hildreth, more than I would admit at that time. In rereading some of my BMC writing class stories, I find myself struggling with this theme.

13.

BLACK MOUNTAIN COLLEGE SUMMERS

In the years I attended Black Mountain College I had summer experiences in great contrast to the school terms.

FIRST-YEAR SUMMER, 1938

IN THE SUMMER OF 1938, SUE NOBLE, a fellow Black Mountain College student, was instrumental in getting me on a Work Camp payroll as a leader, at $50 a month. (Don't sneer—it included room and board and was not too bad for Depression times.) Dick Gothe, a master mechanic and toolmaker with a Ph.D. in economics, was responsible for organizing the popular Work Camp movement in Germany. Fleeing Hitler, he became involved in Work Camps for America and organized a camp outside of Akron, Ohio. Sue and I hitchhiked out to join Gothe. If you like stereotypes, Dick was a real German—tall, brawny, very disciplined, and very insistent on others being disciplined. For a number of us, this was not a bad thing.

Half the campers were from a settlement house in Cleveland and half were college kids. Sue was leader of the girls, Emil of the boys. The day began at 6 a.m. with strenuous exercises—out on the dawn grass, cold and wet between our toes. The goal was to fashion a summer camp out of a dairy farm for the children of Cleveland. This entailed cleaning up the farming crud, manicuring the grounds, fixing up buildings, and sledge-hammering out concrete milking stanchions in the barns. Under Dick, this was an honest morning's labor!

After lunch, we had a study program. We went to Akron and toured the Goodyear Tire factory; visited and talked to the manager of a small steel fabrication plant; and looked into other industrial plants. The Goodyear labor relations director was invited out to camp to present the company's wage and work policies and be thoroughly interrogated by the campers. The next day, we had the head of the local Rubber Workers' Union. The visits were followed up with long discussions on the relationship between capital and labor . . . the right to organize . . . the right to strike . . . the right to hire scabs, etc. The principal dictum of the discussions: No information or data to be introduced that did not come out of the previous visits and interviews. This put a damper on the college contingent, accustomed to gathering data from books, and sharpened the interrogation skills of the campers from Cleveland.

An intense rivalry quickly built up between college and settlement campers. Although handicapped by the ruling, the college kids were still much more vocal in the arguments. The blue-collar gang was clearly better at physical labor skills. After the head chatter, we piled out for volleyball—Joe college versus blue collar. Evenly matched, we had exhilarating, cutthroat games. When we broke up at the end of the month, it was evident that the college kids were impressed with their blue-collar rivals and the settlement kids were making inquiries about the chances of getting into college in Cleveland. I found the Work Camp concept very impressive.

I was even more profoundly impressed by the second Work Camp assignment. Dick, Sue, and I drove south to our next camp at Highlander Folk School on Tennessee's Cumberland Plateau. (I had visualized mountain people deep into producing baskets, duck decoys, and quilts.) We stopped off in Reading, Pennsylvania, to visit an American Friends Service Work Camp. They were making a children's play park, and we joined them for a few days.

The campers at Highlander were much more homogeneous than at Akron; almost all were college students. In the South, certain species of pine grow so rapidly that they can be harvested in 10 to 12 years. Many farmers planted several acres of these trees as income for their children's college education. It was for future income for the school that several acres were being cleared and planted. The Work Program included cutting trees, clearing land, splitting logs, and planting trees. Creosoting the three-story main building was included—mostly done by me.

Highlander was no arts-and-crafts school. An adult education school, at this time working mainly with industrial unions, it was always strapped for money. For our afternoon study periods, not many management types would come to Highlander, but we did manage to interview the labor relations man from a Chattanooga Hosiery Mill. To follow

Painting at Highlander Folk School.

up, we had members of the Hosiery Workers Union come to talk.

As part of the study program, we would go to a cabin where Jim Dombrowski, a Highlander staff member, lived and worked. We were fascinated by his stories. Surrounded in his cabin by books and papers, and puffing on his pipe, he radiated a calm, deep conviction of the need for radical social change in the South.

Dombrowski received a Rosenwald Fellowship to record the use of convict labor in the Grundy County mines near the school. This grew into a book-length manuscript entitled, "Fire in the Hole." But at the time I knew Jim, it was still research material, much of it based on interviews with neighbors of the school who were survivors of the scheme.

In 1871, the Knights of Labor challenged the Tennessee Coal and Iron Company. The coal miners, protesting the deplorable conditions, went out on strike, and the company leased convicts to use as strikebreakers. The convicts worked until the light failed, six days a week. They worked in the same deplorable conditions against which the miners had struck—dark, wet shafts with water up to their belts, for which they were paid 24.5 cents per day. The convicts were brutally treated and whipped by their overseers. Thousands of miners were thrown out of work as convict labor spread through the Appalachian coalfields.

By 1892, some 320 convicts worked in the Tracy City, Grundy County, mines (six miles from the school). On August 13, 150 out-of-work miners marched on the Tennessee Coal and Iron stockade, demanding employment. When company officials refused to talk with them, they loaded the convicts on a train, sent it off to Nashville, and burned the stockade. Guarded by Tennessee state militia, convicts rebuilt the stockade. Jim tells the story of local boys meeting the militia as they marched up the mountainside and, offering to guide them, led them off into a dead-end wilderness.

The miners attacked a few months later, putting boxes of dynamite under the office building. But the explosives got soaked in a heavy rain and wouldn't go off. A firefight ensued, and some 20 men were shot—one died. When the company's convict contract expired, the convicts were removed.

Dombrowski also took us on visits to abandoned mines that were still being worked by hungry unemployed miners. Starting at the farthest end of the tunnels, the men would work toward the opening, robbing the pillars of coal that held up the roof—an extremely dangerous activity. I again heard the story of Bill Turnblazer, head of the Tennessee Mine Workers Union, being burned out and teargassed in the Cumberland Gap Hotel. He had become a legend.

A strapping young man named Herman took us to an abandoned coal shaft he had been working. A set of narrow tracks led into the tunnel, and a weary looking mule, with a rag tied over his eyes, pulled an iron cart in and out of the mine. Herman sold the bootlegged coal to families in the county. One day, Herman was pinned to the floor of the tunnel by a large slab of rock. Fortunately, it was a low ceiling, and he had his back tight up against the stone when it gave way. "Had it dropped on me," he told us, "it surely would have killed me."

Herman also told us about being bitten by a copperhead. Years later, when I was living at the school, Herman and a group of local lads took me fishing. The stream had cut through ledges of flat slabs of limestone. We sat on these ledges, our feet dangling, casting into the water. Suddenly Herman slammed a club down at his feet. We jumped but said nothing. A short time later, again . . . whap! A chorus of "Cut it out!" "Hey, you're scarin' the fish!

"There's a water moccasin under this here ledge, and I'm gonna get 'im." Hoots of disbelief. But he did "get 'im," and it was a water moccasin. Feet ceased dangling.

Dombrowski took the work campers to Tracy City, where we could see the remains of the old stockades, the coal tipples, and the coke ovens. The coal mines around Tracy City were named Rattlesnake, Wildcat, and Possum Tail. Mining history, here, was still a living thing!

In *The Arts at Black Mountain College*, Mary Emma Harris reported:

> Unlike Black Mountain, several other experimental communities and schools were created to educate the mountain people of the area. The Highlander Folk School and Work Camp in Monteagle, Tennessee, also served as a political training ground with a strong Marxist orientation

Not so! Highlander never preached any doctrinaire political system; its main drive was toward a more democratic (which in the South meant interracial) society. In the 1930s and 1940s, anyone left of center and interracial was considered Communist. Eleanor Roosevelt was a patron of HFS. I was not at the school when Black Mountain College opened its student body to include blacks, but I suspect it, too, was accused of being Communist.

Dick Gothe, our Work Camp director, was hired by BMC in the summer of 1941 to organize a Work Program for the college. (No longer at the school by then, I can only visualize it running along the lines of my own experience—an education and work combination.) Dick's methods, which worked so well for us in 1938, didn't fly at BMC, and his contract was not renewed.

I stayed at HFS the summer of 1938 until it was time to go back to BMC. I was enchanted by the Cumberland Plateau, awed by the Folk School, and captivated by the staff and the people of Summerfield.

While the money I earned as a Work Camp leader was pretty slim pickings for my BMC needs, fortunately I was able to get by that year on the fruits of our school printing press. I also got a little gift from the New Deal's Depression relief program called the NYA (National Youth Administration). It paid 50 cents an hour for 20 hours a month. The job was to convert the books in the BMC library to the Dewey decimal system. This was based, of course, on the expertise learned at my prestigious New York Public Library job back in high school days. Years later, I also Dewey-decimated the Highlander Folk School library—at no cost to the government.

SECOND-YEAR SUMMER, 1939

With the sun setting on my Black Mountain College adventure and the dawn of a second world war looming just over the horizon, I spent an unhappy and restless second summer. Chicago's Institute of Design students, under another Bauhaus refugee, Laszlo Moholy-Nagy, had made several journeys down to BMC. Apparently there was little love lost between the two sets of art students, but I knew that Laszlo ran a summer camp, so I thought I might be able to get a job with him. Of course, my main motive was to be in the Chicago area, where I could spend some time with Ruth, a BMC girl who lived there.

I rented a room on Blackstone, in the University of Chicago area, and went up to the institute (nowadays part of the Illinois Institute of Technology). Ushered into Moholy-Nagy's office, I was treated to a lively dialogue on art, the Bauhaus, and the institute. I suddenly became embarrassed, realizing he thought I was a potential student. When I confessed my motive, I was curtly told, "No job," and shown out. In 1945, as Moholy-Nagy lay dying in a Chicago hospital, my friend Bill Reed, as a conscientious objector, was his nurse.

I wasn't doing so well with my friend Ruth, either. We had a strange kind of relationship, blowing hot then cold. It was mostly blowing cold that summer. She had an interesting family. Her mother kept a slot machine in the kitchen, and if you played and won, there would be an expectant silence until you returned the loot to the machine. Her father had been a coach at the University of Chicago and died by suicide when Ruth was 14.

Each summer, Ruth and her family left the heat of Chicago for northern Wisconsin, where they had a cottage. I followed, but slowly, stopping to pick cherries on the Door Peninsula along the shore of Lake Michigan. Learning that a final crop might be ready for picking on Washington Island, the northern tip of the county, I took the ferry there. Of course, Washington Island had a double bonus—cherries and Ruth's family's summer cottage.

We made a tentative peace while I picked cherries on the island, but it didn't last the summer. I wouldn't have stayed, except a young man on the cherry farm was running a small print shop in his barn with a press similar to my Challenge Gordon at BMC. I helped with the work, and he shared some of its income with me. We made the rounds of the three local taverns in his pickup on Saturday nights, and he would buy me a beer or two. It was a great island paradise. You could swim out on the pebbled beaches in those days, and, incredibly, drink the sparkling clear water as you swam. I even grew a beard for the first (and last) time. It was the kind of life to divert a troubled young man. A productive summer, however, it was not.

14.

THE IRON ROAD

RIDING THE RAILS, 1939

THE 1930S WERE DESPERATE TIMES. Thousands of teenagers took up riding freight trains—kids looking for work or adventure (or both), or to get away from cheerless Depression homes. I was none of the above. My initiation to freights was nothing romantic—I was a frightened fugitive from the Arkansas police.

On my April 1939 Easter vacation, I started out on a trip to Denver, where most of my family now resided (except for Pop, staying in exile in New York). A student, Leslie Katz, took me as far as Louisville. The next day, hitchhiking, I made it to Memphis. It was dark, misty, damp, and late when I arrived at the Mississippi River. My only chance for sleeping dry seemed to be under the bridge to Arkansas. Peering under the structure, I found that many homeless folk had made the same choice—living under the bridge like trolls. Their shelters ranged from elaborate cardboard and tin structures to "Hoover blankets" (sheets of newspaper). I had been warned that hobo jungles were dangerous places for young boys. Probably true, but not according to my personal experience. Fully clothed, I rolled up in my canvas shelter-half, completely ignored by my fellow citizens, and slept an uneasy, fitful night.

My first ride the next morning was deep into Arkansas, to a town whose name I should remember but don't. It didn't take long to learn the mood of this town. I had hardly adjusted my pack on my back when a city police car pulled up.

"Outta town, bum! Fast! We don't want the likes of you in this town!"

"Yes, sir. I was just goin'."

On the city-line marker stood an earlier arrival. He was wearing a cap, a dark jacket, and tight dark-purple pants. At his feet was a valise.

"Hi," I said, "not a very friendly town."

He was a man of very few words—in fact, none. He just jerked his thumb down the road for me to get. He struck me as a tough cookie, so I just nodded and went.

About a block from Tight Pants was another character, this one wearing a hard-straw summer hat, an old-style one called a "boater." Combined with a bow tie, it gave him a raffish air. At his feet sat a cheap suitcase. He was a super-friendly man in his late thirties, the opposite of Tight Pants.

"Boy, I'll tell you, it's slow this morning. Been here over an hour and no bites."

"An hour's nothing," was my professional estimate. "Not an over-friendly town, is it?"

"Where you headed?"

"Denver. And you?"

"Just west . . . to get away." And he launched into a tale about his wife and his economic woes. I had to cut him off: "Bunched up like this isn't goin' to get us west. I'll just move down a piece. Good luck!"

It was not only the town, but the whole state of Arkansas that proved hostile. Drivers passed us by with rigid faces and hard looks—a few shook their fists. I didn't dare go back into town. Fortunately, I had a small box of Velveeta cheese, which I ate for lunch. After an interminable 10 hours, it started to get dark. I walked up to Straw Hat, who suggested we pick up Tight Pants and brave the town for something to eat.

The three of us entered the bus station cafe. A newspaper rack near the door had great black headlines that resolved the mystery of the Arkansas hostility:

Hitchhiker Killer of Prominent
Little Rock Man on Trial Today

We exchanged grim looks. Seating ourselves at a table, we ordered hamburgers and a round of beer. Straw Hat, it turned out, was an undertaker's assistant, and he treated us to a long harangue on his profession. He pulled out a set of papers.

"With these documents I can go anywhere and get a job. So that's what I'm doing." He paused and sighed. "Had to get away from that bum who is my wife." As he whined about his wife, Tight Pants pulled out a pint bottle from his valise and generously splashed a dollop of what looked like gin into each of our glasses. After my first sip, I revised the gin to moonshine.

As we finished our beer (but not Straw Hat's sad stories), Tight Pants signaled the waitress for another round. "Hey, no more for me," I pleaded. "I'm just about dead broke." The last thing I wanted was more to drink.

I sat back and watched them empty the liquor bottle. I noticed that Tight Pants had a predatory eye on the activity around us. He seemed to be focused on a single man sitting at the counter. All at once, he jumped up and sat himself next to the man. Silent with us, he was buddy-buddy with his new friend, even to buying him a beer.

Straw Hat, becoming fatherly after his succession of drinks, patted me awkwardly on my shoulder. "Son, if you ever need clothes, go to an undertaker. The next of kin always brings the best suit for the deceased and leaves the clothes he died in. Undertakers are great folk; one might be happy to give you a suit."

He was solemnly informing me that people die, even in an economic depression, and that I should consider following his career, when we noticed Tight Pants and his new friend preparing to leave the cafe. Motioning Straw Hat to come along, he leaned over and whispered to me, "Watch the bags!"

I pulled out my road map, and for the hundredth time that day eyed the distance left in Arkansas. It didn't seem that far, and if worse came to worse, I guessed, I had enough for a bus ticket to Fort Smith. Suddenly the cafe door swung open, my two companions burst in, grabbed their bags, and indicated for me to follow. Well, I thought, things are looking up, I bet they talked the guy into giving us a ride.

Well, I guess not. Tight Pants took us off to one side of town, to the freight yards, where we climbed into an empty. He reached in his coat pocket and pulled out a thick wallet.

"I knew he was loaded when he pulled out this sucker full of bills." He chortled and started to divide the contents into three parts.

"No, no!" I protested. "It's all yours. I didn't do anything to help!"

"You were the lookout," he said.

"You watched the bags," agreed Straw Hat.

"But I didn't even know what was goin' on!"

"To hell with him," said Tight Pants, "two's better'n three." As he counted it out, it did seem like a goodly sum.

Satisfied, Tight Pants laid his head against his valise and promptly fell asleep.

"Boy, oh boy," drooled Straw Hat, feeling his liquor, "that was sure easy. I like that thievin'. I'm goin' out to do some more thievin'. I like that thievin.'"

"You'll just get picked up. Stay here." I urged.

As he started to slide out the door, I tried to grab him, but he got away, staggering up the road and chuckling to himself.

Wow! I thought, best to get the hell out of here. The town had a brick factory—across the tracks were large piles of the stuff. It started to drizzle, so I snugged down between two brick piles, covered myself with my shelter-half, and tried to think.

Straw Hat was sure to get picked up, and they'd come looking for his accomplices. Arkansas chain gangs are said to be no fun. I remembered Paul Muni running through the swamps, dogs baying at his heels. I couldn't hitchhike out tomorrow or even take the bus. But I was innocent, I didn't do anything! HITCHHIKER MURDERS BUSINESSMAN. Not the right climate for a hitchhiker to plead innocence. I would be conspicuous walking . . . maybe just at night on the railroad tracks? I felt paralyzed. That small distance on the road map now loomed interminable. This being a freight yard, my only hope would be for a train to stop here before dawn. Feeling nauseated, I pulled bricks down on top of my shelter-half and, like a sick brick turtle, awaited events.

They were not long in coming. I peered out through a slot in my carapace to see my morning friend, the unfriendly police car, come bounding down the dirt road—with Straw Hat and a cop seated in the back seat. They stopped by the empty and hauled out a struggling Tight Pants. With a swivel light on the side of the windshield, they swept the freight yard. I ducked back under the sweeps as they flooded over my canvas and hoped that my trembling wasn't shaking the bricks piled over me. Following a long period of uneasy silence, I must have fallen asleep.

Awakened by the heavy rumble of a train pulling into the siding, I peered anxiously out into the yard. No activity. I crawled out, shaking my shelter-half, and looked things over. The freight backed into a line of flat-cars loaded with brick. One of the train's cars carried lumber, the top load overlapping the lower planks to form a neat little cave. I lurked in the darkness until the train started moving, then pulled myself up into the cave. Being at the end of the car, I was spared most of the wet as we moved along—but not all. I was soon wet to the skin but happy to be out of that unhappy town. Time passed and we pulled into a large railroad yard.

I arrived in Fort Smith about 3 a.m.—a dismal hour in a dismal town. Toiling up a hill in a poor commercial section, I spotted a small sign hanging from a second-story window: ROOMS. Weary, cold, wet, and on edge from the stress of the night, I realized that for a small fee I could rent a warm, dry room. The impulse was overwhelming, and I decided to splurge. Between two dingy storefronts, a narrow flight of steps led to a narrow corridor of doors. On a small table sat a register and a bell marked, RING FOR LANDLADY. Always shy, I hesitated to ring the bell at that hour, but fatigue brought my hand down on the plunger. The bell was loud but brought no action. Twice again. Nothing. After the third try, I heard a faint stir behind the nearest door, and out lurched a woman, her sole clothing a black slip. Sleep had undone whatever niceties she may have been able to muster in the daytime.

"I'm looking for a room," I mumbled.

"Right down here," she muttered back. Leading me down the corridor, she opened a door and we entered the room. I put my wet pack down in a corner and dashed into the facilities for a long pee. When I came out, to my surprise, the landlady was still there, trying to rake her tangled hair with her fingers.

"How much is the room? Do you want the money now?"

"Naw," she simpered. "I thought we could have some fun first. Only $5 and you can keep the bed the rest of the night."

It belatedly dawned on me that ROOMS might not mean "hotel." ROOMS could mean by the hour as well as by the day—bring your own friend or share it with the landlady.

I groaned. "Please, lady, I'm too tired. I need the sleep."

"Hey, come on, let's have some fun! You'll see . . . . I'll get you goin' in no time." Coyly, she came to put her arms around me.

"Please," I whined, starting to move her out of the room. Her voice became more strident. We struggled, teetering in and out of the doorway.

"Don't be like that! Let me show you a good time!"

We were now in mortal combat, edging out into the hall.

"Hey!" she screamed at me. "Let go a me! Don't ya push me!"

I heard the plod of heavy feet—it was a weighty man, clad for battle in winter drawers.

"Wot's goin' on here?" he demanded.

"He's pushing me out of the room," she cried.

"No, no, it's just that I have a bad cold and hate to spread it to this nice lady," I said, pulling out a wet handkerchief.

"Ah, come to bed, Gladys," he soothed. "Can't ya see this kid's in a bad way?"

The door had a key, so I turned it quickly and went to the bed. There was a suspicious sag in the middle of the mattress, which on closer inspection revealed a large burn hole, which on even closer inspection revealed a colony of small black dots—bedbugs! Was this the bed I fought the landlady for? But I was exhausted. I hung my clothes on the shower rod with wire coat hangers, put my pack into the bathtub, joined it, and fell asleep. My version of fun!

[*Ecological Note:* The bedbug is a camp follower of human poverty. About the size of a tick, it is black and so flat that it is difficult to kill. My technique was to place one between the nails of my thumbs and rotate them under full pressure. Even then, bedbugs are obnoxious, exuding a nasty pungent smell that is hard to wash off. They can insert themselves in the seams of mattresses and under loose wallpaper. Bronx oral history has it that, dehydrated, they can live for years—coming to life only with the proximity of a warm body. A bloodsucker, it extracts a minute quantity of blood, leaving a red, itchy reminder of the deed.

[In the pursuit of natural history (in these days of my retirement), I find the bedbug's reputation is not redeemed. In real life, the bedbug originally lived on bats and probably other denizens of dark, dank habitats, so it was an easy transition to fleabag human hangouts. The male bedbug's penis is a sharp instrument that, even though the female seems to have a normal genital opening, he stabs directly into her abdomen to ejaculate. The act is known to science as "traumatic copulation." To me, it is a form of rape that is better left unknown to the general run of humankind.]

Later that morning, stiff and sore, I could hardly climb out of the tub. First scrutinizing as many of my body parts as possible, I carefully shook out each piece of clothing as I donned it. Ready, I picked up my pack and stepped out into the corridor. Down the hall, I heard chatter and peeked into a kitchen, where Gladys and her man were eating breakfast.

"I'm leaving now. What do I owe you for the room?"

"Come on in! Sit down, have some breakfast," invited the man. "How's ya cold, ya sound better."

"Yeah," said Gladys, eyeing my pack. "Where yer goin'? You're pretty young to be on the bum. Breakfast won't cost ya nothin'. The room is $2."

I looked at my landlady as I ate my eggs and toast. Even with her hair combed, she was rough stuff—but everybody needs to make a living.

The animosities of Arkansas didn't seem to cross the borders of her neighboring states, and toward evening I reached Amarillo, in the Texas Panhandle. This was high-plains country, with few barriers to the sweeping cold April winds. Barbed-wire fences, lined with wind-blown tumbleweed, edged the open terrain. I could see no friendly bushes to den behind. In the gathering dusk, it felt bleak and unfriendly.

Traffic was slow on this road, which led north to New Mexico and Colorado. A freight train, loading cattle cars, was backing and filling across the highway. It gradually came to my attention that among the assorted cars of the train was an empty with its door partially open. At the next opportunity, I climbed into the empty.

Crossing the plain, out of the wind, I stayed snug and comfortable—until we started the long, slow crawl up to the Raton Pass. Then it got cold . . . colder . . . coldest. I stuffed some cardboard into the door track and closed it as far as I could without locking it. Wrapped up in my blanket and shelter-half, I shivered through the night. The next morning, we arrived in Trinidad, Colorado, and the train stopped in the yards. Gathering up my stuff, I slipped out the door and into town.

After hot coffee and a roll, life improved, and I hastened back to catch my train. On the yard edge, a knot of men milled around, each carrying rolled-up blankets tied with rope. I reasoned they were mostly Mexican itinerant workers riding the train north. Figuring that situation looked like trouble, I walked several blocks up the tracks.

When the train presented itself at the yard limits, ready to go, they all piled into my empty, unmolested. The train then started down the track, picking up momentum as it came to me. With my pack on my back, I ran alongside the open door. Reaching up, I grabbed the edge of the car and hoisted myself up on my belly. To my horror, I was unable to pull myself into the car—something was holding me back. As I struggled, I visualized the run of iron switch flags that lined the track but couldn't seem to pull in my kicking legs. Then I realized that I was held back by a strap on my pack that had clipped on some mechanism of the door latch. Suddenly someone leaned over me, cut the strap, and pulled me into the car. WOW!

My savior turned out to be a grizzled old man who sat and glared at me as if I were some kind of obnoxious bug.

"Ya stupid kid," he said in disgust, "do things like that an' ya not gonna live long!"

"I sure thank you," I ventured contritely.

"What the hell wer' ya doin' gettin' in a boxcar on the fly?"

"I saw all the Mexicans waiting within the yard limits for the train and thought there would be trouble."

"Damn," he said, "best ya stayed wid 'em. They's on to pick sugar beets in Nebraska. Railroads let workers ride when there's crops to be picked down the line. Where ya goin'?" he growled, thawing a little.

"Denver."

"Well, guess I got time to teach ya some about ridin' trains."

As he lectured me, the closed boxcar filled with a harsh, acrid smoke, which befuddled me somewhat, but I hung on to his every word as though my life depended on it—which, of course, it did. (I found out later that the Mexicans were smoking marijuana.)

"First, don't carry ya bindle on ya back, carry it on ya shoulder where ya can get shut of it in a hurry," he admonished me. "Nothin' in it is worth ya life. With your legs kicking out like that, ya could have lost them on a gate. I once saw a man get off a train when it was goin' too fast. He ran a few steps and flew into a short switch—it surely killed him."

"When I was yer age, son, we had no luxury fer ridin' boxcars—we had to ride under the boxcars on the tie-rods. In those days, the whole freight crew—brakeman, conductor, fireman—all had to keep hoboes off the trains or it was their ass. It weren't no bed of roses. Today, yard Bulls do the job and most crews don't care if you ride, long as you don't wreck equipment. Young'uns like to race along the top of the boxcars and yell at women at the crossings. Make asses of themselves. Gets the train crew against 'em."

(When the Bonus Marchers went to Washington in 1932, whole families rode the freights. Sympathetic railroad men would, unbeknownst to the companies, add extra cars on the freight trains. Even the railroad detectives, the Bulls, turned their backs—and that's hard to believe!)

By the time we detrained in Denver, I had learned as much about the old man as I did about riding freights and had gained a warm affection for him. I could sense the raw, aching void he carried with him on his endless travels. In Denver, the car emptied quickly, and the old man threaded me through the complex maze of the yard. At the yard limits, he flashed me a quick last look and turned back into the maze. The parting was abrupt and final—one didn't exchange calling cards with a rootless hobo!

When I left Denver to return to college, Mom, Mary, Charlie, and Hedy drove me 100 or so miles toward Kansas City. The family left me on the road but just went back a short piece to wait and see if I got a ride. Mom's influence, to be sure! This made me very uncomfortable—it sometimes took hours to get a ride. Fortunately, a farm truck pulled up promptly, and I was off. I looked back—we were not being followed.

I got to Kansas City by nightfall and headed for the railroad yards. By sheer luck, I found a red-ball express freight and arrived in St. Louis by morning. This was a first test of my theory that by hitching the road in the daytime and beating my way on the freights at night, I could do as well as, or better than, Greyhound schedules.

The next night, wandering around the Louisville yards, I was well aware of the dangers cited by the old hobo. I listened intently for the sound of a car knocker.

"In the yards," he had told me, " your danger comes from white light—battery lamps carried by Bulls. Yard workers carry yellow coal-oil lamps. If you want to know about a train, your best bet is the car knocker. In the dark, you can hear the tap as he checks for cracked wheels and dry journals."

(Each car axle has a journal box stuffed with oil-soaked cotton waste. This is vital to keep the axle from overheating and seizing up. I once was in a boxcar with a flat wheel. It humped and screeched, shaking us like dried peas in a can.)

Seeing a yellow lantern and the comforting sounds of a car knocker, I ran up to walk behind him. I cleared my throat.

"Good evening," I ventured.

"Grunt," he replied.

"Is this freight going to Danville?"

"Grunt."

"Any empties?"

Reluctantly: "The middle of the drag, after the tankers."

"When does she leave?"

He turned to look at me. "They've finished makin' her up—she'll leave about midnight. You'll hear the commotion. Stay outta sight, son, until you hear the highball; we got a real mean Bull in these yards." He waved his lantern in farewell and turned back to work.

Overwhelmed by his burst of loquacity, I stuttered my thanks. I hid in a cul-de-sac made by piles of creosoted railroad ties. I sat up and came to full alert when a deep-throated road locomotive started to dialog with the tiny tooters. When I heard the two blasts of the highball, I jumped up and ran out on the tracks. Keeping a wary eye out for white lights, I raced beside the empty, threw my pack into the car, and boarded—I felt professional, a credit to my old hobo mentor.

I heard the farewell toot of the mule as the engineer turned up the power, and a series of jerks and clanks ran through the train. I have heard that with the slack between cars, the engine of a freight moves 60 feet before the last car moves at all. I can imagine how long it took such a train to stop!

The only one in the car, I pulled the door almost closed, jammed some cardboard into the slide, rolled up in my shelter-half, and slept. The next thing I knew, a bright white light was shining in my eyes, and painful blows rapped against the soles of my feet. In a stupor, I sat up.

"Get ya ass out this boxcar, ya goddamned bum!" It was a loud-voiced Bull pounding my feet with a nightstick.

I gathered up my shelter-half, picked up my pack, and slid out the door. The Bull grabbed me and marched me past the roundhouse and out of the yard, muttering threats as we went. With a final push that almost floored me, he snarled: "And stay out of my yard, you prick!"

From the outside I stood, indecisive, listening to a train making up. A couple of men were leaving the yard. I hesitated and then asked, "Is this Danville?"

"It is."

"Isn't this a junction point for Knoxville?"

"It is."

"Where would I catch a freight going south?"

"Well, young man, that train being made up is heading for Knoxville."

I thanked them and hid in a dark patch of the roundhouse until I heard the compelling highball signal. As I sneaked back into the yard and made for the train, I ran instead into the strong arm of the law. He grabbed me again by my collar and started to shake me violently: "I told you to stay out of my patch, you motherfucker!"

He dropped my shirt and let fly with his fist, knocking me down. I attempted to get up and run. He pushed me down again, scraping my face on the sharp cinders. The train was moving past us, and I got up. Running, I managed to dodge under his arm and clutched the rung of the nearest car. As the uproar behind me rapidly receded, I climbed the ladder. Of all the bad luck, it was a coal gondola! The coal was heaped high in the car, and I figured that the only way I could ride it without sliding off while I slept would be to burrow into it—which I did. Then I settled down to take stock of myself. Fortunately, I had managed to keep my pack . My face was a mess. Nothing serious, but the scraped and weeping forehead, nose, and chin were thick with coal dust and would make a hideous scab.

We were getting into the Kentucky mountains, and the slow going through tunnels was nauseating. Thick yellow smoke eddied around me, and I choked until we finally exited. I was not very happy! At one point, we were shunted off on a siding to wait for a passenger train—which stopped with the locomotive and tender just across from my dirty burrow. I decided on a travel upgrade, dashed across the tracks, and climbed a ladder on the center rear of the tender. With a tolling bell and an eerie, long-drawn-out whistle, we were off to Knoxville.

Afraid of falling asleep, I attached my remaining pack strap to the ladder. When my arms got tired of holding on, I could lean back and let my pack hold me on. After the slow freight, it was exhilarating to go flying through the countryside accompanied by long, mournful whistles and the tolling of crossing bells. But my satisfaction didn't last. I discovered that standing on a rung was bad for my arches; they soon started to ache painfully. I hoped that when we stopped for water, I could find a better place on the train.

Behind the tender was a "deadhead"—part passenger and part baggage car, it was usually empty, hence its name. Where it attached to the tender was a narrow metal ledge, which I eyed longingly. What I didn't know, but was soon to find out, was that passenger trains didn't stop for water.

Speeding down the road, I suddenly got a shocking cold shower. The train was taking water on the fly—scooping it up from a trough in the middle of the tracks. Had I been on the deadhead ledge, I would have gotten the full force of the water head-on. Even though this was the South, it was April in the Kentucky mountains, and I shivered for hours. I still gasped in the yellow smoke and cinders, but for a shorter time as we thundered through the tunnels. I reckoned I still had a lot to learn about riding trains.

In Knoxville, Tennessee (which was to be my future home), I walked down a dirt road along the tracks, looking for the yard limits. Hungry after hanging onto the passenger train nonstop, I stopped at a small store to buy a loaf of bread and sliced bologna.

Just past the yard-limit fence, light flickered in a deep gully. I walked over and looked down in total surprise. A 14-foot-long fire made of parallel heavy trestle ties was filled with glowing coal. Hoboes were sprawled before the fire on corrugated car liners. They looked at me with about as much surprise as I did at them . . . a young boy with a bindle hanging from his shoulder, his face black with scab!

One of the men broke the silence: "If you're waiting for a train, come on down. We're all just bindle stiffs here."

I slid down the bank to the edge of the fire and sat next to the man who spoke. Reasonably well dressed—at least no visible holes or patches—he was working with pliers and wire. On the other side of me were three men whose clothes proclaimed them real hoboes. One handed me a roll of corrugated cardboard and helped me unroll it on the bank. Down the long fire, by themselves, were two bums who looked me over but didn't speak. Straddling the ties were a series of large, steaming #10 restaurant tins filled with eggs and coffee. Off to the side was an egg crate being used as a shelf—with tin-can cups, twists of paper filled with sugar, and several paper bags. It certainly looked a neat and tidy camp. A hobo Hilton.

I made myself a sandwich and added the remainder of my bread and bologna to the top of the crate. One of the men rinsed out a tin can with boiling water, filled it with hot coffee, and offered it to me. Another added a twist of sugar and a spoon. A third shoved a large #10 tin down the long fire to me. It was filled with hard-boiled eggs. I was going to miss my bread before I got over the Smokies to school, so I helped myself to a half-dozen eggs. The railroad, in its largesse, seemed to have furnished these sterling knights of the road not only corrugated liners from furniture vans but valuable trestle ties, coal, and a whole crate of eggs.

The man sitting next to me was twisting wire loops into baskets. They were so neatly hinged that the basket held any shape you wanted to twist it into. The others called him, with some respect, the Crafter.

"I sell them mostly at fairs, where folks use them to display fruit, vegetables and," he grinned, "eggs."

After we sat for a spell, he turned to me. "When hoboes come by here riding coal gondolas, they drop off lump coal as fast as they can. Let's go get some."

We picked up gunnysacks and went down the track together.

"You know, kid," confided the Crafter, "you done good bringing that punk and horse cock [bread and baloney] to the jungle. 'Boes hate buzzards who come, take what others provide, and make no attempt to contribute. I brought you out here to tell you something. The 'boes nearest us are right guys, mostly they're boomers, looking for jobs, but watch out for the two sittin' apart, they're real hard cases. Given a chance, they'll be after your dough or yer ass—or both. At a jungle like this, they usually drink Sterno."

"Sterno?"

"Yeah, canned heat, wax soaked with alcohol. They strain it through a loaf of bread or a handkerchief—it makes them wild."

Back at the jungle, I'm asked.

"How'd ya smash yer face, Kid?"

I told them about my experience in Danville.

"Typical Bull . . . seldom arrest ya jest fer trespassing, but watch out, they can be bullies. Seen 'em beat hoboes half to death."

"Hey," said another, "remember that bastard in Hudson, Ohio? Well . . . . "

After a series of tales about bastard Bulls, we quieted down for a while, listening to the conversation between the yard engines. My neighbors interpreted for me.

"The little yard engines are kind of mules. They shunt the freight cars around, puttin' 'em like ducks in a row. They chatter to keep in touch so's not to wreck each other. Then, when a string is strung and it's time to go, they tootle for the road hog. They call back and forth for a while; the big road engine hooks up and sits waiting for orders. When you hear the high-ball signal, two long blasts, you gets up ready to ride 'em."

"How do you know which is yours?"

"Well, in this case only two lines peel off going east—one goes somewhat northeast, through Bristol, Virginia, and the other directly east through Asheville."

"I'm going to Asheville," I declared. "How do I know which is which?"

"The locomotive light is like a snout that sticks out and shows the engine route number. Yours will be 5462. The Virginia number is 5463. We all wait at the yard limits, catch the number as it sweeps by, and, if it's ours, board it."

"I almost got killed doing that in Colorado," I said, and told them the story.

They laughed. "A lot of the old-timers are just like your hobo," declared the Crafter. "They're proud of their experience and enjoy teaching. Most of us have never had to ride the rods under the cars. It's damn dirty and dangerous. He was right—you don't jump boxcars when the train has hit any speed."

"The engineer can't speed his train over 15 mph," chimed in another 'bo, "until he leaves the yard. Then he pulls the throttle wide open and starts ballin' the jack, so ya better set yerself to grab on real quick. We're right at the yard limits. You'd be a lot safer tonight just reaching for a rung, any rung."

But not just any rung, according to my old hobo mentor: "Ya got two ladders on the sides of boxcars. Always grab the front one. If ya get slammed against the side 'n break loose, you'll be pushed away. Ya grabs the rear rungs and you hit the edge and can drop between the cars. I've seen it. Young kids, mostly."

"Don't wait too long," said another. "It picks up speed fast."

"We don't know what the make-up of this string is goin' to be, but some guys'll race down the top walkway looking for a reefer. I wouldn't advise it in the dark. I doubt if they'll be any empties. It'll be mostly coal, I reckon."

Coal! I groaned. Well, I couldn't get any dirtier.

At one point, the two hard cases picked up sacks and motioned to me to join them.

The Crafter, quickly: "He's done his share."

Another of my friendlies: "He's just a kid—let 'im rest."

They sat back down and glared at us.

Things were quiet around the fire until we heard a dialog between the big road engine and the small yard mules.

"If yer goin', best get ready!"

A few of the men rolled up their bindles, others just moved a little closer to the fire—they were staying.

Last-minute advice: "What did you say the engine number for North Carolina was?" I asked.

"5462," came the answer. "If you find yerself going through Bull's Gap, yer on the wrong train."

The two loud blasts of the highball were unequivocal and arrogant. Then the first charges of steam pushed through the pistons; next came the crash and clang of the chain reaction of cars as the engineer took up slack. I can visualize the big locomotive, straining hard, pouring sand on the tracks to give it traction. Suddenly a dazzling white beam of light pierced the dark—the great engine was breaking the barrier of the yard limits, volcanoes of smoke pouring out of its stack. I was enveloped in a whirl of hot steam as the huge locomotive barreled by, with its eight drivers straining for speed. I panicked. Was that 62 or 63? Huge black coal gondolas flashed by. Take it . . . take it? Virginia or North Carolina? . . . . Just take it! I raced along the front end of a car, reaching for a rung, and then my hands closed on it. Yanked off my feet, I hung tight, my feet groping for the bottom rung of the ladder. I was gasping like a fish out of water. When my heart stopped pounding, I crawled up onto the coal and dug in—by now a veteran of the moving coal pile.

We went through the outskirts of Newport and started the long, tedious ascent of the Smokies. Years later, I learned about Newport—the moonshine capitol of Tennessee. During the war, the moonshiners required so much sugar that a business grew up in counterfeiting sugar coupons. When I was organizing furniture workers in nearby Morristown, many of my recruits still had souped-up cars with heavy springs. They gleefully boasted about transporting moonshine out of Newport, outrunning the revenuers.

On the train, I had a preview of this illicit activity. The train, with a second engine added to push, was manfully and very slowly pushing the long string up the incline. Suddenly a figure appeared on the ladder, carrying a large, rectangular burlap sack. Dismayed at seeing me in the coal, he almost went back down. He hesitated a moment and then put his sack on the coal pile as far from me as he could reach. He quickly dropped back down the ladder. Instant alert! Was he a saboteur blowing up the train? I peered over the edge and there he was—hanging off the bottom rung and reaching for a second gunnysack he had stashed up the track. Back on top, he glared at me with a long, hard look. Tentatively I offered, "Hi," but got no response. He dragged the sacks down the length of the gondola, burying them in the coal and casting glares at me as he worked. I turned away from him and pretended to sleep. It dawned on me that this could be a moonshine delivery to Asheville, and I'd better not appear to be too interested.

The next morning, with the train slowing down for its entrance into Asheville, my bootlegger friend carefully dropped his sacks in some dense bushes along the tracks and jumped off. He had done this before! When I was organizing in Morristown, some of the workers enlightened me about the man's sacks. Each sack contained five one-gallon cans of "white lightning," tightly corked and strapped together. Packed in the burlap "tow sacks," they make an easy bundle to handle.

With the train slowing and my pack slung over one shoulder, I lowered myself down the ladder and braced myself—one hand gripping the bottom rung, the other gripping the next rung up. As we passed a road intersection, I lowered my feet to touch the paving. Running as fast as the train was moving, I slipped my pack free and let go of the train. Just as I picked up my pack, congratulating myself on the performance, a hand clutched my jacket. It was a railroad Bull whose car had been cut off at the grade crossing by the train.

At the train station, I was searched (for railroad property? I'd already eaten the eggs!), grilled, and finally released with the admonition never to trespass again. But I was stone broke, and with my black, scabby face, hitchhiking was out. I hiked out to the yards, hoping to grab the local train that passed Black Mountain. But the yard was huge, with no discernible definition of its limits. I was foolishly wandering around the yard when a car raced toward me, a man on the running board holding a pistol pointed at me. He yelled at me to stop. I stopped.

At the station, there was immediate recognition. This time, I was handled more roughly, fingerprinted, photographed, and told I was to be held for trial. In my first collar, I kept hidden my tenure at Black Mountain College, feeling the college didn't need criminal students to add to its reputation in certain quarters. But this time, faced with building roads for fellow students to travel on, I broke down and confessed. Poor Ted Dreier had to drive in to fetch me. Most humiliating!

Later I learned that some faculty members looked down on my "bumming," thinking it some kind of self-indulgence. This, however, was still the Depression—riding trains for me was a necessity if I wanted to visit my family living in Denver.

During this time, some two million homeless people were on the move—hitchhiking, riding freight trains, sleeping in hobo jungles, flophouses, and jails. These were not bums but the flotsam of the Depression.

Yet I couldn't deny the fascinating adventure of hobo travel—the thrill of mastering the basic rules of the road and exchanging experiences with other travelers. It was the age of steam, and I responded to the powerful thrust of these great engines, the hiss of hot steam, the lonesome wail of the steam-driven whistles. I had no idea that in a few years the steam railroad would be nearly banished from the planet.

Still, I had no trouble pledging: No More Bumming on the Southern! In fact, when I bought my first train ticket at the age of 24, it was on the Southern Railroad. Buying a ticket, I felt, was a waste of talents, but I was going from Knoxville to my draft board in New York, and my country was calling.

15.

PRINTING, 1940-41

SUMMER 1940

WHILE IT WAS UNDERSTOOD THAT I WOULD NOT RETURN to the college for a fourth year, that summer I stayed on to help move Lee Hall to Lake Eden. Classes at Lake Eden were to open in the fall of 1940, and the pace of construction was intense. Part of the time, I drove a dump truck. A young student (from California, I believe) was nimbly scooping out space around one end of the main building with a tractor frontloader. I was hauling it away to fill in a swampy area on the lake's edge. Occasionally I would back too far over my last dump and bog down. Young California would come and, with obvious disdain, pull me out. Even so, I felt I earned my room and board.

LATE FALL 1940 AND WINTER 1941: MY HOLY GRAIL

From Raleigh Archives Notes:

Mangold: He is really productive about the printing, and puts in a great deal of time. He seems to be happier when he is doing manual things.

Albers: Printing seems to have a stabilizing influence on him.

The Black Mountain College faculty was mostly pro-war, and I felt they were wrong about that, but they were certainly were right about my affection for printing. I knew I couldn't make my living by writing, so I pinned my hopes on a high-paying job in the printing trades. The AFL (American

Federation of Labor) is a federation of craft unions. In the printing trades, the union furnishes the skilled workers required by the print shops. The jobs, as they became available, were posted on a board in the union hall. Since the wage scale was very high, my reasoning was that I would work six months or so, bank the surplus money, and then quit to write. When I got hungry, I could go to any major commercial area and check the job boards. An AFL union card in the printing trades became my Holy Grail.

In the fall of 1940, after my stint at Highlander, I returned to New York and went to work for the Columbus Printing Company. My job was to set 6-point type—the type they use on the back of transfers and other documents, where the "small print" is not really meant to be read. Six-point type is *not* easy to handle, which is precisely why I was given the job! I worked at nonunion wages, although this was supposed to be a union shop.

Each letter of 6-point type is marked with a notch that tells you how to place it in your composing stick. Thus, *b-d-p-q* would be impossible to decipher without the notch to tell you which side is up. Different type fonts have different notches. But with 6-point type, even the notch is difficult to decipher. You can understand how careful I was not to "pie" (mess up) this type.

After a few months of this tedious work, I applied for a union card in the Typographers Union AFL. The man behind the desk looked me over and grunted, "Cost ya a thousand bucks for the initiation fee."

[Gulp!] "I can do it." (Yeah, maybe.)

"Then ya gotta go through a seven-year apprentice program to learn the trade."

"But I already know the trade. I'm working now in a shop setting type. Maybe a year's apprenticeship, to fill in the blanks?"

"Nope—rule is seven years. Do you have a sponsor?"

By this he meant you don't have a snowball's chance in hell unless your father was in the union or some big shot took a personal interest. This was and is the nature of many AFL craft unions. They covered certain crafts in factories where most of the other workers worked unorganized. Organizing only the few skilled craftsmen in a factory is precisely what led to the birth of the CIO (Congress of Industrial Organizations).

Sue Spayth was a fellow student at Black Mountain College. She was also a scholarship student and had received National Youth Authority assistance. Her father, George Spayth, wrote about Sue in his autobiography, *It Was Fun the Hard Way*. (I wish I had read this book when I worked for George Spayth. He was an extremely interesting man, and we had many things in common . . . such as riding freight trains.)

> My daughter, Sue, who resigned from her position on the editorial staff of *Life* magazine to work on various newspapers in the vicinity of army camps where her husband [Jerry Wolpert, a fellow student at BMC] was stationed, developed her talents and became a top-notch writer. When her husband, a college teacher, died of polio, leaving her with two infant sons, she joined my staff and for five years handled the news department with distinction, winning a Press Association plaque as the leading columnist in the state.

SPAYTH PRESS, 1941

On Sue's recommendation, I went to work for George Spayth in Dunellen, New Jersey, as a pressman on his union-label newspaper. Newspaper? Four newspapers!

> *The Dunellen Weekly Call*
> *The Piscataway Chronicle*
> *The South Plainfield Chronicle*
> *The Middlesex Mirror*

I don't remember the total circulation of each paper, but they were relatively small townships in those days—possibly a total run of about five thousand. Actually, printing four newspapers was not as daunting a task as it might seem. The *Weekly Call* had the greatest circulation, and after I ran the prescribed number, I would stop the press, open the chase, and substitute a masthead block and an editorial-page block for the *Piscataway Chronicle* . . . and so on. Much of the papers' income came from official county legal notices and real estate sales. Mrs. Spayth would write up social notes from all the townships in the same paper.

Press days were Wednesdays and Thursday morning. I had an arrangement with Spayth: I would print the newspapers, plus a minimum of $500 worth of job printing, and go home to New York City Thursday afternoon. It was a good deal, but what I really was after was my card in the AFL Printing Pressman's Union.

I boarded at the Spayth house; in the backyard, in a large garage-like building, was the print shop. I had arrived at a fortunate time, at least for me. The job press had broken down, and the repairman had just arrived to set it right. The press, called the "Little Giant," was completely automatic—after you gave it the proper instructions. The repairman was a garrulous type, apparently pleased to have me hang over his shoulder asking questions.

The Little Giant made my Challenger Gordon look like a prehistoric oaf. It was a real nitpicker of a machine, but when properly tuned, it had the virtue of running unattended. I was in awe of it and learned to love it. I saved long runs for newspaper printing days, where I could watch it from the elevated platform of the big Cranston Press.

The Cranston was an old-time, hand-fed newspaper press. It had a huge drum, and a long flatbed that contained the type. It was a monster and, after some perfunctory instruction from Mr. Spayth, I was left to its mercy. Mercy, with that machine, however, was in short supply. I had my troubles.

I stood high on a platform above the press, a ream of large newsprint paper on the table before me. With a stick of smooth, hard wood, I raked the paper in a spread, like a gambler with a deck of cards. As the drum rotated, I lifted a sheet to get air under it, which floated it down to grippers that snapped it up against the drum and down to the type. As the bed slid back to be re-inked, a pair of thin hardwood rods, called the "fly," would rise from the bed, engage the paper, rotate it off the type, and gently swing it through the air to deposit it in a bin. The bin opened its sides to receive the paper and then closed to jog it into a neat stack . . . except, of course, when it didn't.

On a cold, dry winter day, when static electricity rippled through your combed hair, the fly would deposit the paper in the bin and then refuse to leave it. I tried grounding the fly to the press with strings of Christmas tinsel. This would work—sometimes. In the back of the shop, I had collected a stack of flat Coke boxes. These I laid around the shop, a boardwalk to key work junctures—the Linotype machine, the Little Giant, and the Cranston. Then I would flood the concrete shop floor. This was the ultimate solution. But even then, although the fly reluctantly released the paper, the jogger never made neat stacks, which meant a messy pile of newsprint when I had to print the reverse side.

The press was motivated by a large electric motor whose speed was governed by a rheostat. The rheostat speed was adjusted by hitting a stiff lever with a rawhide mallet. When everything was functioning well, and I felt sharp enough, I would wallop the lever to make the press fly. It was exhilarating to see how fast you could go, floating those great sheets of newsprint into the grippers. The tin building would start to tremble, and when Spayth was in his office, he would dash out, grab the mallet, and whack it back to a more staid speed. He never said a word to me, just threw down the mallet and dashed off. Of course he was right—it was an old press and the only one he had. By my side was a yard-long iron brake, and if you missed the grippers, it could never stop the press in time. Then there was a long wash-up job, cleaning off the ink with rags and kerosene. Speed kills!

Dunellen had a large shop that printed *Time/Life* publications and a large volume of comic books. It was a union shop, and I showed up one day with my "How about a union card?" routine. They wouldn't even give me the time of day, and when I pointed out that my paper carried the union label, they sent a reluctant old man to take my job. Spayth set up a blistering denunciation of the local, ran off a proof sheet, and sent it over to the union office. Nothing more was ever said, the denunciation was never published, but I was no nearer to my goal. But . . . if the Holy Grail had been so easy to achieve, it wouldn't have been so legendary.

16.

THE LABOR MOVEMENT

EARLY FALL 1940

I FIRST BECAME ACQUAINTED WITH HIGHLANDER FOLK SCHOOL through the Work Camp movement during my 1938 summer at Black Mountain College. More than a little intrigued by Highlander, I had written Myles Horton, the director, about attending a six-week workers' session the fall of 1940. He replied, "We don't usually do it, but we have a rule allowing one non-union, intellectual student at our labor sessions and are pleased to invite you to join us this fall."

I discovered later that Myles made up rules for pretty much anything he wanted to do. I had a good learning experience at Black Mountain College, but I reckon Highlander was closer to my needs at that time. It was just a hop, skip, and jump from where I was working at Black Mountain to Highlander in Monteagle, Tennessee, and I reported promptly as a student to study the labor movement.

There were about 25 students; many were there because they were out on strike—the only way they could get off for six weeks. They were rank-and-file leaders of newly formed locals and without experience. Needless to say, they were all vitally interested in getting the most out of the training program.

The first student I met was a teenager registering students as they arrived. She was from Mobile, Alabama, and her father was active in organizing the shipyard workers for the CIO. When Myles Horton, the Highlander Folk School director, visited Mobile, he signed her up for this term.

According to Woody Guthrie, "Life is the music, and the people are the song." By 1939, Highlander was known throughout the Southern labor movement as "a singing school." Zilphia Horton, Myles's wife, was the heart and soul of music at Highlander. Copies of Zilphia's *Labor Songbook* were passed around after the dinner dishes had been cleared away. Picking up her accordion, she would lead us in rousing union songs. I don't think she brought out any new talents in me, but I bellowed out the labor songs with outstanding enthusiasm, if not musical aptitude! She had collected these songs on picket lines and from students and activists who came to the school. Each union term contributed new lines and new songs to the book.

Zilphia set us up for serious role-playing, and we did numerous improvisations. Since I was the only student not in a union and not on strike, the class thought it great fun to cast me as the villain—boss . . . shop foreman . . . scab. It was good typecasting, I never won an Oscar, but I got to be good at it, and I really made them work hard to get the better of me. The little dramas we put on were in no need of imaginative speculation— they came directly from the students' lives.

Below are excerpts from what the students wrote in their year-book, *I Know What It Means:*

United Mine Workers of America, Appellee, Virginia

I am one of seven children. My father died when I was entering high school for my last year. I went to work as a counter in a paper mill. My father worked most of his life in this paper plant but never received a promotion because he was for the working class and got along with them in a humane fashion. The working conditions here and the rate of pay were two reasons that usually get people into unions and helped me want to join.

I have only been in the CIO union about seven months, and am holding the office of Vice-President. My reasons for attending the Highlander Folk School are to learn more about unions. I hope to see the day when every industry in the South will be organized.

*****

Boot and Shoe Workers, Lynchburg, Virginia

I know what it means to have the government take my father's hoe away because he could not pay the tax on the land and had to move to the city without any hopes of a job.

I know what it means to get a job in a shoe factory at the age of seventeen and dream of making enough money to help my family, and then to find my health would not allow me to stand under the strain of working ten hours a day and then go home and do the house work.

I know what it means to have my seventeen year old brother's body found floating in the river because some hoboes thought he had money because it was pay day at the factory in which he worked, killed him and threw his body in the river.

I know what it means to have my only baby, eleven months old, taken to the cemetery because I had to leave him in care of a young girl while I went to the factory.

I know, now, what it means to have the opportunity to attend Highlander Folk School and to meet Southern people who are trying to prepare themselves to teach workers the things they should know in order to solve their problems.

*****

Steel Workers Organizing Committee, Memphis, Tennessee

The United Rubber Workers of America started a drive on the Firestone plant of Memphis. I was with Bass and Bedgood the afternoon they were beaten nearly to death. We were at the plant gate, when around seventy-five men came out and attacked us.

They were armed with pipes, clubs, pistols, and blackjacks. Ten of the men attacked Bedgood first. I ran to his aid and tried to take a lead pipe from one of the men. They forced me back on the sidewalk. When they left I carried Bedgood to the hospital. Bass was also in the hospital. But the drive is still going on and no doubt will be a victory.

So I am studying here that I may go out into the field once

Work camp at Highlander Folk School, Emil at right with hand in pocket.

more to do my part for labor and for laboring people who are my people from birth.

*****

Textile Workers Union of America, Spartanburg, South Carolina
My mother tried her best to get me to stay in school, but my father died two years before and all the other boys had gone to work when they were fourteen years old, I thought it my duty to follow up. After two years in the textile mill I was making from $5.35 to $9.75—55 to 60 hours a week. I had heard of the union but in my mind the word union was like a very bad cuss word you wouldn't say before a lady.

About this time the CIO was winning great contracts in the steel and auto plants, we began to take notice and soon we knew it was an industrial organization that took in every craft in the industry. We noticed, too, that they did not bar negroes. Lots of us in the deep South did not like this much at first. But when some of the workers brought this up, the organizer explained why the negro was so important to the unions. They were not trying to organize the negro for equality with the whites but only to protect the standards of the white workers as well.

*****

Farmers Union, Green Pond, Alabama

I found that this group of students in my class had no parallel. I was drawn into the union through religion. Many of the students were surprised that church people were friendly towards them. My father helped organize sawmillers. Such a thing wasn't good church policy, he was told, and was forced out of the church. Last July I met Zilphia Horton who interested me in Highlander.

I have found that union doctrine fits in with true religious principles, and certainly no one could hope for more than a successful combination of the two.

*****

Electrical Workers Union, Mexico City, Mexico

The group was exclusively formed of electricians, employees of the same company, and residents of Mexico City only. About 1932 to 1934 our union began to change its organization and a campaign was pushed so that in May 1936 the whole union went on strike and won great concessions. Our union was offered a scholarship for the Highlander Folk School, and I was sent to learn as much as I could about labor problems which happen to be the same all over the world.

*****

The American Student Union, Bronx, New York

To a Bronx radical, the most fascinating aspect of the class was the story behind each of the participants. I'm not so sure that my contribution did the same for them, but I did my best to give some history of the Great Depression as lived in the large Northern cities.

At Highlander, I avidly learned things not taught at Black Mountain College, such as labor history and people's economics. Zilphia asked me to take the class in parliamentary procedure (Robert's Rules of Order), which didn't particularly engross me—little did I know how vital it was to become for me in just a year. I also enrolled in labor journalism—what else for a budding writer? For most students, shop-steward training and negotiating grievances were key courses. These were Highlander's core curriculum, and I could see how my classmates eagerly harnessed them to their own local union needs.

Scattered around the Highlander grounds were a series of small cabins with simple accommodations—beds, bureaus, wash basins (we brought our own water each night). A morning bell woke us, allowing time to wash, shave if necessary, and wander off to breakfast—checking the duty roster to note any assignments for the day.

In the afternoon we had a free-time break to rest, hike, play volleyball. Having had the month's Work Camp experience in 1938, I knew the area and could take the students on short walks to the edge of the Cumberland Plateau. Called the million-dollar view, it looked out over a beautiful valley.

There was no shortage of labor people to come and speak to us. During the term, important CIO officials showed up for panel discussions and weekend institutes, lending importance and weight to our sessions. Bernard Borah, Southern director of the Amalgamated Clothing Workers of America (ACWA), held classes on contracts; Alton Lawrence, Southern director of the LNPL (Labor's Non-Partisan League), talked about the potential political activities of local unions. Paul Christopher, the most open and most personally appealing of the labor leaders, would later become the head of the Tennessee CIO. He led discussions on grievance procedures and shop committees. I was fascinated by Paul and spent as much time as possible talking with him.

Paul was born February 14, 1910, in the little town of Easly, South Carolina. His father was a loom fixer. His mother had to work in the mill for six months to learn to weave before she drew her first pay and before they were allowed to live in a company house. Paul went to work in a textile mill and became an active union member at the age of 14. In 1937, he became South Carolina director of the AFL Textile Workers Union.

In our afternoon study sessions at Highlander, Paul filled us in on the history of the great Southern textile drive of 1934—at the height of the Great Depression. Some 325,000 Southern textile workers spontaneously went on a massive strike to protest their miserable pay and the stretchout of their workload. They left the mills and set up flying squadrons in trucks and autos to move through the textile towns—unbelting machinery, setting up picket lines, and battling scabs and guards. It was a workers' movement of poverty-stricken mill people—and it forced the AFL union leadership to go along

The textile industry, mostly runaway shops from the North, had a bloody history. In the bitter 1929 textile strike, Ella Mae Wiggins (an early day Zilphia Horton) had become legendary for her ability to blend militant words of struggle with familiar church songs. She came to the union when four of her five children died of whooping cough because she had no money for medicine or doctors. Coming into Gastonia, North Carolina, to lead singing for a union pep rally, the truck in which she was riding was fired on by anti-union thugs. Ella Mae was killed by a bullet in her throat.

Zilphia also had a large collection of folk songs, many she discovered on her own. When I was attending this labor school in 1940, Pete Seeger and Woody Guthrie came by to interview Zilphia about her song collection. I was to become a Seeger fan over the next 50 years, meeting him at hoedowns and at Highlander events. My wife and I play his CDs on long Maine winter evenings.

By the 1940s, Highlander alumni participation in the labor movement peaked. Myles reported:

> Rather than train the union members themselves, we spent most of our time teaching people how to do labor education. We ended up having five southern states with Highlander-trained CIO state educational directors, and in the majority of the CIO unions operating in the South, Highlander-trained people were running the educational programs for the union.

In the late 1930s and early 1940s, Highlander had a series of spring and fall six-week terms. By 1940, more than 400 students had attended HFS's residential terms, 1,800 had attended special sessions, and 5,000 had enrolled in Southwide extension courses. More than 50 percent of the school's students left to hold official positions in their unions.

From our 1940 class, a student became a member of the Tennessee state CIO staff; editor of the Tennessee state union newsletter; president of the Knoxville Industrial Union Council; and organizer for the United Furniture Workers Union—all namely me!

TENNESSEE STATE INDUSTRIAL UNION COUNCIL, September 1941
In 1940, Paul Christopher became the CIO director for Tennessee. At the time, the state had fewer than 12,000 CIO members, of whom 7,000 were United Mine Workers under Bill Turnblazer and John L. Lewis. In September 1941, I was waiting to hear from my draft board when Paul made an epic decision: While I waited for the army, he would put me on his expense account at $15 per week.

On September 24, after thumbing my way to Knoxville, I went up to the CIO headquarters and reported for duty.

"Your first assignment," Paul said, "is to get acquainted with the CIO national unions working in Tennessee. Go out with the organizers, attend meetings."

He introduced me to Homer Wilson, an organizer for the Mine, Mill and Smelter Workers. Homer invited me to a big strike rally the next night in Harriman, 50 miles from Knoxville.

"It ought to be a hot meeting," Homer said. "The strikers are getting angry. It's a joint meeting with District 50 of the United Mine Workers. They have a paper plant on strike in Harriman, and we have a copper smelter strike nearby. The bosses in Roane County will stop at nothing to prevent unionism. They've already kidnapped, beaten, and shot some organizers. I'll pick you up here at the office around 5 o'clock—we'll have dinner on the way." Great! I got an advance on Paul's $15-a-week expense account and settled down in the YMCA.

September 25. At the office the next morning, I found that my trip with Homer was out. Paul handed me a large pack of leaflets—the 40-cent minimum wage was a major union victory, and my job was to distribute this great news to two clothing plants about 100 miles to the north. I assured Paul I had leaflet-distribution experience, grabbed my toothbrush and shaving gear, and took off on the morning bus.

My first stop was a blue-jeans factory in Johnson City. (Blue jeans were for working people in those days.) As the workers filed out of the gate, the hands that reached out for my leaflets were stained blue. Handing out leaflets was a skill I had mastered at James Monroe High School—but I had never had the menace of a motorcycle cop at my back. Every time he gunned his engine, the hair on the back of my head stood up. Wait until he hears my damnyankee accent! After an eternity, he roared off. For instructions? Reinforcements? I was glad when the line thinned out and I could leave.

I put up at the Johnson City Railroad Hotel—cheapest in town, I was told. Others had used this hotel before me—many, many others. Fortunately, by this time of my life, I knew how to deal with bedbugs. I quickly stripped and hung all my clothes on wire clothes hangers on the rusty shower rail; my small pack went into the tub. After a careful inspection of the bedding, I lay on top of the sheets, covered only by a light blanket. In the morning, I showered and soaped thoroughly, shook out and inspected each item of clothing as I dressed, shouldered my pack, and carefully slipped out.

September 26. I made the morning shift at the Kingston plant and returned to Knoxville that afternoon. As I stepped off the bus and picked up the *News-Sentinel,* I thought I recognized a picture of Homer on the front page. On closer scrutiny, I realized it *was* Homer—dressed in a coat of tar. Next to him in the photo was Oscar Wiles, organizer of the paper mill. Their car had been shot down, and they were tied to trees, whipped, soaked with gasoline, and tarred. There was room on the page for another body, but he was in Johnson City, combating bedbugs.

A union rally was set up in Harriman, and everyone in the labor movement in the area was to go. We set out from Knoxville in a procession of 10 packed cars. About halfway to Harriman, we stopped at a cross-

road and waited. Pretty soon, a string of old cars came down from the north, miners from the coalfields. The leader of the group was the famous Bill Turnblazer, about whom I had heard from the crippled miner in 1936 when I toured Harlan County. Miners carrying burlap sacks walked along the line of our cars. I cranked down my window, wildly speculating about what I would receive. The miner reached in and offered me a pistol. I declined on the grounds that it would make me a danger to the union cause. The coal miners' guns were part of their union treasury. In my

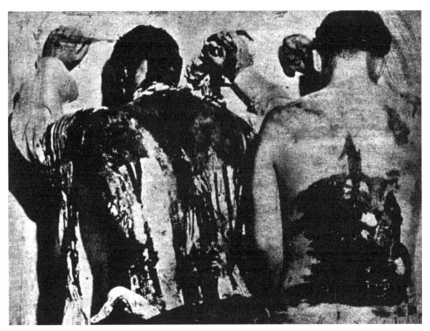

Homer Wilson—dressed in a coat of tar.

youth in the Bronx, it was mostly rocks; knives, clubs, and bicycle chains were also used, but not in my neighborhood. Of course, today's generation is better served.

We swept into Harriman without stopping for red lights and lined up in front of the rally building. On the courthouse roof were local police with rifles peering down at us. The miners posted a squad of armed sentries along the line of cars.

The auditorium was packed with workers, and the tension was electric. I've heard many a good speaker, but no one better than Paul Christopher. In this setting, he was at his best, and he spoke with the conviction of years of struggle in the Southern textile unions. When he sat down, a tense worker came up to him, leaning over and talking rapidly. At one point, they both looked over at the table where the local union officers were sitting. Suddenly, one of the officers jumped up and ran out of the meeting, his face pale and frightened. Paul went down to the table, gathered up a small cadre, and also left the rally. The next speaker announced that the man who organized the beating of Homer and Oscar in Harriman was the secretary of one of the locals who had been in the pay of the company all along. A fierce howl shook the hall, and many jumped up to follow Paul, but they were called back and the meeting went on.

As we were leaving after the meeting, Danenburg, one of the Hosiery Workers organizers, came up to me and suggested he take me home via a detour through the town of Clinton, which also had a strike going. Well, those were Paul's orders—get acquainted with what was going on—so I agreed. When we left the hall, he took me around the corner to where his car was parked. He held me back away from the car. "Wait here a moment—I want to check the car."

He looked under the car, opened the hood, and examined the motor minutely.

"Do you have car trouble?" I asked.

"I hope not," he laughed. "I came late and there was no room in front with the guarded cars. I'm just checking to see if some jackass has put dynamite on my starter!" I stopped breathing until he stepped on the starter and the motor caught.

The road to Clinton went through a series of remote back roads and hills. The union hall was a small building the size of a car garage, and when our wheels hit the graveled lot, the lights in the building abruptly went out. Danenburg quickly cranked down his window and shouted, "It's OK, fellows, only me, Danny!" The lights came on and a pair of men greeted us at the door, each shamefacedly holding a pistol. A group of strikers were seated around a kitchen table playing cards. One opened the table drawer and they put their pistols back in it.

Danny explained: "Two nights ago, some scabs tried to burn down the hall. They got a piece of the corner before they were spotted and run off. We have to keep all-night vigils." He gave me a brief rundown of the mill workers' grievances and the status of the strike. I could see he was talking to the men more than to me. In a short while, we left for Knoxville, this time on a main highway. Pinned to my door at the "Y" was an anxious note: PLEASE CALL NO MATTER WHAT TIME YOU GET IN. PRC.

When I had left the meeting with Danenburg, Paul had still not returned to the hall. It hadn't occurred to me that, with all they had on their plate that night, they might be worried about their newest immature staff member. I hastily called Paul and apologized. They never caught up with the turncoat secretary, Paul reported. Apparently he had left town without even going home. It was a great day of learning, but I was happy to be home—even if it was just a tiny room in the "Y." Both plants were successfully organized, and Homer and Oscar recovered nicely. It took me a while longer!

From time to time, I went with organizers to union meetings and built up a gripping picture of the Southern organizing drive. Riding for hours with these men and women, I became aware of the sacrifices they had to make to do their jobs. It occurred to me one day that I was the only one on the CIO payroll who hadn't been kidnapped, beaten, shot at, or jailed. But as time went on without personal incident, the novelty of violence wore off and I grew familiar, almost comfortable, with the fear. My quest for an AFL Printing Pressman's Union card was all but forgotten.

Just down Main Street from our office was a fairly large brick factory where men's suits were made. It had an active ACWA local, mostly women, and they used our office as a hangout after work. I had a little office of my own where I could write letters, work up and mimeograph leaflets, and put out a monthly newsmagazine of union events. Part of my job, as Paul said my first day, was to become acquainted with the unions. He said nothing about the unionists becoming acquainted with me. This became too easy in my tiny office, with giggling girls crowding in after a strenuous day on the sewing machines, offering to help with my mimeo machine. Men were scarce on the ground, even in those early days of the war, and I seemed to be fair game. Now that I was older than the 14-year-old boy at the Blue Mill Diner, it wasn't all negative.

One day, the men's clothing factory just down from CIO headquarters went on strike. One of the key ACWA organizers was Eula Mae McGill. To me, she was the Mighty Katrinka of the Southern labor movement. (The Mighty Katrinka was a comic-strip character—a large, powerful woman with a Swedish accent who could lift trolley cars with ease. Joanna remembers her as lifting two burly men, one under each arm, and cracking their heads together.) It was a short but emotional strike, with a picket line on the factory's Main Street sidewalk. The police paddy wagon arrived and started to load our pickets as they harassed the scabs. The chief organizer, Ed Smith, said to Eula Mae: "You'd better go along—some of those girls are new and look scared to death."

Eula Mae promptly reached out, grabbed a male scab going into the plant, slammed him against the building, and was hustled into the paddy wagon.

Smith turned to me, frowning, "I didn't mean *that* way!"

Fortunately, the strike was settled on terms favorable to the union.

Paul Revere Christopher was the favorite of every waitress in the restaurants we patronized. I attributed it to his ready smile and humorous banter—until one day I glanced back as we were leaving to see him shoveling all of our tips under his plate. Catching my eye, he gave me a cherubic smile. Don't get the idea that Paul was a tough, burly man hardened by years of hazardous struggle. The opposite. He was short, with blond reddish hair, a friendly open face, and a ready smile. His bow tie completed his disguise, helping to camouflage a man with strong beliefs and a sharp, steely approach to organizing that many employers were to discover. He was one of the best union contract negotiators in the South (in my opinion). During the postwar "Red scare" days, Myles Horton, director of Highlander Folk School, was ostracized by the national CIO because they felt he was too radical—although the Packinghouse Workers and some other national CIO unions stayed with the school. Paul Christopher, who was on the national CIO payroll, opted to stand by Myles and remained on the Highlander board, putting his own job on the line.

On December 7, 1941, the war arrived for the USA. In high school, I had vehemently been both antiwar and anti-Fascism. But the high emotional bitterness of World War I overwhelmed the more political approach to Fascism, and it took me a long time to put the latter in front focus. I finally grew to accept the inevitability of having to face up to Hitler's Europe and reluctantly agreed to go into the U.S. Army. But I still experienced the precariousness of my freedom and had periodic depressions. Living in a tiny, Lysol-disinfected YMCA room didn't help. So I fell back on my favorite remedy for the doldrums—I got a trail map of Mount Le Conte and a Greyhound schedule and planned a rigorous hiking trip to the nearby Smoky Mountains. That planned Sunday morning, I woke up to rain. The gloomy morning passed slowly, but at noon it seemed as though the rain might pass. By all principled evaluations, the time for the climb was far gone, but I took the 1 p.m. bus anyway. The driver dropped me off at the foot of Le Conte. With a major effort, I reached the summit by 6 p.m.

I had planned to memorize the trail map as I walked in the gathering gloom, but the rain started up again, and with it came total darkness. I put my useless glasses in my pocket and, arms outstretched, shuffled my feet in flatfooted circles feeling for the trail's cleared surface.

Once I fell off the trail completely and rolled down an embankment. Crawling uphill in the wet bushes and leaves, I suddenly came face-to-face with a set of eyes. The scene froze. Absolutely nothing moved—least of all me. Are wet bears more aggressive than the berry-picking bear I met back in 1936? After a long stalemate, I decide that the unblinking eyes were nothing personal and closed in—it was foxfire, a phosphorous glow in a shallow overhang.

Frustrated, I figured I'd stay put under the overhang. Shivering in the wet cold, however, I started to worry about hypothermia, so I decided to keep moving. Crawling uphill, endlessly groping, I finally regained the trail and negotiated the abrupt turn that threw me off. Finally it occurred to me that a vague and distant gurgling sound I had been hearing must be the stream the map had me crossing four times. In the endless shuffling, somehow I was making progress. I almost slipped off the first of the four log crossings; crawling across the last one, I found my feet sinking into

ankle-deep sand and bark mulch. I could smell dank horse biscuits . . . ah!
. . . I had discovered the bridle path! I tried to visualize my trail map. This
path was the last third of the trek to the village, and parallel to it was a
macadam road. On the road, for the first time I could actually see the
open sodden sky. On the outskirts of Gatlinburg, I ruthlessly and persist-
ently leaned on the buzzer of a tourist home. Not once had I given a
thought to the war and my depression!

After I had been working about six months, Paul's secretary, a very
efficient and pleasant local girl, left to marry an organizer. We hired a new
secretary from North Carolina named Cathy—college-educated and liberal, a fine young lady about my age. It gave me a friendship on a different cultural level, someone with whom I could exchange books and
records and discuss matters not connected to organized labor.

Soon after her arrival, we all drove across Tennessee to Memphis, for
a state CIO convention. Paul, his wife Booba, Cathy, and me. It was a long
drive, and in the car chitchat, I began to sense that among them was a little something to which I wasn't privy. Not being sure, I kept quiet. Paul
presided over the convention, and at one point, half listening to his talk, I
heard that we were getting a highly qualified new person on the staff.
Aware that Cathy and Booba were grinning at me, I suddenly realized that
this new stalwart was none other than me. I was off Paul's expense account
and on the Tennessee State Industrial Union Council payroll!

For the five or six months on Paul's expense account, I had lived pretty high on the hog. When the local and visiting organizers learned that I
was living on $15 a week, they not only took me out for meals but also
urged me to order steaks and similar upscale menus. When I went on payroll, at $35 a week, not only was I not fed but I was expected to take my
turn at buying beer. I promptly upgraded my living quarters by moving
out of my tiny $3 room at the "Y" into an $8-a-week spare room in a
union member's home—with kitchen and bathroom privileges.

With the increase in pay came an increase in responsibilities. I was
"elected" president of the Knoxville Industrial Union Council. My job was
to preside at monthly meetings at our union hall, summarize any new

Paul Revere Christopher, Myles Horton, Mary Lawrence, and Emil.

events, and introduce visiting speakers—usually this was Paul Christopher. And usually our main audience consisted of workers from the C.B. Atkins furniture company. They were a loyal lot, coming mainly to hear Paul speak. Paul was the kind of speaker who, with the need to fill a time slot, could hold you enthralled yet leave you with little of substance to remember. There were eight deaf workers in the local, and someone would sit in back of Paul, facing the audience, and do "signing." It satisfied them, but I wondered what exactly they got out of Paul's talks. But better Paul than me—I was a dud at public speaking. From time to time, I would entrap an out-of-town organizer in order to give Paul a night off.

In the name of the Knoxville Council, I found myself embroiled in local controversies—defending the CIO against bigots, bosses, and yellow journalists. I must admit I got a charge out of picking up a newspaper to see that Mr. Willimetz "alleges" . . . "claims" . . . "challenges," etc.

More to my taste, I would also announce frequent square dances, bringing my record player and hoedown records and bellowing out calls I learned at Highlander. I depended on the Atkins furniture men and the ACWA girls down the street to fill the floor. With no one "signing" my calls, I also wondered how the deaf ones managed—but dance they did, and very well.

At one point, I set aside a modest sum of money to have a mural of heroic workers painted on the meeting-hall walls. An artistic German refugee, Maria Stenzel, was then residing at Highlander, and I invited her to do the job. She came up, measured the walls, did a rough sketch for my approval, and departed. Weeks later, she came back with a detailed, scaled-down rendering of the mural on butcher paper. She also brought Junie and JD Marlowe to assist her. To inaugurate the completed mural, we advertised a banner square dance and invited the local AFL union folks. With JD on the fiddle and Junie on the guitar, we had a gala party. Although I had specified no alcohol (Tennessee was dry), and there were no bushes to disappear into, some moonshine nonetheless enlivened the event.

I'm ashamed to say that I got a "skinful" and had to be taken home and put to bed. Nothing was ever said—wot a great boss!

One time, Paul was away in Washington on some Union War Board meeting and I was in charge, up front in his big office. Late one afternoon, a committee of workers walked in.

"You the CIO?" asked the leader.

"Yes, sir," I answered.

He looked past me to see if anyone else might be available. Seeing no one, he said, "We want ta join."

"Where do you work?" I inquired.

"We work for the Smoky Mountain Railroad an' we're strikin' fer better money fer our work."

"How long have you been out?"

"Startin' today. Stopped the train on the Tennessee River bridge and pulled the fire into the water. Train's not goin' anywhere until we say so. My name's Murphy . . . Sleepy Murphy."

"Mine's Emil Willimetz. Let's all sit down, and tell me the whole story."

The story, it turns out, started with the short railroad line that went to the town of Sevierville, about 40 or 50 miles from our big city. It was a key factor in the building of the Holston River dam during the early TVA days. The railroad was bought by a steel company for the scrap metal. The government said, "No way!" Not until the end of the war could the rail line be sold—the railroad was the only way to get heavy equipment to the dam in case of emergency. So instead of liquidating the tracks, they had to hire a road gang to maintain the roadbed. This was the road gang sitting in my office—the most vocal element of some 50 or more men. They were getting 40 cents an hour when men in war industries were getting a good deal more.

"Why don't you quit?" I asked.

"Keeps us out of the army and we like the work—it's not too technical."

Not knowing which union had jurisdiction—probably some railroad union not too interested in a hatful of track workers—I handed out National CIO cards, figuring this would hold them until Paul returned. I agreed to meet with the whole gang the next morning at the near side of the railroad bridge. I had seen the bridge many times but had concluded that the sign saying, "SMOKY MTN RAILROAD" was an ancient entity. Civil War? Did it ever go as far as the Smokies? I never thought to ask.

The next morning, I met the gang at the appointed place and talked some more about their grievances and salary hopes. They had a steel-company letterhead with the name of the local CEO. I told Murphy to check with me that afternoon to give me a chance to talk with management.

Talk I did—much to the amusement of the CEO, who acted as though it was all a joke. I asked him to meet with the committee the next morning. He replied, "Tell them to get back to work and we might consider a little something."

I told him the men were not happy and we would be in his office at

10 a.m., then I hung up. When Murphy called, I arranged to meet with the committee in front of the building. I had a feeling that the men had sized me up and knew I was not the type to throw furniture around at the meeting. One told me, "They call Murphy 'Sleepy' because his eyelids sort of hang down. But he's anything but sleepy, has a good temper, so if you feel the need for action or hard words, give him the nod."

Murphy gave me a wolfish grin and up the stairs we went. We crowded past the secretary into the main office, where the boss sat behind his desk.

"What can I do for you fellows?" he asked, looking me over carefully.

"This is a committee representing the work gang, Mr. CEO," I replied. "They've all joined the CIO, every one of them, and we now represent them. I think the first thing on the agenda would be some chairs."

I never looked at Sleepy, but he growled menacingly. "Yeah, chairs." Well, chairs were taken seriously, but not much else. The CEO called in his secretary and had her write down the men's demands. I handed him my calling card. Sleepy turned to the CEO: "The boiler on that engine stays cold until we get our demands!" And we filed out.

I called the CEO every day, and all I got were evasions. The money required to meet the men's demands could have been paid out of the company's petty-cash box, but to him it was a cat-and-mouse game he enjoyed. I was having a hard time keeping the men from tearing up the tracks or damaging the locomotive. Paul was still stuck in Washington.

One morning, out of the blue, I got a very official government document, via cable, that informed me that my little strike was against some serious Railroad Act protocols and I would be liable for some formidable consequences if I didn't cease and desist.

I called a meeting of the gang and exhibited the lethal document: "We have to go back to work. We'll just keep harassing the company until they give in."

After a howl of protest and some hard language, I agreed to visit the company once more with the committee. At the building, I found that my committee had expanded considerably, and we all elbowed our way into the CEO's office. He looked us over in great disgust.

He waved a duplicate of the same document I had received: "Look, fellows, we're going to have to stop playing games. This is wartime and the federal government won't tolerate work stoppages. How about we get serious and negotiate this problem?"

We poured out of his office and into the hallway. I suggested we go back with just the original committee. The result, of course, was a compromise, the men agreeing to a figure they had hoped to get but had inflated for bargaining purposes.

When Paul returned from Washington, I expected to get reamed out for my actions. But he just gave me his cherubic smile, saying, "I should go away more often."

It cost us more to service these men than they paid in dues—but I had a whole railroad under my belt.

In 1943, I mounted my first real union organizing campaign from scratch—two runaway furniture factories from Springfield, Massachusetts, had set up in Morristown, Tennessee. A couple of men from one of the Morristown factories came in to visit us, and Paul assigned the contact to me. Not having a car was a handicap, but Morristown was less than an hour away, and there was frequent Greyhound service. I made an appointment with our contact and showed up one evening at his home. We talked for about an hour, during which I took notes on factory conditions, wages, etc. I noticed a guitar leaning against the wall. He told me proudly that he played it, as did his young son. Being an aficionado of current hillbilly (now called country) music, I quickly had him off on "The Wabash Cannonball." He called in his son and we spent the evening awash in music. My best organizing was done on a personal basis—in homes and sitting around an old school bus telling stories. As a stump speaker, I was no Paul R. Christopher.

The brother of one of my stalwart committeemen had a junkyard that contained a school bus sitting on blocks. This became our union hall; we held our "mass" meetings in the junkyard itself. I began to collect signed Furniture Workers Union cards and soon had enough to show interest, but not enough to hold an election.

When I reported to Paul, he said, "You're off my payroll." My eyebrows went up. "I have something more interesting—you are on the Furniture Workers payroll at $10 more a week."

Now I *really* had to produce. I asked the Springfield local to send me a copy of their contract and called for a meeting in the junkyard, asking my original contacts to bring reluctant fellow workers.

At the meeting, I read contract clauses I knew would excite the men—union-elected shop stewards, paid vacation time, better working conditions. But just as someone asked me to read off the pay scale, it started to rain, and we all packed into the school bus. It had gotten too dark to read the contract, but someone handed me a cigarette lighter. A voice from the dark would say, "What does a sander get?" Flick . . . I would skim down the list . . . 85 cents an hour. "Shit, I'm gettin' 55." "Wot about an upholsterer?" . . . . Shit . . . . "A turner?" . . . . Shit . . . and on down the list. I left the bus with a fistful of signed cards. We were getting close to a majority.

I stayed overnight in an old hotel on the edge of Morristown. I was careful to make friends with the night clerk, letting him know what I was doing. He seemed noncommittal but amicable and enjoyed my spending time with him during his night shift.

One afternoon, a couple of men approached me, suggesting they were interested in the union, but they were from the other plant. They invited me to join them in a beer. During the war, beer came in large bottles, and we had several. A sloppy waitress served us and spent a lot of time hanging around our table. The men's union attention span didn't get past the first bottle, and they spent the rest of the time in man-to-man talk, sordid stories, stupid jokes, and kidding the waitress.

After a while, I suspected I'd better quit this, so I paid the bill and started to leave. They jumped up with me and insisted on walking me to my hotel.

The waitress ran out with us and walked next to me.

"We'll take her home, too," they said. She was a crude, very unattractive girl, and she tried to sidle close to me and get me interested. When we arrived at the hotel, I started up the steps, but she grabbed my arm and came with me. "She likes you," they chorused. "Take her up to your room."

Glancing down the street, I saw the sheriff strolling up the hill. Disengaging, I scooted into the hotel. Stopping at the desk, I called to the night clerk: "If anyone asks for the union man, please call my room before you give them my room number."

He nodded. I packed my shaving kit and what other few things I had and lay on top of my bed, fully dressed. In about an hour, my phone rang: "There's some guys lookin' for you."

"Friendly?"

"Not very."

"I'm leaving," I replied. "Pay you on my next visit with an extra bonus. Thanks."

I removed the screen from my ground-floor window and left. Down the street was a tourist court, and I holed up there for the night. From then on, I was more careful about my beer-drinking companions. I was lucky— still the only one on the staff never hurt.

Several of my most dedicated furniture-worker contacts had been moonshine transporters—liquor runners. Tennessee's moonshine capital, Newport in Cocke County, was close to Morristown. Before the furniture factories came to town, running moonshine was one of the few ways these Depression youngsters could make a living. They worked with souped-up cars, mostly 1937 and 1938 Fords. Moonshine mechanics would bore out the cylinders and increase the stroke or install larger Mercury engines. The cars were equipped with heavy override springs and other load levelers, to the point where a heavily loaded car would hardly sink at all.

"That the car would ride high when it weren't under load was a dead giveaway. Without a load the Revenuers couldn't do ya, but they'd get to know ya. We depended on fast drivin' and usin' the little dirt back roads. I know these little ol' roads like the palm o' my hand."

"I threw my Ford around those narrow curves at over 100 miles an hour—lots a times," laughed another.

They practiced regularly, speeding up and down lanes, spinning on a dime, and making abrupt turnoffs.

"It was great fun, and we made good money, not like in this fuckin' plant, but we began to get caught and get hurt badly in car crashes. Lost a good friend killed one day."

They delighted in a Roy Acuff song and would play it for me frequently. Here's how I remember it:

> *I heard the crash on the highway*
> *but didn't hear nobody pray.*
> *It was whiskey and blood run together,*
> *but I didn't hear nobody pray, dear brother,*
> *I didn't hear nobody pray.*

When we had a comfortable pro-union majority, I petitioned to the NLRB (National Labor Relations Board) for an election. While waiting, I spent as much time with my key people as I could—apparently so did the opposition. On election day, every worker walked into the polling booth with a large smoked ham under his arm.

We lost by a scant six votes.

I filed an NLRB complaint against the plant; introducing gift pigs into the polling place, we contended, was not a kosher tactic. But I was not to stay in Tennessee long enough to see the results.

In 1940, Paul Christopher had inherited 5,000 union workers when he took over the Tennessee CIO. By 1945, the great aluminum plant at Alcoa was organized—more than 7,000 workers—and in 1946 the huge K-25 atomic plant at Oak Ridge. By 1948, he had 100,000 new Tennessee CIO members. This, I'm sure, made Paul very proud—as was I with my Smoky Mountain Railroad!

When shown the "Uncle Sam Wants You!" wartime poster, a little black boy dolefully asked, "Why? What did I do?"

ACTUALLY, THAT LITTLE BOY WAS ALSO ME! In April 1943, the U.S. Army sent an urgent message requesting my services.

ESSAY: UNITED MINE WORKERS OF AMERICA (UMWA)

The miners who came to our assistance in Harriman, Tennessee, must have seemed like a murderous crew. But guns frequently were their only recourse for fighting hired thugs and company-sponsored law enforcers. Company arsenals often contained machine guns. The grim history of the coalfields, from the earliest days, is one of abject poverty and a dogged struggle to unionize. "Bloody Harlan" (Kentucky) was no idle label.

It was the miners, under John L. Lewis, who led the breakaway from the AFL. Always at the bottom of the economic pile, they had to fight hard for any advances they made. I had great admiration for their courage.

Eleanor Roosevelt prodded FDR to have hundreds of small post offices constructed throughout the region. More than the paying jobs, they brought a sense of community to these isolated areas.

Throughout the history of the coalfields in Pennsylvania, poor people and families of the miners picked out coal from the waste dumps. In the 1920s, mechanization was introduced into these fields, and thousands were thrown out of work. During the bitter strike of 1925, thousands more were unemployed. Miners then started to resort to opening small pits on company property, mostly where companies found it unprofitable to exploit, and the bootleg coal industry gained momentum.

About 10 percent of all anthracite sold in the United States during the Great Depression was bootlegged coal—a true Depression industry. The miners were not bootlegging coal because they enjoyed it. They risked their lives at unsafe, backbreaking work, facing frequent crushing cave-ins.

As for the "stealing" part of it, how did the companies get their coal lands? In some cases they paid $6 per acre; was that a fair price? In other cases they stole it from the Indians. Was that a nice thing to do? Well [laughing], we're the new Indians, taking what coal we can back from the companies . . . . We "steal" coal in order to keep from becoming thieves and holdup men, which, to keep alive, we probably would be forced to become if we didn't have these holes. (Louis Adamic, *My America*, p. 320)

It wasn't until World War II that the demand for coal brought full employment to the Appalachian coalfields—but not adequate pay increases. In 1942, Lewis requested a $2-a-day wage increase. It was turned down by the steel companies that owned the mine. The union leadership had taken a no-strike pledge, and by-and-large the overwhelming majority of unions kept it. In 1942, 99.95 percent of the nation's work went on without strikes. In June 1943, John L. Lewis, after trying for months to get the $2 wage increase, called the miners out on strike. The newspapers screamed, "traitors" at the miners.

One U.S. Air Force pilot swore, "I'd just as soon shoot down one of these strikers as shoot Japs." (David Kennedy, *Freedom from Fear*, p. 643)

Harry Truman said, "Lewis ought to have been shot in 1942, but Franklin didn't have the guts to do it." (Kennedy, *Freedom from Fear*, p. 643 footnote)

One might have wished that some degree of passion might have gone into helping the diggers, who suffered from decades of neglect.

Eleanor Roosevelt pointed out " . . . the tremendous risks the miners endured—in 1941, 64,764 miners were killed or injured in the mines." (Doris Kearns Goodwin, *No Ordinary Times*, p. 441)

In any combat army, 64,764 casualties would be considered very deadly statistics. Only $2 a day? What sort of men were these mine owners, who were working on cost-plus contracts? After taxes, profits were $6.4 billion in 1940 and $11 billion in 1944.

Secretary of War Henry Stimson said, "If you are going to go to war in a capitalist country, you have to let business make money out of the process or business won't work." (Kennedy, *Freedom from Fear*, p. 622)

"In perhaps the sweetest deal of all, military procurement agencies let contracts on a cost-plus basis, providing iron-clad guarantees of profits beyond the most avaricious monopolist's dreams." (Kennedy, *Freedom from Fear*, p. 623)

(If business wouldn't work, should we have asked the marines to shoot them?)

The Appalachian (coal-mining) states had the highest rate of voluntary military enlistment in the nation.

In my retirement years in Maine, I took tour groups to marvel at beautiful spots around the world. I should have taken some to Appalachia! Here was a world of mountains, valleys, and waterfalls that matched some of the best scenery worldwide.

On my 1936 Southern trips through Tennessee and Kentucky, I noted large, ugly slag hills dominating small mountain towns. But this ugliness was minor compared to the destruction wrought by the giant strip-mining machines that entered these hills and valleys in 1961. The TVA we venerated as the savior of this depressed Southern region now opened the door to its degradation. TVA is the greatest consumer of strip-mined coal.

According to Mike Clark, then the director of the new Highlander Center at New Market, Tennessee:

> The Tennessee Valley Authority has become a coal-consuming monster to produce cheap electric power. Strip-mining coal companies contracted by TVA are destroying thousands of acres of mountain land—laying waste one section of Appalachia to light cheaply the homes and factories of another section. Only 10 percent of the TVA's electric power is now produced by hydroelectric facilities. (Guy and Candie Carawan, *Voices from the Mountains*, p. x)

To see strip mining on a really vast scale, you have only to visit Paradise, in western Kentucky. Here thousands of acres of land were stripped by the Peabody Coal Company. What Peabody strips, the TVA burns to produce electricity. TVA and Peabody destroyed the entire town of Paradise to fuel the world's largest steam-generating plant.

SONG: PARADISE
"Daddy won't you take me back to Muhlenberg County,
"Down by the Green River where Paradise lay?"
"Well, I'm sorry, my son, but you're too late in asking,
"Mr. Peabody's coal train has hauled it away."
—Words and music by John Prine (Carawan, *Voices from the Mountains*, p. 32)

Since I left the South I have lost two of my favorite heroes. One is the TVA, which renovated an entire region and showed the way for similar large-scale endeavors. I should have known it was too good to be true. Showing tinges of Socialist thinking, it went down the drain, taken over by capitalist avarice.

The second loss was on a more personal scale. In 1936, a crippled miner told me about the courage of one of their leaders, William Turnblazer, whom I later met when I worked for the CIO in Tennessee. In 1969, corruption had taken over the United Mine Workers union in the form of Tony Boyle. A great campaign, led by Joseph Yablonski, was organized to boost him out. About one o'clock on the morning of December 31, Yablonski, his wife, and daughter were shot to death in their beds.

Tony Boyle was convicted of planning these murders and sentenced to life in jail. Nine others were also deemed guilty, and among them was my harsh-voiced UMWA hero, William Turnblazer. (Carawan, *Voices from the Mountains*, p. 191)

BOOK III

THE WAR EXPERIENCE

Because Vietnam, the last large war fought by the United States, was such a brutal failure, a major attempt is being made to rekindle World War II in a heroic vein as "The Good War." Those who fought the war are being billed as "The Greatest Generation." In this I find myself again at odds with my times—as a symbol of the Greatest Generation, I am still a gringo.

Before…

…and after the war. Photograph by Paris street photographer.

17.

WHERE HAVE ALL THE FLOWERS GONE?

I DREAM I'M NAKED IN GRAND CENTRAL STATION. Dream? Nightmare! I *am* naked, and it *is* Grand Central, on a cold April day in 1943. This was the year of the big call-up for massive numbers of infantry troops. The air force wasn't going to win the war by itself after all. Instead of the usual hordes of bustling commuters, the enormous and enormously drafty train-station lobby was seething with naked men taking physicals. I had never been the subject of so much personal attention. As I was directed from post number to post number, clutching my papers to my chilled bosom, I was prodded, probed, stethoscoped, measured, and questioned. My height was noted at five feet ten inches.

"Hey! I'm five feet eleven and a half!"
"The U.S. Army likes to see you grow!"

Finally I was able to sit down, still dressed only in goose pimples, a numbered disk hanging from my neck, to have my schooling and job history recorded. When I mentioned my last job with the labor movement, the CIO, the sergeant put down his pencil and left abruptly. After about a 30-minute wait, the chill of my body having reached and numbed my brain, a sharply dressed Navy officer briskly sat down opposite me and genially announced: "I'm with Navy Intelligence and I'd like to have some more detail on your last job."

Numb as I was, I did my best to play down the virulence of my union career and my previous terrorist activities in high school. It was grossly unfair—sharp, neatly uniformed, patriotic Officer vs. shivering, cowering, nude, un-American Civilian! But army exams are difficult to flunk, and they were pleased to ask me to show up for a journey back to the South via the Southern Railroad to Mississippi—prepaid by the U.S. Army.

I was made part of Basic Training Company E, 272nd Infantry Regiment, 69th Division, at Camp Shelby, Mississippi. The division patch is a snug mating of the "6" and the "9," and the subject of numerous ribald jokes.

Our company clerk, who in real life was an insurance statistician, came to me one day looking very concerned:

"Hey, Willi!" (They couldn't deal with either Emil or Willimetz, so in the army it was Willi.) "What did you do in civilian life?"

"This and that. I did a lot of printing. Why?"

"A guy from Intelligence was picking through your file and made a note on it that you are not eligible for Officers' Training School."

While this irritated me and cost me pay, it very likely saved my life. Lieutenants in combat didn't last long.

Men who had fought in Spain were classified as "premature anti-fascists" and were also discriminated against by the army. But not Communists, not that I knew of, since the Soviets had become our war comrades.

That Navy Intelligence officer, whose eyes lit up when the CIO was mentioned, must have found something really monstrous in my past. Had he found my high school principal, the good Dr. Hein, and learned that Emil Willimetz had been *antiwar?*

CAMP REGULATIONS
IF IT MOVES, SALUTE IT!
IF IT DOESN'T MOVE, PICK IT UP AND PUT IT AWAY!
IF YOU CAN'T PICK IT UP, PAINT IT!

The first thing we learned in basic training was the meaning of chickenshit—a small insignificant turd, a designation in the army for petty acts against those of lower rank. People who were Mickey Mouse types in civilian life had complete control over our lives in the army and resorted to self-gratification tactics of petty harassment. Without a grievance committee or a shop steward, we were at their mercy.

Actually, not entirely at their mercy. Many of our infantry officers lived in Hattiesburg, and on a Saturday they would be out shopping. A group of us on passes to town formed "Submarine Patrols." The mission: torpedo officers found with arms of groceries. Lining up at equal distances along the street, the patrol leader would step up to a burdened officer, stop, and raise his hand in a firm, demanding salute. He would hold it patiently until his target could rearrange his bundles to return it. A number of paces downstream, a second patroller would step up and salute. And so on, until the officer, becoming aware of the harassment, would scream nasty, unsoldierly commands at us. The Submarine Patrol was a great chickenshit antidote—no doubt invented during the Civil War, when it was called the Monitor Patrol (Merrimac in the South?)!

Fortunately, a cadre of old army men, eligible for retirement, had agreed to stay on to help train the enormous, swelling army. Our sergeant was one of these, and he was a caring father figure to the young boys of the company. He took the training very seriously and tried to instill in us survival know-how—although neither he nor anyone else had a clue about what combat conditions would be like. Should one of the recruits ask, "What if . . . ?" The Sarge would inevitably reply, "What if? What if a bullfrog had wings, he wouldn't bump his ass every time he jumped." He'd laugh and try to answer the question.

When I worked for the CIO in Knoxville, I missed Harriett, so occasionally, when I had a three-day weekend, I would ride the Greyhound to visit Black Mountain College. By this time, I knew very few of the students. Harriett was my main motivation for going; she now had a small Ford and could pick me up at the Asheville Greyhound station.

On a romantic impulse one evening, Hattie and I drove over to Lee Hall on the Blue Ridge. The great building was unlocked, but it was dark and empty of everything but the ghosts of our years there. We sat together in one of the large padded rocking chairs in the cavernous lobby and whispered to each other about ancient happenings and present feelings. But the specter of Willis Weatherford, the executive secretary of the YMCA Blue Ridge Association and manager of the grounds, hovered just outside, waiting to enter and turn on the lights. So we left.

One Saturday evening, after dinner at BMC, I was asked by Fran de

Tommy Wentworth was an acting sergeant when he was killed in Normandy.

Graaff, a new teacher at the school, to give a short talk on my experiences in the CIO. After the talk, Hattie and I walked out to the lake. Unfortunately, we were joined by Tommy Wentworth, a small, thin, very young-looking boy—and a very persistent one. Tommy was either enamored of Hattie or interested in learning more about the CIO. I favored the former explanation and resented his intrusion, but I couldn't help spouting off about my union experiences.

Suddenly we noticed a hum of excitement in the dining room area. News had come down that there was a fire on one of the nearby ridges, and the school was sending a truck with rakes, shovels, and students to help fight it. Tommy and I jumped aboard, and we spent the night working together. Aside from his being a barrier to romance, I found I enjoyed his company. A good thing, too, because, in one of life's many quirkinesses, Tommy ended up in my infantry training company at Camp Shelby, Mississippi. Tommy made an ideal army buddy for me, someone who shared some of the same interests and was capable of serious discussion.

Sunday was the time for our old army noncoms to swap army stories in the company Supply Room. I hung around, enjoying the talk. One time, they held a competition to field-strip and reassemble a .45-caliber pistol blindfolded. When they were through, I attempted to reassemble the pistol using the *Official Manual.* It proved to be a real challenge—army manual language has truly been mastered by only a select few. Each Sunday, I chose a different weapon to disassemble; M-1 rifle, 30mm carbine, BAR (Browning automatic rifle), machine gun—it was a great way to kill a Sunday. It had a wonderful side effect—I became friendly with the Supply sergeant and learned how to help him run the Supply Room.

If you think I exaggerate the challenge of the Official Manual, please read the following very carefully:

> *Field Manual* 21-100 in the *Soldier's Handbook,* July 1941.
> At the command FORM FOR SHELTER TENTS TO THE LEFT, the second in command moves to a position on the right of the guide, who is on the right of the right man of the front rank . . . . On direction of the platoon reader, the odd numbers draw their bayonets and thrust them into the ground alongside the outside of the left heel near the instep. The bayonet indicates the position of the front tent pole . . . . At the command PITCH TENTS, each man steps off obliquely with his right foot a full pace to the right front . . . . Each odd-numbered man places a pin in the ground on the spot which he previously marked with his left heel . . . the odd-numbered man driving the rear guy pin two-and-a-half tent peg lengths from the rear triangle pin. You will normally pitch your tent where you will be concealed from enemy observation. In combat conditions the principles of tent-pitching will apply, but there may be no attempt to align the tents.

Think about the above also as the army's mental attitude about the war and the kind of training we received for overseas combat. Our tents turned out to be foxholes, and we needed no guidebooks for the digging.

We went on bivouac campouts, sleeping in the piney woods, to learn about field orientation and map reading. Tommy had a small portable chess-and-checkers set, and on rainy bivouacs we played under the kitchen truck.

For many born-and-bred city recruits, the bivouac was not always a happy event. One boy had a buzzing bug crawl down his ear canal. We tried pouring water in his ear to drown it, then oil to float it out—to no avail. He left in an ambulance, moaning in anguish.

The native pine is soaked with turpentine, and we discovered that on cool nights, it makes for a lovely blazing fire. Too lovely! On one trip, a number of army blankets got burned.

"Too bad," said the Sarge, "these guys gonna have to pay for replacements. Hey, Willi, how would you like to take this blanket and these reject clothes to Quartermasters for me?"

Not to bore you with the red tape involved . . . I turned in the clothes and one of the badly burned blankets. On an impulse, when the clerk wasn't looking, I quickly augmented the "1" blanket on the requisition form to "11." When I presented the form at Quartermasters, I duly received 11 replacement blankets. In triumph, I showed up at the Supply Room with this great bag of loot.

"I reckon there'll be no paying for blankets in E Company," chuckled the Sarge. "What if you'd been caught?"

"Well," I replied, "they could ship me overseas in the infantry."

The Sarge was past the retirement age, and gradually I did most of his paperwork. Since I was his acting assistant, he got me excused from drill. But when the call came down to send the Supply assistant to Armorer Artificer School to learn to repair weapons, the captain (over the objections of Sarge) sent the company runner. When the runner returned, he went back to company headquarters. I stayed on in the Supply Room, without corporal stripes or pay as warranted. It didn't irritate me—I had come to terms with the fact that I wasn't going to make it big rankwise in the army.

One major culminating event of our training was a staged series of war games. We maneuvered against the 442nd Nisei Battalion. Ike Nakata, a fellow student at Black Mountain and the subject of previous painful experiences with the U.S. Army, was also at Camp Shelby in the 442nd Battalion. Our maneuvers against them were *not fair*. They used passwords in Japanese but eavesdropped on us in the dark and used our passwords in perfect English. A good percentage of the 442nd Battalion were college students, and no tougher than we were. But whereas we were apt to be goof-offs, they were determined to excel. I saw them on long marches, shoes off, feet weeping with blisters and bloody from walking on rough pavement but not giving in. For those of us who fought, war was bad enough, but the men of the 442nd had the handicap of having to prove themselves over and over again.

A catastrophic culminating event of our training was a 69th Division forced march to Biloxi on the Gulf of Mexico—100 miles over hot pavement in the heat of a Mississippi August. It was to be done in three days, sleeping out on the ground each night. When we were ready to go, inspection was made of our field packs to make sure we were carrying the full load—plus our nine-pound rifles.

The march order was 50 minutes walking, 10 minutes rest. Dehydration was the main enemy, and since some refused to take salt tablets, salt was put into our company water bags at the stopping points. Ugh!

I was a good deal bigger and stronger than Tommy. Under the rigorous training, I had gained 10 pounds, with my neck size going from 15 to 16 inches. I had a feeling that this ordeal might be too much for slim Tommy. As we walked, sweat dripping from every nose, I frequently glanced back to check on him. A pitiful sight, he was panting with open mouth, his hair and shirt soaked with sweat, his face flushed dark red. The pack on his slight frame seemed bigger than all the others, and to carry the weight, he was leaning forward almost to the point of falling on his face. He was in grave danger of heat exhaustion.

At the stops, I urged him just to fall in a ditch and quit, as more and more men were doing. He said no, he wanted to see what his limits were. Curiosity about his limits seemed to be a major characteristic of this young boy. By the third day, our ambulances were extremely busy. Rumor had it that some 35 soldiers had already died from heat exhaustion, and I believed it. It seemed to me to be a senseless abuse of the men.

It was said that our goal, Biloxi, was a cheap edition of Asbury Park in New Jersey. We were not given time to judge the validity of this—we were trucked back to camp the following day.

I can still see Tommy leaning into his pack on the Biloxi road, testing his limits. Tommy was an acting sergeant when he was killed in

Normandy. For all his slight size, he must have made a good noncom, and he probably died trying to do more than his share.

One of the few books I packed to read on the boat to Europe was Jaroslav Hasek's *The Good Soldier Svejk,* an excellent treatise on getting away with murder in the Austrian military by acting dumb. We had a "Svejk" in our training company, only he was from Tennessee. We called him "Tenn." A few late entries came in to fill out the company, Tenn among them. They were to be integrated with troops that had become fairly efficient at close-order drill. Securely entrenched in the Supply Room, I watched the passing comedy from the open door.

Tenn came to immediate notice during his first drill, when, as by command, all rotated smartly left and he alone turned right. This was very unsoldierly, and a threat to the military. Our fatherly Sarge pulled him out of ranks and dressed him down. Tenn hung his head.

His "about faces" were a masterpiece of wrong "abouts" and angry "faces." The lieutenant came to take charge, since officers were created for taking charge. The lieutenant got down on his knees behind Tenn and grabbed both ankles. When the Sarge bellowed, "About," the lieutenant forcefully put one of Tenn's feet behind the other. At "face," Tenn turned the wrong way and collapsed on the lieutenant—none too gently.

The final maneuver that revealed his true character, at least to me, was the marksmanship exercise. Without ammo, we went through the firing drill: wrap the rifle sling tightly around your left arm for steadiness . . . pull the stock against the shoulder . . . lay your cheek against the rifle . . . close the left eye and sight the target with your right . . . squeeze the trigger gently . . . *fire!* Tenn just couldn't learn to sight—it was either both eyes open or both shut. The Sarge had to tie a rag over one eye.

Now I had lived in Tennessee and knew a number of Tennessee mountain boys. They grew up with rifles and most of them could shoot a squirrel in his right eye at 100 yards. So did this Tennessean grow up in a cave? I had my doubts.

The culmination took place on the firing range, shooting at targets with live ammo. Fifty men at a time were sent to line up at the parapets, 100 yards from the targets. In the exact center of the line stood a tower on which a major was ensconced like a beach lifeguard. He, and he alone, controlled this event. Glancing down at us to be certain we were settled to his satisfaction, he picked up his bullhorn. His "READY ON THE RIGHT" released a rapid roll of safety-catch clicks. He turned his head: "READY ON THE LEFT." Instead of safety-catch clicks, he got *pow* . . . *pow* . . . *pow* . . . *pow* . . . *pow* . . . *pow* . . . *pow* . . . and a final *ping* as an M-1 clip sprang out. Well . . . who didn't wait for "FIRE AT WILL"?

"I WANT THAT MAN!" thundered the bullhorn, and up came the Sarge dragging Tenn, his shirt unbuttoned, a dirty rag around one eye, his other eye firmly fixed to the ground. I was too far off to hear the dialogue, but I could see the frowning Sarge taking Tenn off the battlefield. Well, we got ready on the right again and ready on the left and we fired at will. When the targets come up, Tenn's target was blank, but the one next to his had 16 bullet holes.

Finally he wore down the army and got what he wanted—a Section 8 discharge as mentally unfit for army life. He came into the Supply Room before he was to leave, and for the first time I saw a friendly gleam in his eye.

"You heard?" he asked with some satisfaction.

"Yup. Congratulations." I wanted him to know I was on his side, although I was sure he knew that anyway.

"Yer discharged, yer entitled to a full uniform?" he asked.

"Yup."

"Any outfit you want?"

"I guess."

"Winter uniform?"

This, of course, is August. In Mississippi.

"Wow! I don't know, but I'll look it up for you."

He gave me a searching look: "I'd be thankful."

Evidently he trusted me to do this for him—but it took some doing! The regs simply stated that a man discharged from the army is entitled to a full uniform of his choosing, so I ordered him a "full" uniform—from winter long johns to woolen greatcoat. Lots of squawks from Quartermasters and many meetings, but they finally came through. When Tenn came to pack it all in a barracks bag, I got my first smile.

In a photo taken on a postwar Appalachian tour with young teachers is one of two young Tennessee mountain girls standing on a hillside wear-

Could this be Tenn and his winter army coats? (Joanna Creighton, hand on hip.) Author photograph.

ing woolen army greatcoats. It took me back to the Camp Shelby, Mississippi, Supply Room. I scrutinized the photo again. Could this be Tenn and his daughters wearing the army winter coats I delivered? Why not? Stranger things have happened to me—like living with the girl, Joanna Creighton (above in the photo), for more than 50 years.

With a five-day pass, I took a Greyhound to visit Harriett in Montgomery, Alabama. She took me to a country club buffet/dance for the benefit of military personnel. With my modest exception, all were officers of superior rank—a seemingly great number of majors and colonels, with a sprinkling of brigadier generals. From their scarcity on the floor, captains and lieutenants must have been staffing the kitchen. We were in the second year of our share of the war ,and many of the men were Air Corps returnees from the Pacific theater, bedecked with medals, ribbons, and combat badges and dressed in natty, pressed uniforms.

Harriett looked great in a strapless party dress, suspended from her tiny breasts by an alchemy known only to women. In my rumpled summer suntans, I figured in the story of the princess cat bringing home a battered, but still alive, mouse. In some context, which I never did uncover, Hattie had frequent contact with the local military, and many greeted her affectionately by name and were instantly tolerant of her infantry mouse.

My 69th Division patch caused some amusement, but I must confess I didn't notice any negative reactions or disapproving looks on the part of the brass. Actually, I didn't catch any looks at all. Since I didn't fit the picture, I just wasn't there—a non-person.

In the infantry overseas, we learned to hate the "fly boys," envying the fact that they came home every night to a comfortable bed and breakfast, with plenty of booze and girls. In Germany, I witnessed a return flight of bombers. A B-25, trailing black smoke, dropped out of the formation to circle over our lines. We counted only three of the five-man crew who escaped the burning plane. The first was carried back over Germany, the second came down between our lines, while the third's chute never opened. We laid down a barrage of mortar shells to keep the Germans' heads down, and a squad of riflemen went out to bring in the flyer. As they returned past our position, I had a glimpse of a tortured face, covered with soot and blood. Well, every man to his own poison—I had grown accustomed to my foxhole.

However, this was Montgomery, Alabama, my war was still a year off, and the free drinks were getting to us. I in my army clodhoppers, and Harriett so light in my arms, did an exuberant polka, sending officers reeling like bowling pins. In our occasional correspondence, it became the "bump-the-colonel" polka. I sensed that her father, who was on the scene, was less than pleased. But hell, I had a grudge against him anyway.

From Camp Shelby, our training complete, we were shipped off and scattered around the country. I was sent to Fort Meade. It seemed like a deliberate attempt to break up any friendships developed in training, although it was plainly just military bureaucracy at work. Uncertain of the course of events, I felt very much alone. I missed Tommy most of all. But my skills in Supply must have been on my record, because I was given temporary Staff Sergeant stripes (although not the rank or pay) and went to work in the Supply Room.

Shipped to Fort Dix, New Jersey, adjacent to New York Harbor, I was put to work outfitting men to form a shipping company. As an acting sergeant, I was part of the headquarters cadre and could get numerous passes into New York City. At home, I was welcomed, of course, although there was a bit of apprehension concerning my preparations for going overseas. I assured them I was in Quartermasters and would see little or no combat.

It was at the house of my Onkel Franz, under the influence of his infamous brandy/tea, where I was given detailed instructions on war survival—an exercise known as malingering.

I should have written it down and sold copies at the gates of Fort Dix. Entrepreneurship, however, was never my strong point!

His war was in the Austrian Army in World War I. Whenever he wanted to avoid a patrol or other dangerous duty, my uncle would go on sick call with a high fever. This, he said, was very simple. Put a half-bar of yellow laundry soap under each armpit overnight, and in the morning you will have fever. What's in laundry soap? Carbolic acid.

"You would not see me now," intoned my Onkel Franz, "were I not one year of the war in a TB sanatorium."

"You had TB? Like Mom? I never knew it!"

"*Nein*, I never had it," laughed Unk. "The man next to me I got to spit in my little blue bottle."

There was much more, but why give away vital information? I may still do that war-survival booklet!

Most of my New York friends had scattered—many were in the armed forces and some had already been killed. One evening at a Bronx dinner party, I met Hildreth again. She seemed happy to see me, and I her. Nonstop throughout the dinner, we exchanged life experiences of the previous seven years. She had been married but was now separated and had her own flat, to which she invited me—to listen to music.

Side by side, a phonograph needle going through a stack of records, comfortably situated with pillows, we finally became relaxed enough to talk about our "unhappy experience." I told her how devastated I had been and how it had affected my relationship with girls during the past years.

She seemed to be listening very quietly until I became aware that she was silently crying.

"We should have talked, Emil. We each carried the same burden, but yours was so unnecessary."

She reached over and took my hand. "I was the guilty one but didn't know the extent of it until I got married. Don't laugh, but I had vaginal spasms that stopped penetration whenever we tried intercourse. I had to go through a long spell with a psychiatrist to be cured. If we had only talked!"

Needless to say, Hildreth's story had a salutary effect on me, and when I left her apartment the next morning, I no longer carried the stigma of virginity. All I had now was a war to get through!

18.

ENGLAND

JUDAS GOAT, April 1944

STILL A PLAY-ACTING SERGEANT, like a Judas goat I led my shipping company aboard a troop carrier converted from the luxury liner SS *Rotterdam*. Being faster than German subs, we zigzagged across the Atlantic without an escort. The ship cooks were from the Dutch East Indies, so we were fed hearty, basic Java/Dutch dishes—the buns were almost the size of a bread loaf. It was the kind of Dutch luxury liner my uncle had planned to book me on as a busboy—perhaps even the very same one.

We anchored in the Firth of Clyde and came ashore in the town of Greenock, Scotland. Around the docks, barrage balloons dangled cables to keep air raiders from low-level attacks across the dockyards. There was great activity around the port—damaged ships were being repaired, others were being serviced with ammunition and supplies. Small courier vessels were darting hither and yon—with smartly uniformed British sailors in some, greasy shipyard personnel in others. It was all so strange and purposeful. We had arrived in the war zone!

In the railway station, goods wagons were small and dinky—a far cry from the large freight cars I rode during the Depression. The compartmented passenger cars were different but also familiar—we'd seen them in numerous movies. But it was the engine that caught my attention and admiration. In the station, one swept by us with majestic power, all polished brass and red trim, emitting loud hisses and engulfing us with jets of steam. We rode the trains through Glasgow and over endless miles to London and, finally, to Wells, in southwestern England.

The county of Somerset is west of London, just off the Bristol Channel. Like almost all of England at that time, Somerset was one gigantic supply depot, with solid stacks of equipment massed in fields and along the roads. Not all the freight convoys had been sunk by U-boats. We settled down, amid this vast materiél dump, into a drab, damp, quonset-hut life. Our training program consisted of hikes, close-order drills, and little else. It seemed purposeless and desultory in the face of the coming combat.

Being an acting staff sergeant in Supply gave me certain privileges and exempted me from many of the daily exercises. It also gave me more free time to investigate the surrounding area on foot. On the first day of exploring, I walked into the village of Rockwell Green. This tiny hamlet, about five miles from our camp, was too small and static to attract the fly-boys, who, with their natty uniforms, dominated the nearby towns and cities. There was a marked absence of movement on the street, so I opened the door of the only pub in town and poked my head in. At a table sat a circle of ladies (mostly gray-haired) playing cards. All instantly turned their heads to look me over. "Come in, Yank," they chorused. Reserved English they were not.

They pulled up another chair, sat me down, ordered me an 'arf 'n 'arf ale, and proceeded to teach me the basics of British gin rummy. Playing for pocket change, they soon cleaned me out. All through the game, I found myself being thoroughly investigated, a more thorough job than the one done by my Navy Intelligence officer!

"Where you from, Yank? What do you do in civilian life? Married? Girlfriends? Parents alive?" I, in turn, was treated to endless tales of wartime woe and local gossip, but it was all done with good humor and cackling laughter. I guess I passed muster that first day—I was invited back. Being in Supply, I had friends in the kitchen and thus was able to collect and bring packets of sugar, coffee, chocolate, and canned rations, plus my own rations of candy, cigarettes, soap, and toothpaste. I played these against shillings, pence, and 'arf 'n 'arf ale. Not overly surprising, I found them to be shameless gin-rummy cheats. It got so open that it enabled me to parcel out my supplies evenly.

"Yank" very soon progressed to "Willi," and one day I was rewarded with the grand prize, an introduction to a daughter. Mary was young

Mary.

(about 18—it was hard to tell), thin, very nice, but—unlike her mother—very, very shy. I found it difficult to make small talk. I have always had a curiosity about things in nature, so on my second meeting with Mary, it was with genuine interest that I asked her about heather and gorse, two items of flora I had read about in English novels. Immediately her mother boomed out:

"Why don't you take Willi up on the moor, Mary? You need the exercise and fresh air!"

I had struck a rich vein. Mary was indeed interested in English novels, nature in general, sheep in specific, spinning and weaving. We spent several afternoons walking on the moors. Heather, it turned out, has a purple flower. Gorse, blooming yellow, was a wicked bush like a gross thistle. The moor was punctuated by small, rocky hills called tors. Besides the prickly gorse, the hills had sheep; you had to pay attention when you walked, and, most particularly, when you sat down.

One day, Mary took me to the Bristol Channel. We boarded a double-decker bus that seemed to completely fill a narrow, sunken road, lumbering side to side like a top-heavy elephant. Our destination was a seaside resort, out of season and dismal in a dark overcast and light rain. I carried her umbrella and she clung to my arm as we strolled slowly down the boardwalk. We finally stopped under the shelter of a gazebo overlooking the channel and talked about Wales across the water and how great the beaches were in the summer sunshine. I put my arm around her shoulder and by and by she put her mouth up to me and we kissed. But there wasn't much passion in it; she hadn't had much experience with boys and seemed fearful. I wasn't eager to bring home a war bride, so with common consent, we relaxed into a low-key relationship that we could both enjoy.

Some time after these momentous events, I was invited to Mary's house for dinner. Since I had started going out with Mary, gin-rummy games had become an infrequent rainy-day thing. It was to her house that I most often went, and most of my supplies naturally went with me. It was a very modest cottage, thoroughly laced: lace curtains, lace on the backs and arms of chairs and on numerous little tabletops. (They never talked about her father, but there was a picture of him in uniform in the parlor. He had died in battle—I think it was in the desert campaign.) We ate potatoes, cabbage, Spam (my treat), and a very sweet bread pudding made with treacle. Mary asked me when I would be going—I told her I didn't know. I wasn't being secretive—none of us really knew. We just knew it would be soon. It was not exactly a gay evening.

When I left the house, Mary gave me a package she wouldn't let me open—something, she said, to keep me warm when I went to France. It was a gift of a very heavy brown wool scarf, about a foot wide and long enough to go around my neck with both ends touching the floor, and two pairs of beautifully made gray, knee-length stockings, also of soft, super-thick wool. They were products of Mary's knitting skills and a rare, thoughtful gift for an infantryman. (Later, in the bitter cold of the northern plains of Germany, I would learn how great a gift it really was.) I must confess, there were some tears shed at the door, mine as well as hers. A short time later, we were put on the alert and no longer allowed freedom of movement.

19.

NORMANDY, FRANCE

LOADED INTO A TROOPSHIP DEPARTING FROM SOUTHAMPTON, I joined the crowd at the rails as we slid by the Isle of Wight and out into the rough English Channel. At Omaha Beach, we were decanted into LSTs and dropped into the water just short of the sand and gravel—following in the footsteps of the D-Day troops but without the opposition. On D-Day, our forces met up with a crack German division, the 352nd, which had moved into the Omaha Beach area three months previously but had not been detected. As a result, the 29th Division, which we were to replenish, had suffered higher casualties than anticipated, and my replacement unit was enormous.

The 29th D-Day Division was formed from the Pennsylvania/Maryland/Virginia National Guard. Its division patch, Blue and Gray, depicted the Korean Symbol of Life. My regiment, the 115th, was made up mostly of Pennsylvania and Maryland National Guards, and it represented the Blue. The Virginia National Guard, the 116th Regiment, represented the Gray.

The cross-channel attack had been dreamed about, studied, and planned since the beginning of the war—the proud product of many brilliant minds. Hanson Baldwin, in his *Battles Lost and Won,* wrote:

> The concept of the invasion was immense, imaginative, massive. The invaders were to move across the choppy channel with 5,300 ships and crafts—the largest fleet of any time! The greatest aerial armada in history, some 12,000 planes, were to land airborne

divisions in Normandy. 107,000 troops, 14,000 vehicles, 14,500 tons of supplies were to be landed on the open beaches the first 48 hours.

Charles Cawthon, who wrote *Other Clay: A Remembrance of the World War II Infantry,* one of the truly authentic books on the Normandy fighting, vividly described coming ashore:

> With the burst of fire, we all submerged neck-deep in the sea, for Omaha Beach obviously was not a place to stand up and be counted . . . . It was now apparent that we were coming ashore in one of the carefully registered killing zones of German machine guns and mortar . . . . I tried to rise and found I had seemed to be hoisting the English Channel with me . . . . I jettisoned the assault jacket into the litter in the surf and, free of its weight lumbered up the beach . . . . I took my pistol from its holster and from the plastic bag that was to have protected it from the water. The plastic had not availed, and the pistol was sticky with salt and gritty with sand. Up and down the embankment were lying M-1 rifles, Browning automatics and light machine guns, all similarly fouled . . . . The crusade in Europe at this point was, for all practical purposes, disarmed and naked before its enemies.

Cawthon wrote about the men he had been trained to lead: "The members of my boat team had completely disappeared among the debris, I saw nothing alive to either right or left."

The 29th Division had just come from a year of training in an England that was groaning under the weight of stores of war, tanks, Jeeps, weapons, ammunition—all the matériel needed to overwhelm the enemy. When the ramp dropped on their LSTs, however, they faced a desolate beach empty of the needed tools of war and filled instead with useless weapons, sprawled bodies, and hidden enemy weapons firing directly at them. It must have been an overwhelmingly devastating experience. Reading this in more recent years, I felt a deep sense of shock. For the first time since I started my account of World War II, some 50 years after the fact, I felt the sickening emotional memory of my own combat experience pale. I had no single LST ramp drop down like a stage curtain to reveal the ultimate terror of combat.

I had lived for 12 years in the South and had gone to school in North Carolina, and I loved and admired many of its people. Even as a "damnyankee gringo," I had been largely accepted. I was well aware of the Southerners' deep relationship with their Civil War history. Education for many Southern boys is in military-style schools. Confederate flags still fly in the South. At the start of World War II, *Time* magazine reported: "In Washington the U.S. Senate voted that regiments dating back to the Civil War might carry in battle the Confederate stars and bars as well as the U.S. Stars and Stripes." The 116th Regiment, being mostly Virginian, was named the Stonewall Brigade, and it went through World War II comparing its battles to those fought by the Civil War Stonewall Brigade.

So I wasn't startled to read, in *Other Clay:* "There was a vague report that 'A' Company had lost [on Omaha Beach] all of its officers and most of its men. This proved all too nearly true. It had been as costly a day in the regiment's history as Chancellorsville and the death wound of Old Stonewall himself."

No Civil War Blue Coat regimental flag had been conferred on us, the 115th Regiment. Small favor—I had enough to deal with surviving one war.

We marched up from the beach and were led out into a large field, where sergeants with lists of names separated us into groups. Led into a smaller field, we were allotted a buddy and told to dig in. I paired off with one of the men I had gotten to know on the transport ship, a fresh-faced young Swede. We found a hole someone had already scooped out under a hedgerow, and we crawled in to wait—a matter of weeks. They put us to work loading trucks with supplies coming off the beach. It was hot during the day, but nights were damp and cold. Dusk didn't fall until about 11 p.m. and dawn arrived about 4 a.m.—a short night. With two per foxhole, one had to be out of the hole and on guard at all times. It was a severe infraction to stand guard close to a wall or any structure you could lean against—you might (many did) fall asleep. Zonked as I was for sleep, I spent my two hours tracking ghostly Nazi figures creeping around the periphery of my vision, just waiting for my torpidity to take me off guard—even for the merest second. I didn't trust the officers who told us how safe we were "back here." Prey to the wildest speculation and rumors, our anxiety levels, already too high, crescendoed to the point where it seemed even combat would be welcomed.

Every night after dark, "Bed-check Charlie," a remnant of the German *Luftwaffe,* came over to harass us, buzzing our lines and dropping a few bombs—anything to keep us from sleep. A great concentration of antiaircraft weapons surrounded the beaches and the supply lines. At night, when "Charlie" arrived, tracer shells put up a monstrous Fourth of July display that filled the sky. The Germans called it "Golden City." It kept alive the unbearable tensions generated by the long wait.

I have absolutely no memory of the exact date I arrived in Normandy. In fact, my memories of the entire Normandy campaign are made up of fragments. By June 30, 1944, 452,000 replacements had landed in Normandy. I suspect I was included in that number.

We had been delivered to the front-line hedgerows through the offices of the Replacement Depot system—known with little affection as the "Repple-Depple" system. There was a chronic shortage of men throughout the war, the result of a decision to maintain an army of only 90 divisions. Therefore, every experienced combat division, like the 29th, had to stay on the line, leaving no reserves or little opportunity to pull back for rest and refit.

To make up for the Normandy shortfall, General Eisenhower swept up men from the rear echelon. Men who thought of themselves as cooks, mechanics, and clerks found themselves becoming replacements for decimated rifle companies.

In the States, the time of training was speeded up, and men were, much to their horror, taken out of the Air Corps and put into the infantry. They thought of themselves as "Grounded Butterflies." Part of the problem was that one-third of the draftees—men who grew up in the Great Depression—were being rejected for physical reasons.

The Repple-Depple system was grossly wasteful of life. Replacements were sent up to the units sometimes just before or even during a battle. Completely ignorant of battle conditions, men died unnecessarily, even before we had time to learn their names.

Had the Germans been given a free hand to devise a replacement system for the European Theater of Operations, one that would do the Americans the most harm and least good, they could not have done a better job.
—Stephen Ambrose, *Citizen Soldiers*

How much better it would have been to pull units back for a refit—to orient new men into survival ways with battle-wise men. My Swedish foxhole buddy off the beach was taken as a rifleman. He was killed just a few days later. As attrition quickly made us the old-timers, I found it painful to make friends—only to see them as small parts on the battlefield.

One morning, one of the noncoms who worked for the Repple-Depple came walking briskly past our foxholes: "Rise and shine! Drop yer cocks and grab yer socks! Up and at 'em!"

For a hazy moment, I was back in Mississippi—this fatuous humor was pure Camp Shelby training camp. Cheerfully, he informed us that our time had come. His attempt at cheer failed to dent our deeply ingrained apprehension. But at least the suspense was over. We were rounded up, loaded on trucks, and driven past endless hedgerows toward the combat zone. At the ride's end, a corporal with a 29th Division shoulder patch separated about 35 of us by name and marched us down a sunken road. I was amazed by the sight of a French peasant stoically plowing his fields—fields already more than adequately plowed by high explosives, and more still coming in. Spaced out around him, with bloated stomachs and legs held stiffly in the air, were a few of his dead cows. I was subjected to my first sweet-sour smell of putrefying flesh.

Arriving at the division area, we gathered on a grassy knoll to await our assignments. The corporal who led us there was one of the few real bastards I encountered in the combat zone. He bullied us with the many miseries we would be facing at the front and the gruesome ways the men we were replacing had died. It was obvious he had utter contempt for us as replacements.

Sitting on that grassy knoll, apart from the other replacements, was the loneliest moment of my life. Ahead of me was the war I had feared and fought against since high school. It was total entrapment. I was going into the cellar of darkness with little hope of coming out.

Finally, after what seemed an endless wait, the company's first sergeant arrived. He barked at us: "Any of you dogfaces know machine guns or mortars?"

Well . . . hadn't I taken a machine gun apart one Sunday in the back of the supply room? I raised my hand and was told to move to the side. A staff sergeant came up and questioned us as to how much target practice we had had with machine guns. I kept quiet, and he marched his quota off.

"The rest of you," another sergeant said, "are mortarmen." Me? A mortarman? Anything but! This was the only infantry squad weapon I had never touched—the mortar squad kept the weapon in their barracks. I used to watch the mortar squad train. The sergeant would blow a whistle and a man would dash out with the heavy base plate and slam it on the ground. Immediately a man would scurry out with the tube and lock it into the base-plate socket, while a third man would quickly attach the bipod legs. It was all useless training, since the mortar was rarely taken apart in combat—at a crucial moment one part might not turn up. It didn't occur to me until much later, when I watched more unfortunate replacements joining us in the dead of night, how fortunate I was to be assigned my place in the company in the peace of that grassy knob.

Here's Charles Cawthon again:

> In one of the greatest intelligence failures of all time, no one had ever thought to tell the men about the dominant physical feature of the battlefield—the maze of hedgerows that covered the western half of Normandy. The combined skills of all the renowned military engineers of history could not have built a more effective system of field fortification. It was a system ready-made and waiting for a German army that fully understood its uses. The sunken lane plays a heavy role in battle history: at Antietam, Fredricksburg, Shiloh. We were rehearsed endlessly for attacking beach defenses, but not one day was given to the terrain behind the beaches.

Hedgerows are the result of more than a thousand years of Normandy farmers' piling rocks and dirt to mark off small, checkerboard fields. They can be 3 to 4 feet thick, chest and head high, and topped with bushes and small trees. A labyrinth of sunken roads crisscrosses the terrain. Stone houses and barns were easily turned into fortified strong points by the Germans.

This maze of thick earthen walls and sunken lanes was my introduction to combat. It was tedium spiced with high adrenaline. As we left the grassy knoll, we were given ammo and rations to carry up to the combat zone. Immediately in front of us, we could hear the sounds of combat—the ripping force of rapid-fire German machine guns and the explosion of shells. We crept close to the hedgerows, fearfully keeping our heads down. A sergeant led the way, calm and seemingly unconcerned.

Our mortar position was established in a pit dug in the field in back of a hedgerow. The nasty corporal turned out to be the mortar gunner of my squad, The men had foxholes cut into the hedgerow itself, and I was given one, dug possibly by the man I was replacing.

Our squad leader, Sergeant Schwartz, assigned me a foxhole partner. Foxholes, I found, were always occupied on the buddy system. My buddy was a young replacement who must have been 18 but looked younger. That afternoon on line, we were subjected to our first artillery barrage. When the first shells fell nearby, he clutched the edge of my jacket and pulled me to him. While the barrage upset me, too, trying to give him comfort helped me surmount my fears. I tried to reassure him with the notion that this was the safest place to be, under a thick blanket of earth. But the impact of shells, as they pounded our hedgerow and showered dirt down on us, was terrifying. His face became more and more rigid and his eyes more unfocused. His response was to curl up tightly, his face buried against his knees, and shiver. He started up a monotonous chant, which took me some time to decipher. He was intoning: "Bombs are coming, gotta get away . . . gotta get away . . . gotta get away." Suddenly he started to claw his way out of the hole. I grabbed his legs and pulled him back. Fortunately, I was a lot bigger and could hold his shaking body down until the barrage lifted.

When I released him, he swam out of the hole on his belly like a turtle and started crawling across the field. Sergeant Schwartz and I lifted him to his feet and hauled him to the medics. As we dragged him, his body was rigid, his eyes opened and closed spasmodically. We never did see him again. When we returned, the sergeant looked at me very carefully, as though evaluating my survival qualities. "We lose a few this way, but never this soon."

He started to walk away, then spun on his heels, tapping the shovel dangling on his belt. "This is your best friend. Use it!"

I was lucky to get into the mortars instead of a rifle platoon. Mortarmen didn't have to lead the attack or go on patrols. The order of attack, as in the more open fields of northwestern Germany, was usually two rifle platoons in front, the weapon platoon (us) in the center, and a rifle platoon following. We were precious to the life of the company, since our machine guns and mortars were the first line of defense against enemy counterattacks.

Firing our mortars of course attracted enemy mortar and artillery fire. The greatest source of wounds in World War II (as high as 70 percent) came from mines and mortar and artillery shells.

As I sat with my back to the hedgerow, eating my C rations that first night with the squad, word came down that we were to attack in the morning. At this news, my obnoxious corporal, the mortar gunner, and his assistant—who had been joshing with me about being a combat virgin—fell silent. They wouldn't look at me or each other as the sergeant outlined our role in the coming attack. Then he turned to me:

> Your job will be to bring shells up to the assistant gunner, as he calls for them. [We had stacked boxes of shells against the hedgerow wall to be safe from direct hits.] I'll be up ahead with the telephone where I can call in the shots. Since we all will be busy, you have to keep your eye open for any German infiltration on our flanks. This is ideal sniper country—sharpshooters hide in trees and in the hedgerows. Look for them. You may have noticed that our officers hide their insignia of rank. Snipers prefer them to lowly dogfaces.

> As soon as we open fire, the Germans will return mortar fire, trying to knock us out. They frequently counterattack, and it's the job of the mortars and machine guns to stop them. You probably will be scared shitless, but you gotta know that we all will be too. Just do your job.

In the morning, our attack began with a brief artillery barrage. A squad of riflemen had joined us and were nervously peering through the thick hedgerow foliage. The Germans had machine guns at opposite hedgerow corners and men with rifles or semiautomatic weapons stationed along the walls. Suddenly all hell broke loose. Heavy machine-gun fire ripped through the hedgerow, and mortar shells began dropping in the field behind us. Our sergeant, nestled somewhere in front of us, started to call in firing coordinates and our shells were sent flying.

Terrified, I plastered myself against the wall. Who could survive this hell! Then I heard a scream: "SHELLS . . . goddamn it!"

I scurried over with a bag of shells. The mortarman, wearing earphones, was huddled behind his gun, feverishly working the elevation and the traverse according to the sergeant's instructions. His assistant was pulling safety pins and dropping shells down the tube as fast as he could. Both were trying to huddle as low as possible in the pit and still function. I ran back to the shelter of the hedgerow.

As we fired mortar rounds at the German positions, and our machine gunners fired to keep the enemy down, our riflemen crept over the hedgerow. I couldn't believe it! How could they do this? They ran toward the German line, firing their rifles and throwing grenades. Then it all stopped. The Germans had retreated.

We, too, moved up to prepare for the next attack. Medics were tending to our wounded. But hardly had we begun to dig our new mortar pit when we were deluged by artillery fire. The air was full of menace—high-pitched, screaming shells came from all directions. We lay flattened in our shallow pit for what seemed like an eternity. The ground shook with the impact of the shells, and clods of dirt showered down on us. It was as close to the end of life as I could imagine, and it seemed to go on forever. When the explosions stopped, we heard someone yell, "Counterattack!" The two mortarmen jumped to attend our weapon, and I was told to peer through the hedge to see if the action was coming our way. Riflemen were running up to the hedgerow, and in the corner I could see them mounting a machine gun. Gray figures poured over the opposite wall, and there was a firestorm of noise and activity—total bedlam. I knelt down and pressed my head tightly against the wall, trying to squeeze the panic out of my mind.

The Sarge joined me, angrily shaking my shoulder where my light carbine hung. "Use this . . . NOW! We need all the firepower we can get." Putting my carbine on top of the hedgerow, I started firing at the gray figures. The Sarge shouted instructions at the mortar crew and our shells began dropping into the field in front of us. It took some skill and it was dangerous to drop mortar shells this close. Our machine-gun fire suddenly stopped, and I could see the gunner fall away back into the field. Someone else grabbed the gun and the firing started up again. Suddenly, mortar shells other than ours also dropped into the field ahead. The gray figures melted back across their hedgerow wall. I was later told we had been helped by 81mm mortars from our Heavy Weapons company.

In the unsettling quiet after the combat, I looked around, expecting to find most of our company annihilated. Amazingly, our mortar squad had survived intact. Our machine gunner lay dead at our feet, a bullet in his forehead, and in the field in front of us, gray figures were lying sprawled in every position, some still moving. I was totally befuddled. I was not sure if I had killed anyone, but if I had, it was mechanical and impersonal. A young German who had made it closest to our hedgerow lay on his back, his face seemingly at rest. It was only an accident of birth that I was wearing a GI uniform. Had my father not escaped Austria when he did, I could have been wearing field gray on the wrong side of the hedgerow. That young German's face stayed with me all through my combat experience.

As we went back to digging, the corporal jeered at me for my behavior under fire. Sergeant Schwartz said something sharp to him, and he turned away. The Sarge came and sat down:

> You did fine, Willi, for your first firefight. These hedgerows are our worst enemy in attacks and our best friend in counterattacks. Every battle sound seems to be aimed against you, only you. Hang in there, you'll sort it out. Half the noise is friendly—learn that first. An enemy bullet kind of zings as it goes by; if it cracks, take cover, because it's close. The same for artillery. You get to know where shells will land by how they scream. Artillery comes in at an angle, digs into the ground, and most of the shrapnel sprays forward. Mortar shells come straight down and fragments fly out in a circle—daisy cutters. Dive for cover with artillery shells, keep going with mortars. Better to get it in the legs than in the head.

We got guys who can instantly tell you the pedigree of each shell—its caliber, trajectory, and where it will land. Be surprised how fast you learn.

Sergeant Schwartz was a short, stocky man a few years older than the average in our squad. On his square frame, without a discernible waistline, his pants hung as though about to fall down, which could have given him a comic aspect but never did. He was from Brooklyn, but he had all the characteristics of a Bronx boy from my neighborhood. I identified with him, and he had my total allegiance. Having a decent noncom made all the difference in keeping my sanity in those first weeks. I didn't realize how lucky I was in this until I talked with other replacements.

I was lucky, too, in joining a battle-wise company that already had had many miles of hedgerow fighting behind them. As I grew accustomed to the battlefield noise and could sort out friendly fire from enemy, I started to build up confidence. It wasn't until we received another batch of replacements that I realized how attrition had taken its toll, day by day, and my newfound confidence started to erode.

When the Sarge yelled, "Counterattack!" he was courting dark reprisals. Orders from General Gerhardt were to call such attacks "enemy enthusiasms"—the word "attack" had frightening connotations. Was it really believable that someone in a moment of panic would scream, "Enemy enthusiasms"? In my experience, no one ever did.

Listening to the talk of the old-timers, I learned that in many instances the enemy had superior weapons, particularly for hedgerow fighting. "We would be very happy to swap weapons with the krauts," Sergeant Schwartz told me.

Along with the many elite German outfits in Normandy were paratrooper divisions—the best-armed infantrymen in Europe. They had 930 light machine guns, 11 times as many as 29th Division companies. The average German rifle company had 20 machine guns and 43 submachine guns. Our companies had two machine guns and nine BARs (Browning automatic rifles). The BAR fired a stately put . . . put . . . put . . . and was answered with the terrifying shrieking rip of the German guns, a stitch of bullets at 1,200 per minute, which could literally cut a man in half. Adding that they had six mortars to our two, that meant they had 6 to 20 times our firepower. In the close-in spaces of Normandy, mortars caused by far the greatest number of American casualties.

On the other hand, our M-1 rifle, firing eight rounds as rapidly as you pulled the trigger, was superior to the German rifle. We also had air superiority, although with all the tight hedgerow fighting, we seldom had personal benefit from the air force. Besides, that July was the wettest in 40 years, which kept our planes grounded for much of the time.

About our Sherman tanks, the less said the better, but here's the assessment of Williamson Murray and Allan Millett in *A War To Be Won:*

> The real scandal in U.S. equipment was the decision to stay with the M-4 Sherman tank instead of the new M-26 Pershing with its 90mm gun, improved silhouette, and thicker armor. It would have saved many tankers' lives. By the end of the war the 3rd Armored Division with a table of organization of 232 tanks had lost 648 tanks with 700 more damaged but repairable.

One morning, we were told in our briefing that we were to attack from behind our tanks. I was startled to hear a groan go up from the riflemen. Tanks attract lots of attention: mortars, artillery, other tanks—every available weapon. It was like kicking over a hornet's nest. As an antitank weapon, we had the bazooka, which required a two-man team. The Germans had the *Panzerfaust,* operated by a single soldier and far superior as a tank buster.

Normandy was an infantry battle; tanks could do little in closed-in hedgerow country. The light U.S. Sherman tank, with 2-inch armor plating, was no match for the heavier German tanks, particularly the Panthers and Tigers, which had 6-inch plating and superior cannon. The Germans called the Allied tanks, "Tommy cookers." U.S. tankers called them "Ronson Burners," because advertisements for the Ronson brand of cigarette lighters boasted that they faithfully "lit on the first try."

Even where the open plains of northern Germany gave our faster tanks a better chance of survival, we hated to see them. Cowering in narrow slit-trenches with multi-tonned dinosaurs racing around us, we sweated out the odds—would one cross our slit trench the short or the long way? The difference could be worth our life.

How to use tanks in the hedgerow country was one of the many unsolved problems of D-Day planners. It took a lowly sergeant to improvise a partial solution. He welded a steel cutter-bar to the front of a tank so it could tear open a hedgerow. It was only then—as they poked through hedgerows and poured fire on machine-gun nests in the opposite field—that we learned to appreciate them. Occasionally, the tankers had white phosphorous shells, and the carnage they caused the Germans was hideous. The fiery chemical stuck to their clothing, burning deeply into their bodies. Fortunately, the enemy had few of these shells to expend on us.

Many a tank commander was killed peering out of his turret to direct fire. It took an unidentified GI to suggest a solution to that—attach a telephone connection underneath the blind tank so that an infantryman could direct the tank fire. (It was probably a mortarman, since we communicated with our frontline observation post by telephone.)

The German 88 was a cannon that fired in a flat trajectory like a rifle, faster than the speed of sound, 20 shells per minute. It was mounted on tanks as an antitank, antiaircraft, antipersonnel weapon. Being "personnel," naturally we despised and feared it. It was one of the most hated combat weapons. The 88 gunners had few scruples about using their fearful weapon as a rifle against individual soldiers. Once we had to traverse a sunken road and climb over an earthen wall on the far side. An artillery observer had the 88 zeroed in and was playing a cat-and-mouse game with us—trying to blast us off as we crossed the hedgerow. One victim was groaning in the road before us; the 88 shell hadn't hit him directly, but it had sandblasted him with a shower of dirt, stripping him of most of his clothes and much of his skin. He was alive but bleeding from every pore. Although he never returned to the company, we heard that he survived.

It made for anxious moments of decision. Some started and dodged back, hoping to trigger the fire, then climb up and over before the spotter could alert the gunner for a second shot. When my turn came, I took the pack off my back, threw it over the barrier, and dove after it. It reminded me of boarding a moving empty boxcar.

My fellow ammo bearer, at this point, was a nervous, volatile, thin Italian. He said he was a Wall Street runner from New York City. Whatever his work entailed, he certainly didn't fit the description of "runner." He had long, narrow feet and walked splay-footed. We called him Wall Street. Going for rations at night, I would let him lead the way back. If there was a root, stone, or the least impediment in the path, he would trip over it. It was mean of me, I admit, but it saved me some falls!

When our assistant gunner was hit, I moved up to take his place. The gunner—my sour, unfriendly corporal—was one of the few left from the original Pennsylvania National Guard. He kept apart from the rest of the squad and showed little interest in giving me instructions on the mortar. The only instruction I can remember getting from him, since it was my job as assistant gunner to set up the mortar, was: "Watch where yer placin' the goddamn mortar—we lost some men when they elevated the tube too far and the shell hit the leaves of a fuckin' branch overhead."

The ammo bearer who took my place was a coal miner from Scranton, Pennsylvania. He was the opposite of the Wall Street runner—short, square-shouldered, and, of course, strong. They irritated each other fearfully. It got to the point where Miner refused to let Wall Street help dig.

"Just get the hell outta my way, ya damn Wop."

He, of course, was a Pole—but Runner didn't dare swap ethnic insults.

Toward the end of July, coming into patches of more open terrain, Miner was making more and more elaborate foxholes (slit trenches, actually). One night he covered one with twigs and leaves. About 3 a.m., Wall Street decided to get up and piss. On his way back, he got confused and stepped through the camouflage, directly on top of his slit-trench buddy. With the ensuing uproar, half the battalion was up, ready to repel an attack.

"Fuck regulations!" screamed Miner. "We dig fuckin' separate foxholes from now fuckin' on."

We were going through a series of crippling attacks, and tensions were high, yet each of our ammo bearers dug solo holes. At dawn one morning, I was awakened suddenly by a close-by shot. Taut with apprehension, I exploded from my foxhole. It was Wall Street! Holding his carbine in one hand, he was shaking his left hand. "Look!" he shouted wildly. "My finger is dangling!"

He had his first-aid kit out and open. Dropping his weapon, he started pouring sulfur powder on his wounded hand.

"There was a German out there. He shot me," he moaned.

It happened frequently before an attack. Men broke completely under the tension of waiting. I heard of two who committed suicide. We snatched up Wall Street's still-smoking carbine and threw it into the bushes.

Miner looked at us forlornly. I sensed he was feeling guilty about making the nervous Wall Street sleep alone in an isolated foxhole. "The skinny fucker spoke about it, but I never thought he'd do it."

Sarge asked me to take him to the aid station. "Tell them he was shot by a sniper while on sentry duty."

I hoped they wouldn't notice the powder burns on his filthy hand. Many of our wounded returned to duty, but we never saw Wall Street again. Until we got a replacement, Miner shouldered a double load of ammo—as only he could have done.

In the battle for Normandy, the Germans retreated slowly, inflicting great damage on us. The casualty toll for my 115th Regiment in June 1944 (including D-Day) was 1,138 men. For July, in the hedgerows, the body count was 1,414—our highest monthly loss of the war. Since an average regiment was around 2,000 men (and of that, a certain percentage was not in active combat), it would seem that the 29th's rifle companies had had 100 percent casualties in July alone.

Although there were variations, there was a horrible sameness about this combat. There were 20 miles of hedgerows between Omaha Beach and the more open ground, 15 to 16 of them per mile. Slated to be conquered by D-Day plus 5, it took two bloody months. Each combat day, we had to dig two mortar pits and two foxholes—with a small shovel. During the short nights, half the squad had to stay awake on guard duty and two had to go back for supplies. Adding to the tensions of daily combat, every man was in a constant state of complete exhaustion. Sleep was never refreshing. You went to sleep with a dull gray numbness in your head and a heavy leaden fear in the pit of your stomach—and you woke with them perpetually there.

By mid-July, the *Wehrmacht* had lost some 117,000 men, yet the German will to fight never seemed to diminish. Rommel told his young son, Manfred, the grim truth. As Martin Blumenson wrote in *Breakout,* "All the courage didn't help . . . . Sometimes we had as many casualties on one day as during the whole of the summer fighting in Africa in 1942. My nerves are pretty good, but sometimes I was near collapse. I have never fought with such losses." By the end of July, the *Wehrmacht* still had about 750,000 men on the American sector; we had about 800,000. The major difference was that we were getting many more replacements than they were.

One day, the 30th Division relieved us and we pulled back to a hill a short distance away. On the morning of July 25, as we lay on our backs in the sun, we heard the faint drone of bees in the distance, tiny dots that materialized slowly into 12 plane echelons. Filling the sky above us, some 3,000 bombers were coming over in successive waves. They were to pulverize the German front lines for the 3rd Army breakout. German ack-ack fire managed to knock down a few of the lead planes but was quickly vaporized by the tornado of falling bombs. We were on our feet cheering. Then, to our great horror, the smoke that marked the bomb-drop zone started to drift back toward us, and bombs fell on the 30th.

We later learned that 111 of our men died and 400 more were wounded. It killed the highest-ranking officer to die in the war, Lt. Gen. Leslie McNair, who had come up to observe the effects of the bombing. We could have told you, General—war kills! The 30th, between Normandy and the Bulge, was bombed 13 times by "friendly" planes. They referred to the Ninth U.S. Air Force the "American *Luftwaffe.*" There were times when we too were hit by our own planes, and times when our attack planes saved the day, so it was always a matter of mixed emotions when it was announced we would have air support.

Shortly after the devasting bomber raid, my First Army, which had been slugging its way down Normandy, opened the way for General George Patton's Third Army to break through into the more open fields of France.

On August 7, the Germans attempted a breakthrough at Mortain. The concept was to cut off Patton's Third Army from his supply line. For the second time in a few weeks, the 30th Division had relieved us and again suffered the brunt of the counterattack. That afternoon. the U.S. and Royal Air Forces heavily bombed and strafed the road, the British Typhoon attack-bombers being particularly impressive with their rows of rockets secured under their wings. The road was turned into one long, stinking junkyard.

Entrapped by Allied forces in the Falaise Pocket, some 10,000 German soldiers died and 50,000 were taken prisoner. Since much of the *Wehrmacht* equipment had been reduced to being drawn by horses, their bodies were added to the carnage. (The Germans used 2,700,000 horses to move the *Wehrmacht* transport and artillery. Horses, of course, didn't need gas, which was in increasingly short supply.)

In *Crusade in Europe*, Eisenhower commented:

> It was literally possible to walk for hundreds of yards at a time, stepping on nothing but dead and decaying flesh. The smell was all-pervading and overpowering. So strong in fact that pilots of light artillery observation aircraft reported that the stench affected them even hundreds of feet in the air. The unburied Germans, swollen to elephantine grossness by the hot sun, lay with blackened faces in grotesque positions. Here was no dignity in death.

Happy as I was to see the end of the Normandy offensive, it appalled me to see the horrible price paid by the Germans. As we marched past the garbage dump of mutilated bodies, we were very much aware that this could have been us. Nothing beats the indignity of knowing that one day you, too, could be turned into a bad smell!

The charnel house that was Normandy climaxed with a fitting ending at Falaise. It took 80 days of combat and some 637,000 casualties to accomplish what our planners envisioned would take only 20 or 30 days after D-Day. The heaviest casualties were not, as anticipated, on the beach. Not quite the scale of Verdun, but close enough for me.

Unfortunately, the Gap at Falaise took a long time getting closed, and a good many of the enemy escaped—particularly highly experienced senior officers. General Patton, off and running, chased the remnants of the fast-retreating German Army. While this gave the Allied world a huge boost in morale, he was criticized for not aiding more in closing the Falaise Gap.

As the Gap was closed, the 29th Division was pinched out of the attack area, and we had a few days of leisure before the next chapter. To our surprise, it wasn't, "on to Germany"—but then, when were *we* ever consulted?

20.

Fortress Brest

THE FIGHT FOR BREST, August 22 to September 19
> Brittany glowed in the warm sun on August 22 as the 29th's motor convoy rolled westward en route to Brest. From the roadside cheering Bretons hailed the sun-tanned 29th Division soldier in the rushing column . . . waving, cheering, raising their arms in the V sign, tossing flowers into the trucks.
> —*Official History, 29th Division*

POSSIBLY THE OFFICERS' COMMAND CARS RECEIVED FLOWERS; the troops received apples. If the writer of the above poetry had been hit by an apple in an open truck going 35 mph, he would not have mistaken it for flowers. However, it was exhilarating, in the warm sun, to have a tour of scenic Brittany. We passed Mont St. Michel, a dramatic place of history and great tides. The tide was low, and we could see the wet road going out to what looked like a monastery or castle. Without guide service, we knew "from nothing" about what we were seeing.

> The spirits of the men were high. They had been told that the assignment should not be difficult, that the garrison of this fortress was only waiting to give up.
> —*Official History, 29th Division*

What a snow job! When it came to the attack, we faced the bitter truth.

One of the objectives of General George Patton's Third Army was the great Fortress of Brest in Brittany. Patton found the interior of Brittany largely empty of German troops; most of them had gone to the fight in Normandy. When Brest was found to be heavily defended, the Third Army bypassed it, turning eastward toward Paris. Brest was left to the VIII Corps—namely us, the 29th Division—plus the 2nd and 8th Divisions and two Ranger battalions—not a mighty host to bring down the mighty Fortress of Brest.

> The defense of Brest had been constructed to withstand attack by land or sea. An outer band of defenses consisted of an abundance of strong points, heavy in automatic weapons and self-propelled guns, some fortified with concrete and steel. An inner band of ramparts was modernized with steel pillboxes, antitank ditches, road barriers, and mine fields. With months of preparation these positions had become the ultimate in defense. Garrisoned by the German 2nd Parachute Division and units of the German Navy and Marines.
> —*Official History, 29th Division*

Almost every branch of the German armed forces was represented in the fortress. They used their engineering skills to rig devious booby traps and mines—naval engineers buried 350-pound naval shells that they could detonate electrically. What started out to be an estimated garrison of some 20,000 mysteriously managed to propagate itself into 50,000 men. They fought under direct orders from Hitler to hold out until the last cartridge. General Hermann Ramcke, who had also led the long, bloody defense of Monte Cassino in Italy, was determined that Brest become ". . . the same glorious page in history that Monte Cassino has been." He parceled out his fanatical paratroopers throughout the defenses, with orders to shoot any who faltered.

When we came up to Brest, we found with sickening hearts that the outer lines of the fortress were ringed with miles of hedgerows—even better prepared for defense than Normandy.

The first week was a repetition of attacking hedgerows, and the last weeks, the fortress itself.

Artillery and mortar fire failed to do much damage against entrenchments built to withstand aerial bombs. Flame-throwers, mounted on

Churchill tanks towing fuel tanks, were more effective. Huge amounts of smoke were laid down so that engineers could remove mines. The process took endless days, during which time we were perpetually subjected to showers of artillery and mortar shells.

Closing in on the defense rings of the fort, we came at last to the final wall before the submarine pens. The Germans had the wall under intensive fire, and we huddled there with our heads down. Tired as we were, no one bought into the suggestion made by our captain that we vault over the wall and confront the enemy. Suddenly a colonel appeared on the scene, his only weapon a swagger stick, with which he gestured at the wall angrily, exhorting us to fly over and demolish the "boche." He surprised the hell out of us; it was the first time I ever saw him, and I don't think I ever did again.

"Over the wall, men, we've got 'em cornered in their pigpens like a bunch of fuckin' rats. Be a man, be a man, do it! Do it! 29 LET'S GO! Go! Go!" A few men vaulted up on the wall and were promptly blown back by heavy fire. Some of the riflemen laid their rifles on top of the wall and, with heads down, blindly emptied the magazines. Not to be outdone, we lobbed some mortar shells in the same direction. When it became clear that we were depleting our ammo and would soon be defenseless, the order came to cease fire. The colonel's screams of "29 LET'S GO! GO! GO! GO!" fell on deaf ears. Somehow, this magic formula for action—our division slogan— didn't seem to inspire a death rush over the wall. It was a standoff. Short of scaling the wall himself to lead the charge, the officer was stymied. He stamped away, muttering about getting artillery fire. We became involved in tending to the wounded and moving the dead off to the side. It was getting dark, and we dug in along the side walls to wait for whatever horror came next.

Things remained quiet until about 4 a.m., when every weapon the Germans owned started to fire. Machine guns with white tracer bullets cracked overhead; 20mm ack-ack shells and other light artillery shells whistled past in a great flood. Since the fire had to clear the wall, it all went safely over our heads, but it caused our meager supply of adrenaline to pump, and I anxiously took the safety off my carbine. With Sergeant Schwartz, we moved out of our holes to stand by the mortar. The pyrotechnics lasted for some time and then suddenly ceased. Our hearts pounding, we looked for Germans to come pouring over the wall, but nothing happened. It made no sense, but the pure fury of it kept us cowering, wide-awake in our foxholes. Come the dawn and it all made sense, in a mindless sort of way. The defenders had been told to fight until the last bullet, and as they pledged the *Führer,* they spent it all in one last mad bash.

That morning they surrendered, coming out of holes no one knew existed—in uniforms, clean shaven, and carrying satchels and books. There were even some naval types in white, with technical instruments. We sat on a wall and watched them go by. Many were bold and sassy. As they walked past us, they waved and cheered:

"Hey, Yank, we'll soon see the USA, will you?"

"Hope you make it, we did!"

There was a lot of anger in our ranks, but victory had taken the fight out of us.

The division's official history described the end of the battle, which had cost us great casualties:

> The battle-tired 29th Division soldiers, suddenly freed from the danger that had beset them through the three-week campaign, now gave themselves over to vigorous celebration. They sampled freely of the huge supplies of captured wines and cognac. They swept through the submarine pens, and selected the choice souvenirs from the huge stores of materiel and equipment there.
> —*Official History, 29th Division*

Yeah, sure, maybe for the officers and quartermaster types. We, however, were marched back to the rear area to our favorite parkland—the hedgerows. It's amazing how, even after more than half a century, such petty things still rankle.

There was less chickenshit in combat—line officers and noncoms were dependent on their men. Of all the stories about the "brass" that amused us, most involved General Patton. He himself was a dandy, with brilliantly burnished helmet and brass buttons, polished riding boots, and pearl-handled pistols. He made "chickenshit" famous by insisting on proper dress for the men of his command—helmets fastened under the chin, tie tucked between second and third shirt button, daily shaves, etc.

My favorite Bill Mauldin cartoon shows Willie and Joe in a truck parked before a large billboard listing all the rules and regulations to be followed in Patton's Third Army zone. Willie says, "Radio the Captain, Joe, we're making a thousand-mile detour."

Penalties on Patton's billboard
$10 no shave
$25 no tie
$25 no helmet tied under chin
$10,000 no life—the insurance premium paid to the family of a
    soldier killed [not on Patton's board]

Patton was, of course, most infamous for striking two soldiers in hospitals for being cowards. For this, he was disliked by many of his superiors and almost lost his combat command.

Once Patton chewed out a man in a hospital for not standing at attention, and the man replied, "Run along, asshole, I'm from the merchant marine!"

And just think—if it weren't for being rejected by the merchant marine, that man could have been me! Not much has been written about the merchant marine. They had ships sunk before Pearl Harbor, had the highest casualty rate next to the Marines, and lost ships to mines after the war was over.

In the three weeks or so that we spent around Brest, we had opened and closed a goodly number of narrow trenches for the disposal of human wastes. When these were closed, dirt was mounded over the top and a sign was posted. These signs, mounted on a stake planted at the head of the mound like a cross, informed the public:

OLD LATRINE
Opened: 8/25
Closed: 9/18

They had every appearance of small, hastily dug graves, and the French put flowers on them. I like that in a people!

All in all, I would say that for the front-line troops, very little effort was made to entertain them. We were grateful for the few showers and changes of clothes we did get.

The favorite song of the common *Wehrmacht* soldiers—those we mostly faced—was the nostalgic *Lilli Marlene*. It had a catchy, sentimental tune that was quickly translated and adopted by Allied troops. (The tune was first sung in 1938 by a Swedish girl, Elli Anderson, in a Hamburg nightclub. Miss Anderson ended up in a concentration camp for reasons unknown to this writer. But then, when did the Nazis need reason?)

> *LILLI MARLENE*
> *When we are marching in the mud and cold,*
> *And my pack seems more than I can hold,*
> *My love for you renews my might,*
> *I'm warm again, my pack is light.*
> *It's you, Lilli Marlene, it's you, Lilli Marlene.*

According to John Ellis, author of *On the Front Lines: The Experience of War Through the Eyes of the Allied Soldiers in World War II*, German storm troopers had a less-than-charming marching song: "When Jewish blood spurts from the knife, then things go twice as well."

Actually, we could have told them, "Things Go Better With Coke!" We oughta know—GIs downed 10 billion bottles of Coca-Cola at 5 cents a throw.

But don't get the idea that we sat around our foxholes and cellars harmonizing. Singing was the purview of troops who had access to beer, pubs, and leisure—things we almost never had. At least we did have several days of rest, free from the threat of sudden death.

We also saw the rare appearance of a Red Cross wagon. I had a letter from Harriett and knew she was overseas somewhere with the American Red Cross. This wagon, however, was totally without Harriett or news of Harriett. The coffee was fine, the doughnuts divine, but the "pocket books" were *numero uno*. By going through the line several times and approaching different girls, I managed to get many more than my fair share of books—which helped me get through the interminable trip to Holland and beyond.

Pocket books were my salvation during the war. These were the world's first paperbacks—made strictly for the armed forces, to be destroyed after the war. Since the Special Service Division sent four million of these books overseas every month, some of them even made it to the front. There were classics by Henry James, Christopher Marlowe, Charles Darwin, and Ben Johnson. I never saw any books from the Modern Library, but I was told they could be made available.

Some of the most popular titles and authors—although not necessarily my choices—were Emile Zola, Ellery Queen, *Lost Horizons, See Here, Private Hargrove*, and the *Pocket Book of Verse*. I seem to remember reading some Steinbeck, Hemingway, and Mark Twain. I know I read Wodehouse, because I frightened my foxhole mate by laughing out loud. The bottom of a foxhole does not exactly have a book-club ambience.

> Life in the rest area was a rare experience for the men of the 29th Division's fighting units. For the first time since arriving in France, they were actually allowed to rest and were not required to wear steel helmets. The first days in this area were made even more pleasant by the prospect of seven-day furloughs to England. But before the plan could be set in motion, the 29th Division was ordered to Germany, where it was to reinforce the First Army in its attack on the Siegfried Line.
> —*Official History, 29th Division*

Who needed to go to England! Been there, seen that, hadn't we?

Our train consisted of small French "40 and 8" freight cars (40 men or 8 horses)—leftovers from World War I. They were in no way, snob that I am, comparable to the large boxcars of my boyhood. I suppose we should have considered ourselves lucky they hadn't also added the eight horses!

During the day, I wangled a position at the partially open freight door. While it was chilly in the fall air, it furnished the light I needed to stay involved in my books. It actually wasn't as idyllic as it sounds. I was constantly stepped on, and the light was blocked by soldiers needing to piss out the open door. The forward progress was slow, and broken by numerous halts—the right-of-way had, of course, been badly used by Allied bombers and the French Resistance forces. However, there was little complaint about the pace—every kilometer clicked off was that much closer to the killing zone.

One of our longest halts was in the Paris yards, where the division slogan, 29 LET'S GO!, was taken at face value by numbers of men—two from our Company A. The rationale, as they gleefully told us before leaving, was to pick up a dose of gonorrhea, surrender to the MPs, and spend several months in the hospital. Like most things in the army, though, it didn't turn out that way. The cure for gonorrhea was now a single injection of penicillin—and back to work. Well, at least we hoped they had the joy of it!

Actual figures: U.S. Army deserters (not counting those just AWOL, Absent without Leave) were 19,000—10,000 of them that fall to Paris alone. On leaving the hospital, our two AWOL soldiers were returned to duty instead of to the stockade—on the usual supposition, I gathered, that they could receive no greater punishment.

Venereal disease (VD) was a major consideration in the armed forces—not as much, I'm guessing, in the combat units, since opportunities there were scarce. In the Mississippi summer heat, during our training, we were packed into iron-sheeted Quonset huts, made to wait until the heat was unbearable, and then shown films with lingering close-ups of gruesome, weeping VD sores. It was a formula for causing groans, moans, and dead faints. To hedge their bets, the army also issued copious numbers of contraceptives and had to cope with cries of pain from right-wing church groups.

John Steinbeck reported that, in World War II, "when Army Supply ordered millions of rubber contraceptives . . . . it had to be explained that they were used to keep moisture out of machine gun barrels—and perhaps they did." They did, indeed, John!

(Ironically, in 1948 I would find myself working on a documentary film on the penicillin treatment for syphilis—in the Mississippi summer heat.)

When Cherbourg was captured, early in the Normandy fighting, it was thoroughly demolished and useless as a port. Did they expect the port of Brest to be in good shape? Brest had been a particularly grueling battle, with heavy casualties. After the war, I read several accounts of this campaign. Instead of pushing through and rolling up the German retreat, General Omar Bradley turned from the main German forces and engaged in sterile operations against Brest.

The original "plan" called for an advance into Brittany to free the ports, and Bradley clung to the "plan"—despite the fact that the war was rapidly moving northward, away from Brittany. He claimed that it would have tied up troops to have blockaded Brest. But hey, Brad, we endured some 10,000 casualties taking it—10,000 troops even more permanently tied up.

> Brest held out until 19 September. Instead of isolating the large German garrison in the city, Bradley, for reasons he has admitted had more to do with prestige than military value, left VIII Corps behind to deal with the tough German troops. It was far too high a price to pay to maintain illusions of invincibility.
> —Carlo D'Este, *Decision in Normandy*

Your illusions, Bradley, not ours! Brest was never used as a port!

After a time, we left the Paris yards for Belgium on the train that was pursuing the war, and we were not very happy.

21.

COMBAT IN GERMANY

MAASTRICHT, HOLLAND, September 29, 1944

WE DISEMBARKED FROM OUR TROOP TRAIN in Visé, Belgium, and were trucked into Maastricht, Holland. The brass seemed anxious to get me to the Aachen front, the first major battle on the Siegfried Line. Maastricht was our Corps base for the Aachen and Roer River drives. In our few days in Holland, the battalion was brought up to strength and we received a replacement to fill out our squad. He was from the New York town of Canajoharie. He reminded me of Tommy Wentworth—a bit taller but also of slight build, with adolescent pimples, and shy until he felt at ease with you. As wary as I was of letting someone get close to me, I couldn't help responding to his puppy-dog good nature. He took Wall Street's place as second ammo bearer. In moments of exultation, he would bellow out, "CANAJOHARIE!"—his personalized version of the paratrooper's "GERONIMO!" We called him "Can."

This border between Holland and Germany was coal-mining country—in the flat farmland, great piles of slag stood stark against the blue sky. The Germans had pulled back from the first German town across the border, which we promptly occupied. As we dug in our mortar at the eastern edge of the town, we stopped to watch in horror as a lieutenant led a rifle squad around the open face of one of the slag heaps—in full view of the enemy. It wasn't long before they were hit by 88mm tank fire. Great showers of gray slag were thrown into the air, along with the toylike bodies of men.

Company A had taken over most of the houses for shelter and were busy inventorying food stocks the Germans had left behind. In the backyard of our house, a 200-pound pig shared the space where we were to dig in and site our mortar.

The squealer obviously was in the way of our combat efficiency, so someone put a carbine bullet into its head. We hastily dragged it up into the attic (no sense disturbing neighboring squads). Having seen it done on the Cumberland Plateau, I volunteered to butcher it. Bayonets, I found out, are designed to stab, not to slice, and I soon understood what the verb "to butcher" really means. It was the first time any of us had blood on our bayonets. We literally tore that poor beast apart and laid the pieces out on a bedsheet. I wondered at the reaction of the returning German *Hausfrau* as she washed the blood from that sheet! Should she weep? Was it Fritz or Tommy blood?

The Germans had retreated to the next town, which proved to be better fortified. As the German soldiers retreated, the civilians waited out the battle deep down in a mine shaft converted into an air-raid shelter. The captain called me down to interpret for him. As I labored with my not-so-fluent German, I could hear the twang of a guitar deeper down the tunnel. It wasn't until I recognized the piece as a Spanish Loyalist song that my ears really stood erect, and I hurried to explain to these folks that they were obligated to leave the town for someplace in Holland until the front was pushed much farther back into Germany. They protested and they wept, but it was for their own safety, wasn't it? Finally, the captain lost his patience and told me to tell them to shut up and stop sniveling or we would "run them out through the fuckin' German minefields to join their fuckin' retreating relatives." I said it, of course, in a much nicer fashion than he did—I was at a loss for such profanity in my German lexicon.

Freed from duty, I dashed off down the shaft to find the guitarist—who had gone through "Los Tres Insurgent Generales," "Freiheit," and was now on "The Peat Bog Soldiers"—songs from the Spanish Civil War and French concentration camps. It was a German coal miner who, in reply to my excited questions, said that he had learned them in Spain fighting in the anti-Fascist German Thälmann Brigade. (Some 5,000 Germans and Austrians fought in the International Brigade.) He had a long, lean face, a nose to match, and thin, bitter lips—the kind of face that needs time to grow on you. His was not a warm, spontaneous personality, but he seemed pleased to find someone interested in his life story.

We hadn't gotten very far when, behind me, I heard my name being called. He quickly drew me a map to indicate the house he had appropriated, and I dashed off.

That night, I cooked a slab of ham and went for an interesting visit. The ham made the right impression, but he had something to match— a washtub full of mashed sugar beets, which had been fermenting to feed a makeshift still. We sat on the floor before the still and took turns tossing back tiny glasses of raw moonshine as it dripped from the coils.

He was a coal miner, but not in this town—he was from another town on the border with Holland. Since some of their coal shafts opened into the Dutch mines, the German union miners would use them to smuggle political undesirables on the Nazi list out of Germany.

"One day," he said, "they tell me, better get yourself out. I go into Holland, to Spain."

I told him that I, too, had wanted to go to fight in Spain, but I'd been too young.

"Ach, your Lincoln Brigade, great casualties, many too intellectual for war."

Some Spanish Civil War notes: When I met Fernando Saenz Leon, my Spanish ex-schoolmate, at the Black Mountain College reunion in 1995, we talked about the Civil War, and he sent me copies of notes and letters on his experiences. In 1939, the war lost, Fernando fled Spain and crossed over to France. He wrote:

> In Munich, France and England lost the alliance of Czechoslovakia, which was the best armed nation in Europe after Germany; of Russia, which was left out of the Munich meeting; and of Republican Spain, with a fighting army of 600,000 men but without arms. In September 1939, they had to stand up to Germany and Italy alone.
>
> Franco had not received any armament from Germany during the spring and summer of 1938 because the Germans were accumulating it on the border with Czechoslovakia. After Daladier and Chamberlain gave in to Hitler, Germany sent all this accumulated armament to Franco. With this armament, Franco

dislodged the Republicans from the Ebro [River] and had enough to run through Catalonia. From February 5th to 9th—when Franco's troops reached the border—300,000 Loyalists, mostly military personnel, crossed the border. The airplanes, tanks, artillery, machine guns and ammunition which Russia had been sending us since early summer through France, were piled up on the French side of the Pyrenees.

When the Loyalists were defeated, my coal miner, along with remainders of the International Brigades, also crossed the border. The French received them not as exiles but as criminals. Led off to poorly equipped concentration camps, the men had to survive on 1,600 calories per day. When the Germans combed the camps for forced-labor battalions, "I say, I am coal miner, and they send me here—full circle."

In the morning, after a heavy artillery barrage, we attacked across the beet fields. I had no idea whether I was sicker from my usual fear of combat or from my hangover. They were similar feelings. After months of close hedgerows and fortress Brest in-fighting, one would expect the great open vistas of the northern German plains would be a welcome relief. But it was flat, featureless terrain, with no place to hide. Our heavy artillery fire falling on the town kept the Germans down as we staggered across the field. We, however, were getting some fire from hidden tanks and from our German mortar counterparts. Our two rifle platoons disappeared into the edge of the town. As I moved across the field, I was totally absorbed in searching for any slight depression that would at least partially shelter me. I had just spotted a shell hole when I heard Sergeant Schwartz shout urgently: "Gunner's hit! Take the mortar, Willi. Set it up in this shell hole."

I grabbed the mortar where it had fallen and rolled with it into the pit.

"Change helmets with Gunner!"

In the lining of Gunner's helmet was a table of firing ranges. The Sarge and Miner dragged Gunner off to the closest house, leaving me alone with Can and the mortar.

Hunkered down in the shell hole, I read the chart—for XXX yards, it called for elevating the mortar to 45 degrees. As I fumbled around trying to set the tube at 45 degrees, I called for Can to arm four shells.

In town, there was fierce fighting. The Germans had mounted a coun-terattack and we had run into new German tactics—they defended the perimeter lightly and kept their main force in town. Our hold on the town was very tenuous, and when someone yelled, "TIGER TANK!" it was wise-ly decided to pull back. In a panic, I fired off the four shells, hoping they were clearing the village and doing some good. A knot of German prison-ers emerged from the house carrying a huge couch, on which lay our gun-ner. Typical overstuffed German furniture, I foolishly thought! Staggering across the uneven field with the great couch was our sergeant, wedging a fistful of rags tightly in the wounded man's stomach. He motioned for us to join them. I noticed then that our sergeant was also wounded, blood staining his left sleeve.

I folded the mortar, hot tube and all, hoisted it across my shoulder, and lit out in the general direction of the retreat. I moved as in a night-mare, slithering helplessly on mashed sugar beets in my funk. I passed the corporal on his overstuffed couch, the prisoners slipping and sliding as urgently as they could with the panicky knowledge of Tiger tanks enter-ing the town behind them. The great German tanks never made it to this edge of town in time to shell us. I shuddered—next time they would.

Back in our cozy house, Sarge said, "You're the gunner now, Willi. Who's your choice for assistant?"

"Can, I guess. He seemed pretty steady out there. But, hey, I was never really trained on the mortar."

"You'll learn," he said, as he left for the aid station to have his own wounds treated.

Another unrewarded promotion! A mortar gunner rated a corporal's double stripe and extra pay. But not for me! I wondered if my Camp Shelby records had followed me into combat. I was to carry the heavy mortar and fire it with the instructions under my hat as a private.

The next day's attempt at crossing the field was to be a major effort, with more artillery, air cover, and tanks. This time, there was to be no retreat; we were to dig in, if necessary, in the open field. That kind of brief-ing foretold heavy opposition and heavy casualties.

Our seldom-seen kitchen unit had moved up, and we had a rare "hot" meal. Served outside in the dark, we filed by the cooks who filled our mess gear with stuff. Our decimated squad sat around the mortar eating. We felt lost without the Sarge. His leaving left a vacuum that filled us with dread. In the chill October air, the food had gotten cold, and in the dark the mess gear was full of unpleasant surprises. I could identify greasy lamb stew, beets, mashed potatoes—all mixed with dabs of orange Jell-O. Help, Mom!

After washing our gear, we sat around in our cellar, our normal pre-attack queasy stomachs made worse by the greasy dinner. Walled in by our fears, we talked little. From time to time, the others shot me quizzical glances. Could I do it? I stood a two-hour guard duty after midnight, out by the mortar tube. I kept eyeing it. It was my mortar now. I visualized the quick, practiced manipulation of the machine by the Gunner. Could I do it? Could I fend off the rush of a counterattack? I was overcome with the sick stupidity of not having forced my hated Gunner to teach me more about using the mortar. Back at the cellar, the bodies were packed so tightly that I had to quickly slip into my relief's slot before it closed up and disappeared. I fell asleep listening to the grunts and cries of the sleeping men.

In the morning, we took off, as usual, behind our two rifle platoons. Some of the men were carrying long ladders. For what? To scale walls, cross moats? I had little time to speculate. We were instantly deluged by artillery and mortar fire. Automatically, I dove to the ground. But having to dive and rise with the heavy mortar soon exhausted me, so I just ducked my head and plodded blindly ahead. I hissed, "Spread out, spread out," at Can, who tended to drift too close to me.

About halfway across the field, I noticed very few men still on their feet, so I, too, dropped. Tired and numb with fear, I lay still, pressing my body as flat as possible against the ground. I moved very slowly, and shifting my pack and mortar to protect my head, I detached my folding shovel. With a minimum of movement, I started to dig, keeping my shovel handle flat to the ground. With mortar and artillery shells exploding around me and showering me with earth, it took total concentration.

Dimly I became aware of Can calling: "Hey, Willi, what do we do now? Hey, Willi!"

"Stay where you are," I shouted back. "Put your ammo bags and pack in front of your head and play dead. I'll call when the hole is big enough for both of us."

Completely absorbed in digging, I was astonished to find I had excavated a slit trench 2 feet deep and wide enough for two. The shelling had slowed to an occasional round, and all seemed static on the battlefield. I called for Can to crawl slowly to me, and we took turns digging down to 4 feet. I was glad to have him for company. He obviously looked up to me for help.

"What do we do now?" he asked again.

"We stay in this hole until someone whistles us out to attack or tells us to retreat."

Suddenly I became aware of tank noises—our promised tank support had arrived. I had dug my foxhole parallel to the German lines, in the hope that oncoming or retreating tanks would cross my burrow's short dimension. Tanks that came close made a horrible rumble in our slit trench, and dirt dribbled down the sides. We could hear the cough of our Sherman 75mms, the sharp crack of answering 88s of the German tanks, and the rumbling explosions of tanks going up in flames. Finally the tanks left, and a heavy silence settled on the battlefield.

Books were an important ingredient in my surviving the long hours of isolation in these foxholes. Blanketed as I was by leaden fear, I welcomed the short periods of relief they allowed. So now I wedged myself in a corner of the slit trench and pulled out a book. It was Mark Twain, and I found myself snorting at his sardonic humor. Can grabbed my arm.

"Take it easy, Willi, it'll be all right."

He had become uneasy at my withdrawal, so I put away the book and we talked about his part of New York state—the Finger Lakes and the nearby Adirondacks. He had worked in the Beech-Nut plant in Canajoharie, but he hoped to pick up more education when he got home.

I heard the approach of a slithering body and peeked out nervously, revolver in hand and cocked. It was the company runner.

"What's up?"

"The Germans have pulled back in several places. The captain thinks we can gain the town without much trouble. C Company will push through us and we'll follow them in."

"What's left of A Company?"

"Hard to say, with everybody holed up. We lost a few, that's for sure, and some tanks."

Actually, the enemy had withdrawn completely, and we were able to dig in our mortars on the far side of the captured town. Can and I practiced using the mortar. Setting aiming stakes around the mortar, I put Can in a hole to our front with a telephone. In an attack, he would guide our fire in relation to our numbered stakes. "800 yards, stake 2. Fire one. More to the left, fire one. Good, fire 3." As the attack came in closer, I would be able to see my own shell bursts and pull Can back to us. Over the next weeks, we managed to make it as a team. I found that the more responsibility I had, the better I could survive the tension. I never did learn what the ladders were for.

In northern Germany, we frequently attacked across flat open fields, our hearts chugging away a mile a minute. With the expectation of incoming artillery, I would scan the ground ahead of me, evaluating it for even the least depression to dive for. Once on the ground, I would get as close to the earth as my clothing allowed. I quickly learned that there was no such thing as a completely flat surface.

In *On the Front Lines,* John Ellis wrote:

> Being shelled is the real work of an infantry soldier, which no one talks about. Everyone has his own way of going about it. In novels you read about soldiers, in such moments, fouling themselves. The opposite is true. As all your parts are contracting, you are more likely to be constipated.

Completely random and impersonal shell fire is total terror. One day the company was pulled back for a little rest and hot food. The kitchen truck arrived with our barracks bags, a rare opportunity to get at our personal effects. For me, it was a chance to access a few more pocket books. It meant, too, that we could utilize the comfort of our sleeping bags. The kitchen crew set up a chow line and served hot food. At the end of the line, they placed a garbage can with soapy water for us to wash our mess gear. We were sitting around enjoying the break, when out of the blue a single shell whistled in and exploded, a direct hit on the garbage can. One of our men at the can was killed instantly, bloodily ripped apart by the explosion, shrapnel, and pieces of can. No other shells landed. It was completely random, purposeless—more upsetting to us than a deliberate artillery attack. It negated any good the rest stop had afforded.

On their home territory, the Germans made copious use of mines. Our engineers, when possible, marked off paths through a minefield with white tape. We followed the tapes, stepping in the footprint of the man in front with heart-stopping precision, praying his shoe was a larger size. The ultimate horror was getting stuck in a minefield during an artillery attack.

A most bizarre night battle was fought under the auspices of General Bernard Montgomery. The 29th Division, as part of the Ninth U.S. Army, was briefly attached to Monty's drive to the Rhine. We arrived at his command in trucks late in the day. Each of our companies had a Limey guide to take us through the British troops holding the line. These troops, wearing berets in contrast to our large iron helmets, had scooped out pits big enough for five or six men and were busy brewing tea. Each group seemed to be well equipped with hard biscuits and restaurant-size tins of bitter orange marmalade. I am very fond of bitter orange marmalade, especially as made in England. While we waited for darkness, I garnered from our mortar squad an assortment of our rations—cans of meatballs and spaghetti, franks and beans, pork and beans, ham and eggs—and negotiated a swap for a large can of marmalade. It made an enormous heavy hump in my pack but was well worth it.

At dark, a long line of powerful searchlights, mounted on Sherman tanks and directed into German eyes, was turned on, and we attacked down its beams. Talk about chasing your shadow! In the flat Rhineland plain, my shadow was a hundred feet long. We never got to punch out Nazi eyes with light as was planned; instead, we found ourselves silhouetted like moths. Suddenly, German machine guns opened up and the picturesque shadows instantly disappeared. Fortunately, Montgomery, being the careful Scot he was, turned off the lights and aborted the attack before casualties became too high. According to General Montgomery, "A good general must not only win his battles; he must win them with a minimum of casualties and loss of life."

HURRAH, we say, for Montgomery! He himself had been severely wounded in World War I and never lost sight of the ultimate truth of war—battles were won with the lives of men at stake. He was known for his great concern for his troops, careful to have everything well prepared before a battle. He was looked down upon by "aggressive" types such as General Patton, but the average infantryman thought highly of him. The

British had been fighting for several years before we showed up, and their manpower had been seriously depleted. His sparing use of troops was understandable. I certainly understood!

Recently, I came across a clue to Montgomery's odd strategy. It seems that in England, dogs are trained to run down a strong beam of light to catch a hare. In our case, the hare could fight back. It is historically interesting that the Soviet Union's Red Army tried the same searchlight stunt on the Vistula River in Poland, with similarly negative results. Not to be outdone by other military geniuses, the 29th Division also indulged in theatrical stage lighting:

> Perhaps no single soldier's impression of the Division's campaign in Germany will be remembered more clearly than the strong, friendly searchlight beams which pierced the night sky throughout the long months on the river line. The lights were cast by six 60 inch, 800 million candlepower units. Their employment was to provide battlefield illumination by creating "artificial moonlight."
> —*Official History, 29th Division*

Four of the six units were promptly knocked out by enemy artillery. All to the good—the last thing we needed was "battlefield illumination."

With my less-than-perfect German, I was called upon to shout deserters out of their holes. *"Kommen heraus, Hände hoch!"* It was a weird sensation suddenly to see little white rags pop up from holes in the ground where no one was suspected to be—sometimes within a stone's throw of our own lines. I would tell them to come on the run, leaving behind helmets and weapons. And come they did, hustled forward by shots from their comrades. Since most of these surrenders took place just before a German attack, they stood nervously before me, rushing their answers, anxious to get to the rear. No more anxious than the captain and me—the Germans would often spot-check the surrender site with a flurry of mortar shells.

Toward the later months of the war, desertions from the German army increased. Hanson Baldwin, in *Battles Lost and Won,* gave some indication of the frustrations of the German officers. In late November 1944, a German colonel in the 18th Volksgrenadier Division went into a ranting fury about the desertion and surrender of six of his men:

> Traitors have deserted to the enemy . . . deceitful Jewish mud-slingers taunt you with their pamphlets and try to entice you into becoming bastards also. As for the contemptible traitors who have forgotten their honor, rest assured the Division will see to it that they never see home and loved ones again. The true German soldier was and is the best in the world. LONG LIVE GERMANY! HEIL THE FÜHRER!

Some outfits killed prisoners on the spot, particularly snipers, who stayed behind and killed soldiers until they felt discovery was imminent—then they surrendered. Happily, that was not the practice of our 29th Division—at least not often. We heard that some Paratrooper units were known to take no prisoners and as a consequence had heavier casualties. The Germans refused to surrender to them, fighting to the very end.

In northern Germany, one of our many captains, enchanted to have a German speaker in his company, for a time (fortunately, it was short) kept me at his command post as a runner. His observation post was a church belfry, and we spent interminable hours there while he scanned the adjacent town held by the enemy. Belfries were well known to harbor life other than bats, and they were nearly always eventually blown away by artillery. It was a truly nerve-racking time. I missed my foxhole.

Between *our* town and *their* town was a small cluster of about two dozen unoccupied houses, a no-man's land. One day, we had a German civilian in the belfry. He claimed to be the mayor and he was very agitated. He pointed out a house in the no-man's land cluster, where he said some women and children were hiding in the cellar. One young girl was badly wounded, and they wanted to surrender to us and get medical attention. Would we go that night and convoy them out?

Be glad to, said the captain—I'll send a rifleman with Willi here, soon as it gets dark. (Hey, Captain, did I ever tell you I flunked German in high school?)

That night, I was introduced to my armed escort, a young rifleman from the 1st platoon, who seemed to stand scarcely higher than his rifle.

The German mayor was nowhere to be seen. We got to the last foxhole on the edge of town and the rifleman disappeared into it.

"Hey," I said, "aren't you coming with me?"

He popped his head up: "This is where I live, this is where I stay. I don't speak German! Come on in, room enough for two."

I sat down, my feet dangling in the hole. "Hey, I need someone to watch out—I can't go in there alone." (I didn't want to go, even with lots of friends.)

"Don't be a fuckin' asshole! The krauts send patrols in there every night. It could be dangerous to your health."

"Well, I'm going. Don't shoot when we get back."

"The password is WONDERFUL, reply is WELL. Germans find it hard to pronounce their 'Ws'" Tell me! "Stay out of the roadside ditches, they're loaded with Bouncin' Betty and Shu mines." Shu mines were small boxes filled with enough dynamite to blow your foot off. But an S-mine (or Bouncin' Betty) bounced up about 3 feet and exploded in several hundred steel fragments. It could tear off a leg or, worse, castrate you. We were inordinately not fond of Betty.

I don't know what possessed me. It was stupid, I knew it was stupid. Let the Germans take care of their own. Where was the mayor? Walter Cronkite once said that all combat soldiers were heroes . . . hell, no . . . most soldiers are moved by self-survival. But almost all, under a combination of factors I am unable to describe (or understand), can be moved to an action against the instinct for self-preservation. I nonsensically felt, I guess, that in doing something humanitarian, I couldn't get hurt.

The road made a sweeping curve into the houses, and I walked bent over, trying to make as small a target as possible in the gloom. In the dark, the homes had absolutely no relation to the ones I had seen from the belfry. Blundering from house to house, I was utterly spooked by the engulfing silence.

One house had a broken cellar window, and I knelt outside it to listen. Please someone, cry! I willed it with total fervor. CRY! The fruitless silence was becoming more and more menacing. I spoke quietly at the dark rectangle of broken glass. Despite how quietly I spoke, the sound seemed to dominate the little town. Sound was my enemy. I broke away a few pieces of glass, but the sharp snaps were more penetrating than my voice. In desperation, I gingerly worked my head through the broken window and whispered harshly:

"Is anybody here? Please come out. I'll bring you back to our lines. If you're hurt, we have doctors."

I was only too conscious of how bad my Viennese German must be sounding to frightened people of the northern German plains. I could almost see a hand tightly covering a child's mouth. Suddenly I could also see my head as a black silhouette framed in the window—a sure target for anyone inside with a weapon. I yanked my head back and sat for a moment in miserable frustration.

Suddenly I saw a furtive movement at the enemy end of town, a series of shadowy forms slipping into the first of the houses. A wave of fear swept through me. I was engulfed by my childhood—shock . . . guilt . . . disbelief . . . abandonment, emotions that washed over me in continuous waves of paralyzing fear.

My adrenaline started to pump, my mouth went dry, and I quickly slipped out of the garden to the back of the house. It was all I could do not to break into a run. I worked my way carefully through backyards, trying to keep a screen between me and the patrol. When I came to the curve of the road, I was forced out into the open; there was no cover, and the roadsides were mined. In the expectation of rifle fire, my back went numb with tension. I kept saying to myself, "Wonderful/well, wonderful/well," as I neared our own lines. Suddenly a dark figure erupted from a hole, and I almost passed out. It was my rifleman escort, who silently led me back to our company. Letting it be seen that he had been with me, he deposited me at the captain's headquarters and left.

As a mortarman, I wasn't called on to do night patrols. Riflemen in my company often told me how they dreaded these patrols and how fruitless and stupid they considered them. With the chronic shortage of officers to accompany them, the riflemen were less than conscientious about this duty. The reports they turned in were probably as close to reality as if they had really done the tour. I blessed this custom, and I am quite certain that I owe my life to a German patrol that went to ground in one of the first few houses of the little village and missed my furtive retreat.

When I told our captain the reason for my unaccompanied return, he ordered an artillery barrage of the little settlement. If the German patrol had indeed gone to ground, as I firmly believed, I hoped they survived the barrage—at least this once.

The weather was atrocious! The weather in Normandy had been mostly wet and bleak, but it was far worse in Germany. When the ground froze, our little folding shovels were useless. When we attacked, we either made the next town or pulled back to the one we had just left. Freezing rain was more enemy to us than to the Germans. In November, it rained 28 days. To add to bad weather, we had 16 hours of gloomy darkness each night. It was summed up in a letter from a suffering Eisenhower to Marshall: "I am getting exceedingly tired of the weather that has broken records existing for 20 to 25 years."

It wasn't quite as tiring for you, Ike, as it was for us. Proper winter clothing wasn't getting up to the front lines. Our leather boots were almost worse than useless. The leather soaked up the cold water in which we were constantly standing. Thousands of soldiers were being evacuated with horrible cases of trench foot, which crippled some for life. In many cases, a man's toes would come off when medics tried to remove their wet socks. In November 1944, the figure for trench-foot casualties was 5,386 in our sector alone. In northwest Germany, the total was 44,728—the equivalent of three infantry divisions.

I valued my feet too much. Thank you, Mary, for your wonderful gift of wool! I wore one pair of your thick, knee-length stockings under my belt and the other on my grateful feet and legs—and exchanged places every night I could. Your scarf went around my neck and under my coat almost to the ground. I not only cherished the warmth, but more so the human gentleness of the person who made them for me.

This is probably the time to talk about the feelings that fighting men had about rear-echelon troops. It wasn't just that the noncombatants were safe from harm and lived a dry, comfortable life, but that basic items we needed—and had been sent up to us by quartermasters—rarely made it. Supplies were rushed up to the front via the Red Ball Express over one-way roads. While generals screamed for gas and troops desperately needed basic supplies, tons were siphoned off into the black market.

To add to the black-market losses, supplies reached the combat soldier only after every rear-guard serviceman had his share. There were good boots available, of the type made popular by L. L. Bean after the war—well insulated, with leather uppers and rubber bottoms. But to the everlasting disgrace of the quartermasters and other rear-echelon personnel, who were wearing them by mid-December, not until late January did the boots get to where they were desperately needed. We were issued (but never received) warm khaki combat jackets with full-size pockets—as opposed to the short, lightweight gray jackets that shone in the dark and had slit side pockets, out of which everything fell. I'm also talking about extra blankets and, more seriously, having to wear khaki uniforms long after the winter snows had arrived, and white camouflage suits long after the snows had melted. John Ellis, in his infantry-oriented book, *On the Front Lines,* wrote: "PX rations, by the time they have reached a rifle company, had been picked over all down the line. It has ended up with shower slippers for riflemen."

Guess what the punishment was for being caught catering to the Black Market. Right! Being sent to fight on the front lines. Hey! No fair! We had been told that combat, in the scheme of things, was the place of honor! Is facing death an opportunity also given to the criminal, to redeem himself? If so, dear God, what crimes have I committed to deserve the infantry? The black marketeers could, of course, be put into the stockade. But compared to my foxhole, the stockade would be like the Hilton.

At the time, we blamed only the black market and the rear echelon for our lack of proper supplies, but while researching the war, I found that General Omar Bradley himself confessed to holding back these supplies—figuring that the war would be over by winter. This was not the only piece of bad judgment that worked against front-line troops.

For instant satisfaction and a minimum of red tape, our most efficient Quartermaster Corps was the battlefield itself. Hanging on my web belt were the things I had accumulated: two canteens, a second first-aid packet, my mortar sight (a big, awkward box), a 45mm pistol (useless as a weapon, but possibly useful as a club if the Hun fell into my foxhole), and a folding shovel (my closest friend and savior). To carry this heavy load, I requisitioned a knapsack from its dead former owner, cut off the pack, and used the shoulder straps to support my belt.

BATTLE OF THE GUT, December 5, 1944

In the first week of December, Sergeant Schwartz returned, giving the squad morale an enormous boost. We had just come up to a dense line of thicket and were peering down a long slope of pasture to the Roer River. Near the riverbank, a neat cluster of barns surrounded a stone manor house (called a "Gut" by the Germans). For the moment, our immediate front was quiet, but we could hear the sounds of very active engagement off to the north.

Word came down that the weapons platoon was to attack, take, and hold the manor house, while the rifle platoons were to take over the river shore north of us. As usual, our lieutenant had been "loaned" to an officerless rifle platoon, so on our own we thoroughly mortared and machine-gunned the complex. Finally, after much nail-biting, the Sarge led us cautiously down the open slope, trailing a spool of telephone wire. An open-field attack in broad daylight is devoutly to be despised, but to attack and not meet opposition is almost more nerve-racking. Except for cows mooing and chickens clucking nervously, all was deadly quiet in the Gut.

What had once been an elegant stone house was now rubble. The door to the cellar stairs was ajar, and leaning against the jamb was a German rifle topped with a steel pot of a helmet.

"You go in, Willi," said the Sarge. "You speak German."

The others laughed. Was he serious?

He detached a grenade from his belt, pulled the pin, and tossed it down the stairs. The explosion made a dull, damp thump—apparently indicating the cellar was large and full of stuff.

In the smoke and dust, we could see no corpses, but in the back was a white rag hanging on another doorway. This time, my *"Heraus!"* brought a German soldier with *Hände* as *hoch* as he could get them. He turned out to be an elderly farmer, who had been drafted into the home guard and then hid when his troop scuttled off.

Anxious to explore the cellars, we quickly set up our machine guns and mortars and posted guards according to the manual. What to do with our prisoner? We set aside his hiding space for his quarters; he was not to leave that room without permission. At first, we kept a wary eye on him, but soon we shamelessly enslaved our willing charge to help with menial tasks: stoking the stove with coal bricks, watching the cooking pots, washing the cooking pots, etc.

We were, of course, in communication with headquarters via our telephone wire. Sergeant Schwartz assured them that while we had had a brief firefight, we had everything under control and could hold out as long as necessary. No, no need to send down rations—we had potatoes and stuff, plus the slope was thoroughly mined.

The cellar was furnished as an air-raid shelter, and it proved to be a storehouse of provisions worthy of an Inca. A large milk can was filled with eggs preserved in waterglass (potassium silicate), a clear, viscous liquid that envelops the eggs and works by excluding air. Another milk can contained cooked meat with 6 inches of fat plugging the neck. We found flour, sugar, all kinds of condiments, a barrel of apples, and glass jars of preserved fruit and vegetables. No wine or schnapps, but a large jug of hard cider. In the courtyard stood a cartload of potatoes. Since the door to the cellar faced east, we quickly pulled the cart before the door.

We dined elegantly! A trunk revealed an assortment of priestly robes, which we wore for dinner; for our tablecloth, we used a gold-embroidered vestment. Another box revealed opera hats (the kind that folded flat, and you felt very elegant holding the rim and snapping it into shape). There was also an assortment of silk parasols. We became very unsoldierly dandies at dinner.

In the cavernous barn were cow stalls, each with a framed slate for the cow's name, pedigree, and daily *milch* production. The cows hadn't been milked for several days, and their great swollen udders hung almost to the ground. They cried out to us in pain, or so it seemed to a Bronx boy. To get this bedlam out of hearing range, we turned them loose to graze in the lush grass by the river.

There was also a neat henhouse, which served us better than the cowshed. We had a new replacement, Joe, who had taken Can's place as second ammo bearer. Joe was a farm boy, and he went down the roosting row of chickens, goosing them to pick the fattest. The rude awakenings were protested by loud squawks, but the yield was worth the racket. Our German *"Hausfrau"* undressed the chickens, pulling feathers off with the skin. He would boil the chicken whole, giving us both chicken meat and chicken soup.

I had been appointed chef and felt myself a great success. Joe came to me with the exciting observation that we had all the ingredients for flap-jacks but milk, so "why don't we go down and bring back a cow?" Against all my finely honed instincts for self-preservation, we did just that—in full view of the unknown and menacing opposite shore. What was not calcu-lated in this tactical move was that you just don't casually detach one cow from a herd. Back we came, leading a cow followed by a loudly bellowing mob. Even then, we had to wait for our flapjacks, as the first milking from the neglected udders came out bloody and stringy.

Finally I was able to offer a breakfast menu: apple cider (second only to the Normandy vintage), two eggs over lightly, and large pancakes with syrup made from melted sugar and cinnamon. The only item from our own rations was the instant coffee.

Can had found a motorcycle and worked on it diligently for two days. By the third day, he had it going out on the cobblestone courtyard, riding in tight circles and shouting exultantly, "CANAJOHARIE!" Wearing top hats and holding white parasols, we cheered him on. It was a scene of great interest to the battalion commander, who happened to be out surveying the front with his binoculars. Unlike Disney fairy-tale endings, ours was not a happy one. We soon found ourselves marching off to the sound of battle, downriver.

Our all-too-brief spell of R&R was abruptly ended by some of the worst fighting we'd seen to date. The miraculous break in the monotony of dread only served to heighten the terror of our return to combat. This was the battle to take a sports stadium on our side of the Roer from the city of Jülich. The enemy had been driven out of their foxholes and trenches and had holed up in a fortified *Sportplatz* and swimming pool. Caught out in the open fields around the stadium, we were mercilessly bombarded with shellfire, machine guns, and even depressed ack-ack bat-teries. With a number of others, panic-stricken, I jumped into a trench, only to emerge spitting ice water. The Germans, who controlled the dams upriver, had opened them to flood the shores with winter water. Some of the ditches were also mined.

As we were attacking down a sodden road in the dark, shivering with cold and fear, a sudden burst of high-velocity machine-gun fire opened up on us. Dropping to the ground, we crawled off the road. A couple of dark, wet bundles of clothes stayed behind. One turned out to be Canajoharie, who had been stitched through the middle, almost cut in two. The other was Sergeant Schwartz, this time hit in his side. It meant the loss of the two men I cared most about in the platoon, and it put a cap on this night of pure horror.

Regulations state: "No one except a stretcher bearer helps a wounded man out of action." Joe and I extracted the Sarge from the road and helped him to the first-aid station. I hated leaving Can, but the Sarge was our first concern. Helping him was against regulations, but this kind of thing was widely done. What wounded officer would refuse help? But I can't say our action was totally altruistic: we were desperate to get away from the sports stadium.

In the warm first-aid station, I took off my gloves to find one filled with blood. A shell splinter had pierced my numb, cold hand and I hadn't felt it. I stepped up to one of the medics, a friend, and dangled my bloody hand: "Hey, Tommy, how about a bandage?"

"Willi," he exclaimed, "let me look at that!"

Quickly he painted my hand with an antiseptic, wound a huge bandage around my wrist and hand, and made out a tag. "Once you're tagged," he assured me, "it takes a month of routine before you get back to your outfit." He hung the tag around my neck: "Wear it in good health."

Medics were in combat as often as we were, but they received no extra combat pay—"since you don't fight," they were told. We valued our medics highly, and my squad had chosen me to write up Tommy for a medal. It went through, and he was happy to get it. It was the first time anything I had written, since high school, had paid off. Did I feel guilty? Well, yes and no. That night, I was as close to "breaking" as any time in my combat experience.

I was evacuated by truck to a monastery in the Ardennes that had been converted into a military hospital. Clean white sheets. HEAVEN! My hand felt numb and, I convinced myself, useless. Actually, no bones were broken or muscles cut, and it healed quickly.

Some time after I had been hospitalized, I received a letter from Mom. It was postmarked the day after I was evacuated. Very disturbed, she had dreamt that I was lying in a ditch, wounded and in agony. She had never before mentioned her fears for me. (I had told the family that I was in

Supply, safe behind the fighting lines.) Mom was not at home in English, so she wrote me very few letters. Was it telepathic perception or an almost supernatural case of coincidence? Hedy told me later that Mom fainted when she received the telegram of my being wounded. It spooked me that Mom could be attuned to my combat-fear waves—causing her deep pain. I felt pangs of guilt about taking advantage of my minor wound.

Hdqtrs, Allied Expedition Force, *Communique 253:* "Allied forces yesterday repulsed a number of local counterattacks." Not so. Here's what Hanson Baldwin had to say about that in *Battles Lost and Won:*

> From Saint-Vith to Bastone the roads were clogged with snaking columns of army vehicles, mixed in inextricable confusion. And the woods were creeping with smashed and shattered units, men with dazed faces and the gray look of exhaustion and shock, men without rifles, broken men and broken units. Behind the broken units came the Panzers and the guns of the Nazis, smashing through the Ardennes in a final gigantic effort for Führer and Fatherland . . . .

LIÈGE, December 16, 1944

I had been at the monastery about a week and was beginning to relax when I woke up one morning to frantic activity. Medical supplies were being packed up, switchboards were torn down, and patients were loaded into trucks and ambulances. It was December 16, the start of the Battle of the Bulge. We were offloaded in the large general hospital in Liège, Belgium. That night, our monastery was in German hands.

Rumors swept through the wards in Liège: we were to be moved to another, more distant hospital; those of us who were able were to be given M-1 rifles and sent to the front; the Germans had dropped elite, English-speaking troops behind our lines (true) to cause havoc and to assassinate Generals Eisenhower, Bradley, and Patton.

MPs began stopping American soldiers at gunpoint: "Who are 'Dem Bums'?" "Who is Mickey Mouse's girl friend?" Completely unexpected and CRAZY! I certainly would have flunked some of the questions they asked about baseball.

Ruthless storm troopers under Joachim Peiper massacred 86 American POWs in Malmédy, Belgium. After the war, an American tribunal sentenced Peiper to death, but Senator Joseph McCarthy used his influence to get the sentence commuted to life imprisonment because of Peiper's "anticommunism." After serving minimum time, Peiper was let off by the West German authorities for good behavior. He then moved to France, where a few Frenchmen with memories blew him up.

Actually, we were more in harm's way than we knew. Liège was the first objective of the attack to recapture the great port of Antwerp. Hitler had launched three fully equipped armies—20 divisions, 12 of which were armored—and the tide had reached Stavelot, only 22 miles away. Buzz bombs literally rained into Liège. When the motors of these radio-controlled V-1 pilotless aircraft stopped buzzing, we held our breath until we heard the bomb's explosion. We cheered them when, occasionally, they turned back into Germany. Later, when the weather cleared and our air force could function, aerial dogfights took place over Liège and 50-caliber bullets and 20mm cannon shells (instead of just rumors) went zinging through our windows and down the ward corridors. From our hospital windows, we watched 7th Armored tanks (usually attached to our 29th Division) pour through the streets of Liège. They were coming down from the north to turn the German tide. The location of the 29th at this juncture was unknown to us. I now know that the Germans at one time contemplated their offensive along the Roer River instead of the Ardennes. I shudder to think of the fate of the 29th had they done so.

When I returned to the 29th Division in early January, I found it spread out thinly along the Roer River, some 700 to 800 yards between company platoons. It covered the entire former sector of the XIX Corps. Of course, with everyone battling it out in the Ardennes, the Germans were in the same predicament on the reverse shore. The German radio, using a sexy woman commentator, tried to taunt us: "Hello there, Two-Nine! How does it feel to be sitting in those holes by the river with nobody behind you?"

Not having access to a radio, we remained untaunted.

It was a cold winter, with heavy snows on the ground, and we had to patrol the empty space between our platoons. Naturally, no provisions had been made for white camouflage, so we were flies on white icing. Since I returned too late to garner a bedsheet, I had to make do with a set of fine lace curtains. I held the prize for upscale patrolling!

Telephone wires had been laid on the snow between platoons. When my turn came to patrol, I would pick up a wire in a gloved hand and stagger through the snow to its terminus—frequently in a blinding snowstorm. Every once in a while, the wire would be cut, and the question to the splicer would be—how? Was it shrapnel or a German patrol waiting for the splicer? It made for a suspenseful repair job!

I only had a splicing assignment once. As I waded in the deep snow, peering intently through a cold mist from the river, the wire in my hand was suddenly . . . not there. I instantly dove downhill into a snowbank and lay as still as a hunted rabbit. The wily Nazis lay just as still—but where? I could feel my body temperature draining off. Slowly—indeed, very slowly—I eased out a hand grenade from my belt, put the safety pin between my teeth, and lifted my head. White nothing in all quarters. Slithering back up the slope, I found my footsteps and the wire. Keeping a low profile and the grenade handy, I searched and found the severed end, made a hasty splice, and continued on to our neighboring platoon.

Life on the Roer River that January was freezing cold and deadly monotonous—just our luck that it was the coldest winter in 40 years. All during January, we lacked winter gear. I ran around draped in my white lace curtain, my leather shoes always soggy. In February, when white camouflage clothing arrived and our vehicles were painted white, the snow melted—so we still showed up as positives against negatives. Along with the horrible weather, thoughts of the approaching river crossing constantly blanketed us with dread. The one blessing was the gradual return from the hospitals of several old buddies, foremost among them Sergeant Schwartz.

To break the tedium, I made an attempt to aggrandize my reputation as a chef, gained at the manor house. As was commonly done, the cellar of the house we occupied had been fixed up as an air-raid shelter, with basic living quarters. We were in the habit of throwing unwanted elements of our C and K rations into a kitchen cabinet. Into my scoured steel helmet, I put all the ingredients I deemed useful—fruit and chocolate bars, small bags of cocoa, synthetic orange powder, jellies, sugar, assorted crackers and hard-tack. Stirring in some canned fruit and boiling water, I cooked the mixture until it seemed well blended. Inverting the cooled mixture on a platter, I proudly presented my Helmet Pudding, beautifully molded like a British Christmas pudding. It was not universally accepted—but *I* liked it.

With not much to do besides the daily patrol of the telephone wire, the battalion sent us up a daily ration of mortar shells. We worked out a modus operandi with the other side of the river—we would send our shells over at noon, they at dusk. One day, something new was added by our friends across the river—at dawn, a motorcycle dispatch rider started with a loud, throaty warm-up. After disturbing the neighborhood for an unconscionably long time, it took off down some unseen road. When the same thing happened the following morning, we sent over our daily ration of shells early, as a protest. The Germans immediately presented us with their quota. The gauntlet had been thrown down. That day, we sat around drawing an audio-sited map of the road. Our rifle platoon had theoretically patrolled the opposite side, and we invited a couple to join our mapping. While their firsthand knowledge was suspect, we enjoyed getting their input. In front of the mortar pit, we laid out a series of stakes on which we worked out the contours of the imagined road for the firing sequence.

Long before the dawn chorus, we were up, pulling the safety pins and lining the shells on the edge of the pit. I sighted the mortar on the first setting; my assistant gunner, Joe, hovered over the tube with a shell. It was a tense moment as we listened to the dawn bike chorus. We wanted to deliver the shell just as he started to leave. Someone shouted, "Go!" and as the shell exploded out of the tube, I moved the tube to the second position—and so on, down our version of the road. Then we all scrambled for the safety of our cellar as the return mail came in. We could hear the cycle sweetly put-putting off in the distance.

That afternoon, we asked battalion headquarters for a double ration of shells. They indicated their pleasure with our show of aggression by sending us a goodly amount. A mortar shell is a miniature bomb with four tail fins. Between the fins are increments, little bags of extra explosive powder. In the center of the tail is a shotgun shell that detonates when dropped against the firing pin at the bottom of the tube. Distance is a combo of tube elevation and the explosive propulsion of the increment bags. We were warned that a total of four increments was the safety limit. For the next morning's firing, we hung several extra increments on the fins. Tally ho!

That dawn, the dispatch rider gunned his motor extra loudly and extra long. His progress out of camp seemed deliberate and stately. We hoped he was pleased at the extra effort we made to follow him out. Back in the cellar, we discussed his attitude. Was he stalling that morning through fear or just giving us the finger?

"He reminds me of Canajoharie at the Gut," said the Sarge. By making him a "person," we immediately lost all interest in the game (which, I believe, was the Sarge's intention). It was clear we had come to admire the rider. At dawn, when we heard the throaty roar, we wished him Godspeed—at least I did. At noon, we went back to our regular shelling, and so did the Germans. It was acknowledgment by both sides that the dispatch rider had won the game!

As the time came closer for the final assault over the Roer River, word came down to A Company—take prisoners! Information was needed about the enemy forces across the river. Patrols, of course, proved that officers were aggressive, even though they seldom went along. A tried-and-true patrol was put together for this purpose, and, as a final touch, the captain decided I should accompany it.

"Captain," I pleaded, "why me? I have no patrolling skills."

"Your German could come in handy. Just go!"

As I left, I muttered to myself: "I can teach any GI to say, 'Hände hoch!' in five seconds."

So I found myself, at two o'clock one cold morning, boarding an inflatable rubber boat along with five of our Company A riflemen, each with blackened face. They looked at me with some misgivings. One of them wiped some greasy black off his face and transferred it to mine. A long piece of telephone wire, one end tied to a tree, was attached to the rear of the boat. We boarded the craft and pushed off. I surmised that the men were thoroughly briefed and knew what they were doing. The only briefing I got was a terse, "Sit still . . . stay out of the way." Frozen by cold and tension, I had no intention of doing anything that was or was not part of "the way."

The current, at 10 kilometers an hour, picked us up and swiftly swept us downstream, the men paddling hard to move us across. The German shore was dark and lifeless, but up and down the river were random flares and sounds of shots and artillery rounds. I had a sense that the men were not really trying hard enough to overcome the current. Abruptly we hit the end of the telephone wire and flipped over. In shock, I found myself floundering in the frigid water. Completely befuddled, I had lost all sense of where I was in relation to the shore. Someone grabbed me by my coat collar, shook me roughly, and asked me in a harsh but muted tone, "Can you swim?"

I must have said something that satisfied him, and he pulled me around. "This way to shore," he said, and swam off. I made it to the bushes and was pulling myself out of the water when a flare went off. I had recovered enough sense to stop moving and kept my face pressed against the bank. Letting the enemy see the whites of my eyes, I knew, was a fatal no-no. It took all my willpower to wait out the bright white flare, floating down slowly on its parachute. With the return of darkness, I scuttled crab-like through the bushes and onto higher ground. Hearing other bodies scuffling through the foliage, I moved to join them.

Led to the cellar of a nearby house, we were given a pile of blankets and told to strip. We huddled miserably around a hot stove, but it took a long time to feel real warmth. Nothing was said about the misadventure, except that one of the riflemen muttered, looking hard at me, "That current was too much."

"Yup," I replied. I had the feeling that the current was obviously too much before we started, but I had no notion of sharing these feelings with anyone but myself. I was too ecstatic to be off the hook.

But the ecstasy didn't last long. A few days later, I was back on the river, this time with a different and larger crew. The rubber raft had been upgraded to a 12-man pontoon, the kind I had seen engineers use when building floating bridges. Evidently handpicked for toughness, several men had combat knives with brass-knuckled handles on their leggings. Most had tommy guns slung on their shoulders, and all had a hard look of purpose on their blackened faces. All I had was my useless .45 revolver and my poor German.

They evidently had assessed my capabilities, and then carefully sited me in the center of the craft. The noncom in charge told me they were aiming for a place just off the shore, where a couple of sentries had a post. My job was to stay out of the way. Pushing off, unattached, we made good time crossing the river. The noncom indicated we needed to move farther downriver, and we silently let the river take us. Tying up to a tree, five of the men went ashore. Motioning us to wait, they disappeared into the gloom. For an interminable time we sat in the boat, expecting a flare to burst above us and all hell to break loose.

Suddenly the men returned, hustling a German soldier aboard the boat. It was done in great silence; even the German made a special effort to be soundless. I had the distinct understanding that if I had tried to indulge in conversation with the prisoner, I would have been clobbered senseless with a rifle butt. Back on the other side, we were met by an officer and followed him to his company headquarters. The frightened German was seated between two GIs in the back of a command car and driven off. From start to finish, I never said a word—in German, English, or gibberish!

I did, however, ask one of the noncoms about the second sentry. He shrugged his shoulders, casually drew his hand across his throat, and walked away. I had the answer to why the prisoner was so eager to please. I was sickened by the thought—this kind of work was not commonly done by mortarmen.

On February 9, the Germans blew up the Roer River dams, flooding the riverbanks again and putting off our attack for an additional two weeks. Much to our surprise, we surrendered our positions to others and were pulled back to Maastricht, Holland, for showers, refitting, and special river-crossing training.

To men who hadn't taken their clothes off in months, hot showers were a momentous event. The great Dutch miners' hall was awesome. Coming in from the bright daylight into the gloomy hall, we were stunned by the sight of huge, black bats hanging in rows across the high-domed ceiling. It took a spell before we could decipher the objects on the ceiling as coal-blackened miners' clothes. Benches lined the walls, and long chains attached to ceiling pulleys were hooked in rows behind them. Each chain had a four-pronged grappling hook, draped with dirty mining clothes, pulled up tight against the ceiling. When a shift arrived, the miners would lower their mining outfit, swap costumes, and run the clean street clothes back up to the ceiling. The miners' hall had showers enough for the whole shift simultaneously.

We stripped and entered the shower room to luxuriate in a long, stinging flow of hot water. Pure bliss! Back in the great hall, we lined up to throw our old uniforms and long underwear into bins and file past the quartermaster team for clean replacements. Sizes were left up to the team's snap judgment, but, having been in the same game, I called out the sizes I wanted as I passed each station. The line came to a shocked halt when I asked for an overcoat—the largest size available.

"What happened to your overcoat?"

"Lost it in combat."

"But hey, the sleeves would be inches below your fingertips!"

"That's it . . . exactly what I want."

"I can't do it, I'll get in trouble."

"You'll get in a lot more than trouble denying a front-line soldier what he wants. Just do it, man—and make the raincoat the same size or larger."

Well, I never was the Dude type—why begin now?

During an attack, we carried only bare essentials—our weapons, ammo, some rations, shovel, canteen, and an overcoat if possible. Bedrolls and other nonessentials were left behind, in expectation that the kitchen truck would bring them up. These expectations were seldom realized, so at night I converted my raincoat-covered overcoat into a sleeping bag. The large coat collar encased my head to keep my ears warm. I clasped the bunched long sleeves with my hands and pulled my feet under the coat-tails.

The euphoria that came from receiving fresh clothes was diminished somewhat when I found neatly patched holes that had rendered the previous owner incapable of wearing them.

As the leading battalion of the assault regiments, we were trucked to Visé, Belgium, to practice river crossings in 12-man assault boats in the swift current of the Meuse River.

The first night on the Meuse, a runner from battalion headquarters arrived to request my presence. Immediately, my sick dread got sicker. I remembered my extra patrol duties on the Roer. When I arrived at head-quarters, a colonel called me over and, without a word, handed me a phone. Numb and completely bewildered, I heard a soft Alabama voice: "Emil, is it you?"

Well, scarcely—at least not the Emil she knew! It was Hattie! The conversation that followed never registered in my memory, but the upshot was that she had talked that nice Colonel Whomever into allowing her to visit me on the Meuse, and she could do so tomorrow. I apparently said yes and we hung up. The colonel escorted me to the door.

"We'll bring her over in the morning. You'll be excused from the river-crossing exercises." (I forgot to inform him that I was expert in assault boats.) "She can't stay overnight in your barracks. We'll pick her up at 1600 hours. Understood?"

His speech was clipped and clear, as befitted a battalion commander, and it was all I could do to mumble, "Yes, Sir." I left, still dazed, forgetting to salute.

The next morning, a lieutenant brought her over after breakfast. He was a headquarters jock—he in his neat, pressed uniform and me in my oversize Charlie Chaplin coat. Harriett rushed up to me, clasping me by my arms. (My hands, up inside my sleeve, were hard to come by.)

"Oh, Emil, how wonderful to see you!"

"Hello, Harriett."

Lieutenant: "We'll pick you up in the afternoon, Miss Engelhardt. The colonel wants you for dinner." (I'll bet he does!)

Exit the lieutenant—his duty done, he walked away briskly. I could smell his after-shave lotion. I felt a sudden flash of hate. It had been mandated that Red Cross girls could only date officers. I could tell by his manner that he heartily endorsed this edict, and that I was a good case in point.

"Emil, you remember Colonel X?" I shook my numbed head, no.

"At the country club dance on your furlough? He was a major then."

"Yes," I lied.

Hate had turned to shame at the shabby figure I was cutting. Then back to hate. Vanity, self-esteem, and other emotions welled up in me—personal feelings I had tried so desperately to erase during the months of combat. It didn't help to have Hattie turn to me and fumble up my sleeve for my hand. We were under the intense scrutiny of the kitchen squad.

Our bivouac was in some kind of institution, a school perhaps. Balustrades lined sunken gardens, and numerous stairways led to complicated garden walks. The gardens, now covered with snow, were flanked by buildings with doors leading off to who-knows-where—a typical European-style complex dating back to the Hapsburgs. It reminded me of a foreign film I once saw, *Last Year at Marienbad.* Ill-fated lovers moodily strolling around sunken gardens, holding hands and kissing, as we were doing in our own little cinema.

Hattie, I had the feeling, was definitely free of her father's restrictions, that somewhere in her doughnut-wagon travels she had let herself go and would dearly love to with me. But all the doors either were occupied with comings and goings or were locked—we did try a few. At any rate, if she was liberated and free of restrictions, I was still deeply bound by the war and heavy with the coming river crossing. With no private place to go, hugging tightly but feeling little warm contact through our heavy wool overcoats, we kissed and talked.

"Tell me about your Red Cross wagon experiences, Hattie…."

"I've kept up with your 29th Division all through Europe. Tell me …."

Hattie evidently had been with the 20th Corps (Third Army?) in the Saar River area during the capture of Metz. Walking these cold wet paths with her, I tried desperately to be cheerful and loving, to lift myself out of the rigid protective casing I had molded against the war, to respond to her buoyant mood. She must have been deeply disappointed that there was not more there for me to give. I thought about that other gray wintry day at college, when she passed by me on that empty Lee Hall veranda. "Is that what you've been brooding about in that rocking chair?" This was exactly what I'd been brooding about when I fell in love with this little Southern girl walking down the slushy road to the village. I wondered if she remembered.

Finally the troops came back, flashing quizzical looks at us as they marched by. We had lunch with them, and Harriett became more animated. When I was in the hospital, she wrote me that she was thrilled to see them all cleaning their rifles, knowing that we were going into combat in a few days. I wondered how she would have felt seeing them face down in the water, or dismembered on the muddy banks? The lieutenant came as promised and left with Harriett, leaving me with an aching void.

The morning of February 23, in the Ninth Army crossing of the Roer, the 29th Division was to make the main effort. At our briefing, we were told that there was to be a short but powerful artillery barrage at 2:45 a.m., followed by our crossing at 3:30 to assault the defenses on the high ground north of Jülich, just beyond the river.

> Exactly at 2:45 AM the big guns opened fire. In a quickly rising crescendo, batteries, mortar crews and tanks joined their weapons to the violent preparation. Men of the assault regiments, watching and listening, felt themselves intoxicated with a feeling of great power, which identified them as a part of the great destructive bludgeon which was hammering all life and resistance out of Jülich and the east bank. For this brief moment there vanished the dull soldier sickness that precedes the zero hour. They laughed for sheer joy at this thunderous evidence of their alliance with the big guns.
> —*Official History, 29th Division*

This kind of sheer joy was not for everybody—it certainly wasn't for me!

We had trained in pontoon assault boats but crossed the Roer River in "Alligators"—open amphibious tanks. The Roer was perhaps as formidable a barrier as the English Channel on D-Day. It was 6 to 12 feet deep and about 1,200 feet wide, with a current of some 6 mph. The riverbanks were mined and had been flooded, and although the icy water had receded, I still sloshed in my shoes. Some of the men fell into deep holes. My pack was soaked and hung heavy on my back. My mortar, as usual, weighed a ton. We stood around waiting our turn to cross the river, quivering with the cold and fear. Around us was the usual hullabaloo—streams of tracer fire going in both directions, smoke and flares drifting down onto various sections of the river, the splash-bang of mortar and artillery shells, the roar of Alligators.

As we grounded on the far shore, I jumped out in the soft mud and shouted for the Sarge to hand me the mortar. As I felt the bipod touch my hands, I heard a hollow thump, and the mortar dropped onto my chest. A stray bullet had hit Sarge in the head, and he fell back dead.

We were held up by a deep minefield, waiting for passage to be cleared by the engineers. Come the dawn, there we were, the remaining mortar squad, standing around on the riverbank lamenting the loss—this time for good—of our Sergeant Schwartz. In the grief that overwhelmed us, we had ignored the first principles of survival he had taught us—don't bunch up and, above all, dig in! Suddenly someone whistled an alarm call. On the brow of the hill, a German 90mm cannon was slowly tracking us with its mile-long barrel, the kind they mounted on Tiger Tanks.

It was almost as though, for flaunting the sacred survival formula, the gods of war were giving us the almighty finger. It's not every soldier who gets to see the barrel of the cannon that nails him. I was too disgusted with myself to be frightened. As I turned my back to the gun and started a dive, a shell swished over where my head had been, a huge Niagara of sound. With the smell of cordite, I was engulfed in an enormous black flash. I returned to consciousness in a Paris hospital.

22.

Paris: Beaujon Hospital

Incidental information: The British War Museum is now being housed in the Bedlam Mental Hospital.

U.S. ARMY HOSPITAL PLANT 4314, January 23, 1945
MY ONLY MEMORY, between the banks of the Roer River and the Beaujon General Hospital in Paris, was waking up strapped on a train bunk and a medic reaching over to give me a shot—and I'm not sure it's a true memory or what I believe I know to have happened. I apparently slept on and off for several more days in the hospital before they interested me in getting out of bed.

Years ago, on a hill near our house in the Bronx, a car jumped the sidewalk and killed a young child. Walking by after the wreckage was removed, I spotted a fragment of skull with a dab of gray brains. It was my first memory of accidental death, at age eight or nine, and it has stayed with me until this day. But on thinking back over my lifetime, such traumatic experiences of life's casualties are few and far between. Suddenly, in combat, I had been overwhelmed by smashed skulls, decapitations, spilled intestines, broken limbs, dead bodies in every position—a tidal wave of casualties.

Needing gloves on the cold, open plains of northern Germany, I reached down to strip a pair from a dead soldier. But he wore no gloves. Being dead too long, his skin had turned mahogany, and the flesh underneath had putrefied. The skin of his hand slipped off into my hand intact.

331

Beaujon Hospital, Paris.

I was instantly sick and still become nauseous when it returns to memory at unguarded moments.

What was called "shell shock" in World War I was called "combat fatigue" or "battle exhaustion" in my war. The "fatigue" part was easy to understand. It is not the tiredness felt at the end of a hard day's work, but rather a total state of exhaustion, difficult to describe or even to remember. When you live for months in a constant state of tension and fear (especially when you are in an experienced division like the 29th and know you won't be relieved until you are wounded or killed), and add this exhaustion of the mind/spirit/psyche to the physical, you end up in a condition of total disintegration. The horror of the experiences build up to where they become unbearable in their totality. I've seldom talked about this, feeling that it was too stressful and impossible to communicate. I have read numerous narrations in war books, but they fail to ring a bell. My above explanation, I'm sure, falls into the same category. Perhaps the reader needs to have an equivalent experience.

The constant living with death—the sweet/sour smell from decaying bodies that hung over the battlefields—is with you day and night. It has been established that a man, any man, in any army, of any nationality, could tolerate 150 to 200 days of modern combat before starting to slide off his rocker. Combat divisions survive because they are constantly refreshed with new troops.

Our mortar squad of five men was a family—a changing family, since new replacements kept arriving. The senior member of the family, the lieutenant, was almost never with us—he was used to replace the more-than-frequent vacancies in the rifle platoons. Sergeant Schwartz was our true family head and mainstay. Even when he was out wounded, we never received a replacement. When he was hit in October, I became the oldest squad member, and by November it was rumored that I was the last remaining man in the company without a purple heart. Replacements would come up and touch me for luck. It gave me goose pimples. What saved me from a breakdown was my December hospital interlude during the Bulge fighting.

After a few days in the Paris hospital, they operated on my shoulder with a local painkiller. In the overhead light reflector, I could watch them working. Although I knew it wasn't a demanding job for them, I wished they would take it a little more seriously, instead of joshing about dates. But the focus of my hospital treatment was not my injury so much as my mental state, of which I was myself not fully aware until they took me out of the ward and put me into a private room—apparently I had a loud nightlife. Many happenings in combat accumulate in your brain, which stores them where memory can't reach them. Sodium Pentothal was the pick the psychiatrists used to try to dig them out.

Every day, I would wander down to the first floor for treatment. The Beaujon General Hospital was a giant 11-story U-shaped building that took up three full sides of a block. I've read that for every five wounded soldiers, one died and another was a psychiatric casualty.

Sitting next to me on a corridor bench were soldiers who perpetually stared out into space. A young lieutenant kept clutching my arm to tell me, in hushed confidence, that he couldn't remember his name.

My treatment was simple, completely mysterious, and never explained to me. As a shot of Pentothal was being emptied into me: "OK, fellow, lie back and count backward from 100."

After a very few counts, I was led out to my perch on the bench: "Sit here until you feel like going back to your ward. See you tomorrow."

Sighting down the long hallway, I would stagger off. "Hey, Doc, whatever I told you has to be the truth, right? So what did I say, eh?"

Writers have described movingly the comradeship in the trenches in World War I. Did this apply to the isolation and loneliness of the World War II foxholes? The turnover in my division was so great, and the pain of losing buddies so bitter, that I tried to steel myself against allowing fellow soldiers to get too close. Unfortunately, I was not very successful in distancing myself from the exuberant Can—I can still see that heap of dark, wet clothing in the middle of an empty road. As I clung to the side of our metal Alligator, my feet in the cold mud of a hostile shore, I feel and hear the thump of that random bullet ending the life of Sergeant Schwartz. In the hospital, I missed both Can and the Sarge with a truly aching heart. And still do.

During the day, I hung around one of the big wards, where life was more interesting. All kinds of wounds and conditions. There were bandages on every part of the human anatomy.

At four every afternoon, a nurse would come in and ask: "Anyone with a cough?" Immediately there would be a bedlam of hacking grunts and guttural throat clearings. She would count heads and return with a large tray of shot glasses. Codeine all around, friends.

With the war coming to its climax, we learned of its Wagnerian ending in Berlin with the death of the Germanic god, Hitler—all orchestrated by Marshal Kirov and the Red Army. Wagner would have been disgusted by all his Germanic gods slinking off to commit suicide.

As Ulysses S. Grant had done, Eisenhower decided to fight a war of attrition. His orders were for continuous attack. He thought that since our manpower resources were greater than those of the Germans, if their losses were twice ours, victory would soon come. In the Bulge, our casualties were 80,987, the German casualties 80,000 (higher in some estimates, but certainly far short of one to two). In general, our losses were more like one to one, and we began to run out of available fighting bodies. Even by the end of the Normandy fighting, the U.S. Army had a shortfall of some 300,000 men.

William Manchester pointed out: "All who wore uniforms are called veterans, but more than 90% of them are as uninformed about the killing zones as those on the home front." Of the 16 million in American uniforms, less than 7 percent saw combat. Once a division was "blooded," it stayed in combat. In the U.S. Air Force, after a fixed number of missions, you could be rotated home. In Vietnam, it was home after 365 days in country. In World War II, in the combat infantry, you stayed until you were killed or badly wounded. No matter how many people loved you and depended on you, or how valuable you were as a human being—if you were in the infantry, you were expendable. My 29th Division landed on D-Day and was in constant conflict with German armies until the war was declared over. (Even then, in Bremen, Germany, they were being trained for Japan.)

It was said that the 29th Division was in reality a corps (three divisions): one in combat, one in the hospital, and one in the grave. Per unit of time, the 29th Division lost the second-highest number of men in combat in the European theater—20,324 out of the original 7,583 enlisted men and officers.

During my time with A Company, we lost 15 company commanders and so many lieutenants that we hardly had time to learn their names.

> If a division was engaged for more than 3 months, the probability is that every one of its 2nd lieutenants, all 132 of them, will be killed or wounded.
> —Ronald Spector, *Eagle Against the Sun*

I blessed the army for keeping me out of OCS (officer candidate school) but felt pangs of guilt for harassing the poor infantry lieutenants with our submarine patrols in Hattiesburg, Mississippi—I was sure many were included in the above statistics.

We spent hours in our various cellar bivouacs debating the best-possible million-dollar wound. It had to be substantial enough to have you sent home. Think about it! Would it be your left arm? A foot? A buttock? Don't laugh! I was in the Beaujon General Hospital with a boy who had spent months of agony lying on his stomach, unable to move, while they tried to repair a missing buttock sheered off by shrapnel. I'm sure there were many times he wished to be back in combat—or even in the grave. This may all sound like hysteria, but it was as practical as digging a foxhole—a wound was one of the few solutions if you wanted to survive. Not everyone was ready to shoot off an appendage, but I know soldiers who confessed to lying in a foxhole and hopefully holding a hand or foot out of the hole in the line of fire.

Each GI was issued a small first-aid packet. Most of us carried two, one for a fellow soldier. Each packet contained a dozen sulfanilamide tablets and some sulfa powder to dust on the wound. The sulfa was effective against certain systemic infections that penicillin couldn't touch. Even nasty bacteria need vitamins, and they mistook the sulfa for these vitamins. It was a misjudgment that killed them. Nasty trick—but war is hell. Our Wall Street runner, in his self-mutilation, had his kit already opened and had swallowed a few tablets before the "sniper" shot him.

Sometime in April, I was ready to be discharged, although it would still take a number of months for the pus of fear to drain out of my system. (Actually, it took several years.) Able to take day passes, I explored Paris. I took in the Eiffel Tower and the Folies Bergère, but somehow I lacked the tourist fervor. I tried a few restaurants, where I found the bread crisp but the red wine pure vinegar. I had my picture taken by a street photographer. Although the photo showed me thinner and a bit hollow-eyed, it still was me—I had made it through alive!

23.

A Chateau in France

Having been discharged from the hospital as unfit for combat duty, I was put into the Signal Corps—for which I was even more unfit. The European war over, I was anxious to get to Vienna to see my mother's sisters and various other relatives. But I was told: "No, you can't go to an enemy country if you have blood relations there."

"But we have no enemy countries in Europe now."

"Doesn't matter, the rule is still on the books. How about standing guard for just two hours a day?"

"I can't be responsible with weapons." Too true.

"A comfortable desk job?"

"Can't stand the confinement."

This was a new outfit, having arrived in France just in time to see the war end and feeling very guilty. My infantry badge and purple hearts intimidated them, and they just let me run free. A young French boy in the battalion, from this region, had been sent to the United States before the war and was drafted into the U.S. Army. Running free meant the French boy and I would borrow a Jeep and load it with soap, candy, and cigarettes bought in the PX, plus sugar and coffee scrounged from the kitchen. We would race around the Reims *Département*, picking up what Champagne and Cognac the Germans had missed. We found enough to keep the battalion in good humor.

V-E DAY, May 8, 1945

While we wallowed luxuriously in a chateau above Reims, the historic surrender of the German Army took place in Eisenhower's headquarters in a trade-school building in the city below. Feeling frustrated about their tardy arrival, the battalion members held no wild celebrations. Better I should have been in Times Square!

But don't think celebration was foreign to us in the chateau. We did have ample Champagne and a dance every Saturday night for which the USO bused in young French girls and a little French band that played marginally fair American music. Barracks and camps in our vicinity were crowded with DPs (displaced persons) and released prisoners of war. Folks from these camps who found their way to our dances were made welcome. Few could dance to American-style music, but they enjoyed sitting around the hall on benches imbibing Cokes and potato chips.

One evening, I sat next to a released Soviet soldier, a lieutenant in the artillery. His German was on a par with mine, and I was fascinated by some of his experiences. He took great pride in the Red Army artillery. When I tried to tell him about my little 60mm mortar popgun, he went into great details about the Art of Artillery Shell Trajectory. His eyes sparkled and his enthusiasm was such that I had to stay put. While I longed to get out on the floor with the twirling French girls, I hadn't the heart to cut short my comrade-in-arms from the Red Army, whose successes destroyed the *Wehrmacht* and no doubt saved my life.

Being a combat infantryman carried a lot of prestige with the young men of the Signal Battalion. One day a trunk arrived with encoding equipment considered top secret; it had to be guarded by someone armed with a .45 pistol. Sitting in the Supply Room and watching the men playing with the unfamiliar weapon, I remembered the day in my Camp Shelby training camp when we had just received new M-1 rifles and our sergeant gave us the standard lecture:

> This weapon is your best buddy, your closest friend and protector. You will memorize your rifle number, learn to dismount it and put it back together blindfolded. You will clean your piece every day and know that a grain of sand can cause your death.

He snatched up the nearest rifle. With practiced precision, he snapped back the bolt, whirled the rifle up to the light, putting his thumb into the open breech so that the reflected light from his fingernail illuminated the groves of the barrel.

"Fair, only fair. Could be cleaner."

Suddenly he sprang forward and dashed the rifle from the hands of a soldier who was playfully aiming it at a friend. He shouted harshly, gesturing at the fallen rifle:

"Never point a weapon at anyone!"

"But," said the startled soldier, "we have no bullets. It wasn't loaded."

"You never know, you just never know. Don't ever point your rifle at another person—unless you mean to kill 'im!"

So, I gave my Signal Corps friends my sergeant's lecture. They listened gravely. Of course, I then explained the fine points of loading and disarming the weapon. Carefully releasing the magazine and elaborately examining the barrel to make sure it was empty, I put down the pistol and we went on to other things. After a while, I was asked to demonstrate how to hold and fire the pistol. Aiming at the upper corner of the Supply Room, I carefully squeezed the trigger and blew a great hole in the plaster. Someone had replaced the magazine and slid a bullet into the barrel. I lost a good many points with the gang, but I sheepishly pointed out: "See, I didn't aim it at anyone, did I? Just suppose I did?"

That thought hung heavily in the room while the dust settled. I thanked the drill sergeant for his training. Fortunately, nothing was ever said about the missing plaster. It is a memory of which I am not very proud.

The war was going on hot and heavy on the Japanese front, and some combat divisions were retraining for it. For me it was over, although I still had periods of deep depression. Along the ridge in back of the chateau, I found a network of old World War I trenches. Early in July 1916, it had been clear that the Germans were preparing another major assault. I brooded over the mud-drowned, fear-sickened, exhausted men peering down the ridge at death gathering below in the form of German assault troops. I found myself taking frequent walks to those trenches—was I reluctant to give up my familiar combat fatigue?

Harriett came for a visit.

A letter came from Harriett: Could she visit me? She arrived in a small army plane—this, indeed, was Harriett's war. I put her up in a French war widow's house next to the chateau, and she dined with us in the company mess. She had chosen a weekend to visit, so we spent Saturday night, fueled with Cognac, dancing and reminiscing. It was lovely to dance with her again; she clung to me. When I took her across the street to her house, we stood before the door hugging and kissing, reluctant to break away.

The next day, with a picnic lunch, I took Hattie to the old trenches and stunted pines. It was a mistake. I spread a blanket amid those ghostly ruins and we made love, but I couldn't lift my mood to truly meet this long-awaited occasion. In a strange dichotomy of emotions, my heart went out to Hattie, but at the same time, something inside of me wouldn't let go. We talked about meeting again in New York City. "If we live together," Harriett said, "I want to get married."

Until then, I had had no thoughts of a future. This was a first little window opening on a possible tomorrow. But it was too soon, too abrupt. I couldn't make the commitment, at least not in Reims.

"Let's work it out in New York, Harriett," I said. "I never dared think I could survive combat or what I would do after the war. How would I make a living? We have loved each other under such strange circumstances, let's see how we do in normal life!"

She agreed. I don't think Harriett fully expected a firm commitment to marriage then and there. I felt later that I should have been more positive, but it came out of the blue. I still hadn't sloughed off the stink of war, having just come out of the Beaujon Hospital, filled with the debris of wounded soldiers. It didn't help my mood, of course, being in those World War I trenches.

The next day, I drove Harriett down to the small dirt airfield. The same army plane was waiting, and her friend and fellow passenger was standing by with the pilot. The mood was upbeat, and we more than casually kissed goodbye. I waited until the plane was long gone—thinking about Hattie and the future.

It was announced that after V-E Day, two million men would be discharged from the army. Shipment home was based on a point system—length of service, combat time, purple hearts, decorations. Me, surely. But all in good time. First priority was the movement of combat-experienced troops and equipment to the war in Japan.

I would not get home for another year, but that was my own option, since I had signed on for an additional tour. Meanwhile, I was determined to make it to Vienna to see my kinfolk. Hadn't I carried my mother's sister's address in a condom in my belt buckle all through the war? But you can't win against army bureaucracy, and, over time, I found myself heading the lists of unwanteds being shifted from battalion to battalion. Being passed from outfit to outfit, I went from Luxembourg to Bavaria and ended up in Wels, Austria.

990th SIGNAL SERVICE BATTALION, WELS, September 1945

My best friend at this camp—"best" meaning most receptive—was the major in charge of the detachment. Shortly after I arrived, he called me into his office: "I see by your record that you have no Signal Corps training."

Prepared for a "Well, what can we have you do?" interrogation, I had worn my jacket with the 29th Division insignia, my blue-and-silver combat badge, and my infantry hat with blue piping. But now that I was getting close to Vienna, I decided to behave and play the game.

"No, sir, I was medically discharged out of the Infantry."

"Wow, the 29th! Tell me . . . ."

We spent the next hour fighting through Normandy. Because of his technical knowledge, he had been shunted into the Signal Corps, but his first love, he told me, was the Infantry. He related to me as if I were a fellow officer—a unique experience for a lowly GI. After a time, he picked up my papers again and looked through them.

"Your papers indicate Supply experience, so why don't you hang around the company Supply Room and see what you would like to do there?"

The Supply Room was adjacent to the Orderly Room, and I got to know our commanding officer quite well. We spent a lot of time rehashing battles in which I'd fought but hadn't had the foggiest notion of what was going on strategically. But he did, and I was totally astonished by the war I had fought. My main interest in combat had been to keep in touch with the progress Russia was making pushing the *Wehrmacht* westward into Germany, and the number of divisions they were tying up. Had we faced the full might of the German armies, we wouldn't have lasted a day in Normandy.

When they discovered I spoke some German, they were ecstatic—not much German was available in this Signal Battalion. I was put to work as overseer of 15 German airmen, supervising the cleanup and taking inventory of an air depot. Unrepentant, the Germans kept reminding me they would have won the war if they hadn't run out of gasoline. Didn't they have the first jets that could outrun anything we had? And killer rockets? I couldn't convince them that wars were won on the ground, not in the air. But I did learn something from them—how to string words together to make a single entity. A nut, for example, from the bolt of the airplane engine rotor, we might have noted in my inventory somewhat like this: "messerschmitt107enginerotorboltnut—2,316 each."

After the armistice, Europe was awash with rootless humanity. In Germany, the white sheet had replaced the swastika as the national flag. Suddenly, no one was a Nazi—never had been. There were at least three million German prisoners of war, plus several million DPs. Most of these were forced laborers, who had worked in the Nazi fields and factories. They came from Russia, Poland, France, Spain, Belgium, Holland, Norway, and the Balkans—far from home and uncertain of how to get back. And, of course, there were homeless, rootless German soldiers and civilians who fled the massive Red Army advance and had no wish to return home. Ten million hapless people to sort out and repatriate.

The most distressed were those liberated from the concentration camps. Despite medical attention, thousands of survivors died within days of liberation. In the Allied zone, 20,000 of more than 60,000 liberated Jews died in the first week. Many Jews left the camps unsupervised and wandered around looking for food and shelter. Those who stayed in Poland were driven off by the villagers; some, in their anti-Semitic hatred, killed the hapless Jews.

The UN Relief and Rehabilitation Agency (UNRRA) was organized to take this flood of refugees in hand—453 DP centers were set up, but it took four years to do the job.

A DP center was located next door to our unit in Wels. The refugees were living in old forced laborers' barracks, four to six sleeping in each wide, double-decker bunk. Their Yiddish was not exactly from the Bronx, and I had difficulty understanding it, but most spoke some German, and we could communicate after a fashion.

My knowledge of the Holocaust experience at that time was not very profound. What could I have actually known, then, of how to deal with people still reacting to the shock of sudden release from the horror of the camps into the chaos of postwar Europe? I spent much of my free time in the DP center, fascinated by their stories and trying to do what I could to help. The DPs told me how they survived the camps by having medical skills or painting little portraits of the officers or playing musical instruments or by rare sheer chance.

We had a barber and a tailor, both Polish Jews and veterans of the Warsaw Ghetto and German death camps—survivors through their skills in serving the Germans. Great comedians, the two Poles had routines in Yiddish that kept the camp in good humor. Listening to their rapid Yiddish, laced as it was with German, I got the general drift but missed the funny nuances that set the DPs into gales of laughter. Yiddish is truly international, but it was never made an official language by any state. (Unless you count the Bronx as a state.)

Whenever the barber scraped my Adam's apple with his straight razor, I wondered how his late Nazi customers related to this blade? The tailor and I became good friends. When he left, he gave me his photo, taken in front of his camp shop. Personal photos were scarce in the lives of these people—he must have gotten it from some GI in exchange for a clothing alteration. I treasure the gift.

Families living in the Wels barracks were ad hoc—a husband, wife, and children—made up of bits and pieces of humanity assembled as they drifted through various camps. In many cases, the family members came from different countries, bonded by expediency rather than genes or nationality. Each had lost everything familiar: homeland, home, friends and family, furnishings, attic treasures, family albums. The past was a nightmare to be forgotten—or, at least, kept at bay. And the future...?

Even at this historic point, the United States had not relaxed its immigration quotas, nor did Great Britain allow more than a small monthly quota of Jews into Palestine.

I was able to help set up services between the camp and the battalion—laundering, tailoring, hair cutting, etc. Many of the refugees were trying to make their way to Israel via Italy and Cyprus. The British had blockaded Israel and were sinking ships loaded with Jewish immigrants. In the years 1946 to 1948, some 61,000 entered Palestine, most of them slipping through the blockade. Many soldiers had U.S. money in their wallets, and I arranged swaps, as high as ten-to-one, of "occupation marks" for dollars—occupation money being worthless for booking passage to Cyprus. Many soldiers were pleased just to donate the dollars or give them in payment for services. The families had to sneak off at night, leaving me notes about returning clean laundry to soldier clients.

Just as I carried my aunt's address in my belt buckle, the refugees had addresses, and scraps of addresses, of people in the United States. But the only mail moving was army mail, so I sent off many dozens of letters under my APO return address. Some of the addresses were pathetic, half-remembered, and obviously wrong. These I bundled up and sent to the only organization I could remember—the old Jewish Socialist newspaper, *Forverts* ("Daily Forward"). I remembered them because of their loud radio program every Sunday morning—Jewish Socialists, it seems, like their opinions stated loud and clear!

Our Polish barber survived the death camp.

When the first answer came back from the States, they pushed back the bunks, danced the *hora,* sang Zionist songs, and wept. As did I. (I was still trying to dance Israel into existence.)

How many ever made it to the Land of Zion, I'll never know, but in 1948 our efforts come to fruition—Israel became a nation.

One of my buddies, a Jewish boy from Brooklyn, adopted a nice, quiet, middle-aged Jewish seamstress. He somehow had managed to have an apartment in Wels, close to the camp, and his friend came of an evening, sat in his room, and sewed quietly. She also had bathtub privileges. I'm sure there was more to their relationship than met my eye, but he never boasted about her as most soldiers were wont to do. When he was shipped out, he asked me to look after her. I found sewing work for her but had no bathtub to offer.

The battalion had a photographic attachment in Vienna, and my amiable major promised me that I could go in and visit my kinfolk. To this end, I accumulated a barracks bag of flour, sugar, and canned goods—begged, borrowed, and stolen from the kitchen—almost too heavy for me to lift.

A truck was scheduled to leave for Vienna in a few days, and I reminded the major of his promise. He was on his way to Salzburg and agreed to make out a transit pass in time for me to go. But he forgot, and the truck left without me. The next day, with a friend, we carried my heavy bag out to the highway. I stopped a young lieutenant in a Jeep.

"Where ya goin', soldier?"

"Vienna."

"Hop in."

"Hmm, Sir, can you help me with my bag?"

We chattered comfortably, as usual, about my combat experiences. When we arrived in Linz, he asked me if I had a transit pass.

"No, Sir, but my major said to see Colonel Soso at the barrier. Can you wait just a few minutes?"

He could, and I rushed into the border kiosk and asked to see the colonel. As I went into his office, my eyes went to his Combat Infantry Badge and his to mine—he was also an Infantry retread, so I got a sympathetic hearing.

"Remember the 990th Signal Service truck that came through yesterday? Well, Sir, I was supposed to be on it but missed it. My major was away in Salzburg, but he said if I ever had any problem, you might help me out. Incidentally, our unit in Vienna is photographic, and if you need any film, I could drop it off on our way back. Just write what you want on a slip of paper—I'm originally Infantry and know from nothing about photography."

Everyone had liberated German cameras, but film was nonexistent. I got my pass.

It was a dramatic ride into Vienna, and very little of the countryside showed signs of destruction. We passed Mad King Ludwig's Castle, the large monastery at Melk, onion-domed churches, and other Austrian operatic confections. It didn't seem to be the kind of land that I could relate to my parents! Late in the afternoon, we entered the great city— Vienna at last! To this I could relate!

Vienna was the Willimetz version of my wife Joanna's Thomaston, Maine—I was surrounded by kinfolk. And they all refreshingly spoke Viennese Ottakring *Plattdeutsch*. My kind of German, with jazzy Viennese slang. It was music to my ears!

My sister Hedy kept a letter I had written home about my first trip to Vienna.

Emil Willimetz, 32 905 615
51st Signal Base Depot Company
Wels, Austria
12 September 1945

Dear Mom & Pop,
Best news! This last weekend I was able to go into *Wien* [Vienna].
It is *sehr schwer* [very difficult] to get to Wien from here because
you have to go through a Russian checkpoint at Ennes.

The first thing we saw as we drove into the city was hundreds
of people carrying wood on their backs from the famous
Wienerwald [Vienna Woods]. There is no coal for the coming
winter. I learned later that my two uncle in-laws, Abel and
Leutner, worked very hard each day chopping wood for the City,
for which they got a good noon-day meal and some wood for
themselves. They made it sound funny as they told me the story
but it really is a serious situation. Uncle Abel showed me his pants
which could have filled twice the belly he now has. They are lucky
that they still have good housing to live in.

Mom had optimistically given me her sister Rosa's address,
which I kept wrapped tightly in a condom in my belt buckle all
through the war. A Lieut left me off at 42 Hasslingergasse, in the
XVI *Bezirk* [district] as Mom's note said.

In the apartment house I looked for Abel but he didn't seem
to live there. Of course an *Amerikaner* in that French occupation
district drew a crowd and soon I found an aunt (from Rosa's
daughter's husband's side of the family) who directed me to #41,
which was across a small park. I had all kinds of help to carry my
barracks bag!

I don't know who was more surprised when the door opened
and our Mom looked out. It was, of course, your sister Rosa. She
was wearing glasses and looked exactly like our Fanny. I started to
say, "I'm your *Neffe* Emil from America," when she made a grab
for me and hugged me tearfully. Then Uncle Abel came running
out to see what the excitement was all about. They kept saying
how much I looked like Fanny and how *unglaublich* [impossible]

it was that someone from America had made it to Wien.

I stayed overnight with cousin Minni (Wilhemina) and her husband Ferdy (Ferdinand Schober) sleeping under a goosedown quilt, complete with breakfast in bed. Minni took me over to visit Mom's sister Lini (Caroline married to Albin Leutner) and, of course, it was another big surprise, especially since our little cousin Minni hid after she rang the doorbell. Lini was so overcome she cried and kept wringing her hands. I gathered she was especially fond of her American sister.

Well, my points have gone up from 55 to 68, 8 from being overseas from V-E Day to V-J Day and 5 they owed me from a Battle Star back in Normandy. With 80 points I get to come home!

Your loving son,
Emil

On the back of the letter was a note from Hedy: "When you finish with this letter please return it to Mom, she would like to keep it."

I could just see Mom reading and rereading the letter, dreaming of the good old days in Austria, happy that her son survived the war and met her sisters.

A return letter from Pop also survived the years:

Dear Son,
We are very glad and happy you made the trip to Vienna. Yes this was some surprise for our relatives specile for Lina tante, she was very close with yor mother.

When you go to Vienna again, their shouldt show you the Zenner Maries, where I see your mother the first time and gross the street is that church we got married.

I make you some sugjestion you shouldt see Ringstrasse their a few hotel. Hotel Bristol I was working. [A list of other famous places for me to see follows.]

Whish we couldt help as much as possible. Let us now if we can send some money, cash or money order.

Best regards to all my relatives
Love, Pop

The Hotel Bristol on Vienna's Ringstrasse is a large, elegant, Victorian-style hotel. It must have wowed Mom when Pop brought her there as a bride.

Pop's relatives seemed to be scarce on the Viennese ground—especially after I'd met all of Mom's sisters and so many of their kin. But I did learn where the name Hedwig came from: It was Pop's mother's name, his sister's name, and her daughter's name. (Naturally, Pop's sister Hedwig, when I met her, kept saying how much I looked like her brother, Leopold, when he was a young lad.)

Actually, the Willimetz family name disappeared in Vienna—after my father went to the New World, no remaining male Willimetz married and had children. When I visited Vienna a few years ago, I couldn't find a single Willimetz in the city's huge telephone book.

24.

VIENNA, SEPTEMBER 1945-MARCH 1946

51st SIGNAL BASE DEPOT

IN A FEW WEEKS, the whole Wels contingent moved to Vienna. Did the U.S. Army brass know that Pfc. Emil Willimetz was loose in a Vienna filled with "enemy alien" relatives? When all the points indicated I could go home, I signed on for six months of extra duty.

Our battalion took over a four-story school building in Palmerplatz, not far from many Willimetz relatives. In fact, a lady barber across the street, who shaved me every day, was some kind of a cousin "once removed."

The school was not exactly the Reims chateau, but we had a staff of civilians catering to our every need. The sergeant in charge of the civilian staff was from Georgia, and every morning he would greet the cooks with a booming, *GUTEN MORGEN, DU-ALL!* His other favorite joke was to inquire, "What's for dessert? *Gummiräderstrudel* [Bicycletirepastry]?" His German was strictly limited, as was the cook's English, so I was happy to mediate with some frequency. I blush to confess that I was the darling of the kitchen staff. (An American soldier *aus Wien*—how could I miss?) I played it to the limit for leftover cakes, bread, and meals I could take to my relatives.

We also had a lively crew of young Viennese girls to wait on table and the prerequisite band to play for Saturday-night dancing. In playing American jazz, they were on a par with our French musicians—pretty heavyhanded. But they served their purpose . . . indeed they did.

Waitress Mitzi and I had an instant mutual attraction that brightened my remaining months in Austria. After the dances, one of our trucks drove the girls home, and some of us were gallant enough to accompany them. A rare experience—petting in the back of a dark, bouncing army truck.

Fraternization between GIs and German/Austrian women was strictly *verboten,* but the rule was difficult to enforce. It was estimated later that some 30,000 illegitimate children were left behind in Germany. The Germans quipped: "The next war, just send uniforms—you left the army here!"

Mitzi.

I left no soldier/child behind in Austria—I promise! But I had to be careful with Mitzi—I was sure she wouldn't have minded. Her girlfriend was pregnant by one of our soldiers, and they were about to be married.

With the war over, the troops were paid in "occupation marks" instead of dollars. We used the marks locally and to pay for PX shopping. You could, of course, buy postal money orders with these marks and send the money home as dollars. Black-market occupation marks flooded through American hands. For every $1 million of monthly payroll, $3 million was sent home. It was too good to be true, and it didn't last very long—we were soon issued paybooks and couldn't send home more than we earned. None of this affected me, since all my pay ($60 a month!) went to feed the relatives.

The PX was my main source of supplies. Every week, we could go through the PX to buy soap, shaving items, toothpaste, cigarettes, candy, watches, etc. We would buy the full allotment offered, but how much soap and toothpaste can one use in a week? Some of the stuff, mostly cigarettes,

A going away party—with an unhappy Mitzi.

was used to pick up an occasional piece of loot or to buy services in the city. Cigarettes were more of an exchange medium than marks. But most PX stuff just accumulated. Friends in the battalion, on being transferred out, would casually mention: "There's a box under my bed, Willi; pick it up!"

Fortunately, my friend, the major, and other officers were strong partisans of my efforts to feed my relatives, and they allowed me a good deal of leeway. I was known to all as "Black Market Willi." If an officer wanted a camera, he would write the type on a piece of paper: "LEICA 35MM" or "ZEISS IKOFLEX" or "4X5 VIEW CAMERA." I distributed the requests to relatives, who then asked around. Days or weeks later, I would have a deal. The camera owners would request in exchange such things as 10 cartons of cigarettes, 2 kilos of sugar, flour, coffee, etc. I doubled the amounts on all these exchange items, collectible from the requesting officer (who of course got it from the mess and the PX), and divided the loot between the camera owner and my relatives.

War souvenirs, such as German pistols, were worth a fortune to a newly arrived Signal Corps soldier—not to mention the value of a Russian "Red Star" division patch, a German *GOTT MIT UNS* belt buckle, or a Nazi swastika in some form or other. I collected many of these items from relatives and returning soldiers—even Russian GIs I met on the street.

These items I could barter for food, clothes, or blankets that my fellow soldiers had and for which they weren't held accountable.

Vienna was occupied mainly by Soviet partisan troops who had fought for several years in the forests and marshes of western Ukraine and in Poland, cut off from contact with the Red Army supply system. They had efficiently disrupted German lines of communication and created the basis for the passage of the Red Army into Germany. They wore a motley variety of uniforms and were not very disciplined. To make for conformity in occupied Europe, the U.S. Secretary of the Treasury had given the Soviets a set of engraved plates so they could issue occupation marks to their troops. The partisans received several years' back pay in occupation money that was not convertible into rubles and had to be spent before going home.

We were able to buy Timex watches in our PX for $10 or $12. I went around with a watch for barter on my left arm and my personal one hidden on my right arm. Occasionally while passing a Soviet soldier, I would take an intent, lingering look at my watch. This would galvanize attention and elicit the key word, "Uhr." As the Red Army swept through Europe, they picked up a scratch collection of German words—a favorite being Uhr (watch). Watches were one of the few things on which they could spend their money, and they'd offer me large sums of occupation marks. If they spoke enough German, I tried them out for Red Stars or other Red Army souvenirs. If they couldn't communicate in German, I just accepted the marks.

My apex achievement was a contact with the serious black market. A Russian sergeant had a list of written "wants" in exchange for 10 kilo bags (2.2 pounds each) of flour. He seemed to know the American PX contents and wanted cartons of cigarettes, watches, and blankets. A done deal—we met the next day at my aunt's house. He and his buddy manhandled the flour up the three flights. We shook hands on it and they left, happy with their loot. I was scared to death during the whole deal. It was much bigger than I was accustomed to, and, with rumors of black-market arrests, I had felt very uneasy with it. I wanted no more part in it.

It was of great interest to me to see the difference between my maternal and paternal relatives in how they received my efforts. They were all

The Willimetz family. Christmas 1945.

happy to get whatever I could bring and thanked me profusely, but when I appeared at Rosa's house the next day after the "flour deal," she had baked me a cake out of the flour. When I took my Aunt Hedwig her share of the flour, she asked me if I could get some meat. Her daughter was making her singing debut in a few weeks, and "Hedwig needs *kraft* [strength]!" It was not easy, but I managed to trade cigarettes for some horsemeat and cadged some Spam and Vienna (?!) sausage from the kitchen.

Between the retreating Germans and the attacking Red Army, almost all the rolling stock—trains, trucks, riverboats—had been taken or destroyed. All the Danube River bridges had been blown. Vienna was a

The Thoma family.

huge city, with a population of almost two million in a small country of eight million, and getting food to the people was a monumental problem—only 888 calories of relief supplies per person were distributed by the UNRRA famine relief agency. Although I've been bragging about feeding the Thoma and Willimetz families, actually I didn't even come close. The best I could do was take the edge off the monotony of their rationed diets.

When parcels started coming from home to my Army APO number, I happily had more food and clothes to distribute. I must confess, Black Market Willi was not my first or most felicitous persona.

Hedwig's singing debut was a success. It took place in the small chamber of a great music-hall building packed with friends and relatives. It is interesting that there were as many daily music events advertised in Viennese newspapers as movies are announced in New York City papers—and this when they were suffering constant cold and hunger. I'm no music critic—it all sounded great to me. I took full credit, thanks to the horsemeat, for her full-throated arias. Congratulations, Pop—we've at least one Willimetz with musical talent!

Until this time, real money in Austria had been German marks. The Occupation Forces recalled it all and reissued Austrian shillings. To foil black marketers, only $500 worth could be exchanged. Small change, coins, were exempt from the exchange. It was just the kind of situation in which the Viennese delighted.

One night I went to the opera—*Die Fledermaus*. There was a scene where a buddy bailing his friend out of jail offered the jailer a large bill. The jailer sneered at the bill and sang falsetto: "Do you think I'll give you change?" It brought the house down.

Vienna being a Socialist city, trolley fares were cheap, the equivalent of about three *groschen* (pennies). If you liked the conductor, you gave him a 5 *groschen* piece and said, "Keep the change." This turned every conductor into a comedian, and they went through the double cars cracking jokes. Every old woman was lovingly called *"Grossmutter"* (Grandma) , every old man *"Grossvater."* Taking one look at me, one conductor dug his fingers in his ear and examined the result with the comment, *"Erbsen!"* (Dried peas!—the standard food ration of the time was coming out of his ears.) When folks offered to pay fares in large notes, the conductors couldn't make change, and everyone in Vienna rode free for a while.

For a few *groschen*, you could travel worldwide—England, France, America, Russia! So went a song making the nightclub circuit, lampooning the four-nation partition of Vienna. Of course, I might be a wee bit prejudiced, and of course I might be more familiar with the slangy Viennese German than the *German* German I had been translating previously, but I did find the Viennese refreshingly humorous.

During my occupation of Vienna, I met a distant cousin whose husband was a wily Yugoslavian. He made regular truck trips from Belgrade, bartering *slivovitz* (plum brandy) for whatever he could get—shoes, pocketbooks, blankets, cigarettes. As a gift, he gave me a large demijohn of the stuff in a wicker covering. I mixed the brandy with shaved chocolate for Christmas presents. My Yugo in-law was very ambitious—he wanted me to turn my back during guard duty while he stole a Jeep. I told him that my war days were over, but I still was a trained killer and would hate to deprive my cousin of a mate. One has to draw the line somewhere! (I wonder what he would have paid me?)

The farm and the Thoma family at Strass.

(In 1993, a makeshift Bosnian hospital ran short of supplies. Plum brandy was the only antiseptic/painkiller available. I remember its painkilling aspects well!)

One evening at the Thoma household, I entertained the family with the story of my mother making wine. One thing led to another, and my cousin's husband, Ferdy, suggested that we could easily go to Strass and get some of the Thoma wine to take back to the Bronx.

He said, "I have a pass to take me through the Russian zone and could go with you."

We crossed the Danube just after dawn, and heavy mist was swirling around the bridge when we entered the Russian zone. A Russian sentry yelled after us, but who understands Russian? So on we went. Happy to be free, we sped down the road northwest, bound for the hamlet of Strass. In the back of the canvas-covered truck rolled several optimistic wine barrels. Only 50 miles from Vienna, Strass was a famous wine-producing region, and I had persuaded the major that I would return with wine for the battalion.

Halfway to Strass, at Stockerau, our happiness abruptly evaporated. Across our path was a Red Army roadblock. We, of course, couldn't understand the commands, but this time a menacing submachine-gun gesture spoke a language linguistically clear. A Russian army WAC came running up, a German translator. Asked for "papers," our driver handed over a permit he had to go to Styr, where an auto factory was to winterize our vehicle with an aluminum cab. The WAC took the papers and led me inside the headquarters.

The colonel was a hard, athletic-looking man whose sharp, alert eyes measured me carefully as we entered the building. Several other ranks standing around also looked at me expectantly—a GI was a rare commodity. Should I salute? I didn't. Visions of newspaper headlines danced in my head:

WILLIMETZ DISAPPEARS IN RUSSIAN ZONE

15/9/45. Ferdinand Schober, an Austrian citizen, reports that Willimetz was last seen being led into Russian Headquarters at Stockerau . . . .

I explained to the Red Army WAC that we were on our way to Styr to winterize our truck. The colonel nodded slowly at this information and pointed to the west, and then farther south.

Duplicating her commander's gestures, she said, "The colonel says that you are headed that way [points to the west] and Styr is that way, more to the south." I gulped.

"Yes," I admitted, "we were making a small detour. I wanted to visit my mother's hometown of Strass."

The colonel turned and barked an order to one of the soldiers, who saluted and left. All conversation stopped; the scene froze. In a sweat, I pulled out a pack of cigarettes and, starting at the top, nervously offered them through the ranks (or what I thought were the ranks). The colonel gave me speculative glances from time to time and seemed to grow more and more amused at my discomfiture. When the soldier returned and reported, he broke out into a big grin.

"Ha!" he said. "Your mother makes wine!"

"How else," I explained, "could I get my commander to let me detour?"

He seemed to see the logic of that but admonished me to return to Vienna and get official permission from Russian headquarters—something I knew, and I am sure he knew, was not very likely. To certify that we would arrive safely in Vienna, he put a lieutenant on our running board. As I left, he said something to the ceiling that had everyone in stitches. I'm sure it was: "His mother makes wine!"

One incident sticks in my memory. The old city of Vienna was once surrounded by a wall. It held out against the Turks, who besieged it in 1683. (It is said that the croissant was invented by the Viennese so they could devour the Turkish crescent every morning for breakfast.) In 1857, Emperor Franz Joseph authorized the razing of the defense wall around the inner city, to be replaced by a boulevard some 180 feet wide—the Ringstrasse. Along this boulevard were built a series of monumental edifices (including my Pop's Hotel Bristol)!

The four occupying armies in 1945 had taken over some of these impressive buildings for headquarters. Double and triple trams went up and down Ringstrasse, and at the stops were station shelters. One night, I stood outside one of these shelters, waiting for my trolley, when I heard sounds of female distress coming out of the dark interior.

"*Was ist los?*" I asked nervously. Silence. Various rustling sounds, and then a Red Army soldier came bustling out, adjusting his greatcoat. As he left, he glowered darkly at me and crossed the boulevard to the Russian headquarters building (where, I deduced, he was a sentry). Closely following him, a young woman emerged from the shelter. Glancing at the retreating soldier, she looked at me and smiled.

"Are you all right?" I asked.

"*Ja,*" she replied. As we exchanged polite chitchat, I saw the soldier coming back across the boulevard. He had taken his tommy gun off his shoulder and had it cradled it across his chest. Our conversation stopped, and a bit of panic gripped me. What to do? Surely he wouldn't...?

Just then, like the U.S. Cavalry, a tram swept into the station. She and I hastily boarded. More nervous talk. I told her where I was going, she told me where she was going. Her stop was coming up first, and she invited me to her place—"because you are so nice," she said.

I stared at her, uncomprehending.

"I make you a good price," she added hastily.

"Oh, no, thank you. I am already late with my pass and will be in great trouble if I stay out much later."

At her stop, she shook my hand and departed, taking with her all my Sir Galahad, good-deed elation. Was all the fuss in the shelter about payment? Was he coming back to wipe me out or just to get his money back? I was grateful to Emperor Franz Joseph for having made the Ringstrasse 180 feet wide.

25.

MY BERLIN DIARY

In October 1945, Hedwig Willimetz Nimführ, the sister of the nine Willimetz brothers, asked me to undertake a task that first appalled me and then intrigued me. She hadn't heard from her brother, my uncle Josef, since the Red Army had captured Berlin. I didn't dream I'd get permission to go to Berlin, but I did! My genial major got it for me. All my Aunt Hedwig had to give me was Josef's last known address and that of his girl-friend, Sarah, whom he had once brought with him for a visit to Vienna. My aunt said she thought Sarah might be Jewish. What? Although she said it in a deliberately neutral manner, I chalked it up to the evident fact that she didn't like the lady as a provider of future Willimetz genes. Had my aunt been a Nazi? I was reluctant to ask.

After World War I and through the early 1930s, Vienna was a Socialist city—its health, housing, education, and welfare programs were notably advanced for their time. An official in charge of food supplies for the poor wrote:

> . . . before some demonstration, a number of Socialists would come to my office and inform me that the following day they would be demanding that I hand over 200cwt of flour. I was bidden to say I was prepared to release 100cwt, and in the end they would settle for 150. Then they asked which of the rooms in my offices were least used, in case it became strictly necessary to throw stones at a few windows.
>
> —Claudio Magris, *Danube*

Destruction in Berlin.

Uncle Josef, evidently an active party member, had lived in the vast Socialist cooperative apartment complex in Vienna called the Karl Marx Hof. The decade of the 1920s, in postwar Austria, was a time of deep depression, high inflation, and despair. Yet the Socialists were able to build this great housing complex—more than a kilometer long, with 1,325 apartments and interior gardens. It was a monument to the working-class poor who had lived in ratholes without hope or dignity.

In March 1933, a right-wing Christian Democrat Fascist named Engelbert Dollfuss, with the aid of the army, staged a coup d'état. He dissolved all political parties, including the Socialist Party of Vienna. The Austrian National Socialists were the first organized European group to fight the Fascists. They called a general strike. Attacked by the army in bloody street fighting, they holed up in their beloved Karl Marx Hof. The housing project was ordered shelled. Under a white flag, the Socialists requested an opportunity for the women and children to leave the apartments. Being Austrian, despite being a Fascist, Dollfuss allowed this. The men, including Uncle Josef, became transvestites for the occasion and left the buildings in women's dresses. The empty buildings were then thoroughly shelled.

Democracy was crushed by the Clerico-Fascist party of Dollfuss. William Shirer, in his *Berlin Diary*, wrote of the Fascist takeover in Vienna: "I weep for my Social Democratic friends, the most decent men and women I've known in Europe."

Uncle Josef went into hiding. On July 1934, Dollfuss was assassinated by the Nazis, who were then fighting for power in Austria. The Nazis had wanted to annex Austria, but Mussolini immediately sent troops to the Brenner Pass. Hitler postponed his *Anschluss* (annexation), not ready to face an Italian/French coalition—at least not just yet.

Amid the turmoil, Uncle Josef, on the army blacklist, was finding it difficult to stay underground. He went to Berlin and convinced the Nazi *Gauleiter* that he had fled his country because of his involvement in the Dollfuss assassination plot. As a one-armed marked man on the blacklist, he said, he could no longer hide in Vienna. He must have been a good storyteller, as he was given the prized newspaper/cigarette/candy concession in Berlin's major subway station, *Unter den Linden*. Wanted in Vienna as a Socialist, he found that the best place to hide was in the enemy camp. The Germans didn't march into Austria until March 12, 1938.

Although the Austrians greeted the *Anschluss* with Germany with considerable enthusiasm, there were thousands of grieving onlookers. With undercurrents of resistance, some 100,000 Austrians, mainly in Vienna, were imprisoned for political reasons. Some 200 per day committed suicide. Many were executed.

To the man in the street, Hitler brought prosperity and the return of German pride. If these were achieved at a high cost, did it matter? It mattered to the workers in industrial districts such as Wedding, who for generations gave the city its nickname "Red Berlin." In every single election since the very first in 1849, citizens of Berlin had voted overwhelmingly for liberals, Social Democrats, and Communists. In the rest of the country, the Nazis were the largest party in the Reichstag, but almost two out of three Berliners voted against them in 1932. The Nazis needed a special police "paint squad" to erase graffiti.

Hitler, understandably, despised Berlin, so he turned it over to Joseph Goebbels, the Minister for Propaganda and National Enlightenment. Berliners said, "When Goebbels dies, they are going to have to take his mouth out and shoot it separately."

Goebbels was humiliated because his city was not yet *Judenfrei* (free of Jews). On May 11, 1942, he wrote, "There are still 40,000 Jews in Berlin." This was largely because so many were employed in skilled jobs related to the war effort. Despite pleas from many industrialists, Goebbels had his way. In less than a year, Berlin was down to 4,000 to 5,000 Jews, who were called "U-boats," because they lived underground, hidden by sympathetic Gentiles in homes, offices, and stores.

As in Vienna, Berlin in 1945 was divided into four zones—American, British, French, and Soviet—and was surrounded by Red Army territory. I arrived in Berlin with Uncle Josef's addresses and a pasteboard army pass the size of a postcard in four languages—German, French, English, and Russian. At the U.S. Army quarters, where I signed in, I received a transportation map and directions to Josef's address. There was a lot of curiosity about my mission, and they warned me that Berlin was thoroughly destroyed—the most-bombed city in Europe. They were still digging out mutilated derelict children hiding like animals in the ruins. At Uncle Josef's address, in a fairly upscale neighborhood, I drew a blank—his apartment house was a jagged pile of rubble.

Back at my transient quarters, I went back to the great large-scale map of Berlin to look up my last address, that of Sarah in the poorer district of Wedding. Although they obviously were dying to know more about my mission, they pinpointed the address, gave me precise transportation instructions, shook their heads once more at my fragile cardboard pass, and set me free. Walking through Wedding was like walking through a nightmarish Bronx. Fragments of apartments, with all the accoutrements of my Bronx janitorial profession—tangles of plumbing, wiring, pieces of large furnaces, etc.

Pop fled Europe just two minutes before the final hour, managing to stay out of the army and taking me with him in his sperm bank. Otherwise, the Willimetz family (Mom, Pop, Mary, Lee, Hedy, and Emil) could have been incinerated under such debris—only, of course, in the debris of Vienna. Fortunately, parts of the *S-Bahn* elevated trains were functioning, and I took off. People in Wedding, of whom I asked directions, looked at me with great curiosity—this was deep in the Russian zone. Wandering American GIs were scarce on the ground in Wedding. The Russian soldiers occupying Vienna were a ragtag bunch, no two with identical uniforms; the Russians in Berlin, however, were elite Red Army troops, with neat uniforms and beautiful fur hats with red stars. Would my cardboard pass in four languages really see me through?

The test was not long in coming. Four Red Army MPs in a Jeep pulled up behind me and called me over. Their attitude was noncommittal, their German almost nil. The fact that they wanted to see my papers was uncompromisingly clear. It was also obvious that they had never before seen anything like my little cardboard pass. I pulled out Sarah's address to show I had a legit destination. As they passed this around the Jeep, large grins appeared—they knew Sarah!

They loaded me in the back seat and off we went. Sarah's address was a *Kneipe*, or *Bierstube* (a neighborhood bar, of which there was one on every other block in Wedding). Luckily, my troopers had spent enjoyable evenings in Sarah's *Kneipe*.

When she heard the name *Emil Willimetz*, Sarah looked stunned. Finally she turned and shooed out the soldiers with a good-natured German/Russian scolding. Nodding to the barman, she led me upstairs to her flat. Sarah was indeed Jewish. Josef had protected not only her from the Nazis, but also her father and mother. Sarah's father, a burly man in a black sweatshirt, was a fisherman. I puzzled about this—Berlin being an inland city—until I learned that a series of waterways and rivers connected it with the Baltic. At the very least, in his black sweatshirt, he *looked* like a fisherman. Her mother was a small, quiet, sad-faced woman. Neither parent had much to say. From the appurtenances in the room, I could see that they were proudly Jewish. I would have loved to have talked with them in more detail, but I didn't. It might have been the shame I felt for my terrible German and atrocious Viennese accent, or it could have been that their daughter did most of the talking. And, of course, she was talking about what I had come to hear.

The death of Franklin D. Roosevelt in April 1945 put Hitler into seventh heaven. He regarded it as a miracle that meant the turn of the tide. It was the catalyst that caused him to stay in Berlin and inspire his troops. April was also the month of Hitler's birthday.

Bierstube: Josef and Sarah.

"On April 24," Sarah said, "the radio announced that the RAF and U.S. air raids had ceased. We were unaware that it was done in order not to interfere with the Red Army attack on Berlin. The papers announced that extra rations would be doled out, so the streets had been crowded."

She stood up abruptly, went to a desk, pulled out a newspaper, and read the headline: "IN HONOR OF HITLER'S BIRTHDAY EXTRA RATIONS OF A HALF KILO OF MEAT, A QUARTER KILO OF RICE AND BEANS, A HALF KILO OF SUGAR, A TIN OF FRUIT, 3 1/2 GRAMS OF MALT COFFEE WILL BE ISSUED."

Sarah continued: "We could also draw the standard ration for the next two weeks. Josef, however, was not out collecting *Der Führer's* 'great gift'— he was helping a friend, whose apartment had been bombed, to load a car with what was left of the friend's belongings. It was a typical Josef thing to do!

"The Red Army artillery attack was completely unexpected. Caught on the street, hurt and dying people were everywhere. A shell landed in Josef's friend's street, and it killed your uncle."

For a moment, I thought she was going to weep, but her face hardened, and she cried out: "His friends couldn't wait to take all his belongings—whatever the poor man had left!"

She went back to her desk. "I have a list of some of what they took. I don't want his clothes and knickknacks, but shame on them, they shouldn't have them."

She sat and looked over the list and said pensively, "Perhaps his books …maybe something persona…if I could find some photos."

On this note, she got me to agree to go with her the next day—a kind of Salvation Army collection mission. This was not exactly the kind of thing Josef's nephew liked to do—I knew I would be ill at ease and embarrassed. That night, as I struggled with sleep, I reflected that for Sarah it was not very Salvation Army, either. There was real hatred in her voice—she just didn't want anything of Josef's taken away from her.

The next day we made the rounds—subway and trolley rides, knocks on doors, ticking off the list: "I'm Willimetz, Josef's nephew. I would like to collect my uncle's blue suit … radio … books … umbrella … etc."

Looks of great astonishment, hard looks at Sarah. "Come in, come in." "All the way from America, eh?" "Did you know your uncle?" "I took some of his things—better than leaving them for the Russkies, *ja?*"

Many looked like decent types. Under other circumstances, I might have liked to have stayed and talked more personally about my uncle. Finally we were through—not everything on the list, because some friends were not at home, but for my part, more than enough. I left everything with Sarah and took only a few mementos and a radio to his sister Hedwig in Vienna.

With the imminent arrival of the Red Army, Goebbels refused to allow the evacuation of any of the three million civilian Berliners (including 120,000 children). Some 507,000 Germans were killed or captured in the battle for Berlin. German officials, frantic to escape to the Allied West, bought, at premium prices, Jewish yellow stars of David—a passport for sympathy with the Allies. So many German big shots sewed on yellow stars to escape punishment that the Red Army had them interrogated in Yiddish by Jewish soldiers.

On the return train trip to Vienna, I thought about my Berlin adventure. I liked and admired Sarah and her parents. They radiated courage, anger, and a sense of loss (loss of a Germany they thought they once knew and had been part of?). I deeply regretted my superficial command of German. Hundreds of questions surfaced that I hadn't thought to bring up or hadn't been able to express. Exactly how did Josef manage to protect Sarah and her parents from the relentlessly efficient *Gestapo?* Was he a loner or connected with others?

Josef made at least one trip with Sarah to Vienna, openly presenting her to the family as his fiancée. Could he also have contacted his underground Socialist buddies to get false papers for Sarah and her family? The postal ID with a photo was easiest to obtain, and if the seal didn't overlap the photo, it could be steamed off and replaced with a new one. It wasn't certain protection, but it could help in casual street checks. No doubt Josef had a lot of his brother's (my Uncle Franz) street savvy. I gathered that he also radiated Viennese *Gemütlichkeit* (Viennese whipped-cream fellowship). He was, as well, a war veteran with a missing arm and an Austrian hero (however false) of the German Nazi *Anschluss* fight. But still . . . !

Josef was, it seemed to me, a man of principle, a dedicated Socialist who fought the Dollfuss dictatorship, who accepted the Nazis for a job but lived the extreme irony of defying one of their basic principles—racial purity. I had built up a picture and an emotional attachment for Uncle Josef. It might not have total reality, but on the long train ride back to Vienna, I already missed him, felt his loss. How I would have loved to have been able to talk with him! Joseph, after all, is my middle name. Had I known about Josef when the priest blessed and named me, at the age of eleven, I would have dipped into the holy water and blessed him back!

Gentiles who helped Jews, called *Judenknechte,* were arrested and faced imprisonment— even death. That there are now few Jews in great cities such as Berlin and Vienna leaves those cities the worse for it. A creative cultural spark, a leavening of humor has disappeared.

In Berlin, today, there is an Avenue of the Righteous, in honor of Germans who protected Jews throughout the Nazi regime. I like to think of Uncle Josef as having had his newspaper kiosk on that street.

BOOK IV

HOME FROM WAR:
A NEW LIFE BEGUN

On the way home by Liberty ship.

26.

THE WAY HOME

I'm singing in the sun like a cicada
after spending a season underground,
as a homeward survivor of the war.
　　　　—Maria Elena Walsh, *Americas,* June 1995

Locusts stay underground for 17 years—I waited 50 years before surfacing with my story.

With my war ended, I was faced with another great challenge—going home! I wish I could say I sang in the sun like a cicada on my way, but I was still too subdued, uncertain how the recent past would affect my looming future. What future, indeed?

In Munich, I met John Evarts from Black Mountain College. He apparently was doing something at a music academy. Before going to Black Mountain, he had attended *Hochschule für Musik* in Berlin, so I guess he knew German and his way around Germany's music schools. We exchanged information about BMC people.

"Did you know," I asked, "that Tommy Wentworth was killed in Normandy?"

"No, that's a shame," said John. "A great kid. Did you hear about Harriett Engelhardt? She worked abroad all during the war with the Red Cross and also died here in Europe."

Since our rendezvous at the chateau in Reims, I had heard very little from Harriett, neither of us being great correspondents. So it was with a heart-stopping shock I learned from John that Harriett was dead.

371

"She was leaving France to go home and on her way to the airport, the Jeep skidded and flipped over."

Meeting Harriett in New York was my only window opening to the immediate future, and her death settled around me like a cold fog.

A number of redeployment camps set up in Le Havre, France, were, in some weird army quirk, called Lucky Strike, 20 Grand, Old Gold. In the summer of 1945, there was a lack of available transport to the USA from Europe, since most ships were being redirected to take combat troops to Japan. By the spring of 1946, there was no longer a problem. During my extra six months in Austria, the great rush to get home had slowed down, and most of the soldiers had departed Europe. Lucky Strike had the run-down, dejected look of an old amusement park. The only bright spot was an old admonition written large above the chow line. The humorist was long gone, but his sign remained:

> Chow-line sign: IF YOU CAN'T EAT IT, DON'T TAKE IT
> Under it was written: If you can't take it, don't eat it!

It was a dreary, overcast day when we finally cast off and headed for home. This small Liberty ship didn't have the class of the great luxury liner that brought me to the war, but, hey, Mom and Pop, just like you, I went from Europe to New York in steerage! The hold was a jungle gym of piping, supporting a multitude of narrow steel bunks. I chose the bulkhead wall and climbed up 10 levels to the top bunk—hoping to be unmolested in this isolation. Fat chance, as the saying goes.

Our first night out, we hit a violent storm. I clutched the sides of my bunk, trying to hold onto my dinner and praying for the ship to sink and end my misery. In the murk down below, I thought I heard my name being called, but the *me* that corresponded to that name was in no condition to respond. I could feel the scaffold shudder beneath me and heard evil curses as man after man refused to admit to being me. A face appeared before my eyes and barked: "You Willimetz?"

I couldn't deny what my name tag clearly stated.

"Yup."

"Yer on KP!"

"I'm sick."

"So's everybody, fuckface. Come down!"

Not a nice man, but he outranked me and I followed him. Forgotten by the army were my Staff Sergeant Supply stripes, which I had had coming over. My Infantry status allowed me no privileges on this ship. The exact moment I put my hands in greasy dishwater, I threw up. Someone quickly put a bucket at my feet, and I soldiered on—as they say.

The next morning, I vowed to better my servitude and volunteered for midnight KP. This meant cooking breakfast for some 3,000 men, but no dishwashing. In fact, it turned out to be a lovely assignment. We cracked open several crates of eggs into massive double-hulled steam vats, the few shells that made the plunge causing little comment. We laid out kilometers of bacon on flat trays and did the same with bread slices. Then we were told to relax. When the time came to cook, it was all so simple. Using ship's oars, we splashed the scrambled eggs against the hot walls of the steam vats and scraped the instantly scrambled eggs back down. We cooked the long beds of toast and bacon by just flipping the switches on the electric ovens. Others helped with the serving.

What was so heavenly was that we were dealing with the ship's crew, and not the army. A Jamaican steward took us into the huge food locker—a fairy-tale room filled with steaks, poultry, cheeses, milk, ice cream, and even lettuce. All things we pined for and never saw overseas, and we had free rein! Can you imagine, thirsting for milk and lettuce? Not to mention steaks, done to order by the chefs . . . and ice cream!

The ship had its own mysterious bell signal system for marking the passage of time. The U.S. Army had its own . . . "You gotta get up . . . gotta get up . . . gotta get up in the morning" . . . bugle calls. We chosen few were already up, and immediately after serving breakfast, we had a full day of leisure time. We could watch the men going through their own wakee-wakee rituals. The toilet, for example, was one long metal trough, with a constant stream of running seawater under the seats (reminded me of my coal chutes in the Bronx).

Perched on the seats above the riffle was a full house of men—many not truly awake. With eyes shut, they lingered overlong while a line of full-bladdered GIs impatiently waited their turn. In the hopes of a profitable read, one literate soldier had brought a copy of the overseas *Tribune*.

Frustrated, he bundled up a few pages of the sports section, set them on fire, and carefully laid them upstream in the trough. The shock of rude awakening down the line reminded me of the Manor House barn as Joe went down the row of roosting hens testing their rear ends for plumpness.

The ship was still asleep, but we were due to enter New York Harbor sometime in the early morning, and I wandered to the bow. A lone sailor was standing watch, connected by telephone to the bridge. Bundled in a heavy blue pea jacket, a wool hat down over his ears, he was seated comfortably on a stool. He acknowledged my arrival at the rail with a grunt.

"Hi!" I ventured. "When do we see New York?"

"Should get a glimmer in about an hour."

Long pause as we conscientiously scrutinize the darkness ahead. After a while, he glanced at the Infantry patch on my sleeve.

"How long since you been home, soldier?"

"Twenty-two months."

"Seen much combat?"

"Seven months." A pause.

"Ever been torpedoed?"

"Twice."

Our references established, we relaxed, comfortable with each other in the cold gloom. The penetrating cold started to settle in under my light combat jacket. I shivered.

"Hey," he said, "here's a blanket. It's just been paddin' my ass—you need it more than I do." He pulled it out from under himself and I wrapped it tightly around me. We fell silent.

The golden sodium lights of a Brooklyn coastal highway began to dominate the skyline. Homecoming! I was excited, grateful to the sailor for his silence. During combat, I hadn't given much thought to what I would do when I got out of the army. The war had been all full-time present. But I had cheated the war—I survived!

The chatter between the sailor and the bridge heated up. We slipped through the Narrows and into the tranquil inner harbor. My mood swung constantly between exhilaration and depression. What now? What were my options? Stay in New York and write? I could take advantage of the GI Bill of Rights to go back to college.

With the memory of the dissatisfied World War I veterans and the Bonus Army rebellion in Washington, politicians had been leery of the sudden return of millions of youngsters from overseas after World War II. To forestall the possibility of restless rebellion, they pushed through Congress (by a one-vote majority) the GI Bill of Rights. Hundreds of thousands of young people (including women and blacks) took advantage of the education component to go through college. Was this a possibility for me? I guess the family still had my ancient Royal Standard, but did I have the drive? (John Rice had deflated my enthusiasm for writing.) Try again for a printing job? Pretty hopeless. The CIO? The labor movement? Despite the fears of Navy Intelligence, I was really a poor bet as a labor organizer. But first . . . the homecoming.

We anchored within sight of the Statue of Liberty—which my father had passed to *avoid* a war. I passed it having *survived* a war. Well, Pop, we made it, each in our own way.

I was perfunctorily hustled off to Fort Dix, New Jersey, where a sergeant, scrutinizing my records, looked up at me, grinning:

"Combat Infantry Badge, Purple Heart with oak leaf cluster, Overseas Ribbon, Victory medal, American Campaign medal, European Campaign medal. How come you never got a Good Conduct medal?" He reached in a barrel and, pulling one out like a pickle, pinned it on me.

"You have one now!"

At James Monroe High School, for my antiwar activities, I had been given a Bad Conduct Award, 35 points in Citizenship. The U.S. Army was more forgiving.

27.

RETURN FROM WAR

YOU CAN'T GO HOME AGAIN

THE BRONX, IN 1946, WAS A PLACE OF NO RETURN. I felt alien. Mary, married with three children, lived in Bethpage, Long Island; Lee, also married with two children, was in Kansas City; Hedy, now Hedy Paterno, with no children but lots of pets, was living in Queens. Mom and Pop, tentatively together again, were the only Bronx survivors. My childhood friends were all gone—some dead in the war, others who knew where. Hildreth had completely disappeared.

Today the Bronx is even more remote. The house I left to go to war can only be visited by an archaeologist—its dried bones are buried under the Cross-Bronx Expressway. The South Bronx itself looks like a war zone—with empty, burned-out houses and rubble-strewn lots everywhere. Crotona Park is now a battlefield for a very different set of ethnic groups. In September 1979, when I was doing a training program for day-care-center teachers, one of my centers was only two blocks from our janitorial house on Crotona Park North. Walking into the center with my camera equipment, I was confronted by a young black teenager. She took one look at me, snorted "Whitey," and herded her class into a back room. Almost immediately, I heard the defiant strains of "We Shall Overcome" coming back at me.

By 1946, the *Bronx Home News,* my old employer, had ceased publication, trolley cars were replaced by polluting buses, and the last of the Bronx farms had been developed. The sacred nickel bus and subway fare (since 1904) had been raised to become a sizable escalating cost item in New Yorkers' budgets.

I found a cold-water flat on West 11th Street, just off the Hudson River and far enough from Greenwich Village to be cheap. I paid $16 a month for this rent-controlled apartment. Actually, I paid only $8—an engineer on a banana boat needed a mail drop in New York and was willing to pay $8 for the privilege. His engineering duties, he informed me, consisted of monitoring the bananas with a thermometer.

As an apartment, it wasn't much. The combination bathroom/kitchen had an old-fashioned lion-footed iron tub, covered by a heavy, six-foot enameled lid—an adjunct to a sink, fridge, and gas stove. A toilet, serving two apartments, was out on the landing. It took some keen listening for flushes to know when it was available. Open to the kitchen was a living room/bedroom that I had painted flat black and hung with red velvet curtains. Why black? I'm not sure, but I was still going through some dark moods. The red velvet added a touch of Scheherazade!

I had thought I was out of the war scot-free, but the tension in New York caught up with me—I had constant diarrhea. On someone's fickle advice, I went to see a local physician. Equating me with his normal clientele, he tested me for a food allergy. Every two weeks, he supplied a new list of foods not to eat. In a short time, I lost 25 pounds. On someone's more savvy advice, I went to see a former army doctor working at New York University Hospital.

"Ah!" he said. "You should have come here in the first place. You obviously have spastic colitis, a nervous colon. Your body can't stand up under all this sudden tranquillity. I can take you on as a private patient or put you under the GI Bill for a freebie."

"That's no choice—I'll take the freebie."

"But that means my students get to take a look at you, OK?"

The students gathered around—me, practically upside-down, strapped on a tilted hospital gurney. The proctoscope, uncomfortably inserted into where they wanted to observe, was the size of a torpedo— with a light for the end of the tunnel. In those days, they made instruments a lot larger.

"Wow! Look at that colon . . . see those spasms!" "Move over, let me see!" "Me too!"

"Hey, gang, so it vibrates, but I'm hanging here upside-down. Gimme a break!"

During and after the Vietnam War, veterans' hospitals were forced to recognize a war-related illness called post-traumatic stress disorder (PTSD). A study published in the *New England Journal of Medicine* in 1987 stated that the number of Vietnam veterans who committed suicide after the war's end equaled the number of those killed during the war— some 58,000 additional names not included on the Vietnam Veterans Memorial in Washington.

"It's a nerve thing," said the doc, "the aftermath of combat conditions and your concussion. Stress hormones can help you escape a threatening Nazi, but in excess they may do a lot of harm to the brain. Your only recourse is a series of psychiatric treatments."

Studies of PTSD in combat veterans have shown that one side of the hippocampus in the brain was 25 percent smaller than normal. With me, only the discharge end of the alimentary tract, the colon, was affected. Or so I hoped!

The doc set me up with a navy psychiatrist, whose first crack out of the barrel was: "How are you with the babes? Do you like 'em?"

"Do you mean, Doc, do I like boys?"

What I didn't like was being talked down to, and I told him so. Was I still peeved at the U.S. Navy officer who had interrogated me in Grand Central Station? Finally, he decided that my problem might be war-related and, as had happened to me in the Paris hospital, he started me off on a sodium Pentothal series. One day, he let me leave his office still zonked with the Pentothal. I wandered home in a daze through the subway system and never went back to the psychiatrist.

Gradually I learned to control my skittish colon, calming stress by reflecting: "How does this compare with combat?" Of course, nothing came close, so I learned to relax. My attacks gradually became shorter and less virulent. My nightly war noises, however, took a little longer to subside. Living alone, whom would I bother? When Joanna and I were first married, I had some nightly yelling matches, she says, but in a few years they stopped completely.

Some folks go through life with goals. They set them up and with great persistence work hard to meet them. I seem to have the facility to blunder into goals, and they take charge. One day, still facing a blank wall of a future, I met up with a Black Mountain College friend, Claude Stoller.

Claude asked, "Now that you're out of the army, what?"

Cornered for an answer, I didn't have much to say. "No real plans. Eventually I might want to go back to live in the South. I thought I'd gotten away from the war without any problems, but seems like just as soon as I was discharged, I came down with a stress problem. I've started to see a navy psychiatrist and need to stay in New York for a while, I guess."

"Well," said Claude, "my brother Ezra has also just been discharged and is setting up a photographic studio. He's looking for an assistant."

"I don't even own a Brownie," I confessed to Ezra Stoller, already a distinguished architecture photographer.

"Good," he said, "just what I'm looking for. I don't want anyone with preconceived photographic notions!"

Since I had no preconceived, or, for that matter, any other kind of photographic notions, Ezra proceeded to instill some. His first notion was for us to build a first-class darkroom. This was followed by the installation of the latest state-of-the-art equipment. The huge Salzman enlarger, equipped to handle 8x10 negatives, was activated by electric motors.

In the new darkroom, I stood looking over Ezra's shoulder, intently listening and watching as he worked. His normal prints were on large 11x14 paper. As the weeks went by, I grew increasingly impatient. Enough already absorbing first-class notions—I can do it!

Finally, one day, Ezra selected a set of 8x10 negatives, told me to print them, and left the studio. On his return, I proudly showed him my output. He looked not at me, not at the prints, but in the wastepaper bin.

"Emil," he said, "I start off with a negative impression. Where are your rejects? You have very few."

Then he proceeded to load the bin with prints he found faulty. That afternoon, he sent me back into the darkroom with the same set of negs, and I made sure he would approve of my wastepaper bin. But of course he went directly to the wash tray, pulled out the best, and started me again on the unacceptables. He was as great a teacher as he was a photographer—at least he was for me. For the next two years, I did almost all of Ezra's negative developing and printing.

One day, I asked him what he looked for to photograph in a building. He replied: "With a 'good architect,' the dominant architectural idea is usually obvious—with a 'great architect,' I see many dominant ideas." Ezra himself was a graduate of the New York University School of Architecture.

I had no idea of the caliber of Stoller's work, or of the eminence he had achieved in his field, when I went to work for him. *Modern Architecture,* a book showcasing his work, was published in 1990, with photos by Ezra Stoller and text by William Saunders. Paul Goldberger, architecture critic for *The New York Times,* wrote this about Ezra:

> He is perhaps the most celebrated architecture photographer of the 20th century: his pictures are surely among the most reproduced, and they have in and of themselves played a major role in shaping the public's perception of what modern architecture is all about.

Of the many famous buildings designed by Frank Lloyd Wright, Taliesin, just outside of Madison, Wisconsin, was one of the earliest. *Taliesin* is a Welsh word meaning "shining brow"—a spacious set of buildings capped by wide rooftops. Peacocks sat on the edges of the roofs and draped their gorgeous tails over the edge. Very decorative. I mean , Mr. Wright, how do you get them to do it? (I know these birds. At the Bronx Zoo refreshment pavilion each Sunday morning, I had to clean tabletops beneath where the peacocks had roosted in the overhanging tree limbs. Peacocks, believe me, are not sparrows.)

Ezra had an assignment to photograph Taliesin, and we headed west in a Pullman compartment courtesy of *Architectural Forum,* then a Time Inc. publication. Transportation-wise, it was quite a step up in the world for me. Not only was it first class, but we had a compartment to ourselves. A far cry from my youthful boxcars.

When we arrived, I slept in Wright's daughter's bedroom, which had a birch tree growing through the floor and out the roof. The tree had a tight copper collar to keep out the rain. It made a marvelously efficient sounding board that amplified every creak and groan of the tree's nightlife. That first night, the score was tree 100 percent, photographer's assistant 0 percent.

In 1913, a Barbados servant ran amok, killing Wright's mistress, her two children, and four others, and burning Taliesin to the ground.

Misfortune followed the architect, and it burned a second time, destroying a hoard of art treasures Wright had brought back from Japan. When he rebuilt it a third time, he embedded fragments of statuary, vases, and plates in the hallway.

As an architect, Wright believed everyone over 5 feet 6 inches was an excessive use of materials—he was 5 feet 6. You entered Taliesin through a low door and walked down his fascinating long hallway to burst out into a large sunken living room designed to give you a spiritual "lift." Wright's son-in-law, a Wisconsin farmer named Peters, well over 6 feet tall, walked around the property with a stoop, eyes alert for low doorways.

Wright had his art treasures in a large, walk-in vault and gave me permission to load Ezra's 8x10 color plates in it. One time, working in the vault, I learned from the Master a lesson in economics. A delegation of his construction workers had come to his office to bargain for a wage increase. In his most authoritative manner, he lectured them on the inflation spiral, which all started with rising wages. I decided not to ask Ezra for a raise until we got back to New York.

Meals were served in a large dining room and attended by Wright's students. He demanded a strict observance of mealtimes. For several nights running, Ezra and I arrived late, but we had an outstanding artistic excuse. Ezra had noted that far across an intervening valley, a red barn caught the last rays of the setting sun. "That will make a great contrast with the wide sweep of Taliesin's buildings," he said, so up we climbed to the roof, dragging an 8x10 camera, tripod, and film cases. Naturally, a cloud thwarted our efforts, and we were late to dinner. This happened a second night, and from the imperious frown that greeted us, I decided not to use the vault that day when Mr. Wright was in his office.

The third time on the "shining brow" did it—we had the picture. As we arrived late for our third consecutive dinner, the dining room became completely silent—you could have heard a slide rule slide. Wright accompanied his frown with words.

"Mr. Stoller, as you know, I expect my students and guests to be at meals on time!"

I hid behind Ezra, who I assumed would not let me down.

"You are a great architect, Mr. Wright, and we appreciate the opportunity of recording your work." He looked around at the eager students:

"But you are not as great as a teacher of architecture."

Wright: "Explain that, Sir!"

"You are turning out future Frank Lloyd Wrights."

Wright again: "Are you aware, Sir, of the work of Neutra in California?"

"A talented architect, but he had to break away from you to grow."

Ezra, of course was the foremost master of his craft, but it took real *chutzpah* to face down Wright, who has been acclaimed by many to be the greatest American architect (a status expounded even by Wright himself).

Wright later acknowledged Ezra Stoller as the best photographer to properly interpret his work. Stoller wrote: "Wright would have liked a little more subservience on my part, but he appreciated my efforts too much to dismiss me. At one point he suggested that I show his house photographer 'some of my tricks.'"

When the rooftop photos were printed, the speck of red of the barn across the valley was not discernible. Well, we tried!

When I worked with Ezra, we photographed buildings designed by two famous architects I'd met at Black Mountain College—Walter Gropius and Marcel Breuer. I particularly remember a house Ezra photographed out on Long Island. It was a Breuer classic, and prominent visitors flocked to see it. During the "shoot," the poor distraught owner, proud of her house, went around with a damp cloth trying to keep up with a very active three-year-old diligently making his mark on the pure white walls. I was out on the lawn, under the black cloth checking the scene, when the three-year-old walked up to the great picture window and walloped it with a croquet mallet.

We also worked with Carl Koch, who had built an ingenious series of houses on cold, windy Snake Hill in Belmont, Massachusetts, a site previously deemed too steep for housing. He laid two pipes under the road, pumped antifreeze up the hill, heated it, and let it flow back down—two dry tracks, even in the snow. The rooms were heated by hot-water pipes under the floor, and the entrance to many of the homes was through the top story. He incorporated living rock into the houses by setting thermopane glass deep into the stone. He had formed a cooperative of friends for the project, and when it was all well and beautifully done, and with the lowest costs in town, they rewarded him by forcing him out, claiming the property was strictly residential and that he ran an architectural firm. Koch became known for his prefab Tech-built homes and his almost religious dedication to low-cost housing.

Carl Koch became a contributor to the Highlander Folk School and designed several buildings there, including Joanna Creighton's Community Center/Nursery School.

Near the end of my second year with Ezra, I was beginning to think of myself as a photographer. I had all the darkroom skills but lacked picture-taking skills. I had no intention of competing with my boss as an architectural photographer, so I bought what I considered a candid outfit—a 4x5 view camera. Then I bummed down to Monteagle, Tennessee, during one of my vacations and made an agreement to go to Highlander as a sort of unofficial photographer. To this end, they allotted me a small cabin to set up a darkroom. In the interim, before I left New York to work in the South, Ezra agreed to let me have access to his darkrooms.

CIVIL RIGHTS

My renewed contact with Highlander rekindled my interest in the Civil Rights Movement. In March 1948, the Rosa Lee Ingram trial came to my attention, and I made a deal with the NAACP magazine, *The Crisis,* to do a photojournalistic story on her case—my first serious professional photographic assignment.

So it was off to the peanut fields of Jimmy Carter's Georgia. On the train, I sat next to a Georgia state trooper. I had in mind to see if he could get me into the jail to photograph Rosa Lee Ingram, but his opinion of Yankee journalists was soon vehemently apparent. I had the feeling that if I revealed myself, I could end up in jail along with Mrs. Ingram. I decided to forgo his help. Unfortunately, I was still trying to operate with my 4x5 view camera, so I arrived at an Americus, Georgia, hotel with a couple of obvious large camera cases.

I entered the small hotel self-conscious about my camera cases, but probably looking less suspicious than I imagined. I telephoned the head of the local NAACP, a black dentist, who agreed to meet me after dark in his office. We met again at dawn, when he took me to the sharecropper farm where the Ingram children were staying. Sitting on the porch with the children, I was uneasily aware of the jalopies passing up and down the isolated dirt road. The anxiety of the NAACP dentist had rubbed off on me. I thought of Charlie rolling off the raft at Black Mountain to hide from a redneck farmer. Now the shoe was on another foot—mine! This was 1948, and I was well aware that the violence done to folks battling segregation included a scattering of Northern whites. Returning for me after dark, the dentist was a welcome sight. The death-penalty verdict against the Ingrams was commuted to life imprisonment. (The *Crisis* article is reprinted below.)

For the next nine years, I was active in the Civil Rights Movement, with many opportunities to use photography in the struggle. I did a few other minor stories for the NAACP and a bigger one for *Ebony* magazine—the story of a successful black rice farmer in Arkansas.

JUSTICE SLEEPS: THE INGRAM CASE (reprinted from *Crisis* magazine, May 1948)

I first heard of the "Ingram Case," as did most Americans (i.e., those Americans who are in the habit of being aware of such events), by a tiny notice in the papers announcing that a stay of execution had been granted the Ingrams. The "Ingrams" were listed as Rosa Lee Ingram, age 40, mother of 12 children and a recent widow, and her two teen-age sons, Wallace, 16, and Sammie Lee, 14. It stated briefly that they were Negroes, impoverished sharecroppers, and that they had killed a sharecropper neighbor, an old man named Stratford, white, allegedly in self-defense. A stay of execution had been granted pending a hearing for retrial. And this was all.

To one used to southern folkways, the algebraic formula involving the digits Black, White, Justice, and concluding with Death and Injustice, is as mechanically recited as the multiplication table in grade school. To find the same indifference in the liberal northern press was profoundly disturbing. They say that the world's boundaries are growing closer. How close are we now to Georgia? Or Harlem? Or is it because, after a time, we get used to injustice in places where we expect it? After a long period of war, the atomic destruction of Hiroshima disturbed, morally, very few people.

Some day, I believe, we will truly know the meaning of Hiroshima. Just as some day we will truly know the meaning of the histories of families like the Ingrams. When we become used to and indifferent to violence and injustice, our tendency to value life and justice is generally loosened and our moral fiber comes apart in our hands like a wet paper bag. I believe we saw this recently in Germany and Italy.

Because of this interest in the Ingram case, and my desire to learn more about it, I ran into the rare opportunity of receiving an assignment to do a photographic record of the Ingram children for a pamphlet being prepared by the NAACP in New York.

It's a long journey to Atlanta and train riding is inducive to little else but a kind of mesmerizing introspection. The case I was on, although a brutal miscarriage of justice, was certainly not unique. My knowledge of southern race relations, personal and factual, was filled with many such instances of injustice and violence. Yet there was something in the circumstances here which disturbed me deeply. I thought back over the few facts which were known and established truths in the case. Neighbors, both sharecroppers for the same landowner, both equally poor and insecure. The mules or hogs, or both, of one wander into the "property" of the other. Result: violence, death! And then death for the mother and two of her children? Because of a mule? Or because of race hatred?

Then it struck me that during the war I was constantly being reminded of the same juxtapositions. A sudden reversal of normal, domestic, civilized objects into death and destruction—because, again, violence in war is acceptable and natural. A stone wall, a hedgerow across a field—tranquil in the sun—built centuries ago to keep cattle from the garden, suddenly spits death as we approach it. For weeks my regiment bled itself white pitting itself against a fortified sport stadium and swimming pool. A church spire, built high above the town, emblem of man's highest aspirations, is for us, who see it over a rise in the ground, the eye of malevolence and destruction. A mule tramples in another's garden and in a hate and fear saturated world, death explodes!

Land at War

The South today, and in more or less degree, the entire country, is a land at war. Saturated by a blanket of violence. And that seemed to me to be the

Rosa Ingram and her sons.

keynote of my feelings for the Ingram family. Not alone that life on a mined-out, tired farm meant backbreaking, unrewarded toil; not only that the soil you till was not yours or that the improvements you made might benefit another, should, by some whim of the landowner, you be dispossessed; or that you have lost your husband and needs must raise your twelve children alone—but, that you should be equal to this overwhelming task, provide and be a good mother, you must still always be afraid, every minute (like an old combat soldier attuned to the sounds of shells), of the potential violence of your world. Although a shock, it must not have been a surprise to Mrs. Ingram when disaster struck her down.

My stopover in Atlanta gave me the opportunity to meet the people who were leading the fight, locally, to save the Ingrams. Such men as Col. Austin T. Walden, well-known Atlanta attorney; W.C. Harper, president of the Atlanta NAACP branch; Rev. Wm. H. Borders, vice president; Daniel Byrd, NAACP field representative; and others. From them I got a more intimate picture of the case, the names of some local Negro leaders in Americus [Georgia] who might help me, and the feeling that the leadership of the opposition forces in the South was of no mean caliber. I also found that the sheriff had moved the Ingrams to an undisclosed jail and that even her own daughter, as yet, had been denied a visit to her mother. This was blamed on undue (northern) interest in the case.

It was raining the morning I left Atlanta and still raining when I arrived in Americus. The town, especially from the railway station, was old, certainly, and gloomy. The hotel was in keeping with the town. Going through the lobby of the hotel, through the rows of seemingly dormant rocking-chair folk, I was conscious of sharp appraisal. My camera case made me feel as though I was carrying a sandwich-sign lettered FREE-DOM FOR THE INGRAMS OR BUST! NAACP NORTHERN AGITA-TOR. I had the strong feeling of being "The Stranger"—worse, "A Spy." An enemy alien in my own country, where the people I feared most were the forces of Law and Order. Although in no danger I had an unnerving feeling of uneasiness. I decided to have some dinner.

Revealing Talk

In the cafe peacefully eating, my ears cocked to a most enlightening conversation at a table close by on the Truman Civil Rights program, I was suddenly startled by one of the louder of the group, dramatically pointing his finger at me and exclaiming: "Ten years from now," he said ominously, "our sons, like that young fellow over there," I winced a little at the identification, "will be eating at that table and a nigger will walk in and sit down and eat next to him, and it will be against the law to stop him!" He paused for effect, still shaking his finger at me significantly. "What's more," he continued, "there'll be nothing *we* will be able to do about it either." They all looked at me as though I was expected to lose my dinner at this appalling prophesy. I didn't.

While I sat there, struggling to regain my composure and appetite, the debate went on in very much the same vein. It wasn't until somewhat later that I realized this was the first time I had ever heard, at least from this type of Southerner, publicly admit the possibility of defeat for his program of race segregation and hatred. And it made the winning of each case of injustice, the Ingram Case, all the more important. In Wrightsville, close by, the Klan demonstrated the night before the primary and no Negro voted. In Jeffersonville, however, the Klan demonstrated and two hundred Negroes voted.

Very much encouraged, and despite the rain, I called one of my con-

tacts and made arrangements to be driven out to the Ingram children the
following morning.

It rained the next morning—in fact almost all that week. It was only
because of the fine cooperation of the Americus Ingram Committee and
the self-sacrifice of one of them that I was able to get there during the few
hours of rainless sky there was that week.

I was told that the family was living on the farm of a distant relation,
a prosperous farmer named Sam Hill. Prosperous, I found, is a purely relative term. What is meant is that he actually owns his own land (more
than most small farmers in the area who own very little) and some cattle
and equipment. Be that as it may, and although his house was shabby and
unpainted (Negro homes fixed up and painted, in this area, have been
known to be burned down by jealous white neighbors), Mr. Hill himself I
found to be a kindly, hardworking and purposeful man.

We drove around to one of the old cabins on the place where the children were living under the care of the oldest daughter, Mrs. Geneva
Rushin, who had two young tots of her own to care for. The children, not
expecting visitors, and probably suspicious of white people, watched us
quietly as we drove up. However, they recognized my driver, who had
made many visits before, bringing clothes and money from the
Committee, and came over to the car. Geneva Rushin, who had been
scrubbing the cabin, came out to greet us. I was introduced, and after
bringing in some packages of clothing, was left there on my own for the
duration of the afternoon. There is not enough space to tell the full story
of all that occurred there that afternoon, but I would like to include some
of the impressions I received.

Mrs. Rushin, it seemed to me, was a young woman of great courage
and resourcefulness. The cleanliness of the cabin, the orderliness of the
children, and her own innate cheerfulness testify to her character. Her
greatest concern was for the children, many of whom were sick. I would
like to make a plea here for people of good will who would like to make a
contribution, in addition to money, that they send medical and dietary
necessities, such as vitamin and cod liver oil tablets, standard household
drugs, and other items necessary for the proper care of children.

After the initial excitement of opening the packages of clothes and of
being photographed, and after I had shown the more inquisitive of the kids

the ins and outs of my camera, I settled down on the porch with them, pretending to be resting. I wanted quiet, unpretentious shots, pictures of the family as they were. After a while they grew used to me and I was also able to slip around and get some of the pictures I was after. I was able to get some small insight into the effect on the children of the dreadful struggle that took place near their home and of the absence of their mother.

Charlie—His Grief

Most deeply affected was the oldest boy, Charlie, who was also jailed for some time and only released when it was proved that he wasn't even on the farm when the struggle took place. Charlie sat on the corner of the porch all afternoon, not speaking, just looking down at his feet. He had a clean-cut, soft and sensitive face. Whenever I spoke to him he would look up, answer politely and then look down again. Without looking up, I knew that he was aware whenever I aimed my camera in his direction. I felt self-conscious and ashamed, like I was disturbing a very private and personal grief, and it took all my belief in what I was trying to accomplish to do it. Charlie's face mirrored the very same kind of shock I had seen on the faces of young combat soldiers who found it impossible to adjust to the first days of combat.

The other, younger children were to some degree also very much affected. They would play and then suddenly stop and stare at nothing. Even the one with the most puckish and aggressive nature, who examined me and my camera most carefully and who fished out a large straw hat from the clothes package and strutted manfully around the cabin in it, suddenly stopped clowning and curled up in his coat on the porch, looking woefully at me every time I sat down next to him.

The law had moved Mrs. Ingram beyond my reach and I was unfortunately unable to see her. But from her children I know her to be a good and capable mother. The children were intelligent, well-behaved and very close to one another. When a very young one would cry, an older child would pick him up and soothe him.

I don't believe in emotionalism in judging what is or what is not a miscarriage of justice. But this to me, in the face of all the maladjustment and unsatisfactory family relationships of our times, is the crux and horror of the Ingram case. That despite heroic efforts in the face of formidable odds, a woman like Mrs. Ingram, successful in every way as a mother, is doomed to failure because of race.

Judged coldly, by every judicial standard, the crime committed was nothing more odious than self-defense. This was tacitly admitted by the judge who sentenced them, when he changed the verdict to life imprisonment under the steadily mounting protest, with the statement that the evidence was purely circumstantial. What he neglected to add was that the greatest single circumstance was the fact that the Ingrams were black. And the crime connected with the Ingram case (and there was monstrous crime involved) has not only to do with the law forces of Schley County— it has to do with every one of us who does not in great measure bend our energies and resources (yes, money!) to fight this evil and its component parts everywhere.

28.

ENTER JOANNA

LOVE ON A GREYHOUND BUS (Joanna Creighton's version)
"I HAD COME WITH A GROUP of thirty-five student-teachers from the Bank Street School for Teachers in New York to spend a day at the Highlander Folk School. We were on a 10-day trip through the TVA region, viewing mountains, dams and Southern customs and met, among others, many people who pioneered in the Southern labor movement and labor education. As a result of our one-day visit to the Folk School, I applied for the job of nursery school teacher, and a month later joined the staff."

LOVE ON A GREYHOUND BUS (Emil Willimetz's version)
In early April 1948, still in New York, I was approached by Claudia Lewis. Claudia had set up the first nursery school at the Highlander Folk School in 1938, and she was there when I attended a six-week session for union workers. Claudia, now teaching at the Bank Street School for Teachers, told me about a bus trip the graduating class was taking to the TVA. She had routed them to add a visit to the Folk School. Highlander had just completed a new nursery-school building and community center, and would I go along as the photographer and encourage one of the graduates to stay and teach there? I would and did. The teacher I picked was Joanna Creighton. (Kissing her on the bridge and subsequent momentous events were not in the contract.)

Every married couple has ongoing controversies, and I have no intention of airing any in this book—just this one. Joie claims that it was she who picked me out, not vice versa. But here was a bus full of female teach-

Joie with a nursery school child. Author photograph.

ers, and only one of me. So who did the choosing? Who kept whom trapped in the window seat, so to speak, for most of the 10-day tour—not to forget the next 50 or more years? Not that there weren't any other attractive young ladies on the bus. As one of the others said, "If you hadn't talked with Emil all the time, Joie, someone else might have wanted to!"

While my primary mission was to shanghai a nursery-school teacher, as a cover I did take pictures. In my album, I have photos of the great Norris Dam. Standing in the huge chamber of generating turbines, with the full weight and power of Lake Norris bearing down on us, I learned that the toilets didn't flush. Hey, Arthur Morgan, big TVA boss, get with it!

Another photo taken at Norris Dam shows a male student in the class, a Nisei, standing puzzled before a drinking fountain labeled COLORED. I was surprised that the TVA conformed to the racist mores of the South.

The Tennessee Valley Authority was set up to construct dams to generate electricity for the stimulation of industry—to manufacture fertilizer, to control flooding, to create lakes for recreation, and to build a model city, Norris. It was a Great Depression antidote. The few blacks who were hired were segregated in the construction camps. They were totally banned from living in the town of Norris.

Knoxville, for me, had become a second hometown, and I ventured to show Joie some of its salient features. Walking across the bridge over the Tennessee River, I offered her a stick of Dentine gum and took one for myself. After a brief chew, I blew a magnificent bubble. She looked at me with amazement.

"Do that again," she challenged. So I did.

It was much later, when the situation between us was more secure, that I confessed I had slipped in some bubble gum as an adjunct to the Dentine—and admitted that I didn't really like to chew gum. But don't think that blowing bubbles was the only thing that occurred on that bridge that night! Sent to catch a teacher, I got caught!

On the homebound bus, the students sang labor songs they had picked up at Highlander. One went: "You Can't Scare Me, I'm Stickin' to the Union." I could hear Joie, loud and clear above the gang, singing: "You Can't Scare Me, I'm Stickin' to the Bosses." It occurred to me that in this obviously pro-labor crowd, she was clearly the radical. Her sense of humor also came across.

At the TVA headquarters. Author photograph.

Joie's economics teacher at Wellesley told her that she was the pinkest reactionary she had ever had in class. A left-wing fellow student at Bank Street, when he saw my interest in Joie, warned me that she was probably the most conservative girl in the class. To tease her, he would leave copies of the *Daily Worker* in her mailbox at the YWCA—much to the horror of the woman at the desk.

I would have spurned the notion that I could be a victim of "love at first sight," but documentary evidence, in the form of Joie's saved letters of the period, prove that we discussed marriage in New York just a few weeks after we met. I was away much of the spring and summer of that fateful year, working on the NAACP assignment, on a film project in Virginia, and later on a Mississippi film. Joie's preserved correspondence reminds us of that hectic time.

A postcard to her father, an executive at Bethlehem Steel, on the third day of the bus trip:

> April 1948
> Ha! Ha! Ha! Guess who I had a date with last night—an ex-CIO Organizer!
> Love, Joie

A few weeks later, Joie wrote home that she had accepted the challenge of Highlander. Her father was appalled and tried to get Eleanor Hogan, the director of Bank Street, to dissuade her. He questioned his daughter's attachment to me and to Highlander. (Eleanor Hogan! . . . wife of the leader of the New York City Transport Workers Union!)

May 6, 1948
Emil Dear,
Got a letter from my Dad. He's rather scared & unhappy about the whole business. I showed the letter to Eleanor H. & my Bank Street advisor & they suggested things to write him. Eleanor asked me about you since you popped into the conversation at some point. She sugg. that I make it clear that I wasn't getting married right away & would certainly let them know before I did. She felt that was probably the main basis of my father's fears. Anyway I wrote Daddy a long letter . . . .
Love, Joie

May 1948
Dear Daddy,
I'm awfully glad you finally wrote because I was sure you would have a lot of questions. Before the Bank Street staff would give their OK on my application to Highlander I had very serious talks with several of the staff members.

The main point is that I will in no way be affiliated with any union or will not be part of the discussions. My function there will be strictly the nursery school and getting to know the people of the community, parents of my children who are Tennessee mountaineers.

Also—my talking so much about Emil Willimetz may have troubled you. He's a very fine person that I'm sure you'd like very much. I respect him a great deal. He's now in Washington working on a film for crippled children so won't be around more than once or twice until I come home. If you're worried about my serious intentions with Emil, I still don't know him very well but someday might feel that I wanted to marry him. He was an organizer for the CIO in the South before he went to war and had a pretty hard time. He's not an aggressively vicious person or shrewd or hard, but a very kind, tolerant person who wants as many people as he can help to have happy lives.

To me there is everything to be gained by this experience in my own growth. I love you all very much and do not want to worry or disappoint you, but I also feel in being true to myself I am being most the kind of a daughter you hoped I'd be

Much love, Joie

Emil Darling,
My family called last night and they were all excited about a 1st grade job in Hamburg [New York, not Germany!] I could have if I wanted. I told them that the Highlander job was already definite and they were disappointed but awfully sweet about it.

What shall I write them about you at this point? I want to prepare them for your coming but don't want to get them panicky. What'll I do, doc?

I miss you & love you very much,
Harriet Beecher Stowe

What could she do but bring that Emil Willimetz home to meet the family. We went to Buffalo by train, and by the time we got there, I was in a panic—like the night before a major offensive (not really, but I was not happy). Joanna was as steady as a rock. Her father and mother met us graciously at the station and drove us out to Hamburg. Passing the huge Bethlehem Steel plant on the way couldn't help but add to my feelings of angst.

The next day, I met the rest of the family. I got looked over, but everyone was relaxed and friendly. Mr. Creighton offered to show me his steelmaking operation.

"Don't stand between him and the open-hearth furnace," warned Joie's brother Jim.

I was impressed by the fire and brimstone of open-hearth steelmaking. Great cranes picked up huge ladles of molten ore, pouring white hot contents into molds. Multitudes of brilliant sparks were shooting off in all directions as we walked above the furnace. Taking out dark glasses to peer into the fiery heart of the vast furnace, Mr. Creighton was an impressive man, especially in that setting.

Joie's parents took me to a stream to go fly fishing. (Joie had advised me that hunting, fishing, and oatmeal were key to the family's affections.) So I went with great enthusiasm. I didn't catch anything, but then neither did they. I spent some time taking pictures of Joie's siblings' offspring. Fortunately, they came out well and helped to advance my cause.

> Dear Emil,
> After you left, Loie told me Daddy had said he thought you were nice in spite of what he'd expected. He later told me that he thought you had a lot of common sense and seemed in between his position and mine. (I smiled sweetly but chuckled up my sleeve.) The pictures of the kids are excellent. I'll have them sent to Loie right away.
> Love, Joie

On my second visit, I made strudel for Thanksgiving dinner. This was the very epitome of *chutzpah,* since I'd never before successfully made a strudel. But it put me in the kitchen when Joie's mother, Helen, dropped a large pan of turkey gravy. We eyed each other for a long moment.

"That floor sure looks clean," I ventured.

"I scrubbed it only this morning," she said. (Yeah, right!) "We'll give it a good boil."

I helped shovel it up and made an ally by keeping my mouth shut. But I lost ground again when my strudel dough came out not in one smooth sheet but looking like Maggie's old drawers, full of large, ragged holes. It baked like cardboard, but the apple part of the strudel was good—and then there were Helen's pumpkin pies.

Eleanor Hogan and others raised the question of Joie's and my very different backgrounds—would our marriage last? I think the following ditties emphasize our differences:

BRONX DITTY (taught to me by my brother Lee):
In days of old when knights were bold and toilets weren't invented,
you could drop a load in the middle of the road and walk away
contented.

HAMBURG, NEW YORK, DITTY (taught to me by Joanna)
Push the button . . . pull the chain . . . out comes a little choo-choo
train.

Joie really had fallen in love with Highlander, and she moved down that
summer of 1948. Arriving at the school in nearby Summerfield by taxi
from the bus stop in Monteagle, she found the school grounds seemingly
deserted, the building dark. Puzzled, she knocked on the front door. No
answer. She knocked again—louder. The door opened, showing a dark
interior. A hand reached out, pulled her in, and closed the door. The hand
pulled her under a table and whispered urgently, "Stay here—it'll be over
in a minute." It seemed a long minute, filled with squeaks, squawks, and
giggles. Bodies snuggled up to her from all sides. Suddenly the lights came
on, revealing a room filled with people having a good time. They had been
playing "Sardines."

Someone found Zilphia Horton, wife of the director, who was in charge
of the festivities. She took Joie and her suitcase to a room upstairs, saying,
not in the least apologetically: "I have to apologize for your introduction to
the school—you came at a mistimed moment." Hearty laughter.

Zilphia Mae Johnson, from Arkansas, had what I always thought was a
Native American face—black hair, high cheekbones, almond eyes. She was
to become Joie's best friend at the school. If I had written a film scenario for
Joie's entrance to Highlander, I couldn't have improved on this one. It
helped reassure her that union people were not the ferocious types they had
seemed to be—yelling and threatening at her father's steel-plant strikes.

Highlander Director Myles Horton's correct assessment (and mine) of
Joie's ability to integrate the community with the school is borne out by
John Glen, who wrote in his book *Highlander: No Ordinary School:*

Joanna Creighton joined the staff in 1948 to work full-time in the Summerfield community. Creighton, who received her professional training under former staff member Claudia Lewis at the Bank Street School for Teachers in New York, reopened the HFS nursery school and made it the core of a coordinated community program by early 1949.

Glen's report goes on to say that relations between Highlander and Summerfield improved considerably in the next few years, even to the point where the staff believed they had built up enough support to push for greater changes—namely, integration.

Joie had a lot to learn about living and working in a Tennessee mountain community. Fortunately, she took notes on daily happenings in the nursery school; the account below is lifted from her notes. The article at the end of this chapter appeared in Wellesley College's magazine in October 1949.

A CUMBERLAND PLATEAU NURSERY SCHOOL: TEACHER'S NOTES

The nursery school/community building was designed by Boston architect Carl Koch and built by 15- and 16-year-old Unitarian work campers. Another year they came to build a library. Once when I was lying on the roof looking down on construction activities on the other side, two of the teenagers nailed my blue jeans to the roof, lickety-split. Still, they were a marvelous group.

The fathers and mothers of the Cumberland Mountain children work their small subsistence farms with a mule and hoe. They carry water from wells or a nearby "branch" [creek] and have practically no time for recreation or visiting. To these children a nursery school means playmates, more wholesome food, trips to broaden their horizons plus the delights of swimming in the Highlander lake, making biscuits out of sand and swinging higher'n a treetop.

I was expected to raise the funds for my nursery school and community program. I had the use of a 12-year-old Plymouth for my first school bus, which grew more and more unreliable. I raised $750 for a used Jeep station wagon. I doubt if anyone ever raised money with more pleasure and spent it on something they needed as much as I did with my wagon. The children and I were equally ecstatic!

I had a basic routine—pick up the children around the community, teach, serve a simple lunch, clean up and drive them home. But first I had to convince the mountain families that it was a good idea to release their children for this purpose. In some cases the parents were as shy as their children.

Visiting John Jackson's shack: I sat with him on the front porch trying to encourage him to let his little girl come to the nursery school. As we looked at a puddle I saw a tiny inch-long worm writhing and twitching. He informed me it was someone's hair that had dropped in the puddle and turned into a snake. Wisely I refrained from nay-saying him and won his little daughter for my school.

I had one mother who wouldn't send her child to ". . . that nigger-loving school!" Fortunately she was an exception and I soon was able to take on as many as I could handle and peaked at 32 children enrolled—not all at the school at one time. Some of the mothers and older sisters came to assist me.

The first day of school, one of my new students, Freddy, answered everything I said to him, "Shit yes, Miss Joie," or "Shit no, Miss Joie." In those days (1948) this word was never mentioned in polite company and I didn't know what to make of it or do about it.

> Elmer: "By gosh!"
> Mary Lou: "He cussed."
> Elmer (sits for several minutes): "By gosh."
> Mary Lou: "You better whip him."
> Elmer: "When I get big like my Daddy, I'll kill 'im."
> Mary Lou: "Yer Daddy bin in jail."
> Elmer: "Shit. He ain't gotten' drunk no more by God."
> Mary Lou teases him about his father.
> Elmer: "Goddamn son of a bitch."

Elmer's father was frequently drunk and terrified his family with his violence. When the father was on a rampage Elmer would come to the nursery school and paint completely black pictures. Once, when he had threatened his wife with a knife, she sent for me to come sit with her since she knew he wouldn't attack (I hoped) if I were there. And he never did.

Joie with some of her children. Author photograph.

Children sitting in my sandbox. One threw something at the other.

First child: "Stop, you'll be put in jail."

Second child: "Yeah. The sheriff'll sure do it and he won't let you out till you're six years old and workin'."

Bobby stayed home from nursery school so that he, at the age of three, could keep one-year-old Megan away from the hot stove. The mother was driving a tractor for her neighbor.

Freddy and Elmer swinging, trying to go very high.

Freddy: "You'd be scared if you fell outta that tree."

Elmer: "No, I wouldn't!"

Freddy: "You'd be scared of that ol' booger man."

Elmer: "Wouldn't either."

Freddy: "When he comes with his hot chains you would!! [Then to me:] Wouldn't he?"

Pushing Linda on the swing: "She's just like a wind blowin', ain't she?"

Play in Summerfield was directly related to daily rural life. All the children had seen hogs, which they had fed all year, slaughtered in their backyards. One day my three- and four-year-olds spontaneously acted out the whole sequence. One of them shot (with a broomstick rifle) two hogs. Then they pulled them over to our tree platform (helped, of course, by the dead hogs) to drain the blood out of them. Next they were put into two old rubber tires (as black kettles) to be boiled to soften the bristles. Hauled out and cooled, the bristles were scraped off the inert bodies. Each hog was then cut up to be smoked.

After building a barn of blocks around himself, Peter (playing horse) took an arch-shaped block and said, "Could you put that over my neck and plow me?" The children and I walked around the room plowing each other as horses. Peter looked critically at my feet and said, "You don't hold yer feet like a horse. Horses don't clump flat feet—they point their hooves down."

In December, the nursery school began a hot-lunch program, which provided fruit, crackers, milk, soup, and cod liver oil. To gather the food for this program was for me a learning process, a far cry from shopping at the supermarket! From the families who could manage it, I collected 25 cents a week for the milk. Children whose families had cows brought their own milk. We set up a sewing co-op, and proceeds from the sale of quilts and other goods also went into the program. Some parents set out extra rows of vegetables for the lunch program.

One day our neighbor, Mr. H, asked me if I could use some cabbage. Delighted, I said yes, and he took me out into his field. "You can have *that* row." It was more cabbages than I had ever seen in my life, but I picked about 10, out of which I made sauerkraut.

I told one of my nursery-school mothers and she was horrified. "Didn't you know that yesterday the sign was feet? When the sign is in the feet, your kraut will stink."

Fortunately, my innocence of the zodiac signs kept it aromatic. One day, when I was picking up little Eula Mae, her mother asked if I could use a chicken. Delighted, I said, "Yes, that would be wonderful for the lunch program." She came back out of the house and handed me a live and spirited rooster. Off we went, I driving the car with a flapping and squawking rooster held by the ankles in one hand. (And this with a manual shift!) I finally

The home of some of Joie's children. Author photograph

had to drop him, and he flopped around my feet for all of the way home.

I prepared the soup at noon. Our neighbor and very dear friend, May Justus, offered to help by making soup one day a week. May was a prolific author of highly acclaimed children's books—"A great writer but a terrible soup maker." I moaned and did my best to ameliorate the flavors.

At the Highlander Folk School, we could see the fish the Conservation Department was putting into our new lake, or see the Unitarian work campers raising their tents for the summer. Perhaps next year, the nursery-school children would again ask, "When the Indians who live in them tents a-comin' back?" The Unitarian work campers and visitors would bring all kinds of exotic toys, which constantly intrigued the children. They had all been fascinated by an "electric-eye dog." Little Bobby, staring at the light in the eye, said, "Hits got far in it." I told him it was using electricity, not fire. Later, when the bulb wouldn't light up he brought it to me to be fixed. I took it apart and put it successfully back in working order. Bobby said, "That's the way it do, haint it?"

One morning I opened the school and found a long, straight line of mouse droppings down the floor. "Real discipline," Emil said. "These must be army-trained mice." I swept up before I went to get the kids. In the afternoon, news of the military mice brought Bill Elkuss and some work campers to investigate. It turned out that more than 40 bats had gotten in and made themselves at home along one of the longitudinal beams. With a great hullabaloo and many brooms, the invaders were evicted.

Grundy County had no doctors, health facilities, or libraries, but it did have a church for every 122 people—82 congregations in a population of about 10,000. Families tended to gather together in kinship groups. Itinerant preachers—men who rode a circuit every few months—administered to small family gatherings. The circuit rider carried a change of clothes, a bible and a hymn book, staying at the homes of the people he preached to. These men were not trained ministers with worked-out sermons, but rather spoke on their feet spontaneously, being "led by the spirit."

One Sunday morning, the older sister of one of my favorite nursery-school children invited us to join the family for services at her home. We were taken into the family's small cabin and solemnly introduced to one and all. The preacher started off with a short prayer, imploring us to fight the devil and stay clear of sin. Then swaying gently, the group began moaning through a song, interspersed with prayers and Amens. Suddenly the mother started speaking urgently in an unknown tongue, picked up by her daughter. Others shouted out imploring but unknown admonitions, writhing and jumping in ecstasy. We were clearly not in the circuit, feeling more uncomfortable as time went on but trying to appear in sympathy. Shortly after the final song, we assured the family that their preacher had the right spirit and that we were thankful to have been invited. Then we left—aware that for us to be accepted by this family in this context was a compliment and a trust.

[In his April 2000 book, *Snowshoe and Lancet,* Robert Ecke describes a young girl at a Pentecostal church meeting who, in a burst of religious enthusiasm, had fallen to the floor. When a gentleman in the congregation hastened to assist her to arise, the mother intervened: "Don't tetch her, don't tetch her, leave her lay where Jesus flang her!"]

At the nursery school one day, Billy said he'd seen a big man scare someone. "It was the Ku Klux Klan, they never hurt good people, only mean people." There being no blacks living in Grundy County to molest, apparently the KKK confined its activities to righteous issues. One of my nursery-school fathers was taken out and whipped for infidelity. When Highlander arrived, it was great news for the Klan, and they zealously participated in all the anti–Folk School activities.

Many (probably most) of the women in my co-op dipped snuff. But not the sniff-and-sneeze of Emil's grandmother. In Summerfield, snuff is packed between the gum and the lip and left to do its work. When I sat around a quilting frame with my nursery-school mothers, I was the "oneliest" one without a tin can at my feet for tobacco juice.

On February 14, 1949, Grundy County suffered a terrible tornado. Three-year-old Barbara, whose home was smashed to a foot-high mass of rubble, found emotional security in returning to nursery school to play with her friends. She would gradually overcome her terror at each dark rain cloud and sudden noise.

When one of the sweetest and gentlest of my nursery-school children became very ill and died suddenly, the father came immediately to tell me. He said the little boy had been calling for his teacher when he died. He said he knew I loved their boy too, and he'd always be glad to do anything he could to help the nursery school.

Daily summertime ritual enjoyed equally by mother and nursery-school teacher: Manny Lee arrives at nursery school with a bouquet of wild flowers jammed into a jar. At the end of the morning, he grabs up his wilting flowers and returns them to his mother.

*****

AND SOME FEEDBACK . . .

May Justus, Joie's good friend, author of many successful children's books, and infamous soup maker, had this to say:

> Nursery School children under the guidance of an expert teacher have a bigger world and a sympathetic second home. Here they learn to live and laugh together. They romp and play and shout and sing and forget to be shy. They share their playthings, their good food and forget to be selfish. Mrs. H. can turn her attention

to getting out the family washing without the worry of having two little ones under foot in her small crowded cabin. With a washtub on an outdoor fire, and water to be carried from a spring some distance from the house, this freedom is precious.

One of the mothers said, "If you could see the children before the nursery school came and see them now, you would understand why we support it."

"HOW COME ME TO BE HERE?"
by Joanna Creighton Willimetz (1947)

Seventeen years ago a Wellesley alumna and pioneer in cooperatives, Lilian Johnson, ex'85, donated a building and grounds for the Highlander Folk School near Monteagle, Tennessee. Upon making a trip to the school another alumna, Joanna Creighton Willimetz, '47, was so impressed by the venture that she immediately applied for a position there and is now "Director-janitor-cook-plumber" of the nursery school.

Sitting cross-legged on a porch one rainy morning are twelve children in overalls and "flowerdy" flour sack dresses. With them is a mother and a teacher who is about to read a story on bears. She asks, "Does anyone know what a bear is?" There is slight mumbling in the group and a quick reply from a three-year-old. "Yes. There are blueberries and blackberries and you can tell when raspberries are ready because there's a hole in the middle and they fall off."

This conversation took place shortly after I became the teacher-director-janitor-cook-plumber of the Highlander Nursery School, near Monteagle, Tennessee. In mountain jargon, "How come me to be here?" I had come with a group of thirty-five student-teachers from the Bank Street School for Teachers in New York to spend a day at the Highlander Folk School. We were on a 10-day trip through the TVA region, viewing mountains, dams and Southern customs and met, among others, many people who pioneered in the Southern labor movement and labor education. As a result of our one-day visit to the Folk School, I applied for the job of nursery school teacher, and a month later joined the staff.

It has been an ideal opportunity to set up a nursery school, to work with people who are able to plan their own jobs and who practice their ideals continually. The Highlander Folk School is owned cooperatively by its staff and is supported by tuition from school sessions, fund-raising and fellowships. Our building and grounds were donated in 1932 to Myles Horton, the director, by Dr. Lilian Johnson (Wellesley 1885). Dr. Johnson was a long-time pioneer in cooperatives and once organized a community center in this mountain community on the edge of the Cumberland Plateau.

Besides our teaching staff, which numbered five instructors during our last resident session, we have a Film Center (my husband is the photographer), a secretary, a maintenance man and farm manager, and, for three-month periods, an Antioch College student assistant.

During our summer resident sessions, which are usually interracial, the students have classes in union-building, parliamentary law, grievance procedure, political action, recreation, etc. The current Farmers' Union term studies FU cooperatives, insurance, and their own special problems.

It is very exciting to watch the changes in a group during the week or two of the term period. Here the interracial group will be living together but only very gradually do they come to feel at ease for there are not many places in the South where a group is able to participate completely in democratic living.

The Folk School is located in what was about 50 years ago one of the wealthiest counties in Tennessee, but now most of the timber has been cut and the mines worked out. Except for subsistence farming and a little coal and wood hauling there is practically no means of making a living. A Methodist (Chautauqua Plan) resort colony in a nearby town gives summer employment, but there are few regular jobs.

The homes of the majority of the people are small one-, two- or three-room frame houses, mostly without window panes. Families do the washing in big black kettles over fires outdoors. Of the nursery school families, only one has running water. Despite the continual struggle with poor soil and lack of employment, the people still seem to love their land on the mountain and have great pride both in it and in themselves. All the community women spend busy summers canning. In many of the houses rows of beans, kraut, apples and berries are stored underneath the beds. Even the tiniest children have done their share of berry-picking and field work. But this adds only a little variation to the monotonous diet of biscuits and gravy.

The Folk School has, in addition to its sessions and field work, an extensive community program, which provides a library, a small newspaper, square dances, and the new nursery school. It is only with the support of the people in our county and community that we are able to maintain a resident school and to carry on our program. Everyday these people can hear part of our program as our '35 Plymouth "bus" rumbles by with twelve or thirteen little heads yodeling out of the windows. This apparition was too much for five peaceful cows ambling down the road. As we came around the bend toward the nursery, they leaped up a three-foot bank and over a fence into a graveyard. At the rate my children chased them home, they must have given buttermilk that night. On another trip through the cemetery, Buddy perched on a tombstone. I mentioned that people didn't think it very respectful to play on graves and he announced, "Hit's muh granddaddy's and he wouldn' keer."

The nursery school was built two years ago by a group of Unitarian work campers, and its spacious interior, wide porch and big yard are a teacher's dream, providing plenty of room for the work and play of 2–5-year-olds. One of its most delightful features is a flush toilet which is ignored by most of my cherubs! A bitty two-year-old returned from the toilet one day, and, remembering something, rushed back, pulled off an inch-square piece of toilet paper, dropped it into the toilet and smugly marched out again. Her next move was to climb on a stool at the sink and turn the water on full blast. Running water is a constant joy to these children since most of them help haul water up "from the branch" or carry it from a neighbor's well.

The children are mostly blue-eyed blonds of Scotch-English stock, the majority of whom are the happy products of much loving and strong discipline. They adjust to nursery school very quickly, although many of them, like their parents, are shy. In our nursery school, as with children everywhere, a teacher can learn much about the child's home life and problems in connection with school from simple nursery conversations. "She won't never let me come no more if I get paint on me. Hit must be poison. Hit don't come out," was Bobby's rephrasing of his mother's statement. Later I checked with the mother and found her distressed about the washing problem. The next time a friend in New York sent material to be used at the nursery and distributed to families, I gave each mother a special piece to make a smock for her child. Now, despite painted toes and noses, the children go home on paint days with practically paintless clothing.

A knocked-down block building produced another conversation which had much meaning:

Larry: "You tear mine down an you'll git somepin' you don' want."

Buddy: "Yea. Jail! sheriff'll sure do it. An he won't let you out 'til yer six years old an workin."

Here the law doesn't symbolize a friendly policeman who helps a little boy find his lost puppy or cross the street. Instead, "The Law" is a man who comes to take Uncle George to jail for making "moonshine," or a threat of what will happen if a little boy doesn't obey.

Johnny Lee came in gaily one morning and announced, "I quit cussin' today!" As at most nursery schools the children go on infrequent "cussin'" sprees. This was at the end of Johnny Lee's spree which was probably curtailed by a whipping at home. At the end of the morning from our sandbox came a volley of blasphemy. In walked Johnny Lee very quietly, "I ain't quit cussin' yet."

One or two of the mothers or older sisters help supervise the children at nursery school each day, often bringing with them the youngest baby, who is not yet ready for school. These voluntary assistants also prepare our hot lunches. Community people helped start the lunch program by making a star patch-work quilt which was raffled off. The community sewing cooperative sells children's dresses, aprons, skirts, etc., and has rummage sales from which the proceeds are given to our lunch program.

Besides nursery planning with parents, distributing clothing and Christmas toys, visiting dentists and doctors, my job includes such miscellaneous activities as chasing fifty bats out of the school and catching a runaway horse and wagon. It even includes biological research in the breeding of hamsters or rushing expectant mothers to the hospital in the next county.

While the Folk School has contributed a building, a car and a nursery teacher, it does not have the funds for continued subsidy of the nursery school. The community people have cooperated increasingly in running it, but parents can give only food, labor, and moral support. They cannot give financial help. It will therefore be necessary to close the nursery school for several weeks at a time in order to take fund-raising trips. (To keep our car, building and teacher, it costs approximately $2,000 a year.) As long as we continue to find other people as enthusiastic and concerned as we are about our program, we will be able to maintain our nursery and the Folk School program.

Considering our services—better health through good nourishment, and helping children become happier and better adjusted—we feel it is more than worth any money and time put into it. It is very rewarding to work with the people here in our community and with the farmers and workers who come to the school. For, like people everywhere, they don't want or need charity, but rather the cooperation of others in understanding their beliefs and problems.

29.

FILM CENTER

WHEN I RETURNED TO HIGHLANDER from the Rosa Lee Ingram filming assignment in Georgia, I met George Stoney, whom I remembered as a friend of Highlander. He was (or was soon to become) head of the New York University film department, and he had just completed a film on midwifery in North Carolina for the Southern Regional Film Production Service. He put me in touch with them, and I was elated to be accepted and assigned to a film crew.

My first film, *First As a Child*, was shot in Virginia. It was based on the need of a child about to undergo a traumatic surgical experience to be treated first as a child and second as a patient. Being low man on the totem pole, I learned how to load film magazines, pull focus on the camera lenses, and go for coffee. When Claudia Lewis called me about the Bank Street bus tour, I was scheduled to work on *First As a Child* but hastily agreed to go when the film was rescheduled. It is on such slender happenings that life is predicated. How would I have spent the next 50 years had I not met Joanna? And what about our two boys? Love had gotten its teeth into us and did not falter—even when we were parted during *First As a Child*.

I was fascinated by the whole process. The subject of the film was a poverty-stricken 11-year-old boy who was about to have a major operation on his crippled leg. One scene stands out in my memory. The boy had to be built up nutritionally and was given extra food. Told he was to have whipped cream on his pudding, he was elated.

CAMERA: CLOSE-UP, BOY'S EAGER FACE (only to register him

411

trying to hide instant disappointment). CUT! The mother had never made whipped cream and neglected to add sugar. TAKE TWO: Whipped cream with sugar.

In July, I was assigned to a film called *Feeling All Right,* to be made in Mississippi. The film was to demonstrate the first penicillin treatment of syphilis (outside of the U.S. Army in World War II). It was spared a gruesome tone by director Fred Lasse's sensitive treatment of the story. Fred had spent several weeks in Mississippi researching the characters and locations. His sympathetic directing really got the black family involved emotionally in the project. When Roy's mother scolded him, it was with 20-some years of scolding behind her (she was his real mother), and Roy's reactions were genuinely heartfelt. The film won the New York Critics' Award. A lot of the credit was due to the superb camera work by Gordon Weisenborn.

We had no trouble filming in the relatively worldly city of Greenville, Mississippi, home of Hodding Carter's liberal *Democratic Times* newspaper. Then we decided to shoot a street scene of Roy's regular Saturday visit to town in the small hamlet of Indianola. That day, there was a states' rights convention going on in the capital, and every radio on Indianola's main street was blasting forth segregationist anger. This was to be one of the key scenes—where Roy meets his city friend George and is led astray.

We unloaded our equipment on the sidewalk where George was to be seen having his shoes shined. No sooner was the camera assembled and we started shooting when the sheriff sauntered up to us: "What do you fellers expect to do here in Indianola?"

Fred, in his most sincere Chicago accent: "We're doing a film for the Mississippi Board of Health."

"Got any papers?"

"Well, we have a contract, but I don't carry it with me."

Fred's tone was getting just a little defensive, showing a tiny touch of moral outrage. We now had a small mob, and the sheriff was playing up to them.

"Come back when you have your papers, Son. Here in Indianola you need a damn good reason to be filming niggers on our streets." Laughter in the crowd.

Fred Lasse with silk screen.

I cut in hastily: "Let's pack up. We can come back next Saturday with the papers."

We did just that, hastened by crowd sneers.

The incident came out the next day in the *Indianola Enterprise:*

Mystery Involved in Picture Taking Here Saturday Afternoon
Front Street was the scene of a bit of excitement here last Saturday when a crew of men representing the Southern Educational Film Production Service, of Atlanta, Georgia, were asked to stop shooting scenes on this street due to the complaints of several Merchants as to the type of Moving Pitcures [sic] they were making.

The part taken at this location was that of one actor, colored, alighting from an automobile and stepping up on the sidewalk, calling a colored shoe boy and having his shoes shined right there on the street, but as he put his foot up on the shine box he withdrew a newspaper from his pocket and opening it turned the large headlines toward the camera. These headlines read "CIVIL RIGHTS," and seeming to be the main subject of the picture . . . .

Our filming the next Saturday was, of course, back in Greenville. On a side street, we found a shoeshine stand with four seats that had a cardboard penciled sign stating WHITE on one side and COLORED on the other. The sign would be moved back and forth according to demand and with little apparent alienation.

Flash forward to Indianola recent history. A black writer, Tom Dent, in his book *Southern Journey,* writes that Indianola ". . . had been an awful place for blacks; the White Citizens Council was born there. Its large black community fought hard for rights and the ballot. Now, in 1991, white business leaders were supporting the funding of the predominantly black public schools as an 'investment in their town's future.'"

According to Dent, "Indianola had passed Greenville by." This would certainly not have been the prediction of our film crew of *Feeling All Right* in 1948. Yet all was not lost in Greenville. Although its educational system had been losing ground, Mike Espy was elected to Congress in 1986—the first Mississippi black since Reconstruction days. His congressional district was 52 percent white, yet he was reelected in 1988.

This second film, *Feeling All Right,* with a first-rate director and cameraman, was for me a much more comprehensive experience, a much greater involvement with learning film production. But it took me away from Highlander for the critical months of July and August, when my beloved Joie was settling in.

There was no air-conditioning in our little motel in the Mississippi Delta, and no ice for the sulfur-flavored water. After a day in the August heat, we drank quantities of cold beer to get palatable liquid into our dehydrated systems. Alcoholically, the beer seemed to have little effect. Well, perhaps I shouldn't say that. One major effect of the beer was intense speculation on the possibility of setting up a Film Center at Highlander Folk School, and I made one of my several trips back to HFS to try to sell Myles Horton, the director, on the concept (seeing Joie was incidental).

Myles was gregarious and articulate, given to telling stories to illustrate his points, punctuating his talk with loud bursts of laughter. Being a successful motivator of people by the force of his own personality, he felt little need for audiovisual aids. It wasn't easy to convince him that many people, probably most, didn't have his talents, and that good audiovisuals could help carry the HFS message. I pointed to the success of the Highlander film, *People of the Cumberlands,* and argued that the Film Center could operate independently, covering its own costs.

As I spoke, I could see Myles weighing the pros and cons. I am convinced that it was Joie's growing success in her community program, and our obvious mutual attachment, that was a major factor in his final agreement. Promoting interracial living in an all-white county, Myles needed the support of the community. So he agreed to a trial run.

John Glen reviewed the Film Center in his book *Highlander: No Ordinary School:*

> A new feature of Highlander's program in the late 40s and early 50s was a Film Center. Emil Willimetz, a former student who had been working as a photographer at the school, proposed in 1948 that he and two filmmakers produce and distribute low-cost documentary films and other visual aids and train local union leaders in their use. Operating as a self-sustaining group, the Film Center staff gave demonstrations on the use of filmstrips and other graphic materials at residence sessions; showed films and led discussions at education conferences; trained union organizers in photography; established movie circuits for Southern labor and Farmers Union locals; and recorded various events for Highlander publicity and fund raising campaigns.

To help fund the Film Center, Fred Lasse landed a contract to film Elmer Wheeler, who was billed (or, rather, billed himself) as America's Number One salesman's salesman. Wheeler's sales pitch included the well-known, "Sell the Sizzle, Not the Steak."

Dallas, Texas, was paradise for a crew that had just finished filming in the rural Mississippi summer heat. It had air-conditioning! We went from a cool motel via cool taxis to cool restaurants and to Elmer Wheeler's cool ranch house. After a day of filming, we were invited into Elmer's pool, where he floated hamburgers and cold beer to us on cork trays. Sheer luxury—with cool cash at the end of it.

Our income from both summer films went toward setting up and maintaining the Film Center, for which we designed and built a building. It was a complex job, because it had to encompass an office, art workshop, film studio, and photographic darkroom. That summer, I was in and out of Highlander—just enough, I hoped, to maintain Joie's interest in me. That she was able to eke a number of letters out of me that summer spoke to my super high interest in the matter. I bought two sets of nursery-school blocks for her community school from the Macedonia Brotherhood Co-op in North Georgia. It was a gesture on a par with my bubble-gum caper, but much more expensive and meant to impress her. It did.

When Bill and Mary Elkuss, HFS staff members, left the school, their nice upstairs apartment was slated to become an office! It forced our hand. To get the apartment, we announced our forthcoming union.

That night, the entire Highlander staff went to the local Monteagle honky-tonk to celebrate our engagement. I had my camera equipment all packed and was to take off early the next morning, so we opted not to celebrate too late. Coming up to my cabin, I noticed that the door, carefully locked when we left, was wide open. The lock area was completely smashed. The photo equipment was gone! I noticed a whiff of explosives in the room and a series of crescent-shaped holes in the wallboard. Digging out the holes, I found fragments of a hand grenade. In the grass outside, I found pieces of the main stem—familiar equipment to an old infantryman.

In the morning, I called the Tracy City sheriff, who arrived rigidly set to be unfriendly. He took the grenade fragments without comment—doesn't every robber break in that way? His only words:

"Kin get bloodhounds, cost $75, no guarantees."

"No, thank you." He didn't try to sell me on anything else. However, I needed him for the insurance clearance.

What to do? I had still been using my 4x5 view camera, a leftover from my Stoller training—an excellent camera, but clumsy and not ideal for the people pictures I was trying to capture. I decided to return to New York

Emil hoped to impress Joie with a set of blocks. Author photograph.

and get advice from good photographer friends. It kept me away for three months but was a completely liberating experience. I worked for an award-winning photojournalist, Fons Ianelli. For a camera, he used a double-lens reflex.

With the insurance money for the lost camera equipment and my pay from Fons, I was able to buy one. It changed my whole approach to photography—from one geared to architecture to one made to capture people in action.

The inspiration for the fledgling Film Center was, of course, the highly successful film on Highlander, *People of the Cumberlands*. In 1938, Jim Dombrowski, the Highlander staff member I met at the Work Camp that year, persuaded a young Elia Kazan to help write and produce a film on Highlander. (Kazan would later be the winner of two Academy Awards and the director of five Pulitzer Prize plays.) Ethel Clyde, a supporter of Highlander, put up the money, and Kazan recruited top young talent to work on the production. Michael Denning called it, "Perhaps the most successful independent Popular Front film of the period." The Popular Front was a grouping of liberal and left-wing organizations united to fight Fascism abroad and to support Roosevelt's New Deal. From this group also came the successful International Ladies Garment Workers Union musical *Pins and Needles* and Clifford Odets's play *Waiting for Lefty.*

On May 2, 1938, Eleanor Roosevelt invited guests for a private showing of *People of the Cumberlands* at the White House. During the late 1930s and early 1940s, the film was shown widely—helping put Highlander on the map for fund-raising. I carried the film and a movie projector to so many screenings that the narration was engraved in my brain.

We talked the Packinghouse Workers into sponsoring a short film jointly with the Farmers Union. The theme was labor/farmer unity. Called *They Met at the Fair,* it was filmed at a county fair in Iowa. The film was well received, and we helped with the distribution. It was not another *People of the Cumberlands,* but a good beginning for the new Film Center. While Gordon Weisenborn was pleased with his cameraman role for the film, it was about this time that the lure of the big city took him back to Chicago.

When it came to the arts, Fred Lasse was truly a renaissance man with a wide range of graphic arts experiences. To promote our films, we ran off silk-screened posters. Unfortunately, Highlander was entering a dormant stage with the labor movement, so we didn't have the eager clients we expected. This was going into the McCarthy period, and many of the larger CIO unions went along with the senator's Red-baiting. Highlander was frequently investigated, but the Communist charge was never proven—mainly because Myles kept the school aloof from any political doctrines.

Fred Lasse loved Highlander, and he decided to build himself a house on the edge of Highlander property. It seemed an ideal place to raise a family—he and his wife, Babe, had a two-year-old boy, and she was pregnant with another. A hi-fi nut, he was always trying to produce the best acoustical equipment possible. In his new house, he cemented his speakers into the wall.

"I'm going to have rock-steady sound," he vowed.

His set was always dismantled. "It'll be rebuilt when my new Wilkinson amplifier comes in from England. Can I play my new Rachmaninoff on your set, Emil?"

My "set" was an old Sears, Roebuck lo-fi job someone had donated to the Film Center— but it always worked. Fred confessed to me, on a return from Chicago, where he had attended a live concert, that he sat through the performance totally frustrated—he had no dials to control the volume, treble, or bass of the live orchestra.

Fred had leisurely habits and loved to stop and talk. When his wife announced that the new baby was showing signs of arrival, she sent him over to ask Joie to baby-sit for their two-year-old. By the time they returned to the house, Fred, it seemed, had saved himself a trip to the hospital—the baby was resting on his wife's belly.

Norman Alexandroff was a Russian émigré and a longtime Highlander contributor. He owned and ran a Chicago school for actors and radio announcers called Columbia College. Alexandroff confided to us that he dearly needed to get into television training but lacked the cash to buy the equipment. We convinced him that we could make dummy cameras.

Our TV cameras were plywood boxes with metal snouts and half-inch rubber water hoses for cables. Each box had a battery-operated red light to indicate the active camera to the actors. We took them up to Chicago in our old Ford delivery wagon and mounted them on the hydraulic lifts of old barber chairs. They worked with a feel of authentic equipment for the cameramen. The actors could respond to the lights as the cameras were dragged hither and yon. Flush with success, we talked Norman into putting out his first college catalog. I spent several days photographing classrooms and activities. We made giant enlargements (40x60 inches), mounted them on Masonite, and hung them at the school.

As soon as we returned to Tennessee, we had a call from Norman. "Hey, fellers, something's wrong with your pictures. Listen!"

We could hear a crackling noise. "Your pictures are coming off the boards."

So it was back to Chicago to pick up the enlargements. We deduced that the steam heat had caused it. The dry-mounting tissue we were using didn't have a firm enough grip on hard oiled Masonite. We substituted regular, softer Masonite, heavily sanded. It worked. The trip to Chicago took us 26 hours round trip—not an easy way to make a living.

I charged a dollar for 8x10 prints to participants at Highlander sessions and conferences, which barely paid for the expenses of running the darkroom. The only paid photo I ever took in Summerfield, outside of HFS, was commissioned by Old Man M., an elderly fellow known locally as a queer duck. I arrived at his house to find him dressed in his best dark suit. When he asked me to come down into his cellar, my eyebrows rose, and I was glad I was much more agile than he was. In the cellar, he climbed into a metal coffin, folded his hands clasping a lily, and commanded me to snap. Snap I did, but I couldn't resist asking about the coffin.

"My brother never answers my letters," he said spitefully, "and I'm gonna send him this picture and never write to him again!" After that, he kept his potato crop in the tin coffin.

But I had another outside job that made enough to help keep the Film Center going. I took pictures at the Tennessee Copper Company, where my good friend Dallas McKown was in charge of putting out a monthly house organ. I received $10 a shot for straight industrial pictures and $15 if the shot was considered hazardous—such as requiring climbing the 100-foot chimney or going underground. Actually, I got extra expenses for mine shots, since they consumed dozens of expensive 100-watt flashbulbs. This pay was not bad for the early 1950s.

The large, 50-square-mile denuded area around the Tennessee Copper Company was due to the sulfuric-acid–laden smoke that flooded out of the company's tall chimney. Not only did the acid kill the crops in the surrounding land, but it eroded the turbines in a small hydroelectric plant downstream. Sued by both the Bush Canneries and TVA, the TCC was forced to recover the sulfuric acid before it went out in the smoke. The acid recovery plant became the company's major financial asset. It took some 500 men to run this operation.

The copper plant fascinated me—it had its own railroad, deep mines, and crushing and smelting facilities. Of the 3,500-person workforce, the smallest crew was the common labor gang. Because of the complexity of the operation, there was always a need for a goodly number of pictures for the house organ.

When the company's 100-foot chimney became obsolete, it was demolished. Two men with jackhammers were eating the smokestack from the top down, nibbling away like a pair of nervous beavers. Dallas wanted "a sentimental shot" of the plant from the chimney top. To get to the top, I was faced with a series of 12-foot ladders attached to the rungs that originally had been cemented into the monstrous tube. My new 4x5 industrial plate camera and film plates were in a suitcase attached to me by a strap going through the carrying handle and looped over my back. As I climbed the loose ladders, I noticed, with some trepidation, that they were attached to the original rungs by wire coat hangers.

Of course, when I arrived at the top, the light was directly in the lens, so I had to straddle the edge and hitch myself halfway around. The two men, at first startled by my appearance, just kept chipping away with their pneumatic drills. Going down was worse than going up. The photos were not that great, but I made Dallas buy two of them, at an extra cost.

I have no idea when the Tennessee Copper Company mine shaft was sunk—probably at the turn of the 20th century—but it seemed ancient. The old cage in the shaft, however, flew downward at what seemed like a reckless pace. Going down the mine shaft, the men would spook me about numerous disastrous mine accidents—such as the day the lift operator fell asleep and dumped a shift of miners over the top of the tipple and back down the shaft. One day, as we descended and approached our level, my guide reached out to pull the stop cord . . . too late. We passed our level and stopped between levels. The lift man had strict orders (it could be a life-or-death decision) never to move the lift without the proper signal—which could only be made from the tunnel level we had just passed. The men looked at each other. Finally, one climbed out through the top of the lift, scaled the cable to the missed level, and signaled the operator.

As we walked down the tunnel, they pointed to where a boulder had barreled down a vent shaft and killed two miners. Later, I challenged Dallas McKown on mine safety—meaning, of course, that I wanted additional pay *above* the additional pay already provided for underground pictures. Dallas pointed to a his wall, where a series of plaques commended the company for its safety record.

"The stories the men told you are true, of course," Dallas told me, "but they date back to 1920 and earlier. They just enjoy spoofing you!"

Back in 1938, the Tennessee Copper Company miners in Ducktown had gone on strike. The union organizer in charge told me that the furniture-store walls were lined with coffins because of the high silicosis death rate They lost that strike but finally won the union.

In 1952, Highlander made a deal with the United Packinghouse Workers to conduct a month-long training program, choosing five educational representatives out of 100 candidates

These five studied the union's goals, practiced teaching techniques, and wrote two instructor's manuals for shop-steward classes. Part of the training was to take place in Camden, New Jersey, where the union had held a drive to organize workers in an oyster-packing plant.

Fred Lasse and I made a deal to do a short film on the union drive. The oyster gatherers went out daily to harvest the shellfish on the shallow Delaware Bay. The oyster beds were marked off by wooden poles, and the draggers went up and down the beds exactly as a farmer plows a field.

The oysters would be brought in and stacked on a slanted concrete floor to drain overnight. The next day the shuckers, each with his or her wooden stand, would go to work on the shells. Each factory floor played its own music tapes—the workers rocking and shucking steadily to the cadence.

The union gripe to management centered on the fact that the oysters drained and shrank all night and the workers were paid by the pint. The oysters then were placed in large vats, where air was pumped through them, plumping them up for canning—cheating both the worker and the consumer. It was a neat little film, and we enjoyed making it. With just the two of us, it gave me a greater role in the filmmaking process.

But it was the last hurrah for Fred. Prospects for union film projects had become slim indeed, so Lasse followed Gordon Weisenborn and pulled out for Chicago—taking with him our hopes for a second *People of the Cumberlands.*

30.

A MOMENTOUS MERGER

IN 1935, ZILPHIA HORTON took part in a Textile Workers strike in Daisy, Tennessee. Carrying an American flag and leading the parade was our Reverend DeJarnette. For this, he lost his parish. He settled in the area on a small farm he called Fellowship House. More than once, I went over to help him on his farm. Joie and I arranged with this sweet and gentle man to officiate at our wedding. He had also married Myles and Zilphia and Lou and Ursula Krainock.

On the evening of January 28, 1949, the day before we were married, Joie wrote on her calendar: CHANGE NAME.

Joie claims I never proposed, that it was always just understood. She also claims the following exchange took place:

"Emil, why did you want to marry me?"

"Because, Joie, you were the first person I found as interested in me as I am." Can you believe that?

On January 29, Joie's mother, father, and sister Loie arrived for our wedding.

During the debriefing on wedding procedure (Joie's parents and Loie were standing off to the side—just out of hearing), the Reverend DeJarnette earnestly clasped our hands and asked, "Emil, do you want me to dedicate you and your bride to the labor movement?"

"Just to each other would be fine," I replied.

Gordon Weisenborn's time at Highlander Folk School had been relatively brief, but fortunately he had stayed just long enough to photograph, beautifully, one of the school's more memorable weddings.

"Raised in a log cabin"—how many kids can say that these days? After living at the school for a couple of years, Joie and I bought a log cabin, complete with a well and three-fourths of an acre of land, for $1,900. Not exactly in the wilderness, it was conveniently next to Joie's nursery school. The cabin was one room, 25 feet square, with a small kitchen addition and another room the width of the average hallway. You could see through the chinks in the logs until we insulated it and covered the walls with random-width pine paneling. After we rented a sander in Chattanooga, our dirty black floor turned out to be tightly fitted white oak. The kitchen had been paneled with corrugated cardboard painted silver—weird looking but clean and neatly done. The narrow adjoining room became a bedroom for baby James and his soon-to-arrive brother, baby Andrew.

Major furniture included a bureau, a small table, and a couple of crude rockers. A large bed was covered with an elegant, antique friendship quilt made up of squares donated by friends of whoever originally owned it. The quilt once had a strange visitor. Our Summerfield friend JD Marlowe (who was building the Film Center for me next door) had a young pet raccoon that rode to work with him on his shoulder. The raccoon would spend the workday in a tree. One time, on his way home, JD asked Joie, "Did you ever see a raccoon suck an egg?"

Joie, ever eager for any new cultural experience on the Cumberland Plateau, raced into the kitchen and brought an egg from the refrigerator. The little coon was put on the bed and, after fingering the egg for a minute, suddenly clapped his hands together. Splat! Egg all over our elegant quilt. "Well," shrugged JD, "egg must have been too cold for him."

Grundy County had no medical facilities. At one point, a doctor decided to move into Grundy, and he imported several skilled black laborers to build his house and clinic. The men were run out of town and the doc left as well. Grundy had its reputation to maintain as one of the few black-free counties in Tennessee.

Our nearest medical facility was in a neighboring county, where the University of the South, at Sewanee, had a small but decent hospital. Being among the few folks in Summerfield with a car, we were called upon frequently for hospital trips. Our first experience came about 2 o'clock one morning, when a child of one of our Summerfield neighbors woke us up with a rattle of pebbles thrown against our window.

Joie wrote, "Change name." Gordon Weisenborn photograph

The wedding party: Emil, Joie, James and Helen Creighton, and Lois Abbott, Joie's sister. Gordon Weisenborn photograph

Wedding guests. Gordon Weisenborn photograph.

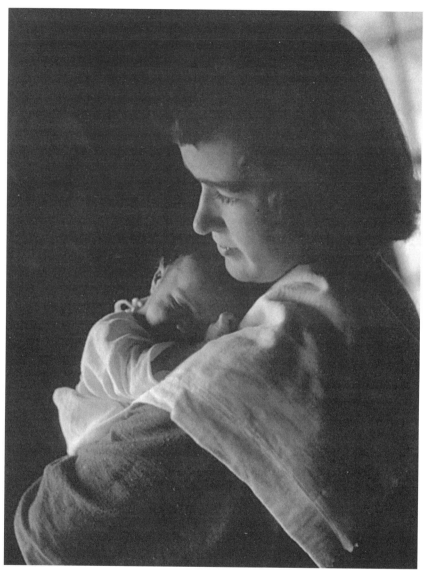

Joie with her own baby.

"Mom sez the baby's a-comin'—could you'uns get 'er to the hospital?"

We dressed hastily and Joie packed some matches, a candle, scissors, and a towel . . . "just in case." Not that we knew much about what to do or how imminent the baby's arrival was. The mother was not nearly as frantic as we were, although the labor pains seemed to be coming closer and closer. (I'll hold the candles, Joie!) But we made it.

The most momentous call of all came early in the morning on May 16, 1951, when the baby to be born was our son James Creighton. It seemed like only a very brief time before a second equally monumental event took place—Andrew Malcolm, October 22, 1953.

Although Joie had help, raising two babies on the Cumberland Plateau along with a gang of local children was no easy task. Finding a nest of baby copperheads in the children's sandbox did add more than just a bit to the glamour of the environment.

Junie, the younger brother of our friend JD Marlowe, just married to a young mountain girl, looked at one of our babies and said mournfully:

"I'd give a million dollars for a pup like that!"

"You'll have a dozen soon enough."

"No, I've been married three months and there's nary a sign."

Later, when asked if his wife was pregnant:

"Pregnant? If she fell on the porch, she'd rock herself to sleep!"

Like almost all the young boys on the plateau, Junie had raised quantities of hound dogs, but as yet no babies. One day, looking thoughtfully at our two infants playing on our large bed, he asked, "How old were they when they opened their eyes?"

31.

ZILPHIA: A SINGING SCHOOL

JOHN L. LEWIS, PRESIDENT OF THE UNITED MINE WORKERS, in an introduction to the 1939 Highlander Folk School songbook, wrote, "Highlander joined the Southern union movement when it was a singing army."

Zilphia Horton, who had rescued Joie on her arrival at Highlander from the "Sardines" gamesters, was almost singlehandedly the dynamo behind the singing at the Folk School and the entire Southern labor movement. She was also a wonderful friend to both Joie and me.

In September 1943, after I had completed basic training at Camp Shelby, and the training slackened off, I had received a three-day pass to the Highlander Folk School in Monteagle, Tennessee. With no classes in session at the school, I slept in a weirdly empty main building. In the morning, Zilphia Horton came over to fill me full of school gossip and buttermilk pancakes with black walnuts, sourwood honey, and wild muscadine grape jelly. There were now 12 members of the Highlander Board, and Zilphia was raising a goose named after each. She served me a single goose egg that filled the platter. This goose, she said, was Board Member Paul R. Christopher, my ex-boss and good friend. It was fitting that it was his goose that sustained me that morning—sort of an extension of his $15-a-week expense account. The memory of that breakfast stayed with me all through my army experience—as it does to this day!

How good it was to be with friends. And Zilphia was one of the best. As we talked, mindless army discipline and chickenshit brass slid into oblivion. I told her about life in an army camp, and we chuckled over the story of my friend the Tennessee hillbilly who was discharged from the army because he couldn't shoot a rifle. Owning and shooting a rifle was as common as chewing tobacco in the mountains. Zilphia admitted modestly that, personally, she wasn't such a bad shot herself.

When I remarked on how empty and quiet the school seemed, she pointed out that Myles, with some kind of medical deferment, was the only male staff member left. Jim Dombrowski had left Highlander in 1941 to head up the Southern Conference for Human Welfare; Bill Buttrick, always frail, had died of a heart attack; and Bill Elkuss had been drafted. Leon Wilson had resigned from the staff in order to register as a conscientious objector. When this was denied by the local Tennessee draft board, he refused to accept his 1-A status, was thrown into a local jail, and then was sent to Alcatraz in California. There, Leon asked for permission to set up and lead a male choir—but he was turned down. They accepted, however, his more orthodox request to play a musical instrument. "When his sister brought him a set of bagpipes," Zilphia gleefully told me, "it wasn't too long before the warden agreed to the choir."

For Joie and me, Myles had the full measure of our respect, but it was Zilphia who had our hearts. A letter that I found and photocopied in the Highlander Center Library gave us our first clues to her Arkansas upbringing and her entrance into Highlander.

> Highlander Folk School
> March 7, 1935
> Dear Dorothy,
> I really and truly don't know where to begin to tell you all
> the exciting happenings at HFS! Yesterday Myles got married to
> Zilphia Mae Johnson, the daughter of a Paris, Arkansas mine
> owner, who came just a month ago this coming Monday.
>
> They were as surprised as anybody else and maybe more so.
> Zilphia is a very capable, calm, determined girl . . . full of poise
> and guts, and at the same time lots of charm. She was the most
> talented girl both at high school and college and has carried on
> radical activities against her father's wishes, till he turned her out
> of the house.
>
> Claude Williams, a radical Presbyterian minister, who sent
> her to us, considers her one of the most vital people he has ever

Zilphia Horton.

known. Her Spanish and Indian blood give her a repose that is very good to have around this excited place. I can just imagine what it would be like to get married among almost complete strangers to a man you had known three weeks! She plays the piano brilliantly and sings well.

[The letter is unsigned, and any subsequent pages are missing.]

"No way on Spanish blood," says Ermon Fay, Zilphia's youngest sister, "although Zilphia did speak some Spanish. Indian blood is more likely, although not proven. My daughter, Claudia, did some research with the Cherokees (the most likely candidates) and did find some family names on their rosters, but these were names not too uncommon in the territories."

Zilphia was a trained classical concert pianist and graduated from the College of the Ozarks, where she studied voice and music. She won a number of awards for her musicianship and taught music in the Sallowish, Oklahoma, high school, where her youthful beauty "attracted the entire football team to her class."

Singing folk and labor songs, she took part in a gala Highlander fundraiser in Washington, D.C., on December 6, 1940. The sponsors of the affair read like a Who's Who of the New Deal and organized labor, including Supreme Court Justice Hugo Black, cabinet members, congressmen, administrators of major federal agencies, Eleanor Roosevelt, and other prominent persons. An audience of around 500 people heard a poetry reading by Archibald MacLeish, Librarian of Congress; a ballad performed by the Washington Choral Society and the Howard University Glee Club; and a collection of folk, blues, and workers' ballads sung by Zilphia Horton and famed black blues singer Huddie "Leadbelly" Ledbetter. The national attention given to the Washington concert improved the public perception of Highlander as a legitimate institution.

Zilphia had a collection of musical instruments that she used for different purposes. The guitar and the zither were for her wonderful folk songs. She had a simple, mountain-made string instrument (a dulcimer, I believe) that she set on the table and plucked as she sang. She delighted in her singing. Frequently she would entertain us by gently singing a few of her mountain folk songs, and she was filled with laughter as she introduced her songs. Her laughter was a wholehearted crescendo of musical notes—she would throw back her head and let it out. When she sang her folk songs with the delicate dulcimer, the atmosphere of the school dining room would respond—we would all be entranced. Even the clatter of the dishwashing would be hushed for the duration. A few strums on the dulcimer and she would be off:

> *I gave my love a cherry that hath no stone*
> *I gave my love a chicken that hath no bone*
> *I gave my love a story that hath no end*
> *And I gave my love a baby that's no cryin'.*

How can there be a cherry that hath no stone?
How can there be a chicken that hath no bone?
How can there be a story that hath no end?
How can there be a baby that's no cryin'?

A cherry when it's bloomin', it hath no stone
A chicken that's a pippin, it hath no bone
A story in the tellin', it hath no end
A baby when it's sleepin', is no cryin'.

And while everyone was savoring the mellow mood of the folk song, Zilphia would slip on her accordion and swing us all into rousing union songs, such as "The Union Maid":

There once was a union maid who never was afraid
Of goons and ginks and company finks and deputy sheriffs who
*   made the raid.*
She went to the union hall when a meeting it was called
And when the legion boys came 'round, she always stood her ground.

Chorus
Oh, you can't scare me,
I'm stickin' to the union
I'm stickin' to the union
I'm stickin' to the union
Till the day I die.

Much has been written about Zilphia's contribution to the Civil Rights Movement of the song "We Shall Overcome." It was one of many spirituals given new words by workers on picket lines. Zilphia heard "We Will Overcome" on the picket line of a Tobacco Workers strike in Charleston, South Carolina, in 1947.

We will overcome; we will overcome;
We will overcome—someday.
Oh, deep in my heart I do believe
We will overcome someday.

No one was as sensitively tuned to the value of songs to be used in the struggles in the South as Zilphia, and she immediately latched onto this one for its power and endurance.

Changing it for use as a union song, she added, "We will win this fight" and "The union will see us through." She taught it to Pete Seeger, who changed it to "We Shall Overcome"—with the feeling, he said, that *shall* opened the mouth more than *will*. He added such new verses as "We shall end Jim Crow" and "We shall live in peace."

Martin Luther King, Jr., first heard it sung (by Pete Seeger) at Highlander's 25th anniversary celebration, and it became the official anthem of the Civil Rights Movement. Today, as the prevailing song of struggle by oppressed groups worldwide, it has been sung and is still being sung in Africa, Asia, and Latin America. The profits from the song—copyrighted and administered by Highlander—go into a fund to support black culture. Dr. King had this to say:

> In a sense, songs are the soul of a movement. "The Battle Hymn of the Republic" and "John Brown's Body" served during the Civil War. The Negroes today sing freedom songs, for we too are in bondage. In Albany, Georgia, we sang:

I'm comin', I'm comin',
and my head AIN'T bendin' low.
I'm walking tall, I'm talkin' strong.
I'm America's NEW Black Joe!
We sang out our determination that "We shall overcome, black and white together."

When Highlander was first opened on the Cumberland Plateau, dancing was considered evil, and play-party games took its place. There was, however, a thin line between the two, and square dancing became the dominant social event that the school offered the community. The Tennessee square dance is far less complicated than the New England and Western styles, so it was quickly learned and enjoyed. Although the dances were not held every Saturday night, they were held frequently—and, sometimes, on the spur of the moment.

At Highlander, I learned to call square dances, such as:

Ladies bow, gents know how.
If this ain't huggin', show me how.
Break that ring with a corner swing
Get your own, leave mine alone.
Swing your corner lady,
And now your honey baby.
If you want your huggin', do it now!
Like that? Do it again!
Circle up four in the middle of the floor.
Ladies join your lily white hands,
Gents your brown and tans.

There's a lot of personal history around that call:
Swing your corner lady
And now your honey baby! (our mountain wedding)
If you want your huggin', do it now! (James Creighton is born)
Like that? Do it again! (Andrew Malcolm is born)

Once my calling made other—less than noteworthy—history! As far as I was told, I called the first interracial square dance at the all-black Tuskegee University in Alabama. The first call from my eager lips was: "Ladies join your lily white hands!" Ouch!

One Saturday night, JD Marlowe, his brother Junie, Joie, and I decided we needed a square-dancing evening. We picked up a neighbor, a banjo picker, and Jim, the best fiddler in the area. Jim had a slight problem—he was missing a string on his fiddle. The only place in town that carried strings was Lacy's General Store, and it was closed. Undaunted, we drove to town, rousted Mr. Lacy from his house, and bought the string. (Being part of the Folk School, which was anathema in the village of Monteagle, Joie and I stayed in the shadows of the car's back seat.) Meanwhile, Junie had circulated around the community, alerting folks to the coming event, and in no time we had a lively Saturday night.

In 1956, Zilphia died of uremic poisoning. Her physical presence is missing from the great Civil Rights Movement, but her songs stand in her stead as a monument to her heart and spirit. Pete Seeger wrote this eulogy: "Zilphia had a beautiful alto voice, an unpretentious rare voice, but not the show-off kind. She sang [folk songs] the way a mother would sing to her child. She brought out the talents of her audience and their enthusiastic participation."

I had always believed that there were no known recordings of her singing. and that her voice endured only in the memories of the few of us still alive. But thanks to the Carawans at the Highlander Center, there is a short fragment of her singing on a tape. It was thrilling to hear it.

Zilphia was a breath of fresh air to Highlander and to the movements it sponsored. Joie and I say Amen to that! May Justus, a Summerfield neighbor and good friend and writer, wrote this on her death:

A SONG FOR ZILPHIA

The music that your music made for me
Was like a singing bird's:
How can I make a song for you
With only words?

32.

SOUTHERN WAYS

"STRANGERS TO OUR LAWS AND CUSTOMS"

Early in the summer of 1717, the Quaker merchants of Philadelphia observed that immigrant ships were arriving in more than their usual numbers . . . a swarm of people . . . strangers to our laws and customs. The men were tall and lean, with hard, weather-beaten faces. The young women startled Quaker Philadelphia by the sensuous appearance of their full bodices, tight waists, bare legs and skirts scandalously short. The speech of these people was English, but they spoke with a lilting cadence that rang strangely in the ear. Many were desperately poor, but carried themselves with a fierce and stubborn pride that warned others to treat them with respect.

—David Fischer, *Albion's Seed*

Those immigrants, from the border countries of England and Scotland, entered America through the port of Philadelphia, from where the Quakers quickly moved them westward to the Appalachian Mountains. The magnitude of this immigration was tremendous—more than a quarter of a million people—the bulk of the flow arriving just prior to the American Revolution. The Appalachians were similar to their Scottish/English borderlands, and the immigrants felt at home. But they were out of the frying pan and into the fire. These rugged mountains were occupied by strong, warlike Indian nations that did not accede easily to white settlement.

MOTHER CORN—GIVER OF LIFE

There's gold in them there mountains,
There's gold in them there hills:
The natives there are gettin' it,
By operating stills.

—John Judge, Jr.

Making liquor from corn was a cottage industry. For many, it was a compact, portable way to bring in cash for the necessities of frontier life. It was also the main ingredient in many home remedies.

When Joie and I lived there, Tennessee had been dry since 1909. In fact, most of the South was still dry. The saying went: "Vote dry, drink wet." Moonshine permeated the culture of the Cumberlands. It was no disgrace to be arrested for the manufacture or sale of the product. Any boy growing up in the region would have felt apart if he had no arrested kinfolk to "brag on." With lumber and mining just about gone, earned income was a hard thing to come by. Much of the annual corn yield was reckoned as so many gallons per acre.

But moonshine can be dangerous. That Prohibition made illegal distilleries profitable also meant a good deal of the product was made from cheap ingredients. People went blind or died from the lead soldering in car radiators, which were used instead of expensive copper for making moonshine. So we depended on our Summerfield friends to guide us through this minefield. Not that we were big consumers; it was more in the line of having some on hand for curious Northern visitors—just as we now wouldn't allow a visitor to leave Maine without a taste of lobster. It also made an excellent eggnog for New Year's Eve and created a first-class party hangover.

One day I went down to the valley with our "cultural adviser," JD Marlowe, and his friend Doc to pick up what they called "shine." We pulled into a remote farm and had our gallon-size Coca-Cola syrup jars filled in back of the barn—$5 a jug. Bell and Ball Mason jars were moonshine standards, but JD preferred the larger sizes. My job was to sit in the back seat with a tire iron to smash the jars should we get stopped by the revenuers. A heartbreaking assignment that, fortunately, I never had to perform.

JD had a young cousin who had found a crevice in the blank-looking wall of a cliff far up a canyon in back of his farm. Squeezing through, he discovered a limestone cave with a running stream—perfect, he boasted, for making moonshine. He improvised an entire still inside the cave. To get a barrel in, he had to laboriously take it apart and put it together, stave by stave. He brought his kerosene in flat, 5-gallon army cans. Elated, he started his first run—and was immediately caught. The revenuers had followed the well-worn path made by his mules between the still and the barn. Baffled by the blank wall, they were about to give up when they spied first an empty kerosene can and then the crevice. "I'll do better when I get out," the youth promised. The sentence was a year and a day.

JD and Doc also discovered a limestone cave with water in remote Hixon Green. JD protected himself by making just enough for himself and a close circle of friends—at a pricey $10 a gallon. He justified this exaggerated fee by explaining the excellence of his product.

"I rectify the raw shine," he explained "in a 55-gallon barrel stuffed with layers of felt and charcoal. It takes all day to go through and it comes out with most of the fusil oils filtered out. And," he added dramatically, "we age it in oak barrels with burnt apricots for six months! The apricots absorb more of the impurities and turn it a rich bourbon color. Try it— it's 113 proof and real mellow." And it was—in small quantities.

Limestone-filtered water, coming out of a cave at a constant temperature, is what, boasts Jack Daniel, makes for their high-quality bourbon. Once, when I was doing some photography in the Jack Daniel Distillery, I mentioned to Lem Motlow, the manager, that he made the best bourbon in Tennessee—next to my friend JD. He took exception to my remark but, in a friendly way, asked me to lean over and take a deep breath of the huge, two-story vat of charcoal in which his whiskey was rectifying. I did—and almost fainted from the heady fumes of alcohol. Great joke! He laughed uproariously and said, "What with your friend's great stuff, I don't suppose you want to take any samples of our poor product? In a storeroom, nodding at a large box of small airline bottles, he said, "Take all you can carry in your arms, none in your pockets." Sorry, JD—I did just that!

On Tennessee's Cumberland Plateau, JD Marlowe was our closest community friend and mentor in all things cultural and natural. The

Marlowe brothers—JD (sometimes Jake) and Junior (always Junie)—had a small cement-block works in Summerfield. JD was an excellent carpenter—bright and sharp and able to construct the complex Film Center building we had crudely designed.

There were things about JD (as there were about life on the Cumberland Plateau) that we had yet to learn. In these times, skilled labor on the mountain was $1.50 per hour; common labor, such as laying concrete blocks, earned 75 cents an hour. JD would submit his week's invoice at $1.50 per hour on a scrap of lumber. At the end of one week, however, he handed me a piece of 2x4 tallied at 75 cents an hour. Surprised, I asked, "Hey, Jake, how come?"

"I wa'n't worth more this week. Couldn't keep my mind on the job."

Well, I had noticed him a time or two, with his ruler against a board and his eyes focused off in the distance.

"Reckon I got to go huntin' for a spell. Mind?"

"Fine," I said, "bring us back a bear."

JD, Doc, and other buddies took off in his Jeep for a completely cut-off and abandoned corner of the plateau called Hixon Green. It had been cut over many years ago, and the ancient logging road that ascended the mountain was hard to find and almost impossible to navigate. I once went with them overnight, and we spent most of our time winching the Jeep up the road.

On these trips, Jake would take little in the way of provisions—some salt, bacon for cooking fat, and a little flour. It was one of the few places in those days where you could find wild turkey and bear; the lakes were well stocked with trout and bass. They had found a cave with a sizable overhang where they could shelter and hide pots and pans and even a kerosene stove to take the chill off cold, wet, wintry weather.

Daniel Boone, I once read, sent a dispatch to England looking for stout, adventurous yeomen to join him in taming the west. JD would have suited Daniel fine. He was a Miniver Cheevy who should have lived in frontier times.

JD, in his camouflage suit and his camouflage-painted Jeep, completely ignored hunting seasons. In fact, I believe he got his kicks more from outwitting the game warden than from shooting game—mostly squirrels.

Country music: Howard Campbell, JD Marlowe, and Ike Church. Author photo.

"I could'a retched out and touched that warden as he went by!"

JD spent quality time on the log cabin he helped us refurbish. He frequently brought dressed-out squirrels (or undressed-out?), and we sat in front of our great sandstone fireplace and barbecued them in the hot ashes. Sometimes Joie would boil the meat into a tasty mulligan stew. But the most memorable evening was spent over a sackful of fried, breaded squirrel heads—about the size of walnuts. We cracked them open and tinkered out the cheeks, tongues, and brains. Barbaric? Maybe, but tasty and fittin' for the plateau culinary arts—especially as washed down by Jake's muscadine wine. In July 2000, the *New York Times* carried an article about the danger of eating squirrel brains. Mad squirrel disease? Now they tell us!

I don't want to give the impression that our friend JD was just a simple mountain boy—far from it. Near Monteagle was a prestigious school, St. Andrew's Academy, where the Marlowe brothers had received a good education. JD was completely literate and made good use of the

Highlander library. During the war, he had gone overseas as a navigator in a Flying Fortress. He never spoke of his war experiences, but I'm sure they affected him deeply. He had seen a part of the world he didn't like and would have none of. Many times, we invited JD to visit us in New York and in Maine, but he never budged. The Cumberland Plateau was home enough for him.

JD was attracted to the girls who came to Highlander to work as staff members or as apprentices from the Antioch College work program. They were attracted to him as well, but they balked at marriage and living out a life in tiny Summerfield on the Cumberland Plateau.

One fall day, JD invited Joie and me to go raccoon hunting. He had a mixed pack of hound dogs—blue ticks, red bones, and beagles.

"I'm breakin' in my newest hound," JD said. "He's a young dog I call 'Trouble.' When you're fox huntin', the fox generally runs in a big sweep around his home territory, so you can always hear your hounds. In raccoon hunting, the coon'll take off in any direction, and the dogs will get out of hearing very quickly if you don't keep right on their tails."

The Cumberland Plateau is edged with a series of escarpments and shelves that step down the mountainside. JD's pack of hounds suddenly went wild, barking and yelping and wagging not just their tails but their whole rear ends with excitement. They had gotten a fresh scent and off they went, pell-mell, diagonally down the side of the mountain to the first shelf. Off, too, went the eager hunters, slipping and sliding in the loose shale.

JD could tell us the status of the hunt by the sounds of the pack. Suddenly the yelps turned into a chorus of wonderful baying sounds. "They've treed the coon," yelled JD. "Now we can take a breather. They'll bay up that tree for a spell."

We kicked together a pile of dry leaves and started a small, smoky fire. As we rested, rubbing our hands together in the cold fall air, we heard rustling in the woods. JD jumped up, shouting, "Trouble, you no-good hound, come here!" Slinking toward us came the young hound, his tail wagging—not in excitement but in supplication. JD grabbed him by his collar and shook him in faked anger. "Go, dog," he shouted, pointing down the trail to where the pack was baying. "You go with the others. Go." And Trouble wandered away, his tail between his legs.

"Well, I guess we'd better take off," said JD. "If the dogs get out of hearing, they'll chase that coon or another for a couple of days. They'll come home exhausted with bloody feet." Carefully stamping out the fire, he motioned for us to go ahead while he damped it down with his internal liquids.

We caught up with the hunt quickly. A few of the dogs peering intently up the tree were still baying, but with diminished ardor. JD had a five-celled flashlight, which he flashed up through the tree limbs.

"I didn't expect to see one," he said. "The raccoon is one smart animal. He'll climb a tree that he knows has connecting branches he can leap onto. Three or four trees down the pike, he'll drop off and run. See that blue tick of mine? See! He's trotting in ever-widening circles. He's an old hand and knows all the tricks."

A second dog joined the blue tick and, all at once, they took voice in the hunting mode and raced off after a new scent. The rest of the pack joined them and, with a forceful gesture from his master, Trouble did too.

"The coon'll run up a stream bed for quite a ways," said JD, "and the dogs will split up to catch his departure point. That coon knows a dozen tricks to confuse the pack."

Off we went after the dogs. It had long been dark, and we followed JD's spot of light like moths. Joie claims that JD and I went down the escarpment and up it at the same pace, and before long she showed signs of stress, so he slowed the pace. The wind had come up and was blowing away from the pack, and we lost them. We gathered again around a leaf fire in hopes the pack might veer back in our direction, but all we got was another visit from Trouble.

As we slowly trekked home and ascended the final edge of the mountain, Trouble suddenly ran up to a large tree, put his paws up on the trunk, and bayed.

"Don't believe it," said JD disgustedly. "He's a fake." But he dutifully flashed his light into the tree limbs to make sure. "Nice try, Trouble, you big phony," he said, scratching the dogs ears affectionately. "He'll learn from the other dogs; he's still young."

Later that fall, JD came over to the school looking sad.

"I almost lost Trouble last night," he said gravely. "He's at the vet's over to Winchester with several broken bones. I knew what I was doin' when I named him 'Trouble.' We have an old boar coon that lives way back of our house by the edge of the mountain. We use him to teach our dogs, and he's usually pretty good about it. But last night he ran with Trouble at his heels for a while and then, slowing down so that the dog was almost nipping his tail, he suddenly turned right and jumped off the edge into a treetop. So did Trouble—only his paws couldn't grab the limb and he dropped through the tree some 70 feet. Gonna cost me a fortune."

"Who learned what lesson?" I couldn't help but laugh. "Put a little overtime on Fred's new house so you can afford Trouble."

"Well," JD smiled ruefully, "the sun doesn't shine on the same hound dog every day."

One Sunday morning, coming back from town with the *New York Times,* I stopped to see the mechanic who did a lot of our car-repair work in his backyard. He was leaning against a rail fence that separated his yard from his brother's, a shotgun at his side. His brother was mowing his alfalfa crop, his tractor going in ever-tightening circles. As we talked, our mechanic kept his attention focused on his brother's work. Suddenly he whipped up his shotgun and . . . pow . . . a running rabbit tumbled dead. My mechanic vaulted the fence and handed me the rabbit.

"Ya like 'em, don't you?"

"Yeah, but it's your rabbit—you been waitin' for it for some time. I wouldn't feel right about taking it."

This kind of thing always put me into a quandary. The mountain folk had very little, but they were extremely hospitable and generous with what they had. When he insisted, I took the rabbit. What else could I do—offer him my *New York Times?*

The mechanic had a young son, a very active child still a little young for Joie's nursery school. It struck the family a cataclysmic blow when the boy came down with polio. He was rushed to the Sewanee Hospital, but by the time they had stabilized the illness, his legs were paralyzed. They were told that without extensive and expensive follow-up treatment, he would never walk.

Sixteen years later, when we had returned from Peru, we visited the mechanic. When asked about the young boy, to our astonishment they proudly showed us a picture of him in a marine uniform. It turns out that the boy had had a large, shaggy-haired dog that adored him. Clinging to the dog's bushy hair, the boy had been dragged all over the yard. And the boy had helped by pushing with his legs, which gradually grew strong enough to walk again—strong enough to join the marines when he was old enough!

A favorite expression when visiting and saying goodbye to Summerfield neighbors was a warm and friendly, "Come spend the night or somethin'." From time to time, young students from the Antioch College work program were helping in the community. They would discomfit their host by asking. "When would it be convenient?" One of the students helpfully sprayed a chicken yard with DDT, and the poisoned flies killed all the chickens.

The mechanic's dead wild rabbit was a far superior gift than the live, fat, domestic one given me by my son's baby-sitter. She had borrowed some money and offered to pay me back with a rabbit. I agreed and was handed a live-and-kicking white rabbit, held by its ears. Well, I had been rigorously trained to sneak up and knock out hefty German sentries with a deadly "rabbit punch," so I stiffened my right hand and chopped the poor creature a deadly blow on its neck. It turned its head, trying to look at me, and gave a weak bleat. A second blow had the same result. Desperate, I finally "rabbit punched" him with a tire iron and praised the good fortune that never put me in the way of a stout German sentry!

One more animal disaster story and I'm through. In a dip of the land just below the school, we built a three-acre lake and stocked it with bass and bluegill. In the second year of the lake, I tried my skill with fishing and, much to my astonishment and chagrin, laboriously dragged in a snapping turtle about the size of a dinner plate. Where did it come from, full grown? The nearest lake was Tracy City, some six miles away.

A snapping turtle is a dangerous-looking beast with a nasty reputation for never letting go of a bite. According to my mountain companions, it made good eating, tasting of any of seven different flavors—fish, beef, chicken, and I can't remember the rest—everything, of course, except turtle! You kill it, they said, by holding it by the short tail and lowering the body to a chopping block. Its head will stick out at a right angle and you whack it off with a quick blow of an axe. Sure, if you are a mountain boy! For a Bronx boy, the turtle instantly pulls its head in, every time. After numerous tries, I had a brilliant idea. In Maine, we killed lobsters by dropping them into boiling water. Lobsters give up the ghost easily.

So into a big kettle of boiling water went the turtle. I clapped the lid on and, horrified, had to hold it down to keep the turtle from getting out. It seemed like hours—certainly more than just minutes—before it gave up the ghost. There is very little of that quick Maine lobster surrender in Southern snapping turtles!

I didn't want to stew the creature without cleaning it, so when I was sure it had died, I dumped it into the sink, cooled it down, and cut it up into solid chunks. We were going to invite JD over to give a demonstration of the seven flavors, so I bottled the parts in salt water and left it on the table to rest (me to rest, not it).

In the living room, Joie looked at me quizzically.

"I hear a funny noise in the kitchen, like scratching on a pane of glass."

Rushing back into the kitchen, I found that the muscles of the turtle were jerking spasmodically, the claws rasping against the bottle. The salted water must have activated nerves and muscles. What a primitive beast!

We seemed to be oriented to Chicago, and a friend of Fred's, Haskell Wexler, loved to visit Highlander. It was said that Haskell's father owned a large company but that Haskell would have none of it and had gone his own way. His major idiosyncrasy was powdered coffee—a new item in those days—and Haskell sprinkled it on everything.

Haskell's Chicago apartment was Fred Lasse's and my headquarters for much of our involvement with Columbia College. He was a conscientious cameraman, and I watched fascinated as he stripped his camera, cleaning it and lubricating it with a special light whale oil. That Saturday, at a frigid, below-zero football game, he was the only one to get good footage.

Going on to become one of Hollywood's top cameramen, Haskell received an award for filming *To Kill a Mockingbird*, with Gregory Peck, an early film on racial tolerance. This was followed by *In the Heat of the Night*. Unlike many others who were seduced by Hollywood, Haskell maintained his radical view of politics, and he became famous in liberal circles for his *Medium Cool,* a film on Chicago police brutality during the 1968 Democratic Convention street riots.

Haskell told us the story of filming in a synagogue and yelling to his assistant, "Kill the juice!" The audience suddenly became deadly quiet. Desperately, Haskell repeated, "Turn off the electricity!"

Fox hunting was a big thing on the Cumberland Plateau—almost everyone on the mountain raised hound dogs. On hunt day, they assembled with their dogs to form a frantic, barking pack. Off they would go, a great jumble of yelping hounds. The men followed the hounds until high-pitched baying indicated a fox scent had been discovered. The men then hunkered down, built a fire, passed around Mason jars of moonshine, and listened to the music of the chase. Suddenly, one of the men bounced up in great excitement—his dog was leading the pack. Taking off his hat, he whacked the man next to him: "I'll be a god-damned curly-headed son-of-a-bitch, he never done hit before!"

Happy laughter, more passing of Mason jars . . . more intent listening. "Hey, listen! They gonna be runnin' past the cemetery in jest a few minutes—they've roused up ol' Slewfoot [a fox with a missing paw]."

The hunters knew all the local foxes and could predict the circular route each would take before getting tired and denning up. The fox was never killed. The men took great pride in their dogs and could sit and tell the whole race by listening to the excited voices of the hounds—the baying and yelping changing with the fortunes of the hunt. They would have you believe that the fox enjoyed the chase as much as the men and dogs. Perhaps it did!

This, then, was what Haskell came down to film. His story revolved around a young boy about to enter his first dog into the hunt. Through his young eyes, we see the fascination of raising different breeds and training them for the hunt. Ol' Dad Horton, Myles's father (whose family were Lincoln Republicans), was supervising the dog's training, and Haskell got great footage of the proceedings. He had advertised for a fox, but none came in, so he shot the whole hunting scene, the gathering of the men (no moonshine), and the running of the dogs without the main actor.

Finally, on a rainy Sunday, a neighbor arrived triumphantly, with a fox he had trapped. Gordon Weisenborn (of Film Center fame) was the cameraman, and he opted to try out the small dog harness they had brought from Chicago. With heavy gloves, they stuffed the fox into the harness, attached a long nylon fishing line, and turned him loose. The fox made a swift dash for the woods and then hit the end of the line, which threw him into a back flip. The fox flattened down in the grass, then eased himself backward and out of the harness. A small Chicago dog is not a Cumberland mountain fox!

The film crew had to leave, but Gordon wrote me that they were able to film a fox in a zoo in Chicago, cornering him in the crotch of a small tree.

Haskell came down to Highlander to screen the film for all of us. He had edited the footage so that you could almost believe you saw a fox ghosting through the bushes ahead of the hounds. The zoo fox, peering apprehensively down at Gordon's camera, was intercut with shots of excited Tennessee hounds supposedly jumping up at the foot of the tree.

One day, coming home from a photo assignment at the copper mine, I was feeling no pain. Going through the gorge of the rushing Echo River set me in tune with the wild nature of the region in which we lived. The sun was bright, and I had a great batch of copper-smelter photos in my camera box. When I passed a sign saying, BEAGLES FOR SALE, I felt obliged to turn in and spend some of my earnings. After carefully inspecting the half-dozen puppies, I picked one and paid the farmer $20. I must have impressed the man with my close inspection.

"Why did ya pick that 'un?" he asked.

I just shrugged my shoulders as if to say, "This knowledge dies with me," and left. I couldn't tell the man that I picked the one that licked my hand.

We called the puppy Bagel, short for the Bronx version of the Voice of Bugle Ann. We loved the dog almost as much as we did our two boys. The puppy, in turn, loved the two boys, since they were not much more than puppies themselves. When we left the mountain to move to Knoxville, we donated Bagel to JD.

When the boys were about ten or eleven, we took them on a trip South and stopped to spend the night with JD. He had bought the old Hennessy farm adjacent to Highlander Folk School and had married Mikii Fawlkes, a young college-educated girl with true Indian parentage and a fascination with the mountain culture. Mikii was a social worker in Chattanooga (a 50-mile commute), and JD worked as a carpenter in the construction of a gigantic TVA atomic-energy plant. They had two boys about the same age as ours.

We pulled into their yard in our old DeSoto Firedome V-8, which I had bought in Miami.

"Where's our beagle?" demanded our two.

JD just smiled, picked up a cow-hunting horn, and blew a few blasts. Beagles came running seemingly from every bush.

"There she be," laughed JD. "The old lady is gone, but there she be."

He had put up a tent for the four boys to sleep in. It was to be an adventure—but more of one than our two boys could stand. Dark clouds had rolled up the mountain slopes, and the sky was getting blacker and bleaker. Then came lightning and thunder. The wind had picked up, and it started to rain in big, wicked slanting drops. James and Andrew streaked for the house.

Joie and I made numerous trips back to the South to see friends and do some serious Easter-vacation birding, visiting JD as frequently as we could. He had built a huge fireplace, open in three directions, in the center of the house he was rebuilding for Mikii and their two boys. After Mikii left him, the rest of the house remained unfinished. We made our last visit to the plateau around 1995. It was typical JD—muscadine wine with a dinner of deer steaks, home-grown vegetables, and corn bread.

After dinner, with moonshine by his great fireplace, his two sons played the guitar/fiddle/banjo, exchanging instruments back and forth. They played our old square-dance airs and sang our favorite folk songs: *Freight Train Blues*, *Cotton-Eyed Joe*, and *Uncle Dave Macon's Tennessee Fox Hunt*. In 1997, we learned that JD had died of prostate cancer. His brother Junie had died of the same disease several years earlier. But nothing was ever mentioned during our visit. JD just sat there sippin' moonshine and looking with pride at his boys—"I may be about gone, but there I be."

33.

HIGHLANDER FOLK SCHOOL

By CHANCE, MYLES HORTON met educator Dr. Lilian Johnson, who had built a set of buildings for a school and community center for Summerfield, on Tennessee's remote Cumberland Plateau. By 1932, at the age of 68, she was ready to give Myles her buildings for a year's trial run. It was a tribute to her steadfast character that she stood by Highlander in spite of a considerable amount of negative "Red-baiting" that was leveled against it. She deeded him the buildings and property.

Myles and friends moved to the Johnson house on November 1, 1932, and started immediately to make the house into a residential center. The spacious attic was turned into a dormitory. Extra beds were added in the three bedrooms on the second floor. The living room became a place for classes, meetings, and square dancing.

Highlander staff frequently took turns doing household chores, including cooking. We all became very fond of Lilian Johnson, and when I was there in 1938, one night she dropped in unexpectedly and caused a little panic for that evening's chef—namely, me. I had just cooked a pumpkin pie liberally enriched with dark Jamaican rum. The question arose: Should we serve this sinful alcoholic dish to our Women's Christian Temperance Union friend? Should we warn her? It was decided that the heat of cooking surely had driven all the spirits out of the pie, so serve her we did—to high praise.

Myles was a graduate of Union Theological Seminary and had done his thesis in Denmark on the Danish Folk School movement. It was his inspiration for calling his venture the Highlander Folk School. From his experiences in Denmark, Myles had worked out his statement of purpose:

The times, the Great Depression, call for an affirmative program, based on positive goals. By broadening the scope of democracy to include everybody . . . the army of democracy would be so vast and determined that nothing undemocratic could stand in its path.

Broadening the scope of democracy in the South meant including blacks, which meant raising the flag of danger, and it took real courage.

One week, we had an invasion of Danes on the Cumberland Plateau. I have no idea what year the great Dane invasion took place, but it seems to fit nicely at the beginning of this saga . . . .

The Danes were a lusty group—they drank their own brand of gin and the women smoked black cigars. Being an occasional cigar smoker myself, I tried one of theirs; it almost killed me. It caused a round of amusement, but nothing like the uproarious laughter continuously caused by their own attempts at broken English. Nothing ever matched that week at Highlander. They were full of song, and Zilphia managed to salvage one of the songs—in full-throated Danish, they sounded like religious hymns compared with the militancy of: "I'm stickin' with the Union till the day I die."

> Men of the soil! Now the torch we have lighted,
> Kindles fire in every land where rings the harvest song!
> Shoulder to shoulder in courage united,
> From every race we come to join the tillers' mighty throng.
> Earth never shall eat again;
> Bread gained through blood of man,
> We have sworn to right forevermore the ancient wrong.

What had intrigued Myles about the Danish movement ". . . was that each Folk School identified the life problems and cultural strengths of the people it served. It would define what it was for and what it was against: for example, for the peasant and against the landlord; for Danish control and against German control; for worker control and against capitalist control. A fishing community, a farm community, an urban community could tailor its Folk School to its own needs and not worry about a nationally imposed curriculum."

When they sat down with Myles in the evening sessions to evaluate *his* Folk School, the Danes were all business. I could sense a deep interest in what Myles had accomplished. In the broadest sense, Highlander was a Folk School built on the Danish pattern—for democratic popular control against demagogic and racist controllers. It was an intriguing, fascinating interchange, but I found it difficult to follow. Not only was the discussion heavily larded with Danish, but it assumed a detailed knowledge of the Danish movement. Danish Folk Schools still exist, and I'm convinced that they helped the Danish people to resist the Nazis and protect their Jews. The Danish king wore a yellow Star of David as an example to his people. It was a high standard for Myles to follow.

The concept of starting a community-based school in 1932 was ludicrously insane. Myles had raised $1,300, but he must have known that in the depth of the brutal Depression, the times would not be right for fundraising. Nor was Grundy County, on the Cumberland Plateau, an ideal location for his Folk School. The acidic soil made for poor farming, the valuable timber had been cut, and the once-abundant coal in the county was running out.

James L. Nicholson, in his 1982 book *Grundy County,* assessed the situation:

> The 1930s were for Grundy County the very worst of times economically. In December of 1935 there were just eleven counties in the nation with a relief rate as high as 30 per cent. Grundy was not only one of these, but its relief rate was running 60 per cent!
>
> The number of homicides has always been great . . . . When Atlanta was being billed as the murder capital of the U.S., the rate in Tracy City [only six miles from Highlander] was 15 times greater. [While the threat was always present, the violence centered mostly on the production of moonshine and other local problems and didn't affect the school until the Tennessee Coal and Iron Company organized a campaign to run Highlander off the mountain.)

According to Nicholson, "There had been 436 blacks in Grundy County in 1890; 39 families were numbered in a relief survey as late as

1935. However no blacks have lived in the county for about the last 25 years."

We were told that in the late 1930s, there was a sign on the main highway: "Nigger don't let the sun set on your head in Grundy County."

The practice of prohibiting blacks from letting the sun set on their heads holds strong. Even by the late 1960s, blacks who came into the county to work as maids or gardeners had to leave by nightfall. Yet Myles was to dedicate his school to racial democracy in a lily-white county that was determined to stay that way. Segregation in the South at that time was a sacred institution, held in place by legal and terrorist practices. It is no dramatization to say it could be worth your life to challenge the system.

In the late 1940s, the Southern CIO unions were making constant use of Highlander's interracial facilities. When they arrived at the school, Joie and I and others would take them up to the large attic dorm and assign them beds. We would have them plunk their bags on a bed in a random way, making it seem totally casual and inevitable that black student beds would be intermingled with those of whites. The same was true of eating together and helping with clearing the tables and other chores. One black woman student laughed, saying, "It's the first time I worked in a kitchen while a white man was doing the dishes."

I met and photographed Rosa Parks at the first Civil Rights Workshop in 1955. She remembers talking to Myles about her first time at Highlander Folk School: "You could just enjoy the relaxing atmosphere without having the color lines drawn anywhere. I remember the statement you gave the press when they wanted to know how did you get white and black people to eat together. You told them, laughing, 'Just put the food on the table and ring the dinner bell! We were too poor to segregate—we only have one bathroom.'"

Eliot Wigginton, a Highlander board member and generator of the Foxfire method of experiential learning, observed: "It's amazing to think that with that simple gesture of having blacks and whites eating together you were breaking the law."

We were trying to create an environment in which the total absence of Jim Crow was the norm, but it wasn't always easy. At one shop stewards' session, a group of black laundry workers from a Chattanooga union were mixed in classes and at the dining room table with white workers from

Alabama. After the second day, Joie took me aside after dinner to tell me that the organizer from the Chattanooga local had to take one of her members home—she threw up after every meal she had to eat with the whites.

Singing militant union songs after dinner really turned the students on and got people talking. One evening, when we were sitting around in the living room, while others were still doing the dishes, a shop steward from Bessemer, Alabama, told a story about the boilermakers at his plant who went out on strike.

They asked a black boilermaker, Bob, if he would join them. He asked them if there was a chance for him to join the union, and the answer was always negative. He stayed on the job. They lost the strike and approached him again: "Well, Bob," they said, "we lost the strike, didn't we?" Bob's reply was, "Yes, sir, but next time, captain, take me with you."

In the ensuing silence, a Birmingham striker suddenly spoke up and confessed to us that he was a Klansman: "Being at Highlander has turned me around; this is the first time in my life I have able to see the man behind the skin."

The next day in class, he stood up and again admitted his Klan affiliation. A mumble went through the class, and I had the impression that more than one student had had some dealings with the Klan. It was a great kickoff for a discussion on the racial problem.

Myles told the story of an incident during a residential Packinghouse Workers session at the school. A white organizer from Texas frequently called a black packinghouse worker from Chicago "Boy" and blacks in general, "Nigrahs." Finally, the black student had had enough. He stood before the organizer: "This is a school and I'm going to educate you. Don't call us 'Nigrahs'; call us 'Negroes.' And don't call me 'Boy'—my name is Charles Hayes. That is the education part. And if that doesn't work, then I'm going to beat the hell out of you."

"This, of course," laughed Myles, "was not part of our shop stewards' course, but it does illustrate a hardening of the blacks to Jim Crow."

Clifford and Virginia Durr were good friends of Highlander, and I worked with them on several occasions. Clifford was from a prominent

Montgomery family, but because he was a defense lawyer for blacks, he was always broke. Studs Terkel called the Durrs "premature integrationists." Virginia helped Rosa Parks attend the Highlander Civil Rights Workshop in 1955. At Highlander, Rosa Parks found a role model in Septima Clark, the school's black Director of Education: "I only hope that there is a possible chance that some of her great courage and dignity and wisdom has rubbed off on me." It had. Just a few weeks after leaving Highlander, Rosa Parks refused to move from her seat on a segregated bus. Writers have said that she refused to stand because her feet hurt. Nonsense! It wasn't her feet that hurt. When once again, after so many times, she was forced to give up her seat for a white person, the very center of her being cried out.

Having been an activist in Alabama for 30 years, E.D. Nixon was solidly prepared in 1955 when a Montgomery policeman arrested Rosa Parks on a segregated bus. Nixon was the instigator of the bus strike and was instrumental in involving a new young minister in Montgomery, Martin Luther King, Jr. Under their leadership, the Montgomery blacks stayed off buses for 381 days and changed the face of the Civil Rights Movement in the South. After December 21, 1956, blacks and whites rode desegregated buses.

Rosa Parks also became a familiar symbol of freedom for South African blacks in the anti-apartheid movement. When the great African freedom fighter Nelson Mandela came to the United States after his release from prison, he made a stop in Detroit. Rosa Parks, put into the reception line, was nervous and uncomfortable.

In his book *Rosa Parks,* Douglas Brinkley described the scene:

> Mandela slowly made his way down the steps and towards the receiving line. Suddenly he froze, staring open-mouthed in wonder. Tears filled his eyes as he walked up to the small old woman with her hair in two silver braids crossed atop her head. And in a low, melodious tone, Nelson Mandela began to chant, "Ro-sa Parks, Ro-sa Parks, Ro-sa Parks," until his voice crescendoed into a rapturous shout: "Ro-sa Parks!"
>
> Then the two, their lives so distant yet their dreams so close, fell into each other's arms, rocking back and forth in a long, joy-

Rosa Parks, from Highlander Report.

ful embrace. And in that poignant, redemptive moment, the enduring dignity of the undaunted afforded mankind rare proof of its progress.

Studs Terkel once asked, "Had Rosa Parks not attended Highlander? It's one of those conjectural matters, you know—the role of Highlander in the psyche, the mind, the will, the gallantry, the deed of Rosa Parks. And multiply this by the thousands who have attended Highlander over the years."

A PBS film on Eleanor Roosevelt (titles shown against a visual of a Klan cross burning) documents that the KKK had singled her out as their enemy number one. The documentary mentions, as an indication of her dedication, that she flew from Washington to Nashville, where she was met at the airport by a black woman (Septima Clark) and driven through the mountains, in the darkness, to Highlander Folk School. On viewing the film, Joie and I were thrilled to see her standing next to Myles Horton and talking to Highlander students. The *Chattanooga News-Free Press* reproduced a copy of Eleanor Roosevelt's $100 check to HFS, to bolster their allegation that the First Lady was financing subversive activities. The check was shown to them illegally by the cashier of the bank in Tracy City.

In the state of Tennessee's campaign against HFS and Martin Luther King, Jr., large billboards were put up on Tennessee highways showing King at an integrated workshop at the "Highlander Communist Training School."

When Bobby Kennedy, as attorney general, forced the FBI to investigate HFS, the FBI admitted that Highlander was not a Communist school, but unfortunately the epithet had stuck.

"They called us Communists," Myles said, "but they misunderstood. We've always been pursuing something much more radical than Communism. What we've been after from the very beginning is democracy."

By 1948, there developed within the CIO a growing concern over Communism, a concern that grew more intense with the advent of the McCarthy witch hunts. As reported in John Glen's 1975 book *Highlander,* some elements within the CIO wanted to know "whether the school would alter its policies to conform more closely to changes in CIO policy, including the ban on activities with organizations not approved by the union. Highlander would not. Horton insisted that they could not shape their policies to satisfy the 'whims of any particular person or group' without impairing the school's overall effectiveness."

The national CIO withdrew its support from Highlander, although several of the international unions, such as the Packinghouse Workers, continued to work with the school.

In 1956, when Septima Poinsette Clark was fired from her school in Charleston, South Carolina, for organizing teachers and being a member of the NAACP, Myles asked her to be Director of Education at Highlander. It was through Septima that Myles became instrumental in the lives of many of the most important black women of the Civil Rights Movement—Bernice Robinson, Dorothy Cotton, Fannie Lou Hamer and others. He was astute enough to step back and let them run the program.

Septima Clark, from Highlander Report. *Ida Berman photograph.*

On July 31, 1959, some 20 armed Grundy County and state law offi-cers raided the school. Obviously aware that Myles was absent, they asked for Septima Clark and told her they had a warrant to search for liquor. Finding no liquor on the school premises, they broke into the Hortons' private cottage and found open bottles of rum and gin. Then they arrest-ed Septima, a teetotaler, for possessing whiskey.

Following the raid, Highlander became involved in a three-year legal struggle to save the school. Although the offense obviously was running a desegregated school, the charges held against the school narrowed down to Myles's operating a school for his own profit and selling beer without a license. Of course, it was not possible for black students to go to local honky-tonks for a beer (or anything else). Joie blushes to admit she ran the soft drinks and beer concession, using the profits to buy food for her children's hot-lunch program. Being in Peru by the time of the legal case, she was not subpoenaed.

The KKK marched on Highlander. from Highlander News.

By April 1961, action by the state of Tennessee closed Highlander—lock, stock, and barrel. Myles said, "Highlander is an idea; you can't padlock an idea." He immediately applied for a new charter in the name of the Highlander Research and Education Center. On August 28, 1961, this was granted, and the school was set up in a large building in downtown Knoxville. There, however, they were completely open to attacks by local bigots and the Klan.

Frank Adams, in his 1975 book on Highlander, *Unearthing Seeds of Fire: The Idea of Highlander,* described one incident:

> The Ku Klux Klan marched on the school in full regalia. Myles and

the school staff sat on the front stoop and cheerfully waved as they went by. Students attending a workshop had ice picks jabbed into their tires, sugar dumped into their gas tanks, and paint smeared on the bodies of their cars. Crank telephone calls came in day and night. Mrs. Walter McCormic was serving as the school's secretary. Once, when an anonymous voice asked, "How many little mulattoes have you got running around down there?" she replied without pause, "I don't know. How many have you lost?"

Fortunately, the Highlander Center was able to find land in a rural area 30 miles from Knoxville, where they have been able to develop programs in relative peace to this day.

At the end of a Highlander workshop, each student often would be asked what he or she could do back home. Esau Jenkins, from the South Carolina Sea Islands, said, "I need to get my people to register and vote. They got to read a part of the Constitution and they don't know how to read." Esau drove a bus to take Johns Island people to work in Charleston, and he had turned it into a "bus school." His riders learned to memorize the required section of the Constitution, but he felt it wasn't enough; they really needed to learn to read and write.

Myles hired Bernice Robinson as the first teacher in the Citizenship Schools that opened on Johns Island, South Carolina. Bernice worked out the details of how the teaching could be done. Myles credited much of the success of the schools to Bernice's skills as a beautician—her ability to converse easily with other black women—and the fact that she had no formal training in teaching. She participated in a number of Highlander workshops and in two years became the director of Highlander's Citizenship Schools field program, which then spread its concepts to all the Southern states.

On April 11, 1956, Zilphia Horton's death, 20 years after her arrival at Highlander, had left a singing vacuum in the school's educational program. When Guy Carawan came to Highlander in 1959, his great musicianship restored Highlander's role as a "singing school." He was instrumental in spreading "We Shall Overcome" and other civil rights songs to the Sea Islands Voters' Rights Movement and to the Freedom Riders and the student lunch-counter sit-ins throughout the South. Guy went to

Johns Island from the Highlander Folk School to learn about the Sea Islands culture and to serve as chauffeur for Septima Clark, who did not drive. He stayed with Esau Jenkins: "With these two beloved leaders to vouch for me, I've had the inside track in getting to know people who might have been suspicious and unfriendly."

Guy developed a singing program as a feature of the Citizenship Schools. One goal was to keep alive the islanders' beautiful singing traditions and the other was to develop group consciousness and boost morale by singing the old spirituals, protest songs, and other folk songs.

In April 1960, Candie came to Highlander to attend the first gathering of sit-in students—a fateful meeting that joined Candie and Guy and kept them active at Highlander for more than 40 years.

In 1963, Guy and Candie moved to Johns Island with their small son, Evan, and spent two years working more intimately with the community. Sponsored by Highlander, they organized a number of "Songs for Freedom Workshops" around the South.

In the 1960s, the highly successful program was passed by Highlander to the Southern Christian Leadership Conference (SCLC), under the leadership of Septima Clark, Bernice Robinson, and Dorothy Cotton. By 1970, SCLC estimated that approximately 100,000 blacks had learned to read and write through the Citizenship Schools.

Living in the South for 12 years, I found numbers of people who never identified with the Klan-type "nigger hatred." I felt that many Southerners felt imprisoned by the environment of hatred and were relieved when Jim Crow was largely run out of town.

Highlander had worked with a good number of Southern people— not all reaching the same public prominence that Rosa Parks did, but each adding impetus to the change. According to the theory of "the point of critical mass," when enough people become convinced of the need for change, something tips the balance and there is a sudden shift in attitude. This is what happened throughout the South, and I believe that Highlander deserves a good deal of credit for the shift. It could (and should) be said that Highlander helped lay the groundwork for the Civil Rights Movement of the 1960s.

Testimony to the change of attitude that Highlander brought about is

Septima Clark, who made Charleston history. Fired by the school board in 1954 for her civil rights activities, she ended up elected to the school board. Today, Charleston has a Septima P. Clark Expressway. On the Johns Island/Charleston road, there is an Esau Jenkins Bridge.

The bus on which Rosa Parks was arrested was part of the Cleveland Avenue line. Today, Cleveland Avenue is named Rosa Parks Boulevard.

Myles spoke of Highlander's history as the weaving of a tapestry. The main threads (the "warp") of the loom, which traveled through its history, were always the efforts to broaden the scope of democracy in the South through desegregation. The cross threads (the "weft") of different colors represent the various programs throughout the years. Here's the way he explained it:

• The very first years of the tapestry show Highlander settling into the Summerfield community. A total of eight young men and women enrolled in the first residential term between November 1932 and April 1933. A summer residence school was more successful, with 18 full-time students from East Tennessee and members of local unions. One of the courses they studied was the link between white and black workers. These were hungry times for the school and the community, and a cooperative cannery was organized. By November 1934, 18 families had canned more than 1,100 jars of vegetables.

• The second larger band covers Myles working on the organizing staff of the Textile Workers Union, successfully winning a contract with the mill in Lumberton, North Carolina. This led to the successful establishment of training schools for CIO educational leaders in the late 1930s and through the 1940s. In 1938, Emil Willimetz, as a 30-day work camper, was added to the tapestry. In 1940, Willimetz returned as a student for a six-week union training session.

• In the late 1940s and early 1950s the next large band was created when Highlander took over the organization and educational programs of the Southern National Farmers Union. In 1948, Joie Creighton joined the Highlander staff, running a community program, and Emil set up a Film Center. These two were married and had two children.

• The most successful band was the South Carolina Voters' Rights schools and working in the Civil Rights Movement of the 1950s and

1960s. Joie and Emil Willimetz, having left the school in 1955, went to live in nearby Knoxville, where they engaged in civil rights activities, returning to Highlander to photograph workshops through 1957.

• In the 1970s, and 1980s, in New Market, Tennessee, the Highlander Research and Education Center became largely an Appalachian school working with local communities to get potable water, stave off dumping of toxic wastes, stop strip-mining, and get better working and health conditions for the mine workers of the region. Highlander studied the 1984 Bhopal (India) disaster, where the Union Carbide pesticide company leaked 40 tons of chemicals that killed 2,000 Indian workers. It was revealed that the disaster was the result of conscious decisions to scale back safety and alarm systems in order to cut costs.

• Today the schools mission has spread to working with the Mexican border *maquiladoras,* making contact and holding workshop sessions with workers' organization throughout Latin America. All Highlander literature is issued today in both English and Spanish. John Gaventa, then director of the Highlander Center, called 1990 "the busiest year at the Center—over sixty workshops and gatherings were led by our staff, involving some two thousand people from forty states and a dozen countries."

According to Myles's biographer, Herbert Kohl: "Myles was convinced the existence of multinational corporations, which controlled international communications . . . and which functioned beyond the laws of nations, made it necessary for working-class people to develop new means of organizing and educating themselves."

Myles Horton spent much of his last years helping Highlander develop working partnerships with similar popular education centers in other parts of the world. He went to the Ulster Peoples College in Belfast; to the National Union of Miners in Wales; and to Nicaragua. The Highlander Center used these networks to help develop educational exchanges between communities affected by Union Carbide's toxic chemicals in West Virginia and India; between women textile workers in Tennessee and in the *maquiladora* zone in Mexico; between popular educators in Appalachia and Nicaragua; and between human rights activists in the South and in Latin America.

Dale St. John White, at the Wilgespruit Fellowship Center, came to know Myles when he visited South Africa at a time of crisis and government persecution. "His warmth, humor and instant appreciation of the pressures we had to endure lightened our burden and strengthened our courage to persevere."

The alumni of Highlander Folk School are now spread all over the globe. For more than 60 years, this powerful institution has served as a beacon that shines brightly, illuminating the awesome power of human potential.

In the last years of his life, Myles debated with Paulo Freire, a Brazilian educator and kindred spirit, about educational methods for social change. In December 1987, these two pioneers came together to "talk a book," *We Make the Road by Walking*. Speaking about their book, Budd L. Hall, secretary-general of the International Council for Adult Education, said: "Their talks represent some of the most important educational conversations of the twentieth century. This is the first book since Freire's *Pedagogy of the Oppressed* that I have said must be read."

In early January 1990, Paulo returned to Highlander for a final review of the manuscript. In the fall of 1989, Myles had undergone surgery for a brain tumor. As his mental and physical strength slipped away, he focused on rereading the edited transcript and on the possibility of another meeting with Freire for final changes. He rallied for the meeting.

Myles: "Well, you feel contented that we've done all we can do?"

Paulo: "Oh, yes. Maybe I'm totally wrong, but I think that it will be a beautiful book."

Myles: "Yes, I don't see any reason for having any more discussions."

Paulo: "It is more or less structured."

Myles: "Let's have a drink."

Paulo: "Yes."

Three days after this last visit with Freire, Myles slipped into a coma. He died a week later at the age of 84.

"It was an honor to participate with him," said Paulo. "He's an incredible man. The history of this man, his individual presence in the world, is something which justifies the world."

Although many people worked at the school and contributed, Myles *was* Highlander—from its birth in 1932 until he died in his house on the hill at the Highlander Center on January, 19, 1990. It is gratifying to us, Joie and Emil, that Myles attained recognition and praise as what W.H. Auden called a "vertical man."

Sue Thrasher of the Highlander Center staff wrote: "He worked right up until the final weeks of his life, saving some of his last energy for a meeting with Paulo Freire so that the two of them could discuss their forthcoming 'spoken book.' He battled cancer with the same ferocity that he had battled all of life's other injustices, and doing so, continued to teach all of us around him about the value of life. His 'ideas' will go where all of us take them."

TRIBUTES TO MYLES HORTON

> *Let us praise if we can*
> *The vertical man*
> *Though we honor none*
> *But the horizontal one.*
> —W.H. Auden

> *The Greatest Education Comes from Action . . . .*
> *The Greatest Action Is the Struggle for Justice.*
> —Myles Horton

Andrew Young: "Myles Horton had a vision of justice in the South long before it was deemed possible."

John Dewey: "One of the most important social-educational projects in America."

Bill Moyers: "Few people I know have seen as much change in the American South, or helped to bring it about, as Myles Horton." (Moyers did a one-hour TV interview on Myles, "The Adventures of a Radical Hillbilly." He liked the material so much that he did a second hour-long interview.)

Studs Terkel: "Were I to choose America's most influential and inspiring educator, it would be Myles Horton of Highlander. His life has touched those of John Dewey, Jane Addams, Reinhold Niebuhr, Martin Luther King, Jr., Rosa Parks, Eleanor Roosevelt, Pete Seeger, and scores of others."

Myles Horton. Candie Carawan photograph.

Pete Seeger: "There weren't many places in the South where you could go and find blacks and whites sitting down eating together and kidding each other and teasing each other, and dancing together."

Beginning in the late 1970s, Myles finally started to be recognized by prestigious institutions. He received the Martin Luther King, Jr., Award from the Fellowship of Reconciliation, a Lifetime Achievement Award from the American Civil Liberties Union of Tennessee, the Literacy Education Award from the International Council of Adult Education in Paris in 1982, and the Rothko Chapel Award for Commitment to Truth and Freedom in 1986.

He used these occasions to advocate his concepts of social change.

34.

THE FARMERS UNION

THE FILM CENTER AND THE FARMERS UNION, 1944-1952

THE NATIONAL FARMERS UNION, based in Colorado and the Dakotas, once tried to organize the South. In 1944, it tried a rerun, and Highlander offered its facilities and staff for the drive. The Tennessee Organizing Committee of the National Farmers Union designated Myles Horton as director of organization and Ermon Fay Johnson as state education director.

Ermon Fay was the youngest of the four Johnson sisters, and the only one besides Zilphia (Horton) to work at Highlander. Ten years older, Zilphia Mae acted as a mentor for Ermon Fay as she was growing up, and they were very close at Highlander. The national organization consisted of large, all-white locals. As education director, Ermon Fay, dealing with the small family farms of the South, felt hampered by the educational directives coming from the western-based organization.

The Southern Farmers Union drive gave the Film Center (namely, me) grist for its mill, but with Fred Lasse gone, it was just photography and filmstrips.

Greeneville's Borden's Milk plant became the site of the early organizing drive. The farmers were paid not only on the quantity of milk but also by the butterfat content. This required a milk checker at the plant who took samples and rated the milk. The farmers were not so much concerned about the price as getting a fair butterfat-content measurement. To this end, through the Farmers Union, they were able to install their own checker in the plant.

I had met N.C. Hatley at a Highlander Farmers Union school session,

A meeting of the Farmers Union. Author photograph.

and he invited me to come stay with his family and photograph a local meeting. As a Bronx boy, I was curious to see what a farmer prized most on his farm—Mr. Hatley was proudest of his new silos. Lined with chocolate-colored tiles, they were indeed things of beauty, and I duly took a number of photos. Then he took me through his milking shed to exhibit his herd. Finally, he took me to his house to meet his wife and children. I spent the next day and night photographing other Farmers Union members and the monthly meeting. As I was leaving, Mr. Hatley asked me if I would like some books he had on photography.

"Last year I raised Poland China pigs," he said, "and won some prizes at the fair, so I bought a camera. Then I bought these books to teach me how to use the camera. Well, I don't raise Poland China pigs anymore. and you can have the books."

Of course, I showed the proper enthusiasm, but I assumed he would bring out some Kodak booklets, most of which I probably had. He came back out of the house with a rather large corrugated box and dumped it on my back seat. When I opened the box back at school, I found it contained a full set of the *Photographic Encyclopedia,* more than a dozen volumes containing the most complete articles and instruction on anything one would want to know on the subject of photography, written by top experts in each field. It was expensive, and invaluable to someone as isolated as I was in Summerfield.

A second Borden's Milk plant was in Abingdon, Virginia, right on the Tennessee border. I stayed with a dairy farmer whose name I can't remember. He first took me down to his spring house, where he kept cream, butter, and other perishable items. Surrounded by slabs of stone, it had a picturesque little shed around it, and a pool of spring water. What he wanted me to see was a single trout swimming in the pool.

"I want to tell you why I became a Farmers Union member," he said. "This stream goes through my property, and one day the head honcho, a lawyer of this Commonwealth [a county in Virginia], came to see me. 'If everyone cleans out his part of this stream,' he said, 'we're going to stock it with trout. Will you do it?

"Well, sure. I put in a lot of time, but it was well worth it when the trout showed up. Then one day I noticed a fish belly-up . . . then another and another. I figured it must be the chemicals from the Borden plant.

"I went to the Commonwealth office and complained about the plant. The lawyer said he'd look into it. Fish were still dying in my stream, so I went back.

"'No,' he said, 'I checked with Borden's, and there is no problem there, nothing from the plant is killing the fish.'

"So I came home, filled a burlap sack full of dead fish, and dumped them on the Commonwealth office's beautiful carpet. 'Something killed these fish!' I told him. Angry with the Borden plant, I did what I had long expected to do—I went home to join the Farmers Union!"

We stared down at his spring. The lonely trout was endlessly circling the circumference of the pool. "This," he said pensively, "is the last one."

At breakfast next morning, the farmer said, "Mom, we don't have any kids and Emil, here, is already fully grown, so why don't we adopt him and turn this blankety-blank farm over to him to struggle with?"

Laughter at the table.

"Yeah," I thought, "now that all the fish are dead!"

The educational director of the National Farmers Union, Gladys Talbott Edwards, wrote that she was impressed with the determination of South Alabama Farmers Union members: "The courage of this little band of folks in the South who are building this cooperative out of their dollar shares is like nothing else I have ever known."

In the piney woods region of southern Alabama, the sandy soil was very poor for farming and required a judicious use of fertilizer. The Farm Bureau recommended the purchase of 100-pound bags of phosphate—20 percent phosphate mixed with 80 percent fine Florida silica (sand!). Few of the small farmers could afford to buy Florida sand at retail prices, and the great need for a fertilizer co-op was apparent. The Farmers Union started a campaign to organize locals based on railroad sidings, with the aim of pooling their financial resources to order carloads of pure phosphate from Florida. In places where only a few blacks lived, they would attend local meetings, staying in the background. Where only a few whites were in a local, they too stayed in the background, cultivating black leaders to get their needs represented.

Other fertilizers, nitrates and potash, however, were also needed, and plans were drawn up for a fertilizer mixing plant. The leader for these activities was J.D. Mott (nicknamed "Motto"). I met Mott at a Highlander training session, and he invited me down to Andalusia, in southern Alabama. Mrs. Mott (who had also been at Highlander, along with their oldest son) invited me to stay at their home and made me welcome with a glass of cold lemonade. Their parlor was typical rural South—a little-used room with plastic flowers, lace doilies, and plastic-covered furniture. What was not typical, here in the deep South, was the framed photo on the mantelpiece. On closer inspection, it turned out to be one I had taken of Mr. Mott seated in a Highlander class with other farmers—many of whom were black.

Mrs. Mott noticed my interest and smiled: "When neighbors come in, the first thing they do is stand in front of that picture. 'What in hell, Mott,' they'll say, 'are you doing with those niggers?' And then," she laughs, "that tetchy old man of mine sits 'em down and tells 'em."

Highlander had not, of course, given J.D. Mott his humanity. But Highlander had provided him an experience that Southern custom had denied him all his life—the opportunity to face a black man on an equal basis. And I was proud to have given him an instrument to spread this experience. At that moment, I felt as if I'd been given a Nobel Prize for photography.

In the morning, I was in the kitchen enjoying my favorite pastime—watching an expert cook. Mrs. Mott was preparing breakfast. Her kitchen counter had a 100-pound bin of flour, which narrowed downward to a hinged edge. Tilting this bin forward, she dropped in some buttermilk, baking soda, salt, and lard (none of the ingredients being measured). Stirring this around in the flour, she came out with a ball of dough, threw it on a bread board, and fashioned from it a series of biscuits. In my honor, she sprinkled in a handful of lard cracklings. Eggs, thickly sliced bacon, grits, freshly churned butter, and several jams completed the meal. As she deftly threw the meal together, I chattered about my mother's skills. Mrs. Mott seemed intrigued, maybe a little flattered, by a young man's interest in matters of the kitchen.

Calling Mott and two young children, she laid out the breakfast. When I was asked to say grace, I was prepared—not taken completely by surprise and rendered mute as per earlier experiences. I started out with a robust, "We thank thee Lord . . . ." Occasionally the host would start a set of "favorite quotes from the bible" going around the table. As a photographer, I got away with ". . . and the Lord said, 'Let there be light!'" Once I learned what was required, I never felt hypocritical—it was all part of a culture I was required to learn in order to work with and enjoy the people.

When they shooed the two children out to play, I remarked, "Your son must be happy to have you take care of his little ones!"

"They're not Johnny's kids, they're ourn," said Mrs. Mott. "J.D. missed having young-uns around, so we started a second crop."

Mott just looked proud.

To construct the large cement-block fertilizer plant, each local sent a daily quota of men, black and white. Southern Alabama can get insufferably hot, and this was August. After a few hours of manual labor, water is vital. But the water had a high sulphur content that required ice to make it palatable. It was Motto's task, around 10 a.m., to fetch ice for the water barrel.

One morning, as I was busily poking around with my camera, I noticed the men getting restive, glancing anxiously at Motto and the water barrel. By 11 a.m., the mutiny started—these people, after all, were rebels! Shouts of "Where's the ice, Mott?" became an insistent chorus. Finally they forced Motto into his pickup, and he reluctantly left.

After a prolonged absence, he returned to ice the water barrel. All work stopped, and the men crowded around. Mr. Mott held up the two water dippers and announced: "I noticed that some of you are getting careless about who uses which dipper."

Holding up a pencil, and with a great show of concentration, he wrote, "COLORED" on the black-enameled handle of one dipper. As he handed them out, he emphasized, "This one's "white" and this one's "colored." Within minutes, in the desperate grasps of the hot and sweaty hands, the pencil marks were gone. Mr. Mott would stop some hapless member's hand in mid-drink and earnestly ask, "Are you sure you have the right dipper?"

Soon his ploy became obvious to one and all—hand grabbing and joking became the order of the day. "Are you sure you have the right dipper?" became the catchword whenever anything negative arose between the races. Lincoln couldn't have done it better.

Unfortunately, the Farmers Union, successful as it was with a few locals, was not able to ignite the South, and it pulled out in 1952. It apparently required more investment in time and money than the western-based organization was willing to spend.

The programs at Highlander dealt with people relating to people—which in the South boiled down to race relations. As late as 1940, when I attended a six-week labor school, the CIO had come to the point of sending black members. When it was seen that Highlander was able to handle the mix, even to the point of converting Klan members, the sessions almost all became interracial. The Farmers Union sessions were interracial from the very beginning.

In the summer of 1953, Highlander scheduled a workshop on deseg-

The Farmers Union unloading fertilizer in Alabama, from Highlander Fling.

regation. Seventy-one people attended, racially mixed, mostly communi-ty leaders from nine Southern states. This was almost a year before the Supreme Court passed favorably on the decision to desegregate the schools.

It was out of this session that I designed a guide for action—"Working Toward Integrated Public Schools in Your Own Community"—along with a filmstrip, "The High Cost of Segregation," also complete with a guide.

In 1954, a second desegregation workshop was the main (only) ses-sion for the year. It was not enough to keep the Film Center active.

In his book *Highlander: No Ordinary School,* John Glen wrote: "Many of these groups [the Film Center served] were unable to pay for the Center's services, creating a drain on Highlander's resources . . . until per-sistent financial difficulties finally closed the Center."

Not so! The Film Center more than paid its own way—underwriting the construction of two buildings with its own resources and using the money earned on outside film and photographic jobs for operating funds. None of us received more than room and board. Joie and I had bought a cabin next door and were living apart from the school. Joie, a staff member, received $50 a month, and we did eat some meals at the school—hardly a drain on Highlander's resources.

But with few unions using Highlander by this time, and the Farmers Union leaving in 1952, there was little for the Film Center to do. Short of staff, Myles pulled Joie off her community program and had her working full time in the office as the executive secretary of the school, doing fundraising and administration.

With Joie unhappy, having had to give up her beloved nursery school and community program, we decided it was time to leave, closing the Film Center in 1954 and leaving for Knoxville. But it was without rancor, and we remained good friends with Myles and Zilphia. We had a good, fulfilling life at Highlander. It had been a comfortable nest for our growing family and gave Joie and me the opportunity to do our jobs. Now we had to open a new chapter.

35.

FAREWELL, HIGHLANDER
FOLK SCHOOL

HELLO, KNOXVILLE! WE MAKE THE BREAK . . . .

FORTUNATELY, THE FILM CENTER AT HIGHLANDER had traded in our old delivery van for a station wagon. It had a good deal more power, and we fitted it with a trailer hitch. With JD Marlowe's help, we built a trailer to carry our stuff to Knoxville. For his help, he inherited the trailer. Knoxville was a good choice for us—it was only five hours from Highlander, so we could still work with the Folk School programs.

Much to our horror one day, an IRS agent tracked us down. It seemed that we owed the government $2,000 in back taxes. WHAT? At $50 per month? How come? Well, we didn't factor in our free room and board, which seemed to be worth a good deal of money. Seven years of noodle casseroles, beans, and meat loaf! No way! Was there a bigot somewhere in the IRS? (We had become super-sensitive about these things.) The IRS had tried three times unsuccessfully to revoke the school's tax-exempt status. What they hadn't added into our back taxes, however, was the very rich cultural life we had enjoyed—tax-free—at Highlander.

Seeing the looks of dismay on our faces, and Joie's tears of anger and frustration, but mainly because we obviously didn't have anywhere near that kind of money, the IRS agent showed his good heart and allowed us a schedule of small monthly payments.

Needing a place to hang our hats in Knoxville, I took advantage of my first and only benefit from the GI Bill of Rights. We found a builder who was putting up a modest development in upscale West Knoxville. He agreed to take us on via the GI Bill, with nothing down (about what we could afford) and payments of $75 per month, which included mortgage, interest, and taxes. In TVA territory, it was an all-electric home—a neat little house with a carport, which I converted into a darkroom.

Joie insisted that my darkroom was musty and attracted black widow spiders. I pooh-poohed this as nonsense until the night that she served me one on a lettuce leaf for dinner.

Our lot was three-fourths of an acre, somewhat larger than the others because it adjoined a railroad track. They didn't need to give us that extra land. Little did they know how much I enjoyed the rattle of the boxcars going by—the long, drawn-out, lonesome whistle for the crossing was my favorite kind of music.

We found Paul Christopher, head of the Tennessee CIO—and most of the elite of progressive Knoxville—ensconced in the Unitarian Church. We are still in close touch with our youthful Unitarian minister, Richard Henry. Below are excerpts from my fairly recent correspondence with him:

> Dear Dick,
> We joined the Unitarian fellowship in Knoxville because it was the main interracial event in town and all our friends belonged. When my immigrant parents came to visit us, they were astonished on Sunday morning when we announced we were going to church. My mother was raised a Catholic but despised the village priest. When she got over her astonishment she said to my father, "Must be for social reasons." My father, the Austrian Socialist, replied, "Ach, no, for business reasons!"
>
> They were right on both accounts, plus the fact that our children needed to hide behind some religion here in the Bible Belt. We stayed in the church not only because it was interracial, but because you were such a stimulating preacher (and good friend). Our impious leanings were included in the Unitarian openness and we always felt very comfortable belonging.
> Emil

One would think that by joining a church, we would get some relief from the bigots. But not so! Dick Henry's response reminded us that we had not left Tennessee and these were still the McCarthy days.

Dear Emil:
You know I'm really a blank when it comes to remembering the early days of our Knoxville life. I recollect Paul's [Paul Christopher] recounting how, when he ran once for re-election [a textile plant, probably for shop-steward representation], by way of doing him in, his opponent put a photo on a conveyor belt of his shaking hands with a black . . . tho it didn't work.

I remember the day Jim Person, our first black member joined . . . and the school board voted (in secret summer meeting) to deny us further use of the Christenberry School, where we were paying rent to meet. Our opposing the nature of the vote led to the *Knoxville Journal* headline: RED QUESTION RAISED ABOUT UNITARIANS.

I remember working for integrated lunch counters and drinking fountains at Rich's new department store in 1957. I like to tell the story of seeing two little black kids, aged about 9-10, when the store opened: one challenging the other to go on and drink from the integrated fountain. He looked around to see if anyone was watching, quickly ducked to get a drink . . . and came up with a crestfallen look. "It tastes just like ours," he told his buddy . . . and they ran off.
Regards, Dick

My photographic career in K'ville, at the time, appeared to be limited. The TVA had its own staff photographer—a good one, unfortunately. Oak Ridge, the Atomic Energy Station, was not about to hire me with my CIO/HFS background, and the huge aluminum plant in Maryville also had an in-house photographer. That left me such potential clients as the hosiery mills and underwear factories, and shooting pots and pans for Rich's Department Store.

In the church, as my parents observed, we quickly made lifelong friends—people who worked for the TVA, Oak Ridge, and the University

of Tennessee. I kidnapped their kids for pay—kidnapping being a photographer's term for taking pictures of children at home or in natural surroundings instead of slick pics in a studio (my only option, since I had no
studio). We found that unposed, active kid shots were highly prized by the
parents and financially rewarding for me.

Joie, her usual energetic self, took on hyperactive troubled kids as her
Unitarian Church assignment and, because she enjoyed eating regular
meals, took on a number of other jobs. She ran the interracial Fellowship
House Day Camp one summer, the Beech Hill Day Camp another summer, and a day-care program for the Knoxville Evening High School. She
also set up and ran the Methodist Social Center Nursery School.

Joie worked on the board of the interracial Fellowship House with
Mrs. Ted Wilcox. At one dinner meeting, a black board member, O.B.
Taylor, came in late and sat next to a prominent local white lady.
Astonished, she turned to him and asked, "Aren't you colored?"

His answer, "Just a little!" so tickled Joie and Ted that they had to grab
each other's arms to keep from bursting into laughter. This cemented a
growing relationship, and we were invited one night to dinner. Joie
warned Ted that her husband (me) was the quiet type. True, frequently,
but when we met Jack, Ted's husband, the head of the economics department at the University of Tennessee, he and I monopolized the evening
swapping freight-train and Depression stories.

As we left, Ted smiled at Joie: "Was that your quiet husband?"

The Wilcoxes became close friends, and we would visit them frequently in their family house in Highlands, North Carolina. Ted and her
two daughters were theatrical types, active in Knoxville's excellent
Theatre-in-the-Round. I did playbills, posters, and cast photos for the theater. Ted's older daughter, Colin, was talented and fast becoming a professional actor. I did her first composite (a full page of assorted poses). Her
initial Hollywood assignment was the major female part in *To Kill a
Mockingbird,* with Gregory Peck. She followed this with a number of successful roles. The last one I remember seeing was as one of two leading
young ladies with Jessica Tandy in *Fried Green Tomatoes.*

Joie's best job (most remunerative) was in the United Mine Workers
Welfare and Retirement Fund office—working as a clerk in preparation

for an assignment as a social case worker. She was overjoyed one day to hear her fellow Tennessean workers, forgetting Joie's antecedents, discussing a new employee as "a typical damnyankee."

Life in old Knoxville began looking pretty good. We had paid off the IRS, were both earning modest incomes, and had a neat little house in a lovely neighborhood. In truth, I also began to have more appealing assignments. I was learning new audiovisual techniques and producing interesting materials for professors at the University of Tennessee, doing filmstrips for the Knoxville United Way, and working with local businesses and the CIO.

I now had an office downtown, and the commute in the spring was pure exhilaration. The roads were lined with flowering redbud, magnolia, and dogwood trees; the houses of the affluent competed among themselves with lush gardens of azalea and rhododendron bushes; the air was balmy, and, in the near distance, lay the majestic Smokies.

Living in Knoxville, we maintained a close connection with Highlander. In 1955, I went down to HFS to photograph a workshop on school desegregation attended by Rosa Parks and again in 1956, to photograph workshops on school integration.

I realize now that we left too soon. The short 1954 and 1955 sessions on segregation were to become the forerunners of Highlander's successful involvement with the Civil Rights and Voters' Registration Movements.

Traveling through the South in 1970, Joie and I were profoundly moved by the changes. Sitting in a Georgia restaurant, we watched a young white waitress serving a black family. We couldn't help but feel that these young Southerners' lack of concern for "the right dipper" was a contribution to the new society that Highlander helped make and is still making.

In the nearby town of Clinton, in the fall of 1956, there had been a bitter battle to integrate the school system. Bigots and segregationists invaded Clinton to whip up race hatred. State troopers were called in to quell the rioting, but for months, the young black high school students and their families bore the brunt of these attacks.

Rosa Parks at Highlander with students from Clinton, Tennessee.

We worked with Highlander to bring those students to the school for a weekend retreat. A tutorial program was designed to help the students who rode the torment until the end of the school year. In 1957, one of the students, Bobby Cain, graduated—Tennessee's first black graduate of an integrated public school. Courage about facing up to desegregation was spreading rapidly.

Not far out of the West End of Knoxville was a park with swimming pools, to which I went on Sundays with our two young boys. I spent my time sitting in a foot-deep kiddie pool in a circle with other young fathers, hashing over politics with our little ones clinging to us like baby possums. Knoxville was where I started to learn about parenting.

In our little log cabin at Highlander, our only source of heat had been a huge sandstone fireplace. We learned the technique of maximum combustion with minimum effort, using a large log as a backpiece and burning split wood against it. At night, we threw ashes on the log, and in the morning it would still be hot enough, with proper coaxing, to burn anew.

Jamie with his "camera."
Author photographs.

"Ready on the right!"

"Ready on the left!"

Andy. Author photograph.

I like to think of myself as an old backlog—banked at times but never out. I could keep my backlog glowing by writing, photography, and taking part in activist community and world concerns. I am just as angry about the world's injustices now as I was at 18. I am no longer the Gringo of "Green Grow the Rushes"—"where one is one and all alone and ever more shall be so." With a family of four, I am certainly never alone.

But was I still a Gringo? One good Unitarian friend, Nelson Robinson, absent on leave from the University of Tennessee, was teaching in a university in La Paz, Bolivia. He had written to me, suggesting I get in touch with an Ed Movius, who was running a successful documentary-film company in Lima, Peru. Ed was looking to expand but was having difficulty finding the type of recruits he needed. It could be another Ezra Stoller–type training apprenticeship, but in filmmaking. Nelson suggested I might be interested. Was I?

Suddenly I had these choices to make—time was pressing. After all, I was now 39 years old!

INDEX